Contributions to Management Science

The series *Contributions to Management Science* contains research publications in all fields of business and management science. These publications are primarily monographs and multiple author works containing new research results, and also feature selected conference-based publications are also considered. The focus of the series lies in presenting the development of latest theoretical and empirical research across different viewpoints.

This book series is indexed in Scopus.

Hongmu Lee · Gianni Nicolini
Editors

International Comparison of Long-Term Care Insurance Systems

Springer

Editors
Hongmu Lee
School of Commerce
Waseda University
Tokyo, Japan

Gianni Nicolini
Department of Management and Law
University of Rome Tor Vergata
Rome, Italy

ISSN 1431-1941 ISSN 2197-716X (electronic)
Contributions to Management Science
ISBN 978-981-95-7780-4 ISBN 978-981-95-7781-1 (eBook)
https://doi.org/10.1007/978-981-95-7781-1

This Springer imprint is published by the registered company Springer Nature Singapore Pte Ltd.
The registered company address is: 152 Beach Road, #21-01/04 Gateway East, Singapore 189721, Singapore

Preface

Life expectancy is increasing worldwide, and the population is aging along with the declining birthrate. To cope with this aging population, countries are developing long-term care insurance systems and nursing care facilities. The long-term care insurance system in Japan was introduced on April 1, 2000. The reasons for the introduction of a public long-term care insurance system in Japan are as follows.

First, the rapid increase in average life expectancy has led to an increase in the number of bedridden elderly and those suffering from dementia, and the need for and importance of long-term care has grown. Under these circumstances, women, who had been responsible for caring for the elderly, increasingly entered the workforce, and the nuclear family has become more common, resulting in the problem of "elderly nursing care," in which the elderly care for the elderly.

Second, it was necessary to eliminate social hospitalization. Social hospitalization refers to a condition in which a patient is not in need of medical care but remains hospitalized in a medical institution for compelling reasons such as family circumstances. Under the circumstances of low medical costs for the elderly based on Geriatric Health Care Law, medical institutions bore less of the costs than nursing homes, and the welfare service system was inadequate, resulting in many long-term hospitalizations (social hospitalization) in general hospitals.

Third, medical costs for the elderly were increasing rapidly. It was necessary to control the increase in medical costs by separating medical care from long-term care.

Some countries, however, have not introduced a public long-term care insurance system as in the U.S., but instead use medical insurance and welfare programs to cope with the situation. In such countries, it is reported that many long-term care services are provided by private long-term care providers.

The purpose of this research is to compare public and private long-term care insurance and long-term care services in these countries and to make policy recommendations to cope with the aging society. This long-term care insurance includes public and private long-term care insurance, and the roles of each will be clarified. An analysis of these public and private long-term care insurance systems will also be conducted.

However, public long-term care insurance does not exist in the United States or China. For such systems that differ from country to country, classification and other adjustments are made at editorial meetings, as well as an international comparison of long-term care facilities and long-term care insurance programs.

In the global aging society, the biggest challenges are long-term care and retirement funds. Some countries have established public long-term care insurance systems to address the risk of long-term care. Unlike medical insurance, which allows people to receive medical services as and when they need them, public long-term care insurance sets a limit on the amount of care that can be used for each level of care that has been certified in advance. If the amount exceeds this limit, or if the service is not covered by long-term care insurance, the full amount is paid by the user. On the other hand, the number of elderly people using private-pay nursing homes, which provide higher quality services than public facilities, is rapidly increasing.

We are confident that this book will be useful in finding directions for coping with these retirement risks.

Tokyo, Japan
Rome, Italy

Hongmu Lee
Professor of Risk Management and Insurance

Gianni Nicolini
Professor of Finance

Contents

Long-term Care Needs and Issues 1
Gianni Nicolini, Hongmu Lee, and Soyoung Lim

An Analysis of the Long-Term Care in Italy: Financial and Non-financial Issues 13
Gianni Nicolini

Long-Term Care in Poland 43
Anne-Marie Weber and Hanna Salera

Long-term Care Insurance in the US 71
Peter J. Morgan

Exploring the Long-Term Care Partnership Program in the United States: Challenges and Lessons from Connecticut 91
Shangzhu Huang

Role of the Public and Private Sectors of Long-Term Care Insurance in Japan 107
Hongmu Lee

Private Long-Term Care Insurance in Japan 123
Akio Hoshino

Long-Term Care Insurance in South Korea 141
Soyoung Lim

The Roles of the Private Long-Term Care Market—Focusing on Comparison of Japan and Korea 155
Seungho Hwang

Social Long Term Care Insurance in China 183
Chao Lu

Long-Term Care Insurance in Malaysia and the Role of the Public and Private Sectors 211
Mohamad Fazli Sabri, Husniyah Abd. Rahim, and Maheswaran Periasamy

Long-Term Care for the Aged Population the Case of Bangladesh 245
Muhammad Ziaulhaq Mamun and Md. Zahid Hossain

Long-Term Care Insurance in Vietnam 285
Huong Thi Thu Phung, Van Dinh, and Thai Hong Le

Responding to Long-Term Care for an Aging Society: Insights from Medical and Care Platform Initiatives in Asia and Europe 323
Kayo Uemura

About the Editors

Hongmu Lee is a professor of risk management and insurance at Waseda University, Tokyo, where he received his Ph.D. He is also the president of the Insurance and Risk Management Institute of Waseda University. The institute aims to carry out research internationally in cooperation with industry and the academic world on insurance and risk management. He has authored several books and articles in academic and professional journals, mainly in Korea and Japan. He also serves as the president of IAFICO (International Academy of Financial Consumers). This book was authored as an outcome of IAFICO's Book Project.

Gianni Nicolini, Ph.D. is a full professor of finance at the University of Rome 'Tor Vergata', Rome (Italy). His main research interests involve personal finance and consumers' financial wellbeing, and his publications include studies on financial literacy, financial education, and the functioning of pension systems. He is Past-President of the ACCI (American Council on Consumers Interest) and Vice-Chairperson of the IAFICO (International Academy of Financial Consumers).

Long-term Care Needs and Issues

Gianni Nicolini, Hongmu Lee, and Soyoung Lim

1 Long-term Care Needs and Characteristics

Long-term care needs (LTCNs) refer to the requirements of assistance with daily living activities and/or medical assistance over a long period of time (European Commission 2021). Examples of people with LTCNs are the elderly, including those that need assistance for bathing, dressing, or other activities of daily living (ADLs); people recovering from injuries or other health issues (e.g. stroke); or people with cognitive impairments who require assistance for most standard living activities.

The main characteristics of the LTCNs are the duration of the needs, the inner nature of the services required, the different locations that can be used to aid, the emotional and psychological issues related to the personal conditions of those with LTCNs, and the financial aspects of long-term care conditions.

About the duration, we refer to LTCNs when the person's condition is long-term, sometimes undefined, and is frequently permanent. Recovering from a stroke or a heart-attack can be a long process, the duration of which can vary a lot from case to case. In the case of inability in dealing with activities of daily living due to aging, the needs for assistance tend to be permanent, and it is likely that they will grow over time. Similarly, people with dementia or Alzheimer's disease will require assistance for the rest of their lives.

G. Nicolini (✉)
Department of Management and Law, University of Rome Tor Vergata, Rome, Italy
e-mail: gianni.nicolini@uniroma2.it

H. Lee
Professor of Risk Management and Insurance, School of Business, Waseda University, Tokyo, Japan

S. Lim
Assistant Professor of Risk Management and Insurance, School of Business, Waseda University, Tokyo, Japan

H. Lee and G. Nicolini (eds.), *International Comparison of Long-Term Care Insurance Systems*, Contributions to Management Science,
https://doi.org/10.1007/978-981-95-7781-1_1

The inner nature of the LTCNs includes a variety of needs that are not always related to medical needs. For instance, the elderly can be in good health, not showing any disease, but can be in need of support for cooking (or even just eating), dressing, or bathing, showing needs that belong to the LTCNs category. People recovering from severe injuries could be able to take care of themselves for eating or dressing, but they could need assistance with their mobility, and they could need physiotherapy for a sustained period. People with cognitive impairments will show other assistance needs (e.g. help for grocery shopping, money management, supervision, etc.), while people with dementia or Alzheimer's disease will show other and different (long-term care) needs.

The long duration and the variety of needs of LTCNs suggest considering different locations to deal with different LTCNs. In some cases, home care is the most appropriate solution (e.g. elderly with difficulties with ADLs), while in other cases the need of a specific location—like community centers or nursing homes—is justified by the need of medical assistance that cannot be provided at home. However, a critical point in dealing with LTCNs is the need to avoid the needs of long-term care patients hosted in hospitals and other medical infrastructures shrinking the reception rate of those medical venues, especially when the long-term care patient's need for medical treatments is limited or null. People with LTCNs can be at home, receiving assistance from family members or other caregivers, can be assisted going to community centers—like adult day care—during the day, can be hospitalized in long-term care structures (like those specialized in helping recovery from serious injuries), or can be hosted by nursing homes. Of course, the different combination of needs and the evolution of the LTCNs over time can even require a change of location over time, or a combination of different locations (e.g. hospital for specific treatments first, then home assistance, or home assistance overnight and community centers during the day).

Another characteristic of the LTCNs is the attention required to psychological and emotional aspects of the individuals that require such needs. Especially in the case that the individual is aware that the need for personal care is not temporary, and it requires serious efforts for the caregivers (e.g. family members, volunteers, nurses, doctors, etc.), the risk is that such individuals will show depression, or they will isolate themselves, being shy of asking for needs or feeling guilty for the burden generated by the caregiving.

About the burden of caregiving, it represents another characteristic of the LTCNs. The undefined length of the needs which are typically lengthy involves costs for assistance that can be hard to manage. Such costs are not only monetary (e.g. medical checks, treatments, prescription, hospitalization, etc.) but include the time that family members spend in home assistance, for the mobility of the long-term care individuals, and time constraints that such systematic support involve in people's lives (e.g. matching working hours of the day with the home assistance, deficit in career developments, difficulties in planning for holidays, etc.). The need to deal with such costs and the pressure that LTCNs put on both individuals and the welfare systems are some of the reasons that bring the attention of researchers to studying LTCNs.

The tendency of life expectancy to grow, low fertility rates, changes in family structures and the job market—with the all the individuals of a family group (singles, partners, children) not being at home for large parts of the day—are elements that already highlight the growing needs to deal with the management of the LTCNs. The increase in life expectancy involves an increasing number of people that will need assistance for aging related issues. The low fertility rate involves sharing the burden for a family member in LTCNs between a smaller number of individuals, compared to the past. Thinking about the home assistance of aging parents by children, in the case of two children, the care duties can be shared between them, while a single child could struggle to take care of all the needs by him/herself. Of course, the lack of children increases the complexity of managing people with LTCNs even more, requiring external support from the society (e.g. government, no-profit Organizations, charitable groups, etc.). Moreover, if previous generations typically managed the caregiving required by the elderly at home, thanks to the presence of housewives, the change in the job market and the need to be employed (being out of the house) for all family members increased the demand for new and alternative solutions for people in LTCNs.

The aim of this book is to analyze how the demand of LTCNs is managed in different countries, being aware that the age structure of the population, the role of the welfare system, and the varieties of solutions potentially available can differ a lot from case to case. The knowledge about how different countries deal with the LTCNs of their populations can help identify best practices and stimulate the discussion about the adequacy of current public policies.

2 Summary of Book Contents

Long-term care insurance (LTCI), which is a social security system that provides services or financial support regarding basic living and medical care for individuals who have physical or mental disabilities due to aging, illness, and so forth, is an important guarantee to meet the LTC needs of the increasing elderly population. Most countries in the world are facing an aging population problem and changes in family structures. Consequently, there has been a growing demand for long-term care insurance and services.

2.1 Italy

In Italy, long-term care insurance and services are provided by the public sector (government agencies), the private sector (insurance companies), and single individuals (usually family members of the LTC individual, providing—directly or indirectly—informal care). Compared to other countries, Italy does not have any single organized system of LTC services providers, but services are provided by different entities, sometimes operating on a national level, sometimes on a regional scale, with different criteria for being eligible for assistance. The public sector offers its services to any individual that needs assistance and that is officially resident in the country (regardless of his/her nationality).

The recipients of LTC include individuals across different ages, including people that are unable to work due to injuries or sickness, people dealing with drug addictions, people with blindness or deafness, or people with mental diseases. From the public sector, individuals can get money allowances and direct services. The main money allowance program is the IDA, acronymous of "Indennità di Accompagnamento (accompanying allowance)." Direct services contain health-care services and socio-assistance services, and they can also provide residential or semi-residential services. Private sectors can provide private residential facilities and private insurance policies. In Italy, private long-term care insurance policies can be a "term-LTC insurance policy" or a "whole-life LTC insurance policy." Lastly, single individuals can provide informal care for those who need long-term care. Mostly, caregivers do not have specific healthcare or medical skills, nor medical education; they are normally females, and foreign workers.

2.2 Poland

In Poland, public long-term care services have been established like in most OECD countries and they are structured across two primary sectors; the health care sector and the social assistance sector. Institutions involved in the public long-term care system at the central level of government include the Ministry of Health, the Ministry of Family, Labor, and Social Policy, and the National Health Fund (NFZ). These organizations mainly define the guidelines for funding long-term care services and monitor the quality of services provided. The legal frameworks governing public long-term care provision in Poland are the social welfare act and the act on publicly funded health care services but no specific legal provisions have been established to regulate the right to long-term care, its scope, methods of implementation, administrative competencies, or financial structure. The methods of providing public long-term care can be broadly categorized into the provision of services and the disbursement of financial benefits. The provision of services includes in-kind benefits, such as direct caregiving, medical assistance, rehabilitation, and other forms of professional support for individuals in need of long-term care: social assistance centers, support centers, nursing homes, and family care homes.

On the other hand, the payment of financial benefits involves monetary support provided to beneficiaries or their caregivers to help cover the costs associated with long-term care. These payments are intended to supplement household income, allowing recipients to either arrange for private care services or cover specific caregiving-related expenses. The primary sources of funding for LTC services are public funds, which include contributions from the state budget, local governments, and the National Health Fund. Regarding LTC at home, 90% of older people need to use their wealth to pay for these services. Individuals residing at LTC facilities are generally responsible for covering the costs of accommodation and meals. In Poland, the private sector of long-term care has rapidly expanded since 2010 but there is no official register for private providers offering home-based care. The absence of regulation for private in-home LTC services creates significant challenges for both consumers and regulators. Without a centralized, publicly accessible database, it becomes difficult for individuals to find reliable service providers or compare quality across options.

2.3 United States

In the United States, most individuals who need long-term services and support are cared for in their own homes with the assistance of informal caregivers such as family members or friends. There is no general public long-term care insurance system in the US. The states and the federal government became the largest payers of long-term care services and support. Medicare is the main public health insurance program for individuals over age 65, but it is oriented primarily to cover acute conditions, not chronic illness or disability. Medicare does not cover nursing home stays longer than 100 days, and individuals must shoulder a substantial copayment on the portion of the stay beyond 20 days. Medicaid programs that cover long-term care for seniors aged 65 and over include Nursing Home Medicaid, Home and Community Based Services (HCBS) Waivers and Aged, Blind and Disabled (ABD) Medicaid. The Medicaid system provides long-term care insurance for people with low income and assets.

Unlike Medicare, Medicaid will provide indefinite coverage for a variety of needs, including custodial care. Medicaid covers children, adults, and seniors who need long-term care services because of disabling conditions and chronic illnesses. However, Medicaid faces numerous structural issues. The burden on households for both formal and informal care is quite high, especially for middle-income households that do not qualify for Medicaid. The private long-term care insurance has been provided in the US for over 30 years but the private system is small and stagnating. With the development of private long-term care insurance and due to the high cost of long-term care insurance, private insurance companies develop a combination of or hybrid products which combine life insurance or annuities with long-term care insurance. However, the supply of health care workers is inadequate due to low wages and difficult working conditions, and results in many deficiencies in care delivery. Also, the number of insurers offering LTC products has been steadily declining. There are five major categories of long-term care facilities in the US: nursing home, assisted living, home care agency, adult day care canter, and hospice.

2.4 Japan

In Japan, the problem of aging is considered more serious than in other countries because Japan has one of the highest rates of aging in the world, as a result of declining birthrates and an increasing life expectancy. Long-term care insurance and services are provided by the public sector and private sector. Public long-term care insurance premiums must be paid by all residents of Japan from the age of 40 until death. When receiving public long-term care insurance services, the user pays 10–30% of the total service cost as a self-payment depending on his or her income, and the remaining costs are supported by 50% each through taxes and insurance premiums. For receiving public long-term care insurance services, a private person should get prior certification of the long-term care grade by the municipality. Public long-term care services are categorized as in-home services, institutional services, and community-based services. From the in-home services, people can get home-visit services, day-care services, and short-term residential services. Institutional services are provided in welfare facilities for the elderly requiring long-term care, health care facilities, and integrated facilities that provide both medical and long-term care.

Community-based services have been in existence since 2006 and are an intermediate concept between in-home services and facility services. Community-based service centers are designated by municipalities and are available only to those who have a certificate of residence in the area. About the long-term care facilities, the capacity of long-term care facilities is increasing, especially the capacity of Toll Homes for the Elderly. It is because public long-term care facilities are not fully equipped to meet the needs of the elderly and the demands of the elderly are becoming more diverse compared to the past. Private long-term care insurance provides supplemental coverage in Japan and it is offered by life insurance companies and non-life insurance companies. Private long-term care insurance is provided by fixed amounts and reimbursements. Fixed-amount policies pay fixed benefits and reimbursement policies pay actual costs within the amount insured and generally life insurers are focused on fixed-benefit policies and non-life insurers are focused on reimbursement policies. Also, most private fixed-amount LTCI insurance products link payment conditions to public LTCI (a five-level graded system).

2.5 South Korea

In South Korea, similar to other countries, long-term care insurance and services are provided by the public sector and private sectors. The South Korean government established long-term care insurance in 2008 as the fifth social insurance system. The national health insurance service performs the main roles as an insurer, long-term care institutions are established and designated in accordance with the Elderly Welfare Act and the Elderly Long-Term Care Insurance Act and local governments establish and implement detailed implementation plans. Currently, subscription to long-term care insurance in Korea is mandatory by law, and those who are enrolled in health insurance are automatically enrolled in long-term care insurance. South Korea collects long-term care insurance premiums and health insurance premiums together, and long-term care insurance premiums are 6.55% of health insurance premiums.

The Long-Term Care Insurance Act in South Korea is not a pure form of social insurance but rather a hybrid system that includes government subsidies (taxes) and insurance premiums for social insurance subscribers. Similar to Japan, public long-term care insurance and services will be provided by five different categories. Long-term care insurance benefits are divided into three categories: home care benefits (home-visit care, day and night care, short-term care, other in-home benefits); facility benefits; and special cash benefits. However, there are some limitations such as rapid increases of certified people, lack of supply of long-term care facilities compared to demand and balance deficit. In South Korea, public health data has been available to insurance companies since 2021, and to fulfil that purpose, insurance companies have been able to develop dedicated products for the elderly and the sick, as well as provide healthcare-related flat form services through deregulation. So, some insurance companies and other financial institutions have recently entered the nursing care service industry.

2.6 China

In China, long-term care insurance is still in the pilot stage at present. In 2015, the Fifth Plenary Session of the 18th CPC Central Committee addressed that China should establish the LTCI system to meet the essential needs of the aging problem. After that, in 2017, the Ministry of Human Resources and Social Security issued the Guiding Opinions on Pilot Implementation of the Long-term Care Insurance System to launch the pilot program in 15 cities and designate Jilin and Shandong, two northern provinces of China, as key regions for special focus. As of the end of December 2023, the LTCI in China has already covered 49 cities and 170 million elderly people. Chinese governments are responsible for selecting the most suitable partners and integrated management through tenders or purchasing particular services from commercial insurance institutions. The long-term care insurance pilots are financially supported by diversified channels for the fee, such as funds transfer, government subsidies, personal wages, employing unit payments, medical insurance fund transfers, public welfare funds of welfare lottery, and social donations.

Among them, the transfer of basic medical insurance pooling funds is the main source of capital and is contained in the LTCI funds with respect to all pilot cities. Long-term care insurance funds in China are as follows: single-channel, dual-channel, triple-channel and quad-channel. The funding level of long-term care in China is currently influenced by various factors such as the economic development circumstances of each pilot city and the scope of LTCI coverage. Overall, the funding level is relatively low and still needs to be improved. Since long-term care insurance is in the early stage, it concentrates primarily on alleviating economic problems for the severely disabled elderly who are in critical need of basic living conditions and medical care.

2.7 Malaysia

In Malaysia, long-term care policies are overseen by the Ministry of Health and the Ministry of Women, Family, and Community Development. For Malaysia, some of the life insurance products include medical treatment with home nursing care for a limited time such as for a maximum of 180 days in their lifetime and coverage until the age of 100. For senior citizens in Malaysia, there are insurance options that can help cover medical expenses and nursing care facilities. Medical cards offer coverage for hospitalization fees, surgical procedures, outpatient treatments, medications and other healthcare services and are subject to a limited age coverage. Some of the insurance plan that covers up to at least 80 years of age also include home nursing care or nursing care facilities.

However, in Malaysia, private long-term care insurance has some issues such as affordability of the insurance plan, eligibility of the potential policy holder, the coverage limitation and increase of the premium throughout the enforcement of the insurance plan. For public care facilities, the Malaysian government established the Elderly Division and it oversees the operation, administration, and financial management of public facilities for the elderly. As a public long-term care facility, the Malaysian government provides five different types: Senior Citizen Activity Centers, Senior Citizens Care Unit Program, Respite Care, Home Help Services, and Senior Citizen Club. For the private sector, the Malaysian government permits private firms to participate in supplying care services to older persons under the Care Centers Act 1993. Also, to regulate private care facilities, the Ministry of Health introduced the Private Aged Healthcare Facilities and Services (PAHFAS) Bill in 2017. The PAHFAS Act 2017 aims to set higher standards for long-term and health care delivery to older persons. Admissions to government care facilities can be voluntary or through court orders for destitute individuals.

2.8 Bangladesh

In Bangladesh, most long-term care has traditionally been provided at home by family members, relatives, and friends, along with domestic helpers. Long-term care can also be provided in institutions such as nursing homes or in adult daycare centers, which are yet to be established and operated effectively in the country. Most nursing homes in Bangladesh offer only housing and housekeeping, with a few providing personal care and medical services. Specialized programs for Alzheimer's and dementia, as well as rehabilitation services like physical, occupational, and speech therapy, are not widely available in Bangladeshi old homes.

2.9 *Vietnam*

In Vietnam, public long-term care insurance in Vietnam is primarily governed within the comprehensive social insurance framework, regulated by the Ministry of Labour, Invalids, and Social Affairs (MOLISA) and implemented by Vietnam Social Security (VSS). The system operates through a network of local social insurance offices that oversee the execution and administration of long-term care services across various regions. There are no financial resources specifically allocated for long-term care by the Vietnamese government so the funding for public long-term care insurance comes from several sources such as payroll taxes, general taxation, specific premiums, and government subsidies. Vietnam currently lacks a standardized and formalized system for certifying long-term care needs.

Consequently, the process of assessing an individual's need for long-term care and issuing the corresponding certification remains undefined and is not widely implemented. Long-term care services in Vietnam are provided through a mix of public and private systems and include various forms of care depending on the individual's needs and preferences such as in-home services, facilities services, and community-based services. The main issues regarding public long-term care in Vietnam is limitation of public financial budgets to cover the expenses for elderly and disabled people in the future. Private long-term care insurance in Vietnam is a relatively new product, emerging in the 2010s from the growing demand of the population for comprehensive and long-term healthcare services. At present, private long-term care insurance in Vietnam remains in the developmental stage.

3 Issues and Prospects for Long-term Care

Rapid aging is progressing in many countries, and approaches to addressing the care risks for the elderly vary. For example, some countries rely on self-help efforts, such as family caregiving, seen in many developing nations. Others, like the United States, rely on public and private health insurance. Still others, such as Japan and Germany, primarily rely on public long-term care insurance systems.

Furthermore, eldercare costs typically increase from the initial stages of care through to the later stages when care needs intensify. In contrast, pension amounts are fixed, leading to a growing funding shortfall for care expenses over time (Fig. 1). Meanwhile, the number of elderly individuals utilizing fee-based nursing homes, which offer higher-quality services than public facilities, is rapidly increasing. Given these changing circumstances, there is a strong demand for creating systems that enable efficient selection of eldercare risk management approaches capable of addressing the diverse needs of the elderly.

On the other hand, many countries have public pension systems, supplemented by corporate pensions, and additionally offer private pensions that individuals can choose to join voluntarily. These pensions are intended to cover long-term care

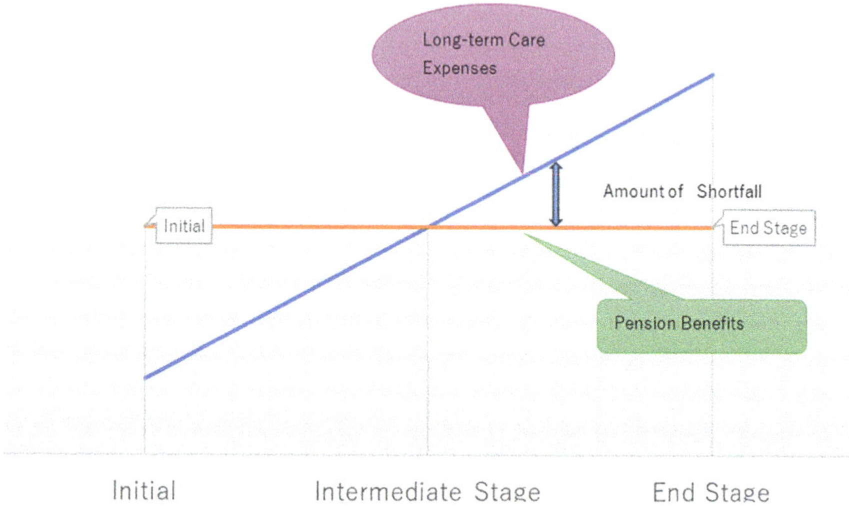

Fig. 1 Relationship between long-term care costs and pension benefits (conceptual diagram). *Source* Created by Lee

costs and living expenses in old age, but the amount received is fixed. Therefore, when relying on pensions to cover long-term care costs, the shortfall increases over time.(Fig. 1) Addressing this shortfall becomes a major challenge.

Second, as confirmed by the following trend in the capacity of Japanese nursing care facilities, the capacity of each facility is increasing, but the capacity of paid nursing homes is surging (Fig. 2).

The primary reason appears to be the diversification of needs among elderly individuals seeking admission to high-end facilities. Private pensions and private long-term care insurance are necessary to address this diversification of demand for care services.

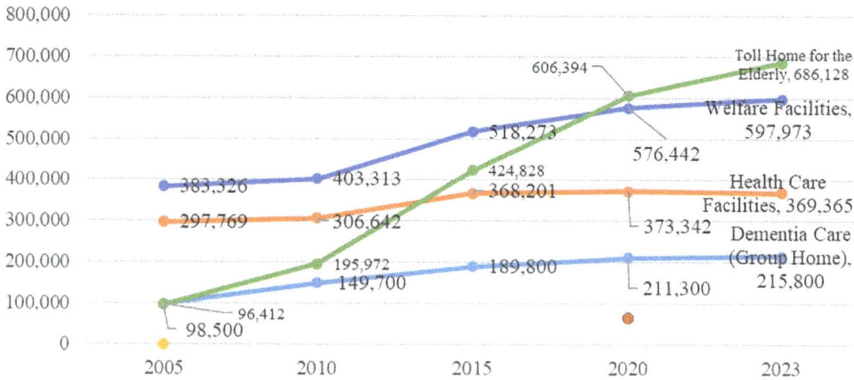

Fig. 2 Trend of capacity of long-term care facilities in Japan. *Source* Cabinet office of Japan

Meanwhile, while 55% of individuals aged 85 and older are said to have dementia (Japan Ministry of Health, Labour, and Welfare), the care system for dementia is not sufficiently developed. For example, if an elderly person's cognitive abilities are deemed insufficient due to dementia, financial institutions may freeze their accounts. As a result, funds set aside may become inaccessible for use as care expenses.

The central issues in caregiving are the increasing burden of care costs alongside aging, the choice of care facilities, and the response to dementia.

References

ADBI/OECD/ILO. (2023). Labor migration in Asia: Changing profiles and processes, Asian Development Bank Institute. https://doi.org/10.56506/lhmv144

Annual Report on the Ageing Society. (2019, June). Cabinet office of Japan.

European Commission. (2021). 2021 Aging report: Ageing in populations and fiscal sustainability. https://economy-finance.ec.europa.eu/system/files/2022-05/2021_ageing_report_0.pdf

Lee, H. (2022). Retirement income security in Japan: An overview of the public and private pension system. International comparison of pension systems: An investigation from consumers' viewpoint. Springer.

An Analysis of the Long-Term Care in Italy: Financial and Non-financial Issues

Gianni Nicolini

1 The Demand of Long-Term Care: Who Are Those in Need?

An analysis of the Long-Term Care needs (LTC needs) of a population requires a preliminary definition of those needs and an identification of the services and the target of recipients to satisfy those needs.

The concept of LTC is related to the impossibility or difficulty in self-managing normal Activities of Daily Living (ADL), like bathing or showering, dressing, getting in and out of bed or a chair, walking, using the toilet, and eating (European Commission 2021). People lacking in even just a few of these activities become dependent individuals, requiring external support. However, the loss of independency for an individual, and the demand for external supports, can be related even to Instrumental Activities of Daily Living (IADL) (ISTAT 2021). The IADL are all those activities needed to live as an independent individual, and refer to cooking meals, using telephones, grocery shopping, taking pills, (light) housekeeping, seldom domestic hard work, and self-financial management. If limitations due to the lack of abilities in doing IADL are less severe than those related to ADL, in both cases it emerges due to the need of external supports. When the need of external supports extends over time, it is the case of LTC needs.

From these definitions it follows that an individual can start being dependent on others for the lack of different abilities, and the degree of dependency can be more (or less) severe, according to the number of limitations, and the amount of help required to make up for a deficiency.

The reduced degree (or complete loss) of functional capacities can be due to physical or cognitive reasons. An injury can temporarily limit the walking ability of an

G. Nicolini (✉)
Department of Management and Law, University of Rome Tor Vergata, Rome, Italy
e-mail: gianni.nicolini@uniroma2.it

H. Lee and G. Nicolini (eds.), *International Comparison of Long-Term Care Insurance Systems*, Contributions to Management Science,
https://doi.org/10.1007/978-981-95-7781-1_2

individual, while aging can involve a long-lasting limitation. At the same time, mental diseases (e.g. dementia, Alzheimer's, Parkinson's, etc.) causes the same limitation, but for different reasons. Hence, there is not a perfect overlap between dependent individuals and those requiring LTC. The temporary and reversable limitations of some dependent individuals stress how in the case of LTC individuals, the length and the gravity of these limitations make the real difference. A broken leg or a spine surgery can temporarily limit the ability to walk, or to do grocery shopping, making the individual a dependent individual. The loss of walking abilities due to aging or mental diseases will make the dependent individual in need of LTC.

So, there is not a single target of recipients for LTC services, but the long-term loss or reduction in abilities in dealing with activities of daily living (ADL) makes the elderly, people with mental diseases, people with severe mental or physical disabilities (regardless of their age) the main reference points of LTC scenarios. Another point to stress regards the chance that an LTC need is not necessarily related to sickness or requiring (acute) medical treatments. An elderly person that needs help for showering or bathing, and that requires support for eating (or just cooking), is an individual with LTC needs, even if those needs are not caused by a sickness. It follows that an approach to the LTC needs of a population should include health issues but not be limited to those needs, and it should keep in mind the chance that an individual could show a diversity of needs, caused by different things.

2 The Growing Demand of LTC Services

The number of individuals with LTC needs and the ability of the LTC system of a country to deal with them is one of the challenges of several developed countries. Data shows a growing demand for LTC services in the recent years, and the projection on the future is even more demanding. Within the reasons for the number of individuals with LTC needs, and the efforts required to deal with those needs which are growing, there are: (1) the aging in population; (2) the changes in family structures; and (3) the change in the roles of females in the society.

The aging in the population is a general phenomenon in most of the developed countries (Fig. 1). The causes of this average increase in the average age of a country are the increasing life expectancy and the decreasing fertility rates. People tend to live longer than previous generations thanks to the scientific progress (e.g. achievements in medicine, technology, etc.) and a better quality of life (e.g. nutrition, housing, access to medical treatment, decreasing job wear and tear, etc.). meanwhile, the average number of children in a family decreased after the 1960s, remaining below the natural replacement rate after the 1980s (Fig. 2).

The projections at European level report a population to grow in some countries, and to shrink in others (Fig. 3), but to age in all (Fig. 4).

Projections on data on fertility rate confirm a trend of average numbers of children in families quite below the natural replacement rate, even if the downward trend that started in the 1960s seems to be inverted in the last 20 years (Fig. 5).

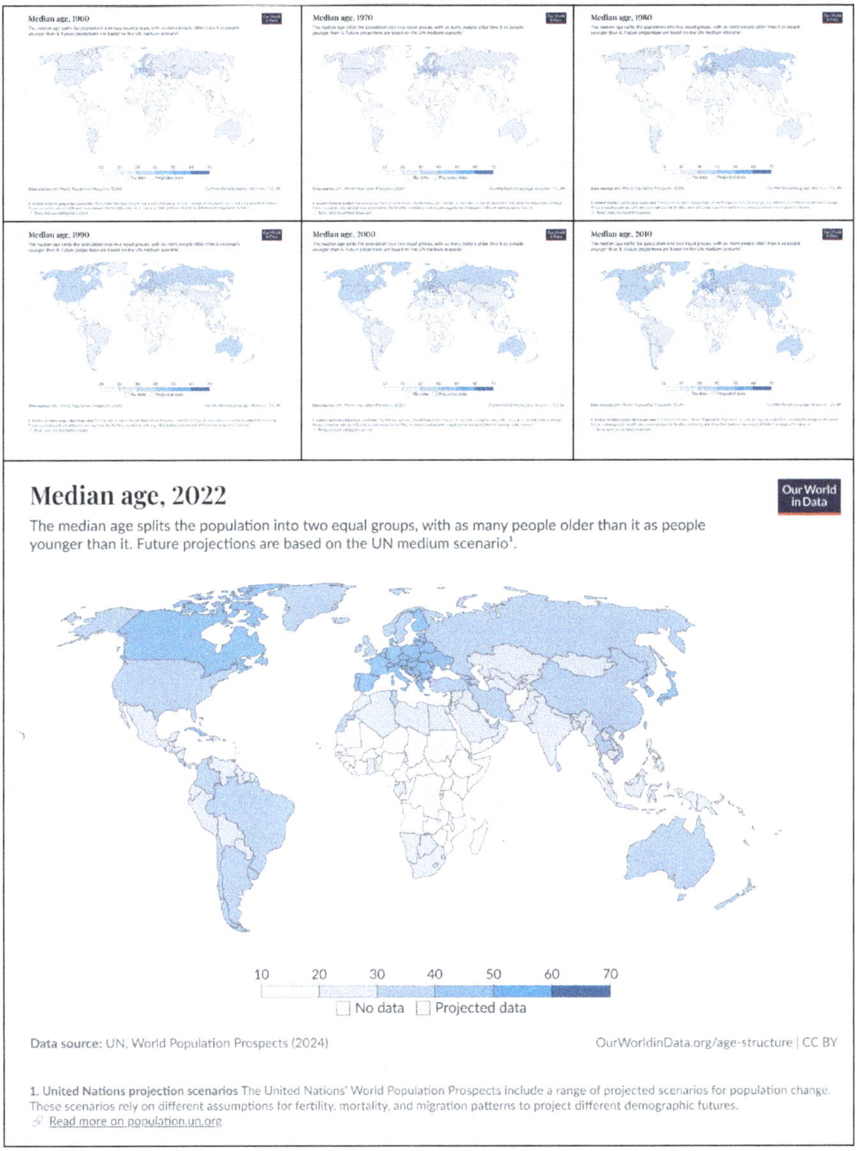

Fig. 1 The aging in population. *Source* Our World in Data (2024)

Crossing projections about life-expectancy with those on fertility rates, we obtain the projections on the share of people 65+ on people in their working age (20–64): the so called "old-age dependency ratio" (Fig. 6).

Data from Italy (Fig. 7) shows a growing life expectancy, both at birth and at 65. The life expectancy at birth for males in 2019 was 81.3 years (85.7 years for females)

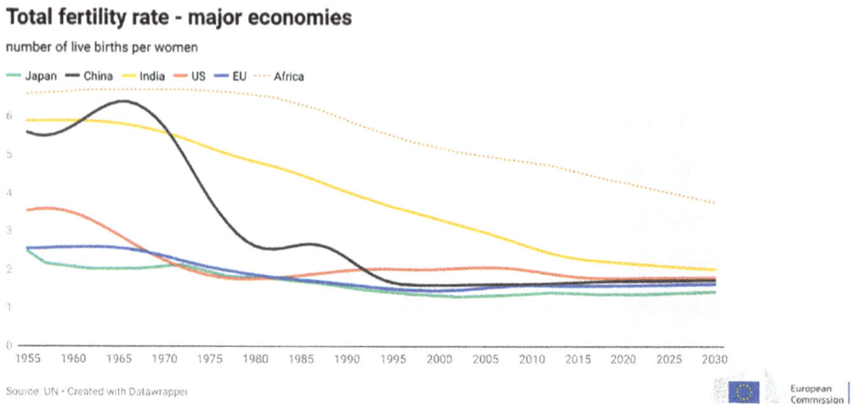

Fig. 2 The fertility rate—major economies. *Source* European Commission (2021)

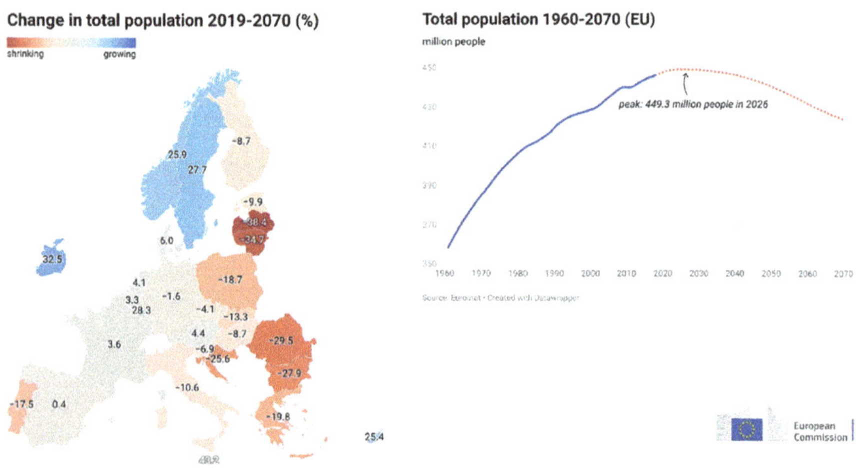

Fig. 3 Expected changes in population in Europe (2019–2070). *Source* European Commission (2021)

with an estimated increase from 2019 to 2070 of 5.7 years (5.2 for females). The same positive trend is reported for the life expectancy at 65, that goes from 19.6 years for males in 2019 (22.9 for females) to 23.9 years in 2070 (27.2 for females), with an expected growth of 4.3 years (for both males and females).

The fertility rate seems destined to remain quite below the natural replacement rate. Its value in 2019 was 1.31, with an expected value in 2070 of 1.52.

The combination of those factors involves an old-age dependency ratio, given by the ratio of number of individuals aged 65 and over per 100 people of working age (age 20–64)—equal to 38.9 in 2019 but expected to be 65.6 in 2070. Hence, a first

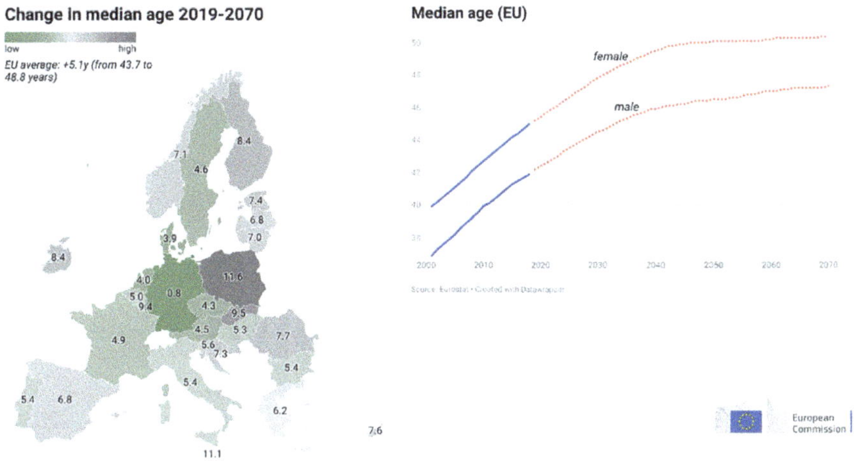

Fig. 4 Expected changes in population in Europe (2019–2070). *Source* European Commission (2021)

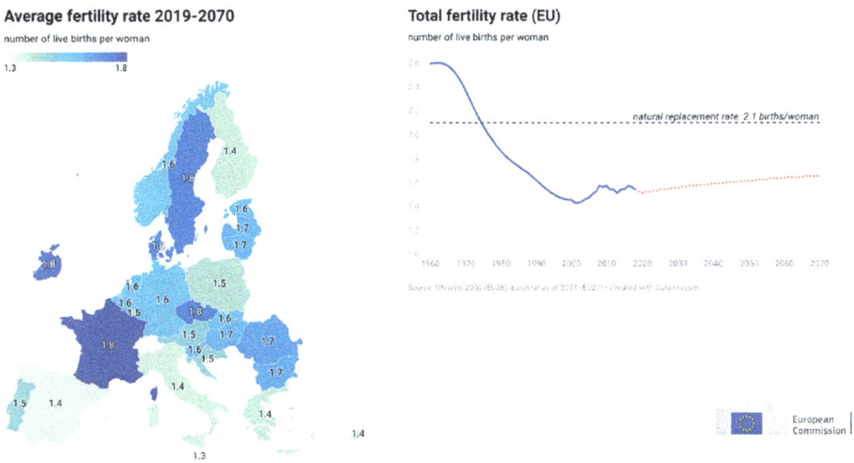

Fig. 5 Average fertility rate 2019–2070. *Source* European Commission (2021)

factor that affects the demand for LTC services is the growing number of elderly people and a decreasing number of young people (potentially caregivers).

A second factor affecting the demand for LTC services regards the changes in family structures. The shrinking average number of people in households makes the chance that one or more family members become caregivers (individually or by sharing their care) simply less likely. As reported in Table 1, the number of Italian singles increases over time, while families with three or more members decreases. If families made by many members have the chance to cope with cases of members

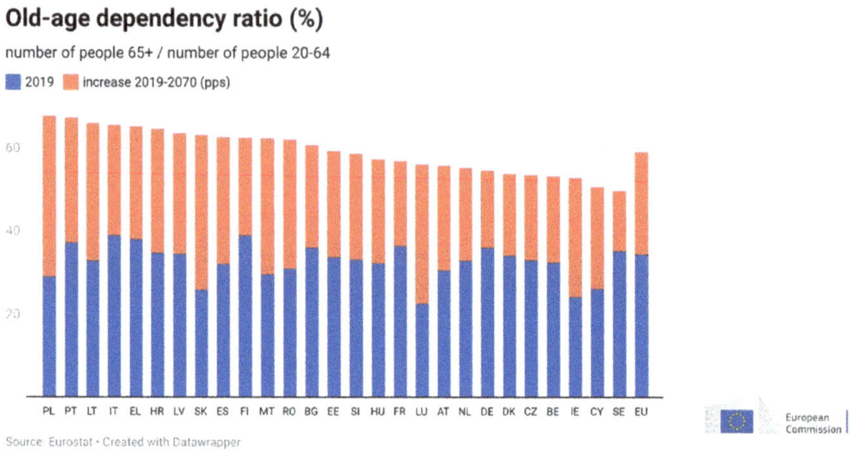

Fig. 6 Old-age dependency ratio (%). *Source* European Commission (2021)

Italy							
Main demographic and macroeconomic assumptions							
Demographic projections (EUROSTAT)	Ch 19-70	2019	2030	2040	2050	2060	2070
Fertility rate	0.2	1.31	1.37	1.41	1.45	1.48	1.52
Life expectancy at birth							
males	5.7	81.3	82.6	83.8	84.9	86.0	87.0
females	5.2	85.7	86.9	88.0	89.0	90.0	90.9
Life expectancy at 65							
males	4.3	19.6	20.5	21.4	22.3	23.1	23.9
females	4.3	22.9	23.8	24.7	25.6	26.4	27.2
Net migration (thousand)	:	134.7	224.0	217.2	214.3	210.5	206.6
Net migration as % of population	:	0.2	0.4	0.4	0.4	0.4	0.4
Population (million)	-6.4	60.3	59.9	59.3	58.0	55.9	53.9
Young population (0-19) as % of total population	-2.1	17.9	15.9	15.4	15.6	15.6	15.8
Prime-age population (25-54) as % of total population	-7.1	40.3	35.8	34.9	34.1	33.6	33.1
Working-age population (20-64) as % of total population	-8.3	59.1	56.8	52.4	50.7	51.0	50.8
Elderly population (65+) as % of total population	10.4	23.0	27.3	32.2	33.7	33.4	33.3
Very elderly population (80+) as % of total population	7.2	7.3	8.8	10.5	13.8	15.3	14.5
Very elderly population (80+) as % of elderly population	11.8	31.7	32.2	32.6	41.0	45.8	43.5
Very elderly population (80+) as % of working-age population	16.2	12.3	15.5	20.0	27.3	30.0	28.5
Dependency ratios	Ch 19-70	2019	2030	2040	2050	2060	2070
Share of older population (55-64) (2)	2.4	23.5	27.9	25.1	24.1	25.1	25.8
Old-age dependency ratio 20-64 (3)	26.7	38.9	48.0	61.4	66.5	65.5	65.6
Total dependency ratio (4)	27.6	69.2	76.0	90.7	97.4	96.1	96.8
Total economic dependency ratio (5)	-6.7	159.3	149.1	157.1	161.7	156.7	152.6
Economic old-age dependency ratio (20-64) (6)	23.7	58.5	65.8	81.0	87.0	84.2	82.2
Economic old-age dependency ratio (20-74) (7)	16.7	56.9	61.7	74.5	80.1	76.5	73.6

Fig. 7 Demographic projections for Italian population 2019–2070. *Source* EUROSTAT (2019)

requiring LCT, the shrinking size of the Italian families tends to make this option no longer available, increasing the demand for external supports.

A third factor in the growth of demand for LTC services is the change in the roles of females in society. In the past, the case of single-income families, with the men being the only income provider and the woman being the housewife, represented a standard. In that case women usually start being the caregivers when one (or more) family members quit to be independent, requiring LTC.

Table 1 The composition of Italian families over time

Years	% of families (by numbers of households in the family)						Total	Average number of people per household
	1	2	3	4	5	6+		
	Percentage							
1961	10.7	19.6	22.4	20.4	12.6	14.4	100.0	2.761
1971	12.9	22.0	22.4	21.2	11.8	9.7	100.0	2.778
1981	17.9	23.6	22.1	21.5	9.5	5.4	100.0	2.704
1991	20.6	24.7	22.2	21.2	7.9	3.4	100.0	2.644
2001	24.9	27.1	21.6	19.0	5.8	1.7	100.0	2.503
2011	31.2	27.1	19.9	16.2	4.3	1.4	100.0	2.326

Source ISTAT (2012)

However, the change in the family structure and the increasing participation to the job market by female workers make the assignment of the role of caregiver to housewives no longer an automatic consequence of having a family member with LTC needs, because women cannot be full time at home anymore. As reported in Table 2, the percentage of Italian women active in the job market (looking for a job or working) increased over time. It was below 40% until mid-80s, being around 60% in recent years.

The growing participation of Italian women in the job market is not only part of the evolution of the society but is frequently a necessity, due to a decreasing purchase power of salaries in Italy. As reported in Table 3, Italy is within the group of European countries—with Greece and Spain—where average real salaries (accounting for inflation) decreased across the last 20 years. From 1997 to 2019, the average purchase power of the Italian salaries decreased by 6%. In case of families where the loss of purchase power was above the average, it is likely that the need of a double income (so the need of women to get a job and leaving their full-time housewife status) became a necessity.

Hence, the combination of an aging population, a family size (on average) smaller than before, and the chance that most of the family members in working age are not at home defines a scenario where the demand of LTC services of the population grows, and the subjects that traditionally played the role of caregivers are not available anymore. The result is the need to find alternative solutions to the LTC needs of the population while respecting traditional options.

Table 2 Female participation (age 25–64) in the job market in Italy

Years	Workers (%)	Unemployed (%)	Active (looking for a job) (%)
1977	33.7	5.5	35.7
1978	34.3	5.4	36.3
1979	34.8	5.5	36.9
1980	35.9	5.5	38.0
1981	36.4	6.1	38.7
1982	36.7	6.2	39.1
1983	37.2	7.1	40.0
1984	37.9	7.3	40.9
1985	38.1	7.3	41.1
1986	38.6	7.7	41.9
1987	39.4	8.6	43.2
1988	40.0	8.9	44.0
1989	40.6	9.2	44.7
1990	41.3	8.5	45.2
1991	41.7	8.7	45.7
1992	42.1	8.6	46.1
1993	41.7	9.8	46.3
1994	41.5	10.8	46.5
1995	41.7	11.5	47.2
1996	42.4	11.5	48.0
1997	42.7	11.8	48.5
1998	43.6	12.2	49.7
1999	44.6	11.9	50.7
2000	45.8	10.9	51.4
2001	47.5	10.0	52.8
2002	48.6	9.4	53.7
2003	49.0	9.4	54.2
2004	49.5	8.7	54.3
2005	49.8	8.4	54.4
2006	51.0	7.3	55.1
2007	51.4	6.6	55.1
2008	52.2	7.2	56.2
2009	51.5	7.8	55.9
2010	51.3	8.2	56.0
2011	51.9	8.0	56.4
2012	52.7	10.0	58.6
2013	52.2	11.1	58.8

(continued)

Table 2 (continued)

Years	Workers (%)	Unemployed (%)	Active (looking for a job) (%)
2014	52.7	11.8	59.8
2015	53.2	10.8	59.7

Source ISTAT (2015)

Table 3 Percentage change in the average real salaries in Italy (1997–2019)

	Average real salaries in Italy (% change, 1997–2019)
Lithuania	258
Latvia	195
Estonia	177
Slovakia	100
Malta	46
Ireland	34
Finland	17
France	17
Luxembourg	17
Cyprus	16
Portugal	14
The Netherlands	12
Austria	10
Germany	10
Belgium	9
Slovenia	5
Spain	-2
Italy	-6
Greece	-18

Source OCPI (2022)

3 The Response of the Italian System to the LTC Needs of the Population

The solutions adopted in response to the LTC needs of the population in Italy come from the public sector (government agencies), the private sector (insurance companies), and single individuals (usually family members of the LTC individual, providing—directly or indirectly—informal care).

With respect to other countries, there is not a single organized system of LTC services providers, but services are provided by different entities, sometimes operating on a national level, sometimes on a regional scale, with different criteria for being eligible for assistance.

3.1 The Public System

The approach of the public sector with the LTC needs of the population is not based on specific targets (e.g. elderly, people with dementia, etc.), but it offers its services to any individual that needs assistance and that is officially resident in the country (regardless of his/her nationality). It means that the recipients of LTC include individuals across different ages, including people that are unable to work due to injuries or sickness, people dealing with drug addictions, people with blindness or deafness, or people with mental diseases. If, in some cases, the LTC need can be reversible (e.g. people can recover from an injury or be out of a drug addiction), while in others the system should be able to provide aid for an unlimited amount of time.

The support provided to LTC individuals by the public sector is based on (1) money allowances, and (2) direct services. Within the direct services, there are health-care services and socio-assistance services. The main money allowance program is the IDA, acronymous of "Indennità di Accompagnamento" (accompanying allowance). The IDA is paid to any individual—regardless of income—that is 100% permanently unable to work, or those that are not able to walk without the support of a caregiver or those incapable of doing daily basic activities. The amount of money paid monthly for the IDA is (in 2024) equal to €534.76, and it is tax-exempt. To receive the IDA, it is necessary to submit a request to INPS (Istituto Nazionale Previdenza Sociale), the national agency responsible for social care and (public) pensions. Every applicant is evaluated by a commission every 12 months (except the cases of irreversible conditions). The IDA is not based on a budget, so any applicant that is eligible according to the evaluation criteria will receive the allowance, and it does not require any type of accountability for how the money granted is spent.

Within the LTC services, there is the healthcare support (e.g. medical treatment, psychological support, rehab, etc.). With respect to the IDA, that is administered at a national level, the Italian healthcare system is on a regional base. One of the main consequences of that difference is the chance that different regions define different criteria to access (free) healthcare services, and the criteria of a region cannot overlap with those set for the IDA money allowance.

An additional service included in the LTC list of services are residential or semi-residential services. The first one includes the chance to be hosted in a healthcare residence called RSA ("Residenze Sanitarie Assistenziali"... "healthcare support residence"). This option is provided in case a homecare solution is not feasible but there is no need for hospitalization. There are four types of RSAs: intensive care RSA, extensive care RSA, extensive care for serious behavioral cognitive disorders SBCD-RSA, and maintenance RSA.

Intensive care RSAs host people with serious disabilities requiring high levels of medical cares and continuous assistance (e.g. assisted mechanical breathing, enteral nutrition, vegetative state, prolonged coma, etc.). Extensive RSAs regard people with high levels of medical care that need a functional stabilization aiming for the homecoming of the patient or a transfer to a maintenance RSA. In case of extensive care for serious behavioral cognitive disorders SBCD-RSA, the residents are affected by dementia requiring a protected environment for the patients. For both the extensive RSAs (standard or SBCD-RSA) the patient does not stay on average longer than 60 days in the facility. A maintenance RSA hosts people in need of long-term assistance with standard medical assistance. According to the level of assistance needed by the guests (more or less intensive), there are maintenance RSA of level A or B.

In the case of RSAs there is an overlap between the public and the private sector, because RSAs can be public, private, or being a private RSA open to patients coming from the public sector and hosted thanks to an agreement between the two counterparts. It is even possible that a residential structure is privately owned and only some of the available slots are reserved for guests coming from the public system. The overlap between public and private sectors affects even the pricing of the service. The daily fare for an RSA is fixed by the regional council. It follows that the price for the service can differ from region to region. For intensive and extensive RSAs that are public, and for the slots of private RSA used for patients coming from the public sector, the cost of the service is fully covered by the public system, while for maintenance RSA, 50% of the daily fare (representing the healthcare quote) is charged to the public system, and the remaining 50% (the living costs) is charged to the guest. However, there is the chance for low-income individuals to be waived (fully or partially) from the payment of the living expenses, in case of contributions from the local administration (municipality) of the city/town of residence of the patient.

Semi-residential facilities regard meeting centers, where LTC individuals can be hosted only during the daytime, with no chance to stay overnight. An additional type of semi-residential assistance is the home assistance. In that case the support to dependent individuals is provided at home. The patient remains in his/her residence, receiving visits from caregivers in order to receive help (so-called "nursing at home").

An additional option for those that have to deal with LTC patients is the care leave program. The law 104/92 (usually reported simply as "legge 104", meaning "law 104") allows one family member of a LTC individual to use up to three days a months of care leave with no income deductions (the cost is covered by the national social security agency "INPS"), with the chance to fraction this time in certain situations.

If the public sector can provide support to LTC individuals in the abovementioned ways (except for the IDA money allowance, and the care leave program "104," that are administrated at the national levels), the availability of other services can vary greatly from region to region, as well as the quality of those services, and the criteria to access could not be the same.

Some data can help to figure out the relevance of the LTC support provided by the public sector.

According to the Italian Minister of Finance (MEF 2023) the public expenditure on LTC in 2022 was equal to 1.73% of the GDP, equal to (around) 33 billion euro.

Half of that money (50%) regards money allowances (Table 4), residential and semi-residential assistance accounted for 33.8% of the public expenditure on LTC, while only 4.8% regards the house assistance programs.

A comparison between 2012 and 2022 (Table 5) shows how the public expenditure on LTC decreased. The total expenditure on GDP was 1.84% in 2012, dropping to 1.73% in 2022. However, referring to the part of that money spent on people 55+, the 1.27% of the GDP in 2012 raised to 1.28% in 2022. It is even interesting to note how the composition of this expenditure changed over time. The money allowances decreased (from 0.81% of the GDP in 2012 to 0.74%; and for 55+ it changed from 0.63% in 2012 to 0.56% in 2022), while residential and quasi-residential solutions and house assistance supports increased (from 0.17% to 0.28%; for 55+ from 0.13% to 0.25% of the national GDP).

The fraction of the GDP spent on LCT is not itself enough to assess the role of the public sector over time. In fact, accounting for the increase of the elderly population

Table 4 LTC public expenditures (year 2022)

	Total			65+ years		
	Expenditure in EuroBN	Expenditure/ GDP (%)	% on total	Expenditure in EuroBN (%)	Expenditure/ GDP (%)	% on total
House assistance	5.3	0.28	16.20	4.8	0.25	19.30
Residential and quasi-residential assistance	11.1	0.58	33.80	7.2	0.38	29.70
Money allowance	16.6	0.87	50.00	12.4	0.65	51.00
Total	33	1.73	100.00	24.4	1.28	100.00

Source MEF (2023)

Table 5 LTC public expenditures in 2012 and 2022

	Total		65+ years	
	Expenditure/ GDP 2012 (%)	Expenditure/ GDP 2022 (%)	Expenditure/ GDP 2012 55+ (%)	Expenditure/ GDP 2022 55+ (%)
Healthcare services	0.86	0.70	0.50	0.47
Money allowance	0.81	0.74	0.63	0.56
Other services (residential, quasi-residential, house assistance)	0.17	0.28	0.13	0.25
Total	1.84	1.73	1.27	1.28

Source MEF (2023)

Table 6 Public expenditure on LTC on GDP in the European Union in 2019 and forecasting at 2070

Country	2019	Forecasting 2070	Country	2019	Forecasting 2070
Greece	0.2	0.2	Slovenia	1	2.1
Bulgaria	0.3	0.4	Malta	1.1	2.5
Cyprus	0.3	0.6	Ireland	1.3	2.6
Croatia	0.4	0.6	Czech Rep	1.5	2.9
Estonia	0.4	0.7	Germany	1.6	2.3
Romania	0.4	0.7	Italy	1.7	2.7
Portugal	0.4	0.8	EU 27	1.7	2.9
Latvia	0.5	0.6	Austria	1.8	3.6
Hungary	0.6	1.2	France	1.9	2.8
Spain	0.7	1.5	Finland	2	4.2
Poland	0.8	2.3	Belgium	2.2	4.3
Slovakia	0.8	2.5	Sweden	3.3	5.7
Lithuania	1	1.7	Denmark	3.5	7.5
Luxemburg	1	1.7	The Netherlands	3.7	6.4

Source MEF (2023)

from 2012 (12,639,829) to 2022 (14,177,000) and the increase of 12% of dependent people[1] makes the reduction of the assistance to the LTC population more evident.

Looking at the data from other European countries (Table 6), the Italian total expenditure in LTC (1.70% of the GDP) is in line with the average of the European Union (1.70%). However, the EU average is made by quite different values. The total expenditure on GDP is equal to 0.2% in Greece and 3.7% in The Netherlands. An additional note is about the different levels of GDP from country to country: for example, the Italian 1.7% and the German 1.6% seem very close but when rescaling the money expenditure of the public German system to the Italian GDP, it is equal to 2.2%.

Beyond the money spent in LCT by the public sector, it is interesting to check how the supply of services is able to cope with the demand of the population. Looking at the number of available beds in residential facilities, in 2022 there were 12,576 residential facilities, offering around 414,000 beds, equal to one bed every thousand residents. The number of available beds is bigger in the north-east of the country (10 beds every thousand residents) compared to the south (three every thousand residents). Maybe even due to the more available beds, the number of elderly hosted in residential facilities is bigger in the north-east (28 every thousand) than the south (eight every thousand). Details about the guests of the residential facilities (Table 7) highlight how most of the residents are elderly people—independents (13.46%) or dependents (60.78%)—followed by people with disabilities (7.64%), children (5.29%),

[1] MEF (2023).

and people with mental illnesses (4.84%). It is interesting to note that within the elderly group the number of independent individuals hosted by residential facilities is much bigger in the center and the south of the country with respect to the north.

3.2 The Private Sector

The provision of LTC assistance by the private sector refers essentially to two kinds of solutions. The first one is the management of private residential facilities that can be offered directly to private users or being rented to the public sector. At the end of 2020, 75% of the 12,630 residential facilities in Italy ("RSAs") were managed by private institutions (mainly no profit organizations).[2] Some 44% of the residential facilities were managed by no-profit private institutions, 24% were managed by for-profit organizations, and 12% by religious communities. Hence, 80% of the residential facilities belong to the private sector, with the remaining 20% owned by the public sector. However, there is the chance that a public residential facility is managed by a private entity (most likely a no-profit organization).

The great heterogeneity of the Italian LTC system requires stressing the differences between different areas of the country. For instance, in the north of the country, 70% of public residential facilities are—directly or indirectly—managed by public entities, with 26% by no-profit organizations. No-profit organizations in the center manage 41% of the public residential facilities, and 36% in the south. Hence, the big picture is that most of the residential facilities are managed (or both owned and operated) by the private sector.

The second solution to LTC needs of individuals provided by the private sector are insurance policies.

The LCT insurance policies offered by insurance companies guarantee a periodic income when the insured individual loses his/her self-sufficiency. The instalment received from the insurance companies can be prefixed or tuned accordingly to the degree of dependency from external cares. An alternative insurance agreement can replace the money allowance with a lump sum, or the reimbursement of the expenses for external cares, or it can guarantee direct assistance in hosting the insured person in a residential facility.

The LTC insurance policies can be a "term-LTC insurance policy" or a "whole-life LTC insurance policy." In a term-LTC insurance policy the loss of self-sufficiency that triggers the payments by the insurance company must happen in a specific time frame. After a deadline (the "term" of the contract) the insurance company has no more obligations in case the self-sufficiency of the insured individual will be lost. In whole-life insurance the insurance company is obliged to pay from the time the insured individual loses his/her self-sufficiency, regardless of the time it happens, for the whole life of the insured individual. To avoid opportunistic behaviours, insurance companies usually accept requests of new insurance only if the insured individual is

[2] Source: ISTAT (2022).

Table 7 Types of residents in residential facilities

	Children	People with disabilities	People with addictions	Dependent elderly	Independent elderly	Immigrants—foreigners	Adults with social problems	People with mental illnesses	Victim of gender violence	Multiple conditions
North-west	3.13	7.3	2.25	10.78	69.88	0.38	1.87	3.6	0.12	0.69
North-east	4.35	7.23	1.07	6.37	73.83	1.39	2.77	2.62	0.06	0.32
Center	6.95	7.94	3.98	20.42	46.48	1.9	4.18	6.15	0.21	1.78
South	6.56	10.35	6.16	24.74	37.64	2.42	3.23	8.24	0.11	0.54
Isles	13.54	6.38	2.29	21.47	32.91	4.38	4.75	11.18	1.56	1.53
Italy	5.29	7.64	2.63	13.46	60.78	1.45	2.87	4.84	0.23	0.81

Source ISTAT (2023)

younger than 65,[3] even if that threshold can be different from company to company, with a range that goes from 60 to 70 (years of age). As with any insurance policy, increasing the risk, the premium to be paid increases too. Hence, for instance, the older the insured individual, the more expensive the premium required by the insurance company will be, due to the correlation between the age and the likelihood to require LTC assistance. However, in case of whole-life LTC insurance policies, premiums have to be paid only until a certain age of the individual (e.g. 65 years or 70 years), even if the coverage of the insurance is extended to the whole life of the individual.

It should noted that the insurance market offers even LTC insurance policies that cover only medical expenses (within a maximum amount of money).

An incentive to develop private solutions to LTC needs is the tax shield on premiums paid on LTC insurance policies. Those payments are deductible at 19%, with a cap on the amount of the premium of €1,291.14. It follows that the maximum deduction is €245.32 a year.[4]

Few numbers can help to figure out the role LTC insurance policies have in the LTC Italian system. The public expenditure on LTC in Italy in 2023 was 38 billion euros (including healthcare services, money allowance, other services), while the private expenditure (for residential facilities and home assistance) was 33 billion euros. In the meantime, the premiums on LTC insurance policies were 0.17 billion euros, representing only 0.2% of life insurances (IVASS 2023). This data highlights the characteristic of the Italian insurance market, featured by a large under-coverage of private individuals in both life- and non-life risks.

3.3 *The Self-Made Solutions*

The set of options to deal with individual requiring LTC assistance includes all areas of informal care. This includes the chance that family members (especially if co-habiting) of an individual that starts to lose independence become caregivers. This option was a traditional solution to the LTC needs of the elderly in the past. However, as it was stressed in previous paragraphs, this option becomes less and less likely, due to the lack of individuals at home, especially in daytime. If women (as housewives) typically became in the past the caregivers of the elderly living at home, the will or need to work out of home makes this option not available anymore. In the meantime, the low fertility rate reduces the average number of components in the family structure, reducing the chance that the burden of the cares could be shared between multiple members (e.g. mother, fathers, sons, daughters).

In this new scenario, the need to cope with dependent family members at home—as co-habiting members of the family or as individuals living in different houses—pushed Italian families to develop an alternative solution, based on professional caregivers, privately hired (and paid) by the households. The term used to identify

[3] Source: Comitato EduFin (2024).

[4] Source: Altroconsumo (2023).

this new job figure is "badante" (the Italian word identifying who is taking care of another individual, the plural of which is "badanti"). These caregivers, in most cases, have no specific healthcare or medical skills, nor medical education (they are not nurses or social workers); they are (on average) females and foreign workers (Fosti and Notarticola 2019). This practice started in 2000s and developed over time. This innovation did not require the development of infrastructures or new regulations, and it was essentially based on word on mouth. People rely on references of other families that hired a badante before, or the request of a new badante is satisfied by new ones, contacted and recommended by a current badante. This phenomenon was initially based on foreign workers looking for a job to last for a few years and aimed to support family members at home (especially education of children). It then developed into making a badante a real professional, permanently living in the country, not necessarily living anymore with the care receiver but having their own independent living venue. The end of assistance to an individual (due to the death of the caretaker, or his/her transfer in hospitals, needing medical assistance) sees the badante come back on the job market looking for a new position. The fact that these working relationships could not always be supported by a regular contract makes the estimation of the total number of this kind of (professional) caregiver challenging. According to Fosti and Notarticola (2019), more than a million professionals operate in the country. This number, compared to the number of beds available in residential facilities (the "RSAs")—around 400,000—and the number of workers in these structures (225,000) stresses the pivotal role of the badante in the Italian LTC system.

4 The Big Picture

The heterogeneity of the LTC Italian system suggests an analysis of the relevance that each of the available solutions has in the system. However, the scenario can differ a lot from region to region, producing a different mix between solutions that belong to the healthcare system, those based on residential facilities, on home assistance, or others.

Figure 8 presents the number of services provided (for each hundred 75+ individuals) by all the 20 Italian regions in 2016.[5]

The fact that the total benefits received for each hundred 75+ individuals is bigger than 100 is due to the chance that one individual receives multiple services. Some regions seem to be more active than others (see Lombardia, and Emilia-Romagna) and the composition of the mix can also be different from region to region. For instance, the number of beds in residential facilities is a relevant factor in the offer

[5] In the cases of Trento and Bolzano, they do not refer to "regions" (together they represent a single region called Trentino Alto Adige), but their special status of border provinces gives them a degree of autonomy in the management of the healthcare system, comparable to those of regions. In the rest of the study they will be addressed as independent regions, even if they represent provinces.

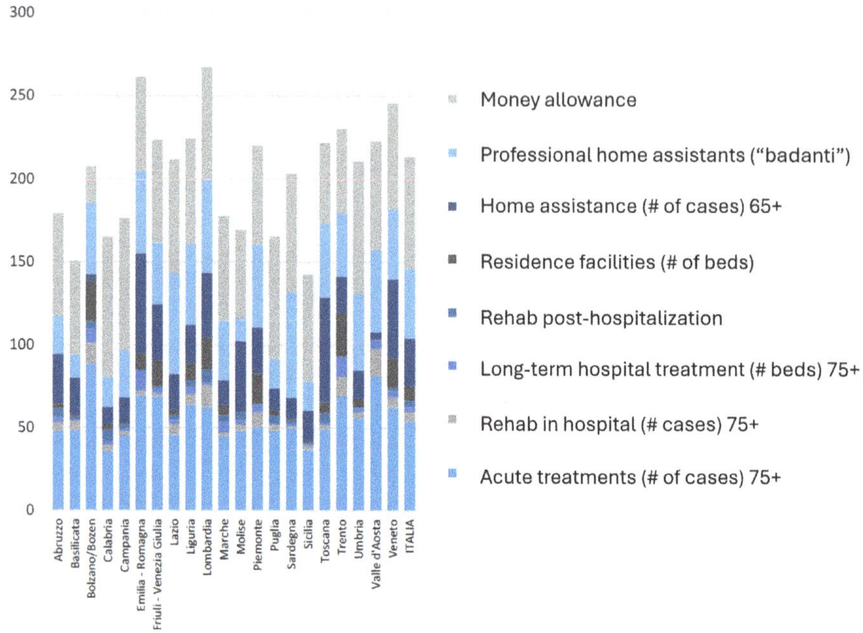

Fig. 8 Number of services provided for each hundred 75+ dependent individuals. *Source* Fosti and Notarticola (2019)

of LTC care in Bolzano or Trento, while it is almost absent in Sicilia (Sicily) ad Sardegna (Sardinia). In the meantime, the money allowance—that is administrated by the central government—plays an active role in every region. Looking at the role of the badanti in the system, it is clear how this solution is quite common, especially in areas where other services are not available or not as common as in other regions.

The role of different solutions in each region is even clearer in Fig. 9. Regions from the South (e.g. Calabria, Campania, Puglia) strongly rely on money allowances, while it is not the case in the upper part of the country (e.g. Bolzano, Trento, Emilia Romagna).

Regardless of the differences in the mix of solutions offered by the Italian LTC system in different regions, it is critical to estimate how much the system is able to deal with the demand of LTC service coming from the population.

Table 8 reports the estimation—made by Fosti and Notarnicola (2019) on 2016 data—of the coverage rate of the Italian demand of LTC services.

The data confirms the differences between the North (with high coverage ratios) and the South. However, even the best case (Veneto) is able to cover, by the residential facilities and the professional home assistance ("badanti"), around 78% of the estimated needs of the 75+ dependent individuals. Due to the small dimension of the LTC insurance market, it is likely that the gap between the above-mentioned services and the demand of the market is covered by informal assistance provided by

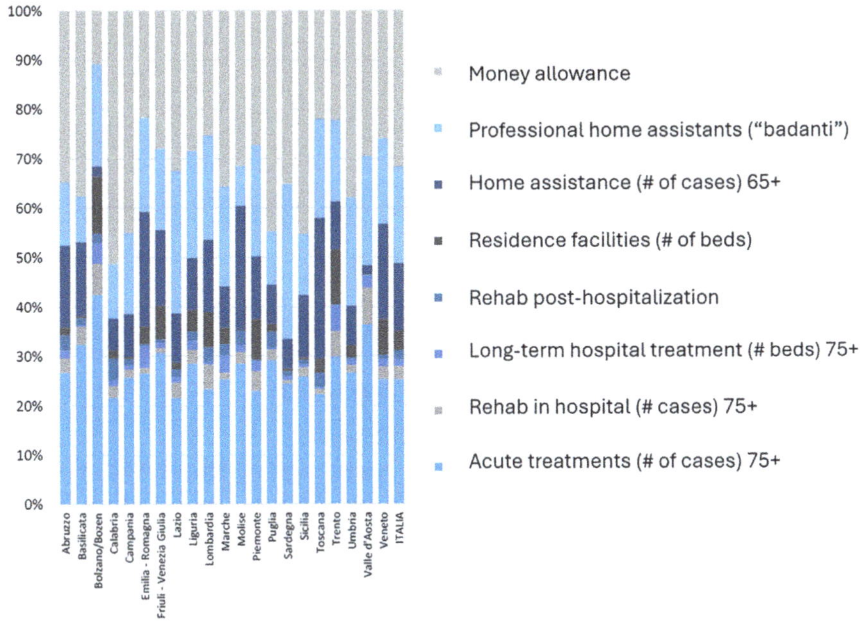

Fig. 9 Distribution of LTC services provided for each hundred 75+ dependent individuals. *Source* Fosti and Notarticola (2019)

family members. We cannot even ignore the chance that part of the demand remains uncovered.

More recent data (from 2021) confirms the small coverage of the public LTC system to the market demand (Table 9). That the most recent trend is to invest in home assistance provided by nurses and social workers, in order to reduce the pressure on hospitals and other LTC structures, is confirmed by the coverage provided by this service to the total coverage ratio.

This trend was encouraged by the COVID-19 pandemic, where the ability of residential facilities (the "RSAs") to protect the resident (fragile) individuals from the spread of the virus was in many cases jeopardized. Table 10 reports the number of guests in the residential facilities in 2021.

Regions from the North (e.g. Bolzano and Trento, Veneto, Lombardia) are able to cover (by residential facilities) around 20% or more of the 75+ dependent individuals. It means that this option is used for around one out of five of the potential targets. That sounds like a low coverage ratio but, of course, the use of a facility depends on the fact that it is available, and the attitude of individuals (and their families) to consider this as an option. The differences between the North and the South of the country are evident looking at the coverage ratio in Sicilia (Sicily 2.1%), Sardegna (Sardinia 1.4%), Basilicata (1.3%), and Campania (0.9%), where, in practice, residential facilities play a very marginal role in the LCT assistance system.

Table 8 Coverage rate of the LTC service demands (public and private) in 2016 (by region)

Dependent 75+ individuals	Coverage ratio by public services (residential facilities—"RSAs") (%)	Coverage ratio by private services—professional home assistant ("Badanti") (%)	Total (%)
Molise	0.26	13.72	13.98
Basilicata	0.65	13.98	14.63
Sicilia	0.69	17.54	18.23
Puglia	2.57	17.76	20.33
Calabria	2.78	18.12	20.90
Abruzzo	2.73	23.05	25.78
Campania	0.73	28.92	29.65
Marche	5.89	35.90	41.79
Valle d'Aosta	0.25	49.28	49.53
Toscana	6.28	44.40	50.68
Umbria	5.12	46.19	51.31
Friuli-Venezia Giulia	15.36	36.88	52.24
Liguria	9.73	48.64	58.37
Emilia-Romagna	9.61	49.71	59.32
Trento	25.66	37.96	63.62
Lazio	2.85	61.08	63.93
Sardegna	1.03	63.60	64.63
Bolzano/Bozen	24.21	43.07	67.28
Piemonte	18.15	49.79	67.94
Lombardia	18.97	56.41	75.38
Veneto	17.88	60.42	78.30

Source Fosti and Notarticola (2019)

Table 9 LTC needs coverage ratio by the public system (2021)

Estimated potential need (market demand of LTC services) (2021)	Service	Total number of individuals in charge of the public system (healthcare and social service)	Coverage ratio (%)
3,959,395	Residential facilities	284,141	7.18
	Semi-residential facilities	16,225	0.41
	House assistance (by public healthcare professionals and/or social services)	879,030	22.20

Source CERGAS-Bocconi (2023)

Table 10 75+ dependent individuals LCT services coverage ratio by resident facilities (RSAs) (2021)

Region	Guest of residential facilities (RSAs)	Dependent 75+ individuals	Coverage ratio (%)
Bolzano/Bozen	5642	20,791	27.1
Trento	6290	23,250	27.1
Marche	11,383	59,613	19.1
Veneto	40,908	219,697	18.6
Lombardia	79,070	440,295	18.0
Toscana	26,145	148,551	17.6
Friuli-Venezia Giulia	10,062	63,346	15.9
Liguria	13,099	92,152	14.2
Piemonte	28,355	219,890	12.9
Emilia-Romagna	22,918	210,822	10.9
Valle d'Aosta	596	5735	10.4
Umbria	3424	35,723	9.6
Calabria	5975	102,756	5.8
Lazio	10,202	192,551	5.3
Abruzzo	2959	80,552	3.7
Puglia	7034	219,831	3.2
Molise	463	19,652	2.4
Sicilia	5488	257,172	2.1
Sardegna	1322	97,825	1.4
Basilicata	423	33,018	1.3
Campania	2383	252,061	0.9
ITALY	284,141	2,972,326	9.6

Source ISTAT (2021)

The role of home assistance and the recent trend in favor of this option is evident by data in Table 11.

The coverage ratio of the 65+ dependent population by professional home assistance (e.g. nurses, social workers) provides a better picture of the coverage of LTC needs by the Italian system, compared to the data on residential facilities. The very high coverage rate of Molise (71%) is not representative of the country—the average coverage ratio of which is 22%—but in several regions more than 20% of the 65+ dependent individuals receive professional home assistance (e.g. Basilicata 20%, Lombardia 26%, Trento 26%, Friuli-Venezia Giulia 30%, Emilia Romagna 32%, Toscana 45%, and Veneto 52%).

Regardless the presence of some regions with better coverage ratios than others, the offer of residential facilities and professional home assistance is far from guaranteeing a complete answer to the LTC needs of the population. Data about the home

Table 11 A 65+ dependent individuals LCT services coverage ratio by home assistance (2021)

Region	65+ population	65+ dependent individuals		Home assistance to 65+ individuals (# of cases)	
		(#cases)	(%)	(#cases)	(Coverage ratio) (%)
Molise	76,120	19,639	25.8	13,965	71
Veneto	1,142,745	270,831	23.7	140,049	52
Toscana	952,609	255,299	26.8	115,951	45
Emilia-Romagna	1,073,202	354,157	33.0	112,642	32
Friuli-Venezia Giulia	319,340	69,297	21.7	20,827	30
Trento	121,842	29,364	24.1	7759	26
Lombardia	2,286,466	557,898	24.4	146,498	26
Basilicata	131,267	43,318	33.0	8671	20
Abruzzo	316,711	103,564	32.7	17,679	17
Liguria	436,284	94,674	21.7	14,970	16
Sicilia	1,079,447	373,489	34.6	55,392	15
Marche	381,162	123,115	32.3	17,360	14
Lazio	1,293,472	347,944	26.9	48,902	14
Umbria	227,477	68,926	30.3	9398	14
Piemonte	1,112,287	254,714	22.9	34,567	14
Campania	1,118,545	380,305	34.0	51,606	14
Puglia	909,396	298,282	32.8	38,749	13
Sardegna	401,716	141,404	35.2	12,023	9
Calabria	425,625	151,523	35.6	10,724	7
Bolzano	105,549	25,437	24.1	1106	4
Valle d'Aosta	30,269	7265	24.0	192	3
Italy	13,941,531	3,970,445	28.5	879,030	22

Source ISTAT (2021)

assistances stresses how the innovative solution of the badanti helps to fill the gap between demand and supply of LTC services (see Fig. 10).

The north is the area of the country with the highest number of home assistant workers, followed by the center and then the south. However, looking at the data from single regions, two of those (Lombardia and Lazio) are the ones with the highest numbers. Looking at the socio-demographic characteristics of those professional workers, data from 2023 reports that almost nine out of 10 are females (88.6%), and almost seven out of 10 are foreigners (68.9%), with a prevalence of Eastern European countries like Romania, Bulgaria, and Ukraine (35.7%). Italians are even well represented (31.1%), while those from South America (8.1%) and the Far East (5.8%) are smaller groups (Assindatcolf 2024). These statistics refer to the category of

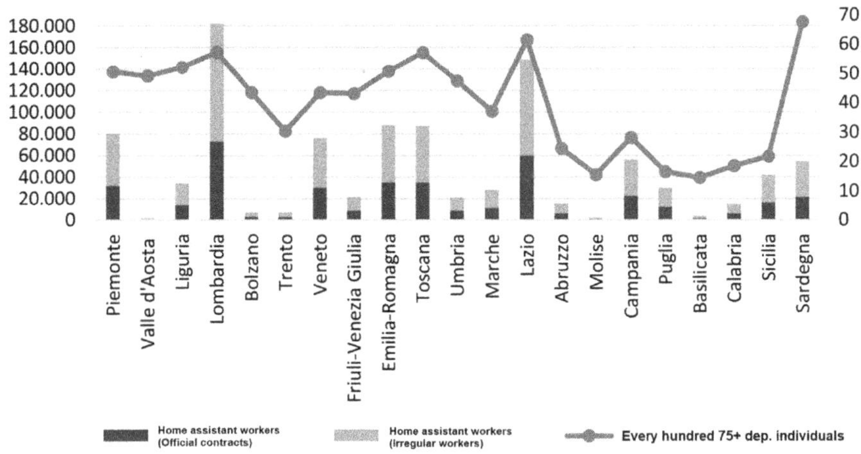

Fig. 10 Number of private home assistants and coverage ratio on 75+ dependent individuals. *Source* CERGAS-Bocconi (2023)

"home assistant workers." Both housekeepers and the badanti belong to this category, even if the services provided by the first group (e.g. house cleaning, cooking, ironing, etc.) are not necessarily provided for dependent individuals. Additional statistics (Table 12) help to disentangle this overlap, showing how the total number of home assistant workers is almost equally split in the two categories.

Table 12 Number of home assistant workers and weekly working hours ranges

Average weekly working hours ranges	Professional work		
	Badante	Housekeeper	Total
Less than 4	7398	37,900	45,298
From 5 to 9	18,291	75,463	93,754
From 10 to 14	21,804	53,330	75,134
From 15 to 19	26,614	38,603	65,217
From 20 to 24	27,503	38,603	66,106
From 25 to 29	70,421	106,514	176,935
From 30 to 34	36,487	26,124	62,611
From 35 to 39	20,156	10,974	31,130
From 40 to 44	37,772	21,169	58,941
From 45 to 49	12,958	2643	15,601
50 or more	133,753	8854	142,607
TOTAL	413,157	420,177	833,334

Source Assindatcolf (2024)

The same Table 12 stresses how the average week's workload can vary a lot. A badante can easily work even more than 50 h a week, while housekeepers tend to work less than 30 h a week.

Data about the numbers of weeks of work in a year (Table 13) highlights how those who refer to the badanti (so related with LCT care needs of dependent individuals) tend to do it on a continuous basis, hiring professionals for several months a year (if not for the entire year). However, there is even the chance to rely on a professional home assistant (badante) only in emergencies, especially when the main caregiver is a family member.

The analysis of the large use of badanti by the Italian families dealing with LCT needs of dependent individuals has to be completed with an analysis of the costs of this solution. If, in case of a money allowance received by the Government (the "IDA—Indennità di Accompagnamento"), this money can be used to cover the cost of a home assistant (or at least a part of it), in many cases the burden of the service represents an out-of-the-pocket expense for the household budget. Of course, the cost of a badante depends on the number of working hours a day and the number of working weeks a year, but some data (see Table 14) can help to figure out how much Italian families spend to fill the gap between the LCT needs of their relatives and the services provided by the public system.

The number of cases where a family pays more than €13,000 a year represents the 24.7% of the cases. Extending the case to those who spend at least €10,000 a year, we find that they represent the 40.5% of the cases. That cost can be a source of concern on a household budget, especially when a single family has a deal with it (e.g. elderly parent with just a single son or daughter).

Table 13 Number of worked weeks by "badanti" (2023)

Average worked weeks in a year	Badante	
	# of professionals	%
Less than 4	17,939	4.3
From 5 to 9	34,754	8.4
From 10 to 14	37,176	9.0
From 15 to 19	25,130	6.1
From 20 to 24	23,175	5.6
From 25 to 29	30,819	7.4
From 30 to 34	23,858	5.8
From 35 to 39	32,038	7.7
From 40 to 44	19,187	4.6
From 45 to 49	26,390	6.4
From 50 to 52	143,231	34.6
Total	413,697	100.0

Source Assindatcolf (2024)

Table 14 Number of "badanti" by annual gross salary ranges and by gender (2023)

Annual gross salary of "badanti"	Badante	
	Female	Male
Up to €999	22,755	2802
From €1000 to €1999	28,340	2947
From €2000 to €2999	25,528	2547
From €3000 to €3999	23,395	2259
From €4000 to €4999	21,689	1892
From €5000 to €5999	20,197	1815
From €6000 to €6999	20,742	1750
From €7000 to €7999	20,844	1807
From €8000 to €8999	21,278	1709
From €9000 to €9999	22,186	1936
From €10,000 to €10,999	20,372	1558
From €11,000 to €11,999	20,317	1515
From €12,000 to €12,999	19,469	1331
€13,000 or more	94,352	6365
Total	381,464	32,233

Source Assindatcolf (2024)

The cost of a badante cannot be affordable, or it can be related to assistance requested to temporarily replace the family member who is the usual caregiver, and that could not be available for some time (e.g. vacation, business trip, emergencies, etc.). An analysis of the informal caregiving in Italian families is reported in Fig. 11.

Figure 11 reports, within those that provide cure or assistance at least once a week to a family member, the age groups of these caregivers. The evidence is that those between the ages of 45 and 54 are the most likely caregivers, followed by the 55–64 group. However, we have to keep in mind that more than one family member can be involved in home caregiving at the same time, and that the available family members in a certain family can belong to only some of the possible age ranges. Another evidence is that the family caregiving to 65+ dependent individuals can be provided by peers too. It could be, for instance, the case of partners (e.g. wife or husband). In those cases, the likelihood that a female will be a caregiver is bigger (7% in case of 65+ individuals, 4% for 75+ individuals) than the case of a male caregiver (5% in case of 65+ individuals, 3% for 75+ individuals).

According to the Italian national institute of statistics (ISTAT 2021), more than 50% of the elderly—regardless of their health status—receives help from family members (even if not just from them), while 17% receive a paid assistance and 6.4% receive help by others (e.g. friends, caregiver organizations, etc.). In general, 65.2% of individuals age 65+ with some personal limitations receive help from at least one of the above-mentioned categories. Restricting the analysis to dependent individuals age 65+ requiring LTC assistance, the average percentage of individuals receiving

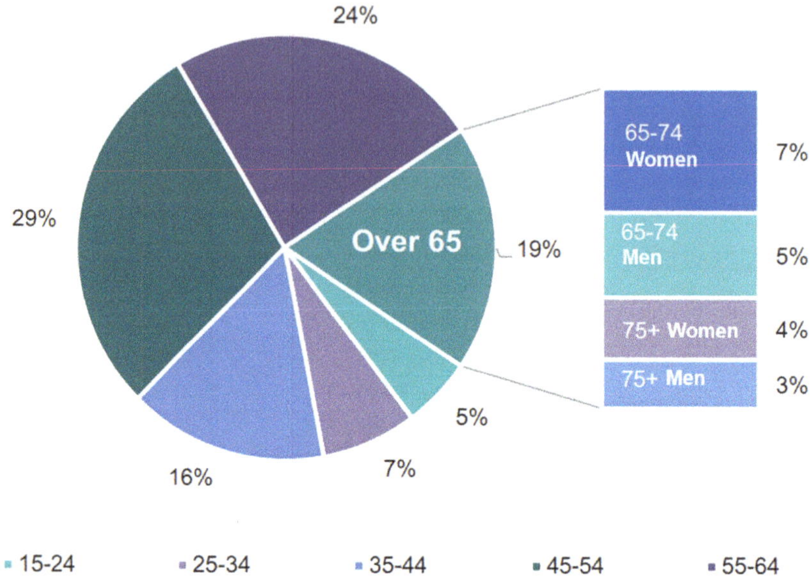

Fig. 11 Informal caregiving to family members with LCT needs (aging, chronic diseases, etc.) in Italy (2015). *Source* ISTAT (2015)

help from family members raises to 84.4%, and the average percentage of those receiving paid help raises to 35.8%. Figure 12 shows how the presence of family caregivers is consistent across geographical areas, while some differences exist for paid assistance, with an average use of this service of 26.6% in the south, compared to 41.9% in the center, and 42% in the north. However, those differences can be explained by the above-mentioned cost of the service (and the affordability for the family) and income differences across the country.

5 Conclusions

The analysis of the Italian LTC system allowed some key points to be stressed about the current and the future scenario in the country. Like in other countries, the aging in population, due to the growing life expectancy of living individuals and the low fertility rate, raised the need of LTC in the population and the demand for solutions. This demand is expected to grow in the coming years, requiring planning a development for possible solutions, from both the public and private sectors.

The current scenario sees different solutions being available, from both the public and private sectors. However, with respect to other countries, there is not a single system planned to guarantee transparency and easy access to the available solutions. The central government provides money allowance-based solutions, but medical

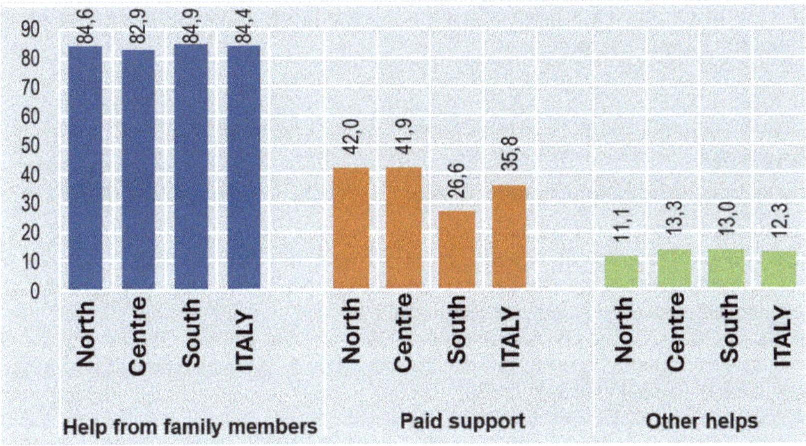

Fig. 12 65+ dependent individuals with LCT needs: support received by different groups (geographical distribution). *Source* ISTAT (2021)

treatment and healthcare solutions in general are administered at the local level (regional level), making the rules of access, the types of services provided, and the cost of those solutions different across the country. In the meantime, the insurance market devoted to deal with LCT needs is not developed yet, playing a marginal role in the current system. However, it cannot be excluded that the growing demand for LTC services will stimulate the demand for insurance coverages too. This option is to face this with a low level of use of private insurance by Italian financial consumers. In the meantime, the downward trend in the generosity of the welfare system—including the public pensions system and the healthcare system—could trigger the demand for solutions from the private sector.

An interesting solution developed by the Italian LTC system being is represented by the so called "badanti." This solution is based on hiring, directly by the family of a dependent individual and most of the times by an out-the-pocket money expense, a person that provides home assistance to people in need. These workers are not medical professionals but allow families to cope with the need to assist for several hours a day (if not 24 h a day) dependent individuals. This solution started in the early 2000s, and it is now one of the main solutions adopted in the country to assist LTC individuals, with more than a (estimated) million workers. The fact that the majority of the "badanti" are foreign workers can be an issue in the future, due to the chance that restrictions in the immigration policy could cap the number of available professionals, putting pressure on the whole LTC system.

The number of residential facilities (so called "RSAs") and their distribution across the country struggle to deal with the current demand for LTC services. Moreover, the recent trend of the healthcare system is pushing toward an increase of the home assistance, made by professionals (e.g. nurses, doctors, and social workers), in order to limit the need for hospitalization, so the future development of residential facilities for LTC is unclear.

References

Altroconsumo. (2023). Terza età in serenità: cosa sono e perché sono utili le polizze Lont Term Care ("Third age in serenity: what are and why are the LCT insurance policies useful"). https://www.altroconsumo.it/soldi/assicurazioni/news/una-polizza-per-anziani-non-autosufficienti. Last Accessed February28,2026.

Assindatcolf. (2024). Calano i domestici regolari ("Regular home assistants decrease"). https://lavorodomestico.assindatcolf.it/calano-i-domestici-regolari-76-in-un-anno-pubblicato-il-report-inps/. Last Accessed February28,2026.

CERGAS-Bocconi. (2023). Rapporto OASI – Osservatorio sulle Aziende e sul Sistema sanitario Italiano ("Observatory on Health Companies and Italian Health System"). https://cergas.unibocconi.eu/sites/default/files/media/attach/0026_Rapporto_OASI_2023_Capitolo_5.pdf. Last Accessed February28,2026.

Comitato EduFin. (2024). LTC insurance. Comitato per la programmazione e il coordinamento delle attività di educazione finanziaria. www.quellocheconta.gov.it. Last Accessed February28,2026.

European Commission (2021). 2021 aging report: Ageing in populations and fiscal sustainability. https://economy-finance.ec.europa.eu/system/files/2022-05/2021_ageing_report_0.pdf. Last Accessed February28,2026.

EUROSTAT. (2019). Projected old-age dependency ratio. https://ec.europa.eu/eurostat/data/database?node_code=tps00200. Last Accessed February28,2026.

Fosti, G., & Notarticola E. (Eds.). (2019). Il futuro del settore LTC. Prospettive dai servizi, dai gestori e dalle policy regionali. 2° Rapporto Osservatorio Long Term Care ("The Future of LTC sector. Perspective from services, managers, and regional policies"). https://cergas.unibocconi.eu/sites/default/files/files/fosti_notarnicola.pdf. Last Accessed February28,2026.

ISTAT. (2012). Censimento generale della popolazione ("General census of national population"). https://seriestoriche.istat.it/index.php?id=1&no_cache=1&tx_usercento_centofe%5Bcategoria%5D=3&tx_usercento_centofe%5Baction%5D=show&tx_usercento_centofe%5Bcontroller%5D=Categoria&cHash=ac047678dfcd1a32f2e1ae225122c17e. Last Accessed February28,2026.

ISTAT. (2015). Tassi di occupazione, di disoccupazione e di attività per classe di età e sesso - Anni 1977–2015 ("Occupational rate, unemployment, by gender and age ranges").

ISTAT. (2021). Le condizioni di salute della popolazione anziana in Italia ("The health status of elderly Italian population"). https://www.istat.it/wp-content/uploads/2021/07/Report-anziani-2019.pdf. Last Accessed February28,2026.

ISTAT. (2022). Le strutture residenziali socio-assistenziali socio-sanitarie ("The health- and socio-residential facilities"). https://www.istat.it/it/files//2022/11/REPORT_PRESIDI_SOCIO-ASSISTENZIALI_2020.pdf. Last Accessed February28,2026.

ISTAT. (2023). Le strutture socio-assistenziali e socio-sanitarie ("The health- and socio-residential facilities"). https://www.istat.it/wp-content/uploads/2023/11/Report-presidi-assistenziali-Anno-2021.pdf. Last Accessed February28,2026.

IVASS. (2023). Long term care. Dove siamo e dove Andiamo? Intervento del Consigliere dell'IVASS Prof. Riccardo Cesari al Senato della Repubblica (17 luglio 2023) ("The LCT: Where are we and where are we going?"). https://www.ivass.it/media/interviste/documenti/interventi/2023/rc_17_07_2023_ltc_lavorowelfare/RC_LTC_17.07.2023.pdf. Last Accessed February28,2026.

MEF. (2023). Ministero dell'economia e delle finanze. Annuario statistico della Ragioneria generale dello Stato – 2023, 2023a ("Official statistics of the Central Accountancy agency of Italy"). https://www.rgs.mef.gov.it/_Documenti/VERSIONE-I/Pubblicazioni/Studi-e-do/annuario_statistico_della_ragioneria_generale_dello_stato/2023/Annuario_statistico_della_RGS_2023.pdf. Last Accessed February28,2026.

OCPI. (2022). Osservatorio Conti Pubblici Italiani ("Observatory of national public budgeting") on Eurostat data. https://osservatoriocpi.unicatt.it/ocpi-pubblicazioni-le-retribuzioni-e-i-profitti-in-italia-e-nell-eurozona. Last Accessed February28,2026.

Our World in Data. (2024). Age structure. https://ourworldindata.org/age-structure. Last Accessed February28,2026.

Long-Term Care in Poland

Anne-Marie Weber and Hanna Salera

1 Introduction

Poland is undergoing a profound demographic transformation influenced by several interrelated factors, including increased life expectancy, the aging of the post-war baby boom generation now entering retirement, and persistently low birth rates below the level of population replacement. Currently, individuals aged 65 and older comprise 19.5% of the population, while those aged 80 and above represent 4.2%.[1] In 2023, life expectancy in Poland stood at 73.4 years for men and 81.1 years for women.[2] Older adults were particularly impacted by the COVID-19 pandemic, which temporarily reduced life expectancy rates. Projections from the Central Statistical Office (GUS) indicate that the aging trend will intensify in the coming decades. By 2040, the proportion of individuals aged 65 and over is expected to rise to 24.6%, with those aged 80 and above increasing to 8.7% of the total population.[3] This is a positive effect of conducting an effective public health policy involving treatment and

[1] Report, "Przegląd Strategiczny Systemu Opieki Długoterminowej w Polsce," World Bank, June 2024, (hereinafter: World Bank Report, 2024a), p. 15.

[2] World Bank Report, 2024a, p. 15.

[3] World Bank Report, 2024a, p. 15.

This chapter presents the results of research project no. UMO-2023/51/D/HS5/1563, "Combatting financial exclusion of the elderly in the digital era - a regulatory roadmap," funded by the National Science Center, Poland.

A.-M. Weber (✉)
Faculaty of Law and Administration, University of Warsaw, Warsaw, Poland
e-mail: a.weber@wpia.uw.edu.pl

H. Salera
University of Warsaw, Warsaw, Poland

H. Lee and G. Nicolini (eds.), *International Comparison of Long-Term Care Insurance Systems*, Contributions to Management Science,
https://doi.org/10.1007/978-981-95-7781-1_3

prevention, and at the same time a challenge to improve health care and functional efficiency of the elderly functioning in social life.[4]

Poland's demographic dependency ratio[5] is projected to rise significantly, doubling from 30% in 2022 to 60% by 2060.[6] This shift will substantially increase the caregiving burden on the working-age population. Compounding this challenge is the prevalence of chronic health conditions among the elderly, including cardiovascular diseases, cancers, diabetes, and fall-related injuries, which remain key contributors to morbidity and mortality within this demographic group.[7] Survey data commissioned by the World Bank highlights a pronounced decline in self-assessed health status with age. Respondents expressed particular concern regarding physical impairments, cognitive decline, and the prevalence of chronic diseases, reflecting the multifaceted health challenges faced by aging populations.[8]

These health challenges are often exacerbated by economic hardship, as older adults face disproportionately high rates of relative poverty.[9] Many also endure substandard housing conditions, further compounding their vulnerability and diminishing their overall quality of life.[10] Gender disparities are pronounced, with life expectancy differing significantly by gender.[11] While women, on average, outlive men, they are more likely to experience chronic illnesses and report poorer health outcomes during their later years.[12] The population over 65 is characterized by an overrepresentation of women. The phenomenon of feminization promotes the singularization of old age and the running of households mainly by women and, thanks to the increase in life expectancy and healthy life expectancy, the number of people living long lives is increasing. Feminization and longevity in this population entail a need for different medical care, as the number of people around 100 years of age is increasing, which entails an increase in age-specific morbidity and multiple organ failure with the need to include dementia and an increase in gender-related morbidity. The group over 90 is not only characterized by greater infirmity; it is also a qualitative change, that is, the specificity of the disease. There are specific changes in the body of the elderly related to the aging process: these are different in the 65+ group and different in the 90+group, in which these processes not only accelerate, but qualitative changes will also take place (which should be given more attention).[13]

[4] Kawałko, S., Istota i zadania współczesnej polityki ochrony zdrowia, Studia Gdańskie. Wizje i rzeczywistość, Vol. 11, 2014, p. 335.

[5] The dependency ratio is an age-population ratio of those typically not in the labor force (the dependent part ages 0 to 14 and 65+) and those typically in the labor force (the productive part ages 15 to 64). It is used to measure the pressure on the productive population.

[6] World Bank Report, 2024a, p. 15.

[7] World Bank Report, 2024a, p. 16.

[8] World Bank Report, 2024a, p. 16.

[9] World Bank Report, 2024a, p. 50.

[10] World Bank Report, 2024a, p. 16.

[11] World Bank Report, 2024a, p. 15.

[12] World Bank Report, 2024a, p. 15.

[13] Kuncewicz, D., & Pabiś, M., (2016), Potrzeby osób starszych w zakresie opieki zdrowotnej—konteksty, Pielęgniarstwo XXI Wieku, *15*, no. 4 (57), 58.

As the population ages and chronic health issues become increasingly prevalent, the need for coordinated, accessible, and sustainable care services will intensify. The outlined demographic challenges, therefore, necessitate a comprehensive response in the field of long-term care (LTC). Long-term care, as understood in this chapter, aligns with the 2022 EU Council Recommendation and the 2021 Social Protection Committee's definition[14]: LTC encompasses services and support for individuals who, due to frailty, illness, or physical or mental disability, require assistance with daily living activities or continuous caregiving over an extended period. Addressing the growing demand for LTC services requires a robust system capable of meeting the complex needs of aging individuals while ensuring that care delivery remains equitable, high-quality, and financially viable.

This chapter examines how Poland is addressing these demographic challenges through various modalities of LTC provision. The chapter outlines the functioning of LTC in the public and private sectors. It also identifies existing weaknesses within Poland's LTC system and evaluates potential instruments for improvement. The analysis is structured into four sections. Following this introduction, Section II examines the functioning of public LTC schemes, with a focus on their two main parallel pathways: the healthcare sector and the social assistance sector. Section III explores LTC within the private sector. In Sect. IV we address the challenges the Polish LTC system faces and discuss several thematic areas of potential improvement measures. Finally, Section V concludes with a summary of our findings.

2 Public Long-Term Care

2.1 Constitutional Foundations

Like most OECD governments, Poland has established publicly funded programs that cover certain LTC services.[15] The state's obligation to provide long-term care for its citizens derives directly from the Polish Constitution (hereinafter: "PC").[16] According to Art. 68 (1) PC every person has the right to health care. This provision should not be regarded merely as a general policy objective but rather as establishing an individual's concrete entitlement to health care provision.[17] All citizens are guaranteed equal access to publicly funded health care services, regardless of

[14] World Bank Report, 2024a, p. 144.

[15] Colombo, F., et al., Help wanted? Providing and paying for long-term care. OECD Health Policy Studies, (Paris: OECD Publishing, 2011), p. 15.

[16] Konstytucja Rzeczypospolitej Polskiej z dnia 2 kwietnia 1997 r. (Dz.U. z 1997 r. Nr 78, poz. 483) (hereinafter: "PC").

[17] Bosek L., in: M. Safjan, L. Bosek (eds.), Konstytucja RP. Tom I, Komentarz do art. 1–86, Legalis (online) 2016, commentary to Art. 68, par. 2, see also in jurisprudence: judgment of the Constitutional Tribunal dated 7.1.2004 r., K 14/03, OTK-A 2004, Nr 1, poz. 1; judgment of the Constitutional Tribunal dated 24.3.1999 r., K 2/98, OTK 1999, Nr 3, poz. 38.

their financial situation (Art. 68 (2) PC). The specific conditions and scope of these services are determined by law (Art. 68 (2) PC).[18] Furthermore, public authorities are expressly required to provide special health care for children, pregnant women, persons with disabilities, and the elderly (Art. 68 (3) PC).

The Polish Constitution does not provide a substantive definition of "health protection." In particular, it does not allow for the precise constitutional determination of the types or categories of services encompassed within the right guaranteed under Article 68. As a result, the constitutional guarantees in this area shift towards the procedural dimension. The key issue, therefore, is the legislator's proper regulation of the organizational framework, ensuring that the health care system is structured in a precise, unambiguous, and functionally coherent manner. Notably, the constitutional legislator has explicitly rejected the establishment of a fully market-based health care system based on self-financing. Beyond this constraint, the ordinary legislator retains broad discretion in shaping the specific model of health care provision, in accordance with its political and social objectives.[19]

The constitutional concept of health care provision must be interpreted broadly, encompassing not only strictly medical services but also social care and charitable assistance. It does not entail an abstract guarantee of a specific health condition for individuals but rather ensures access to a health care system functionally designed to combat and prevent diseases, injuries, and disabilities.

2.2 *Structure*

The public LTC system in Poland is structured across two primary sectors: the health care sector (sektor ochrony zdrowia) and the social assistance sector (sektor pomocy społecznej). This duality inherently generates challenges in coordination and the harmonization of standards between the two sectors, which is essential for fostering the effective provision of LTC.[20] Much like a structure built upon two supporting pillars, each sector plays a vital role in sustaining the overall framework, yet their divergent functions often necessitate careful alignment to ensure seamless integration. The successful operation of the public LTC system relies on the strength and cohesion of both pillars working in tandem, balancing the complementary and sometimes substantively overlapping roles of health and social assistance services and benefits.

Institutions involved in the public LTC system at the central level of government include the Ministry of Health, the Ministry of Family, Labor and Social Policy, and the National Health Fund (NFZ). These bodies play a central role in the formulation

---

[18] Berezowski J., Guzak B., Realizacja prawa do opieki długoterminowej, Wydawnictwo Państwowej Wyższej Szkoły Zawodowej w Raciborzu, 2016, p. 133.

[19] Lenio P., Publicznoprawne źródła finansowania ochrony zdrowia, Wolters Kluwer, Warszawa, 2018, p. 64.

[20] See further a discussion of challenges in sec. 2.3 below.

of policy related to LTC services. They are responsible for proposing changes to the legal framework governing the system. Additionally, they establish standards for the provision of services across the country. These institutions also define the guidelines for funding LTC services. Beyond policy and funding, they are tasked with implementing mechanisms to monitor the quality of services provided. These monitoring mechanisms are designed to ensure that care services meet established standards and remain effective in addressing the needs of the population.[21]

Local government units (jednostki samorządu terytorialnego) at the level of voivodeships (województwa), counties (powiaty), and municipalities (gminy) play a pivotal role in the implementation of public long-term care services in Poland.[22] Their responsibilities mainly center on the social assistance sector and encompass the administration of resources to organize, provide, and finance various forms of LTC services, including day-care residences, support centers, and care services. Furthermore, local government units collaborate closely with non-governmental organizations (NGOs) and private sector entities to ensure a comprehensive approach to care for the elderly and dependent individuals.[23] A core function of local government units is to assess and identify the care needs of the local population. Through regular demographic and social analyses, they can prioritize services and allocate resources effectively. In addition to direct service provision, local government units are responsible for overseeing cash benefits provided to beneficiaries. They also organize training for caregivers and support staff to maintain high-quality care and adapt to the evolving needs of society.[24]

2.3 Legal Framework

The legal framework governing public LTC provision in Poland is characterized by its complexity and fragmentation, encompassing both organizational and financial structures, as well as service quality standards.

The primary legal instruments regulating this area are the Social Welfare Act (hereinafter: "SWA")[25] and the Act on Publicly Funded Health Care Services (hereinafter: "APFHCS").[26] These statutes form the foundation for the organization and delivery of public LTC services, shaping the operational landscape of both the healthcare and social assistance sectors. However, within this system, long-term care is not

---

[21] World Bank Report 2024a, p. 57.

[22] Voivodeships are the largest administrative units below the national level, with a total of 16. Counties form an intermediate tier within the system of local government units, numbering 380 in total, while municipalities are the smallest units, with 2, 477 in total.

[23] World Bank Report 2024a, p. 174.

[24] World Bank Report 2024a, p. 254.

[25] Ustawa z dnia 12 marca 2004 r. o pomocy społecznej (t.j. Dz. U. z 2024 r. poz. 1283 z późn. zm.).

[26] Ustawa z dnia 27 sierpnia 2004 r. o świadczeniach opieki zdrowotnej finansowanych ze środków publicznych (t.j. Dz. U. z 2024 r. poz. 146 z późn. zm.).

distinctly recognized as a separate category. Most notably, there is an absence of any normative statutory definition of long-term care. No specific legal provisions have been established to regulate the right to LTC, its scope, methods of implementation, administrative competencies, or financial structure. This regulatory gap significantly impacts health care across all dimensions, making it part of a broader pattern of legal ambiguity in this sector.[27]

The SWA establishes the regulatory framework for the social welfare system, which encompasses the provision of care services and support for individuals requiring continuous assistance due to age, illness, or disability. Article 50 of the SWA defines care services as benefits that include assistance with daily living activities, such as meal preparation, housekeeping, and shopping. These services may be provided either at an individual's place of residence or within inpatient facilities. Additionally, the SWA outlines the organization of specialized services for individuals with more complex needs, including those experiencing mental health disorders.

In practice, the services governed by the SWA are delivered through various institutional forms, including nursing homes (Domy Pomocy Społecznej, DPS) and family support homes (Rodzinne Domy Pomocy, RDP), both of which offer round-the-clock care in environments adapted to residents' specific needs.[28] The SWA also establishes regulatory standards and certification requirements to ensure the quality of services provided. These standards cover personnel qualifications as well as the conditions under which care is delivered. Regional social assistance centers are responsible for conducting regular inspections to monitor and enforce compliance with these standards.

The APFHCS regulates the financing and organization of healthcare, including long-term care (LTC) services. This encompasses nursing and palliative care, as well as physical rehabilitation, which are provided through specialized institutions such as nursing and therapeutic institutions (Zakłady Opieki Leczniczej, ZOL) and nursing care institutions (Zakłady Pielęgnacyjno-Opiekuńcze, ZPO), or through home-based nursing care. The law stipulates the methods for financing these services via the National Health Fund (Narodowy Fundusz Zdrowia, NFZ). Additionally, the APFHCS requires regular inspections to ensure compliance with established quality standards.

2.4 Methods

The methods of providing public LTC can be broadly categorized into the provision of services (świadczenia rzeczowe) and the disbursement of financial benefits

[27] Berezowski J., Guzak B., Realizacja prawa do opieki długoterminowej, Wydawnictwo Państwowej Wyższej Szkoły Zawodowej w Raciborzu, 2016, p. 11.

[28] Report "Opieka długoterminowa w Polsce", World Bank, June 2024, (hereinafter: World Bank Report 2024b), p. 12–13.

(świadczenia pieniężne). Cash benefits include nursing allowances paid by the social security system and nursing benefits available through social welfare. In contrast, benefits in kind encompass various forms of nursing and care services provided by both the health service and social welfare system.[29]

Health care services are contracted by the National Health Fund (NFZ) and are referred to as products. The products contracted by the NFZ primarily include inpatient long-term care, nursing home care, as well as palliative and hospice care.[30]

2.4.1 Provision of Services

The provision of services includes in-kind benefits, such as direct caregiving, medical assistance, rehabilitation, and other forms of professional support for individuals in need of long-term care. Within the social assistance sector, various institutional modalities are essential in delivering LTC services, including:

Social assistance centers (OPS–ośrodki pomocy społecznej) or social services centers (CUS–centra usług społecznych), which provide caregiving services to individuals who, due to age, illness, or disability, require assistance in fulfilling basic life needs and cannot rely on family members for such support. These services are typically delivered at the beneficiary's place of residence (home care) and encompass basic assistance with daily activities, such as maintaining personal hygiene, providing medical care as prescribed by a doctor, assisting with household tasks, and, where possible, facilitating social interactions and connections with the wider community. OPS and CUS also offer specialized care services, tailored to meet the specific needs of individuals based on the nature of their condition or disability. These services are provided by trained professionals with expertise in addressing the complex needs of beneficiaries.

Support centers (OW–ośrodki wsparcia), including day care homes, shelters for homeless individuals, and entities offering specialized services for people with mental health disorders, such as self-help clubs and community-based self-help homes. These facilities focus on non-residential, day care services, which may include therapeutic activities, meal provision, and, in some cases, specialized caregiving services. Approximately one-third of individuals receiving support in this form are individuals with disabilities and mental health disorders.[31] The second largest group (22%) consists of older adults receiving services from OWs.[32]

Nursing homes (DPS–domy pomocy społecznej), which provide residential care for individuals who are unable to live independently due to age, illness, or disability. They offer round-the-clock care, including medical and personal assistance. These

[29] Mitek A., Finansowanie i organizacja systemu opieki długoterminowej w Polsce, Studia i Prace Wydziału Nauk Ekonomicznych i Zarządzania, Vol. 34, No. 1, 2013, p. 225.

[30] Mitek A., Finansowanie i organizacja systemu opieki długoterminowej w Polsce, Studia i Prace Wydziału Nauk Ekonomicznych i Zarządzania, Vol. 34, No. 1, 2013, p. 225.

[31] World Bank Report 2024a, p. 69.

[32] World Bank Report 2024a, World Bank, June 2024, p. 69.

facilities offer round-the-clock care, including both medical and personal assistance. Nursing homes are typically large institutions; in 2021, the average capacity of a nursing home (DPS) was 98 places.[33] In 2021 there were 826 DPS in Poland, with elderly individuals comprising half of the residents.[34] While DPS facilities offer a range of services to their residents, medical care is not among them.

Family care homes (RDP—rodzinne domy pomocy), which similar to nursing homes (DPS), provide services for individuals requiring round-the-clock care due to age or disability. However, the environment in RDPs is more intimate and personalized than in DPS facilities, as they typically accommodate between three and eight residents. In 2021, there were only 44 RDPs in Poland, housing a total of 322 residents.[35]

In the healthcare sector, LTC encompasses a wide range of medical and social services aimed at providing continuous nursing care, rehabilitation, and therapeutic interventions. These services are specifically designed for individuals with chronic illnesses and disabilities who do not require hospitalization but still need ongoing medical treatment, including pharmacological management and dietary support. The primary goal of LTC within this sector is to help individuals manage their conditions, promote a level of independence, and ensure that their healthcare needs are met outside of hospital settings. LTC services in the healthcare sector are delivered by various medical providers operating under contracts with the National Health Fund (NFZ). The key modalities of LTC provision in this sector include:

1. Nurses providing LTC services (pielęgniarki świadczące opiekę długoterminową), who offer LTC either as part of an employment contract or through self-employment. These services are delivered at the patient's residence, with access to home nursing care granted upon referral from a doctor. The qualification criterion for receiving nursing care at home is a poor health condition that leads to significant functional limitations. The services provided include activities such as wound treatment and dressing changes, administering medication, giving injections, assisting family caregivers with nursing tasks, conducting respiratory and general development exercises, and advising on obtaining medical support and appropriate rehabilitation equipment. Nurses are also authorized to prescribe certain pharmaceutical products, issue referrals for specific tests, and prescribe medical devices (e.g., adult diapers). Visits are conducted regularly, at least four times per week, and are documented in the patient's medical record.
2. Teams for long-term home care (zespoły długoterminowej opieki domowej), which provide care for adults, youth, and children who require mechanical ventilation. These services are typically offered after acute respiratory failure has been treated, usually in a hospital setting, and when a pulmonologist or

[33] Report of the Ministry of Development and Social Policy [MRIPS-05] for 2021-selected information on social welfare homes with municipal, district and regional coverage, as well as on 24-hour care facilities run as part of business and statutory activities.

[34] World Bank Report 2024b, p. 65.

[35] World Bank Report 2024b, p. 32.

anaesthesiologist recommends home ventilation based on appropriate diagnostic tests.

3. Nursing and therapeutic institutions (ZOL-zakłady opiekuńczo-lecznicze), which provide residential, specialized medical, and nursing care for patients requiring continuous medical attention and supervision. Within a ZOL, medical and nursing assistance encompasses a range of services, including consultations with specialist doctors, nursing services, rehabilitation, dietary support, occupational therapy, and pharmacological treatment. Most ZOLs operate within hospital structures, facilitating integrated care for patients with complex health needs.
4. Nursing care institutions (ZPO-zakłady pielęgnacyjno-opiekuńcze) which focus on providing long-term care for individuals who do not require acute medical treatment but need ongoing nursing and personal care services. Unlike ZOLs, most ZPOs operate independently, outside of hospital settings.

It is important to note that the length of stay in a nursing and therapeutic institution (ZOL) or a nursing care institution (ZPO) is determined on an individual basis. This decision depends on the patient's health status, which is assessed using the modified Barthel scale. The assessment is conducted by the doctor and/or nurse at the time of admission and at the end of each month. For a patient to be eligible for services at a ZOL or ZPO, they must score between 0 and 40 points on the modified Barthel scale. In the case of long-term inpatient care, the primary criterion for discontinuing services is an improvement in the patient's health condition, resulting in a Barthel scale score exceeding 40 points.[36]

2.4.2 Financial Benefits

The second category of LTC provision, the payment of financial benefits, involves monetary support provided to beneficiaries or their caregivers to help cover the costs associated with long-term care. These payments are intended to supplement household income, allowing recipients to either arrange for private care services or cover specific caregiving-related expenses.

Financial benefits for LTC are administered by various institutions, including the Social Insurance Institution (ZUS), the Agricultural Social Insurance Fund (KRUS), the Pension and Disability Fund of the Ministry of Internal Affairs and Administration (ZER MSWiA), as well as local government units.

[36] Lamont M., Efektywność zespołu terapeutycznego w zakładach opieki długoterminowej, Uniwersytet Medyczny w Lublinie, 2021, p. 19.

2.5 Financing

The primary sources of funding for LTC services are public funds, which include contributions from the state budget, local governments, and the National Health Fund. Regarding LTC at home, 90% of older people need to use their wealth to pay for these services.[37]

Individuals residing at LTC facilities are generally responsible for covering the costs of accommodation and meals.[38] A key feature of the system is the dual, two-pillar allocation of funds between the healthcare and social welfare sectors, with regional funding mechanisms designed to ensure equitable access to services across the country. As noted earlier, the distribution of public funds between these sectors is governed by separate regulations. Additionally, the eligibility criteria for publicly funded LTC services differ between the healthcare and social assistance pillars.

In the healthcare sector, eligibility for LTC is based on a medical assessment conducted by doctors, nurses, and treatment teams. In contrast, LTC services in the social assistance sector are granted following an interview with a social worker who assesses the beneficiary's health, income, and family situation.[39] In this sector, eligibility is determined by both the beneficiary's income and a functional assessment of their care needs.[40]

The National Health Fund is primarily responsible for financing healthcare services, which encompass in-home nursing care, physical rehabilitation, and care provided in nursing care facilities (ZOL) and nursing care institutions (ZPO).[41] In contrast, the social welfare sector is allocated funds for services such as nursing homes (DPS), support centers, and residential care services. This dualistic funding system, while essential for addressing different aspects of LTC, often leads to fragmentation and a lack of coordination between the healthcare and social assistance sectors.[42]

Regional funding participation plays a significant role in shaping access to public long-term care services. Local governments are responsible for co-financing services within the social assistance sector, such as nursing homes (DPS) and support centers.[43] However, disparities in the financial resources of these local governments result in significant variations in the availability and quality of services across different regions of the country.[44]

---

[37] OECD 2024, p. 17.

[38] Kilian J., Ćwirlej-Sozańska A., Wiśniowska-Szurlej A., Wilmowska-Pietruszyńska A., System długoterminowej opieki domowej nad osobami starszymi w Polsce i wybranych krajach europejskich, Niepełnosprawność—zagadnienia, problemy, rozwiązania, Vol IV, No. 29, 2018, p. 116.

[39] World Bank Report 2024a, p. 82.

[40] World Bank Report 2024a, p. 72,

[41] World Bank Report 2024a, p. 57, 143.

[42] World Bank Report 2024a, p. 133.

[43] World Bank Report 2024b, p. 13.

[44] World Bank Report 2024a, p. 188.

The role of social insurance, encompassing health insurance, is fundamental to the LTC system. In Poland, healthcare services are predominantly financed through health insurance premiums paid to the NFZ, ensuring universal access to medical services for the insured.[45] However, the absence of a comparable mechanism in the social assistance system means that care services are more reliant on local budgets and the decisions made by local governments.

In the case of LTC provided within the health care sector, the cost of medical services is generally covered by health insurance, with specific services determined by a medical certificate that verifies the individual's dependency or the presence of a chronic illness requiring long-term care. Patients are charged fees for accommodation and meals. For example, in a nursing and therapeutic facility (ZOL) accommodation and meals are subject to a fee, with the monthly charge set at 250% of the lowest pension. However, the fee cannot exceed 70% of the patient's monthly income. Health services, including specialized medical products, are provided under the coverage of health insurance, ensuring that patients receive the necessary medical care without additional financial burden beyond the accommodation fees.

In the social assistance sector, private co-financing for services is typically required, with the fee structure varying depending on the type and location of services provided. For instance, the cost of staying in a nursing home (DPS) is capped at 70% of an individual's income. If the individual is unable to cover the costs independently, the responsibility for payment falls to their family (spouse, ascendants, or descendants). If the family cannot contribute, the local government authority that issued the referral to the DPS facility assumes payment responsibility.

Certain long-term care initiatives are supported by European Union (EU) funds, aimed at expanding the availability of services and promoting the deinstitutionalization of care. These projects are financed through the European Social Fund (ESF) and the European Regional Development Fund (ERDF), which provide financial support to enhance the accessibility and quality of LTC services across Poland.

3 Private Long-Term Care

3.1 Structure

The rapid expansion of the private LTC sector in Poland since 2010 reflects the increasing demand driven by an aging population and the insufficient availability of services within the public sector. According to data from the World Bank, the number of private long-term care and nursing facilities grew by more than 30% between 2010 and 2021, highlighting strong interest from private investors in this market segment.[46]

---

[45] World Bank Report 2024a, p. 143.

[46] World Bank Report 2024a, p. 15.

While statistics are available for facilities providing private LTC in residential settings, there is no official register for private providers offering home-based care. In 2021, Poland had 704 registered private LTC facilities, accommodating 20,894 residents. However, the full extent of the private LTC sector remains unclear due to the lack of comprehensive data on private home-care providers.[47]

Private LTC can be delivered either independently or in cooperation with the public LTC system. In the first scenario, private providers offer both home-based and facility-based services as part of their business activities, with payment typically made directly by clients or their families.

In the second scenario, private providers enter into agreements with public entities under public procurement laws, often through a competitive tender process. This allows LTC services to be "outsourced" to private providers, effectively integrating them into the public system through formal contracts.[48]

In addition to commercial private LTC providers, other non-public entities play a significant role in delivering these services. Non-governmental organizations (NGOs), including the Polish Red Cross, Caritas, and various local organizations, also contribute to the provision of non-public LTC services. These entities typically focus on offering care aligned with social assistance goals, targeting individuals who may not be adequately served by the public LTC sector and who cannot afford care within the private commercial sector.

3.2 Legal Framework

One way to regulate the activities of private LTC facilities is by requiring the issuance of permits for their operation. This ensures that these facilities meet specific standards of care, safety, and quality before they can provide services to individuals. The provisions of the Regulation of the Minister of Family, Labour, and Social Policy, dated August 28, 2020, govern the issuance and withdrawal of permits for business activities related to the provision of 24-hour care services.[49] Under this regulation, the voivode (regional governor of the voivodeship) is responsible for reviewing applications for operating permits for private LTC facilities. The process involves an inspection of the facility, which must be completed before the application is reviewed. The voivode has 14 days to make a decision after the inspection, taking into account the results and assessing whether the facility adheres to the care standards outlined in Article 68 of the Social Welfare Act (SWA). This regulatory

[47] World Bank Report 2024a, p. 267.

[48] Jurek Ł., Zmiany stacjonarnej opieki społecznej nad ludźmi starymi w Polsce i wybranych krajach, Uniwersytet Ekonomiczny we Wrocławiu, 2009, p. 219.

[49] Rozporządzenie Ministra Rodziny, Pracy i Polityki Społecznej z dnia 28 sierpnia 2020 r. w sprawie wydawania i cofania zezwoleń na prowadzenie w ramach działalności statutowej placówki zapewniającej całodobową opiekę (Dz. U. poz. 1532).

framework ensures that private LTC providers maintain quality services and meet the necessary care standards, contributing to the protection and well-being of residents.

As a result, information about licensed private LTC facilities can be accessed through their registration with the local voivodeship authorities. Publicly available data typically includes operational details such as the facility's address, the number of available places, and any other relevant licensing information. Additionally, private LTC facilities must undergo regular quality audits, which they are required to submit to the relevant regulatory bodies for evaluation. These audits ensure ongoing compliance with care standards and help maintain the quality of services provided to residents.[50]

The absence of regulation for private in-home LTC services creates significant challenges for both consumers and regulators. Without a centralized, publicly accessible database, it becomes difficult for individuals to find reliable service providers or compare quality across options. Moreover, the lack of standardized quality control means there are no consistent benchmarks for the care being delivered, which could result in variable levels of service across providers. This regulatory gap could put vulnerable individuals at risk and undermine the effectiveness of long-term care in the home setting.

3.3 Methods

The methods of LTC provision in the private sector encompass both in-home and facility-based services. Private LTC facilities are generally smaller than their public counterparts, with an average capacity of about 30 beneficiaries.[51]

Private in-home LTC services vary widely in terms of the scope of care provided and the associated costs. These services are more prevalent in large urban areas, where demand is typically higher. Private in-home services may include medical treatments, such as nursing and physician care, alongside other forms of support.

Notably, a substantial portion of private in-home LTC services is delivered by individuals, rather than formal commercial entities.[52] This often occurs within the informal sector,[53] where retired individuals or migrant workers from Ukraine or Belarus provide care on an individual basis, often without the oversight or regulation seen in more formalized care systems.[54] In contrast to some other European countries,

[50] World Bank Report 2024a, p. 268.

[51] World Bank Report 2024a, p. 267.

[52] Lewandowska-Szweda Z., Rynek usług opiekuńczych—dynamicznie rozwijający się segment gospodarki, Rynek Pracy, Vol. 3, 2018, p. 27.

[53] Lewandowska-Szweda Z., Rynek usług opiekuńczych—dynamicznie rozwijający się segment gospodarki, Rynek Pracy, Vol. 3, 2018, p. 27.

[54] World Bank Report 2024a, p. 267.

the legalization of care provided by migrant workers has not been specifically pursued through any targeted policy measures in Poland so far.[55]

3.4 Financing

The financing of private LTC services in Poland varies significantly across providers, offering a diverse range of payment options. These include one-time payments for services rendered, as well as subscription-based systems that allow families to distribute the costs over a longer period. Additionally, private health insurance or specialized long-term care programs offered by insurance companies may be utilized to help finance these services.

Subscription care plans, an innovative financing model, are gaining increasing popularity in Poland. These plans provide families with access to customized care packages for a fixed monthly fee. Subscription plans typically combine medical support, nursing care, and assistance with activities of daily living, offering a comprehensive solution to LTC needs. In 2023, the number of individuals utilizing subscription care plans grew by 15% compared to the previous year, indicating a positive shift towards this model.[56]

Despite their growing popularity, subscription care plans face significant barriers to broader adoption. High costs remain a key obstacle, making them unaffordable for the majority of families. Additionally, the lack of standardization among providers complicates the decision-making process for consumers, as they are unable to easily compare offerings and ensure they are receiving the most appropriate care.

4 Addressing Challenges

As outlined above, the Polish LTC system is characterized by its complexity, encompassing various sectors, administrative levels, care facilities, programs, and funding sources. In light of this intricate framework, we aim to highlight five thematic areas that possess the potential to significantly enhance the overall LTC system. These areas represent key opportunities for reform, innovation, and strategic improvements that could address the challenges faced by both service providers and beneficiaries. Such improvements could lead to a more cohesive, efficient, and equitable system, better aligned with the evolving needs of the population.

---

[55] Colombo, F. et al., Help wanted? Providing and paying for long-term care. OECD Health Policy Studies, Paris: OECD Publishing, 2011, p. 197.

[56] World Bank Report 2024a, p. 198.

4.1 A Unified System of LTC

The current LTC system in Poland is fragmented and lacks coherence in several critical areas. First, there is no unified, overarching definition of LTC, which leads to ambiguity in policy and service provision. Second, the public component of the system is divided into two separate sectors: the healthcare sector and the social assistance sector. Third, the public and private LTC sectors operate in parallel without systematic coordination or governance mechanisms connecting them, leading to inefficiencies and gaps in service delivery.

The absence of a unified governance framework is arguably the most pressing issue facing the LTC system. A cohesive governance structure could facilitate the integration of both the public and private sectors, as well as unify the healthcare and social assistance components within the public sector. The existence of dual funding streams within these sectors further complicates the system. Moreover, the legal framework for LTC is dispersed across multiple legislative acts, creating a disjointed and confusing structure that undermines the effectiveness of providing LTC.

This fragmentation leads to complex eligibility rules, a lack of transparency, and insufficient information for beneficiaries. As a result, confusion surrounds the system, exacerbating delays in accessing publicly funded services, with beneficiaries frequently facing extended waiting periods. These delays are driven by both demand-side factors, such as the growing need for LTC services, and supply-side factors, including the limited availability of services and resources. In sum, the current system creates significant barriers to the timely, equitable, and efficient provision of LTC services.

Seniors encounter significant challenges due to the limited availability of clear, accessible, and detailed information about the services available to them. While an individual could potentially benefit from assistance from various sources, the eligibility criteria are complex.[57] Many beneficiaries struggle to comprehend the full range of services provided, the locations where they can access care, and the specific procedures required to obtain assistance within the public system. This lack of transparency not only creates barriers to entry but also hinders beneficiaries' ability to navigate the system effectively and exercise their entitlements. As a result, individuals often experience delays in receiving necessary care, which further exacerbates their vulnerability.[58]

On the supply side, service providers in both the healthcare and social assistance sectors frequently lack a comprehensive, integrated understanding of the services available across the system. This knowledge gap prevents them from identifying which individuals may be eligible for care services in other sectors or how they might effectively coordinate care across different domains. As a result, inefficiencies and fragmentation occur, with care often being provided in silos rather than as part of a holistic, person-centered approach. The lack of coordination between sectors further

---

[57] Mitek A., Finansowanie i organizacja systemu opieki długoterminowej w Polsce, Studia i Prace Wydziału Nauk Ekonomicznych i Zarządzania, Vol. 34, No. 1, 2013, p. 230.

[58] World Bank Report 2024a, p. 242–20.

undermines the quality and continuity of care, hindering the overall effectiveness of the LTC system.[59]

Moreover, beneficiaries of LTC who turn to the private market—whether out of necessity due to the absence of adequate public alternatives or due to insufficient information about existing public options—often find themselves evaluating various options without the necessary knowledge to make informed decisions.[60] Key factors, such as understanding the components of high-quality care or assessing the credibility and reliability of providers, remain unclear. This lack of transparency places beneficiaries at significant risk of selecting suboptimal care solutions, which may not meet their specific needs or quality expectations. As a result, individuals may face unmet care requirements, financial strain, or even potential harm, further highlighting the need for clearer information and better regulation in the private LTC sector.

Unifying the system of LTC should thus become a reform priority. Establishing a singular, comprehensive definition of LTC at the regulatory level, alongside the operational integration of private and public LTC, encompassing the two pillars—healthcare and social assistance—through a unified governance framework and coherent financing scheme could markedly enhance the accessibility and efficiency of services.[61] Such unification could also remedy the institutional complexity of the public LTC sector. Also, unification could help to reduce the overall costs of LTC provision.[62]

Addressing these challenges requires the development of an integrated information system that spans both the public and private sectors. Such a system would empower beneficiaries to more easily identify and access the services they need, while promoting transparency that supports informed decision-making.

A key component of this informational integration could be the establishment of care coordinators, who would act as facilitators between the healthcare and social assistance sectors.[63] Furthermore, the adoption of modern management and monitoring tools would be essential for effectively integrating the existing, fragmented LTC measures. These tools would enable real-time tracking, evaluation, and optimization of services across the entire LTC system, ensuring that care is delivered in a timely, coordinated, and patient-centered manner. Such technological advancements would also aid in bridging the information gap, improving the quality of services and the overall experience for beneficiaries.[64]

Another initiative aimed at fostering integration at the highest institutional level within Poland's two-pillar long-term care (LTC) structure could be the establishment of a Department of Senior Health within the Ministry of Health. It would serve as a counterpart to the existing Department of Senior Policy within the Ministry

[59] World Bank Report 2024a, p. 242–21.

[60] World Bank Report 2024a, p. 242–21.

[61] World Bank Report 2024a, p. 19.

[62] Berezowski J., Guzak B., Realizacja prawa do opieki długoterminowej, Wydawnictwo Państwowej Wyższej Szkoły Zawodowej w Raciborzu, 2016, p. 23

[63] World Bank Report 2024a, p. 60.

[64] World Bank Report 2024a, p. 188.

of Family, Labor, and Social Policy, facilitating collaboration between the two ministries. Strengthening coordination at the ministerial level could enhance policy integration and streamline activities across lower levels of government, ultimately improving the effectiveness of Poland's LTC system.[65]

4.2 *Optimalization of Funding*

In 2022, 10.4% of the GDP of the EU was devoted to healthcare.[66] In Poland, the share of health care spending in GDP was only 6.4%.[67] Additionally, more than a quarter of this share was accounted for by private spending, meaning that public healthcare expenditure in Poland amounted to only about 4.8% of GDP.[68] When specifically examining LTC spending, public expenditures in Poland were also below the EU average. In 2021, Poland allocated just 0.5% of its GDP to LTC, significantly lower than the EU average of 1.7%.[69] This discrepancy underscores the underfunded nature of the LTC system in Poland, which likely contributes to challenges related to service availability, quality, and accessibility. To address this underfunding and meet the growing demographic demands, it is crucial to increase state budget allocations for LTC. Adequate financial support is a fundamental requirement for improving both access to and the quality of LTC services.

Currently, specific government programs aimed at improving LTC in Poland are primarily short-term and aimed at specific beneficiary groups.[70] While a notable source of funding for LTC in Poland are EU funds, a persistent challenge lies in the optimal utilization of these available resources.[71] The current practices contribute to a fragmented financing structure at the regional level, lacking sufficient coordination and strategic alignment of financial flows. This fragmentation undermines the overall effectiveness and efficiency of LTC funding.

A comprehensive review of public expenditures on LTC is essential to assess the cost-effectiveness of current allocations. This process should focus on identifying inefficiencies within the system and proposing targeted budgetary strategies that can ensure the long-term fiscal stability of LTC services. By systematically evaluating funding distribution and its impact on service delivery, policymakers can

[65] Szatur–Jaworska B., Rysz–Kowalczyk B., Imiołczyk B., Sytuacja Osób Starszych w Polsce—wyzwania i rekomendacje, Biuro Rzecznika Praw Obywatelskich, 2020, p. 21.

[66] OECD/European Commission (2024), Health at a Glance: Europe 2024: State of Health in the EU Cycle, OECD Publishing, Paris, doi:10.1787/b3704e14-en.OECD2024,p. 144, (hereinafter: OECD/EU 2024).

[67] OECD/EU 2024, p. 145.

[68] OECD/EU 2024, p. 145.

[69] World Bank Report 2024a, p. 105, 23.

[70] World Bank Report 2024a, p. 105, 24.

[71] World Bank Report 2024a, p. 105, 23.

better prioritize resources, reduce wasteful spending, and implement more effective financial mechanisms.

As noted, in Poland the sector of LTC pre-funding schemes, including insurance frameworks, remains underdeveloped. While private LTC insurance has not established itself as a popular product, a specific public LTC insurance system or pre-funding scheme does not exist outside of the standard health insurance framework.

One critical aspect of reforming the LTC system by fostering pre-funding solutions lies in introducing incentives and financial tools to encourage individuals to proactively plan for their future care needs. Similar to preparing for retirement or unexpected events, it is essential to offer citizens more tools that enable them to save and prepare for their potential dependency. This also includes measures to improve healthy aging.[72] Currently, however, a significant gap exists in this regard. Despite the recognized effectiveness of preventive actions and health-related investments in maintaining independence and delaying care needs, a large proportion of the population remains passive. For instance, 41% of survey respondents reported that they make no effort to stay healthy, fit, or independent for as long as possible. Even more concerning is the lack of forward planning—55% of individuals aged 65 and older have never discussed aging-related issues or future care needs with family or friends.[73] Among those aged 45–64, this number rises to 71%, reflecting a lack of awareness and engagement in long-term care planning.[74]

One potential reform is the introduction of a public long-term care pre-funding system, which would not only stabilize funding but also ensure continuity of services across the country.[75] This system could be structured to ensure equity, allowing individuals of varying incomes to contribute in a manner that aligns with their ability to pay, while providing a safety net for those who are most vulnerable.

In addition to such public system, government initiatives could include tax incentives for savings accounts dedicated to health-related expenditures, which would encourage individuals to save for future care needs in a structured manner. Public education campaigns designed to raise awareness about the realities and potential costs of long-term care could help shift societal attitudes and motivate early planning.

Addressing the issue of underdevelopment in the private LTC insurance sector in Poland requires a multifaceted approach that fosters personal responsibility and encourages proactive planning for future care needs. Costs of LTC can be very high compared to an older person's disposable income.[76] In the absence of a public scheme of funding, most older people would not be able to afford adequate formal LTC at

---

[72] OECD 2024, p. 9.

[73] World Bank Report 2024a p. 105, 199.

[74] World Bank Report 2024a, p. 105, 199.

[75] World Bank Report 2024a p.192; see further: Barr, N. (2010). Long-term care: a suitable case for social insurance. Social Policy & Administration, vol. 44, nr 4, s. 359–374.

[76] OECD (2024), Is Care Affordable for Older People?, OECD Health Policy Studies, OECD Publishing, Paris, doi:https://doi.org/10.1787/450ea778-en(hereeinafter:OECD2024), p. 8.

the time they require such services. By implementing measures that support health-related investments, voluntary financial savings, and innovative private insurance products, the government can empower individuals to take control of their long-term care plans while reducing the financial burden on the public system.

Another critical aspect related to the challenge of funding is the adequacy of infrastructure, particularly in terms of housing.[77] As the elderly population in Polish society continues to grow, housing conditions have become an increasingly pressing issue. These conditions significantly affect the safety and quality of life for older adults and individuals with disabilities, especially as they often face limited mobility. With a significant portion of the elderly living alone, the barriers related to housing become even more pronounced. From the point of view of LTC needs, the place of residence of the elderly matters. In Poland, seniors are more likely to live in urban areas. A similar pattern is found in Slovakia and Hungary, while in most other EU countries, elderly people live in rural areas.[78] This poses unique challenges to accommodating housing challenges in the Polish LTC system.

In response, current policies must be expanded to address the specific needs of an aging population, requiring housing that accommodates the needs of both the elderly and people with disabilities. Accessible, adaptable, and affordable housing options are essential to ensure that older adults can live independently and securely in their own homes or in supportive environments.

While the proposed solutions extend beyond the competencies of the healthcare and social assistance sectors, it is crucial to acknowledge that they belong structurally to the LTC problem. Age-appropriate and disability-friendly housing conditions are fundamental in determining whether individuals will be compelled to move to a care facility prematurely due to the risks posed by unsuitable living environments. Literature on home-based medical care clearly demonstrates that remaining in one's own home promotes well-being and safety, especially for the elderly. It is well-established that health policies for the elderly must recognize that staying in familiar surroundings—especially for individuals with dementia—improves well-being.[79] The availability of housing tailored to the needs of the elderly and individuals with disabilities is essential for the deinstitutionalization of the LTC system, as it reduces the likelihood of beneficiaries being transferred to institutional care and enables care to be provided at home, which should be the preferred choice. Consequently, effective integration of housing policies into the broader LTC framework is necessary to address the full spectrum of challenges facing an aging population.

Key proposed solutions could include the development of housing resources specifically designed for the elderly and disabled, efforts to regulate design standards for buildings and residences intended for these groups and increased funding

---

[77] World Bank Report 2024a, p. 105, 30.

[78] Golinowska S., Potrzeby osób starszych w zakresie zdrowia publicznego, Projekt „Łagodzenie skutków pandemii wśród grup wysokiego ryzyka–osoby 60+" finansowany ze środków Ministerstwa Edukacji i Nauki na podstawie Decyzji Nr 41/WFSN/2021, 2021, p. 4.

[79] Fal A., Rekomendacje zmian systemowych w opiece nad osobami starszymi w Polsce, Spartańska Fundacja na rzecz rozwoju Narodowego Instytutu Geriatrii, Reumatologii i Rehabilitacji w Warszawie, 2016, p. 35.

for adapting living spaces.[80] Additionally, collaboration with LTC facilities is vital for assessing needs and supporting beneficiaries in obtaining funding for housing adaptations. Regular assessment of housing needs based on local conditions, along with the management of housing resources to meet the population's demands, should be prioritized.[81] Lastly, addressing planning issues in accordance with local conditions—ensuring access to transportation, services, social activities, and essential facilities such as healthcare and shopping—will be crucial in fostering supportive living environments for the elderly and disabled.[82]

4.3 Support of Informal Caregiving

In Poland, family members have traditionally shouldered the primary responsibility for LTC, a practice rooted in cultural values and societal expectations.[83] The transfer of "Western care patterns" to Poland is to some extent visible and increases the social acceptance of paid care services and institutions providing assistance, while reducing social pressure to provide personal care for seniors.[84] However, formal care in Poland still accounts for only 20% of the total care provided, while 80% is composed of informal care.

This heavy reliance on informal caregiving highlights the urgent need for comprehensive financial support and training programs for caregivers. The core of Poland's LTC system is largely informal, with care predominantly provided by relatives—family members, friends, and neighbors. While existing financial assistance may offer some relief, it is insufficient to address the multifaceted challenges that caregivers encounter. As the demand for LTC services continues to rise, it becomes increasingly crucial to develop more robust mechanisms that can alleviate the burden on family caregivers and enhance the quality of care they provide.[85]

Many caregivers in Poland are forced to reduce their working hours or exit the labor market entirely, which not only impacts their financial stability but also reduces the overall economic productivity. The financial strain on caregivers is further compounded by the costs associated with care, such as specialized equipment, medications, and necessary home modifications. While financial benefits exist for caregivers of individuals with disabilities, these benefits often fall short of covering the

[80] World Bank Report 2024a, p. 105, 30.

[81] World Bank Report 2024a, p. 105, 30.

[82] World Bank Report 2024a, p. 105, 30.

[83] Łuczak P., Publiczne i prywatne finansowanie opieki długoterminowej. Przykład Europy Środkowo-Wschodniej, Problemy Polityki Społecznej. Studia i Dyskusje, Vol. 33, 2016, p. 36, 38.

[84] Lewandowska-Szweda Z., Rynek usług opiekuńczych—dynamicznie rozwijający się segment gospodarki, Rynek Pracy, Vol. 3, 2018, p. 33.

[85] World Bank Report 2024a, p. 266–269.

full range of expenses, particularly for those who are forced to reduce their income by stepping away from work or cutting their working hours to provide care.

Expanding access to respite care services is critical in alleviating the pressures faced by family caregivers. By allowing caregivers to temporarily transfer their responsibilities to professional services, respite care helps prevent burnout, reduces stress, and enables caregivers to maintain a healthier balance between their caregiving duties and personal well-being. This support not only enhances caregivers' physical and emotional health but also improves the quality of care provided to those in need, as caregivers are better able to recharge and refocus.

Training and support programs for caregivers are essential in enhancing the quality of care and the well-being of both caregivers and recipients. These programs should equip caregivers with the necessary skills to manage medical tasks, navigate the complex healthcare system, and provide emotional support to both themselves and the individuals they care for. In addition to medical and emotional training, it is crucial that the programs address practical skills such as time management. This will enable caregivers to better balance their caregiving duties with professional obligations, reducing stress and improving their overall quality of life.[86]

The demand for long-term care (LTC) workers is increasing across OECD countries, and many are struggling to meet this challenge.[87] However, ensuring a sufficient workforce is an achievable goal through strategic efforts. One approach is to enhance recruitment by expanding hiring pools, including young people and the long-term unemployed, or by attracting migrant workers. While some countries have seen an increase in migrant LTC workers, labor migration programs often fail to address the specific needs of the sector, leading to mixed results. Another crucial strategy is improving retention, as high staff turnover is costly. In the United States, the cost per vacancy is estimated at a minimum of $2500. By offering better wages and improving working conditions, countries can increase retention rates and strengthen the LTC workforce. Countries like Germany, the Netherlands, Sweden, and Norway have successfully implemented measures to upgrade LTC jobs, leading to positive outcomes. Boosting productivity is also essential, primarily through work process reorganization, technology integration to reduce administrative burdens, and delegation of certain nursing tasks to assistants. However, there is limited evidence on the overall effectiveness of these strategies in improving efficiency within the LTC sector. In the long run, enhancing job quality for both local and migrant workers will be critical. Low pay, poor working conditions, and high turnover are unsustainable, as fewer workers may be willing to enter the field. On the other hand, professionalizing the sector could create barriers to entry, reducing flexibility in a workforce that

[86] World Bank Report 2024a, p. 236.

[87] See extensively: OECD (2020), Who Cares? Attracting and Retaining Care Workers for the Elderly, OECD Health Policy Studies, OECD Publishing, Paris, doi: https://doi.org/10.1787/92c0ef68-en.

currently values adaptability. Implementing these improvements requires investment, and any increased costs must be justified by measurable gains in productivity.[88]

Moreover, the role of informal caregivers should be formally recognized within both policy frameworks and societal attitudes. Public awareness campaigns can serve to emphasize the critical importance of caregiving, thereby reducing stigma and fostering a more supportive and appreciative environment. Strengthening both formal and informal social support networks is equally important, as these networks can help mitigate caregiver isolation by offering both emotional and practical assistance. This multifaceted approach will ensure that caregivers feel valued, supported, and better equipped to fulfil their responsibilities, while also promoting a broader societal understanding of the challenges they face.

4.4 Improved Quality Control

Due to the limited availability of quality metrics and inadequate oversight mechanisms, the quality control of LTC services in Poland remains insufficient. Although regulations specify certain standards that LTC facilities must meet to operate legally, there is no cohesive, unified definition of quality that applies across both the healthcare and social assistance sectors. Furthermore, there is a conspicuous absence of universal indicators to consistently measure and evaluate service quality.[89] The existing quality standards are fragmented, and inspections of LTC facilities are conducted irregularly by various entities, including local government units and the National Health Fund. This fragmented approach not only hinders the systematic improvement of service quality but also exacerbates disparities in the delivery of care, further compromising the overall effectiveness of the system.

According to public opinion surveys, nearly half of Polish adults hold a negative view of the quality of LTC services, with dissatisfaction rates even higher among individuals who rely on these services.[90] Addressing these quality challenges will require decisive action from national-level institutions, alongside active engagement from regional authorities. Efforts must focus on creating consistent, enforceable standards, enhancing oversight mechanisms, and ensuring adequate staffing and resources to improve the overall quality of care.

One measure could be the establishment of an expert task force to develop integrated quality frameworks for LTC in Poland, accompanied by a set of key performance indicators (KPIs).[91] The expert group should consist of representatives from relevant sectors, including healthcare, social services, and public administration, as well as academics and civil society organizations, to ensure a comprehensive and

[88] Colombo, F. et al., Help wanted? Providing and paying for long-term care. OECD Health Policy Studies, Paris: OECD Publishing, 2011, p. 15.

[89] World Bank Report 2024a, p. 105, 28.

[90] World Bank Report 2024a, p. 105, 28.

[91] World Bank Report 2024a, p. 105, 28.

multidisciplinary approach. Such an initiative would aim to create a unified definition of quality applicable across both healthcare and social assistance sectors, addressing the current fragmentation. The framework should include measurable KPIs that evaluate the accessibility, safety, efficiency, and user satisfaction of LTC services.

The inclusion of definitions, frameworks, and quality indicators within the relevant legal framework is essential. Additionally, establishing a national monitoring and evaluation mechanism applicable to service providers, institutions, and organizations within the LTC sector is crucial for ensuring accountability.[92] The implementation of surveys on LTC provision, aimed at collecting feedback from both the beneficiaries and their families, will help gauge public opinion on the system. Furthermore, the development of a publicly accessible database with quality indicators for individual LTC facilities, both public and private, would enhance transparency.[93] Regular audits are vital for identifying areas for improvement. The introduction of a central quality management system with data on staff, patients, and treatment results would enable better quality control.[94] The use of emerging technologies to improve data management, beneficiary care, and the utilization of real-time data would contribute to more effective ODT outcomes. Finally, promoting research focused on LTC-related issues is necessary to advance services and optimize the overall system.

Importantly, quality control systems should encompass private LTC services, which currently operate almost outside the boundaries of quality control, leading to private facilities often lacking adequately qualified staff and monitoring standards. The introduction of an accreditation and quality monitoring system could reduce disparities and guarantee uniform standards. An example of good practice can be found in the German system, where private providers are subject to regular audits, helping to improve the quality of services.[95]

The issue of a lack of qualified caregivers is also a critical challenge in both the private and public LTC sectors. Without proper education and training standards, caregivers' abilities can vary widely, which affects the quality of care provided to those in need. The perceived low societal prestige of the profession combined with relatively low salaries stops the necessary inflow of skilled caregivers.[96] The absence of formal (legal) qualifications and oversight for both community and migrant caregivers is particularly concerning, as these caregivers often play a central role in delivering LTC services.

In order to improve the situation, it is necessary to guarantee stability and continuity of employment by increasing salaries and mandatory training to improve

[92] World Bank Report 2024a 2024, p. 105, 29.

[93] World Bank Report 2024a, p.105, 29.

[94] World Bank Report 2024a, p. 237.

[95] World Bank Report 2024a, p. 237–268.

[96] Szatur–Jaworska B., Rysz–Kowalczyk B., Imiołczyk B., Sytuacja Osób Starszych w Polsce–wyzwania i rekomendacje, Biuro Rzecznika Praw Obywatelskich, 2020, p. 30; see also 34. OECD (2023), Beyond Applause? Improving Working Conditions in Long-Term Care, OECD Publishing, Paris, https://doi.org/10.1787/27d33ab3-en

skills.[97] The introduction of formal training standards could significantly improve the professionalism and consistency of care.[98] However, this may also lead to higher costs, which could create barriers for families seeking care. Increased costs might reduce demand for formal care services, potentially forcing informal caregiving responsibilities, leading to economic and social consequences. Consequently, any reform in caregiver qualifications and training standards must be carefully balanced with appropriate funding and public support. Public transfers, in addition to household budgets, are crucial for sustaining a sustainable and accessible LTC system. A combination of financial support, training, and regulation could help develop the care services market while ensuring that caregivers are properly equipped to provide high-quality care.[99]

4.5 Development of the Private LTC Sector

The private LTC sector can effectively complement the public system, either through the development of fully private (commercial) services and facilities or through public-private partnerships. Encouraging individuals to purchase private insurance plans through targeted incentives could further support the expansion of private LTC services. Such insurance mechanisms, by pooling risk across large groups and leveraging economies of scale, can more effectively reduce the financial burden of providing care for dependent individuals.[100] However, it has been rightly stated that private LTC insurance schemes need to be supported by incentives if they are to develop beyond a niche market.[101]

However, as international comparison shows, a market for private LTC insurance has only formed in few countries and faces obstacles both on the demand and the supply side.[102] Importantly, trust in such a system is crucial for its success. Given the long-term nature of LTC needs, the legal framework should address scenarios in which a commercial entity fails to deliver on its private insurance product. A safety net system should be established to protect beneficiaries in such cases, ensuring continuity of care and further enhancing public confidence in purchasing such insurance

[97] Szatur–Jaworska B., Rysz–Kowalczyk B., Imiołczyk B., Sytuacja Osób Starszych w Polsce–wyzwania i rekomendacje, Biuro Rzecznika Praw Obywatelskich, 2020, p. 30.

[98] Szatur–Jaworska B., Rysz–Kowalczyk B., Imiołczyk B., Sytuacja Osób Starszych w Polsce–wyzwania i rekomendacje, Biuro Rzecznika Praw Obywatelskich, 2020, p. 24.

[99] Lewandowska-Szweda Z., Rynek usług opiekuńczych–dynamicznie rozwijający się segment gospodarki, Rynek Pracy, Vol. 3, 2018, p. 34.

[100] Łuczak P., Publiczne i prywatne finansowanie opieki długoterminowej. Przykład Europy Środkowo-Wschodniej, Problemy Polityki Społecznej. Studia i Dyskusje, Vol. 33, 2016, p. 40.

[101] Colombo, F. et al., Help wanted? Providing and paying for long-term care. OECD Health Policy Studies, Paris: OECD Publishing, 2011, p. 15.

[102] Szatur–Jaworska B., Rysz–Kowalczyk B., Imiołczyk B., Sytuacja Osób Starszych w Polsce–wyzwania i rekomendacje, Biuro Rzecznika Praw Obywatelskich, 2020, p. 29.

products. This would create a more stable and trustworthy environment for individuals to proactively plan for their future care needs while reducing the financial burden on the public system.

Cooperation with the private sector can increase investment in infrastructure and increase the number of places in LTCs facilities. One example of effective cooperation is the "Care 75+" program, which enables support for seniors by expanding access to home services.[103] Countries such as the Netherlands have successfully integrated private and public sectors through joint financing and management of facilities, resulting in a more cohesive and efficient care system.[104]

While public statistics provide some data on private care facilities in Poland, little is known about services contracted by public LTC institutions to private providers. Given the presence of various private and third-sector entities, including commercial enterprises and non-governmental organizations (NGOs), the existing challenges in coordinating LTC services become even more pronounced. On the other hand, the diverse service offerings present an opportunity to address gaps and reduce regional disparities. Persistent coordination between both sectors is necessary so that beneficiaries can access these services in the future without concerns about continuity of care or service standards.

The development of private LTC must be accompanied by enhanced quality control measures (see 4.4.). Given that private LTC provision largely operates outside regulatory oversight, it is essential to implement standards that safeguard the rights of beneficiaries. Additionally, establishing information and communication platforms to raise awareness of the rights of individuals in need of care is crucial.

5 Conclusions

In conclusion, Poland's LTC system is deeply entrenched in complexity, encompassing various sectors, levels of administration, and funding sources. This fragmentation has led to inefficiencies, inequities, and accessibility challenges. The lack of a standardized definition of LTC and the absence of a coordinated framework between healthcare and social assistance sectors exacerbate service delays and hinder the effective delivery of care. A unified LTC system should be a key reform priority, focusing on integrating both the public and private sectors, and creating a cohesive governance structure.

One critical area for reform is the optimalization of funding within the LTC system. Poland's public spending on LTC remains significantly below the European Union average, and the current funding structures are fragmented, undermining the

---

103 The "Care 75+" program is an initiative of the Ministry of Family, Labor and Social Policy to support municipalities in providing care services to people aged 75 and over, especially those living in small towns. The program finances or subsidizes care services so that seniors can function in their home environment for as long as possible.

104 World Bank Report 2024a, p. 266.

system's effectiveness. An increase in state budget allocations is essential to meet the growing demands of an aging population. Additionally, the development of a robust long-term care insurance system, alongside tax incentives and savings tools, would help individuals plan for their future care needs, reducing the financial strain on the public system. Addressing the underdeveloped private sector and encouraging proactive care planning through financial incentives could also play a pivotal role in creating a more efficient LTC system.

Equally important is the support of informal caregiving, which forms the backbone of LTC in Poland. The financial and emotional strain on family caregivers is a significant issue, with many reducing their working hours or exiting the labor market to provide care. Expanding financial support for caregivers, including wage compensation and tax relief, is crucial to alleviate their burden. Additionally, increasing access to respite care services, offering training and support, and recognizing the role of informal caregivers in both policy and public perception would significantly improve the caregiving environment. The introduction of a LTC insurance system could provide a safety net for families.

Finally, the quality control of LTC services in Poland remains insufficient due to the lack of comprehensive metrics and oversight mechanisms. The establishment of an integrated quality framework, with clear indicators for both healthcare and social assistance sectors, is essential for ensuring consistency and high standards of care. Introducing regular audits and creating a centralized quality management system would enhance transparency and foster accountability. The private LTC sector requires greater regulation to ensure that services meet the necessary standards. By implementing these quality control measures, Poland can ensure that both public and private LTC providers deliver high-quality care to beneficiaries.

References

Bank Światowy. (2024a). Opieka długoterminowa w Polsce: Raport z konsultacji społecznych. World Bank Group.

Bank Światowy. (2024b). Przegląd strategiczny opieki długoterminowej w Polsce. World Bank Group.

Barr, N. (2010). Long-term care: a suitable case for social insurance. Social Policy & Administration, 44(4), 359–374.

Berezowski, J., & Guzak, B. (2016). Realizacja prawa do opieki długoterminowej.

Błędowski, P., & Kaczmarska, E. (2018). Czynniki wpływające na poziom wydatków publicznych na opiekę długoterminową w wybranych krajach Europy, Ubezpieczenia Społeczne. Teoria i praktyka, Vol. 3, 19–33.

Bosek, L., & Safjan, M. (2016). Konstytucja RP. Tom I: Komentarz do art. 1–86. Legalis Online.

Campbell, J. C., Ikegami, N., & Gibson, M. J. (2010). Lessons from public long-term care insurance in Germany and Japan. Health Affairs, 29, 87–95.

Cho, M., Nicolini, G., & Lee, H. (2022). The national pension systems and financial consumers: An International comparative perspective on the key linkages, international comparison of pension systems.

Colombo, F. (2011). Help wanted? Providing and paying for long-term care. OECD Health Policy Studies. OECD Publishing.

Fal, A. (2016). Rekomendacje zmian systemowych w opiece nad osobami starszymi w Polsce, Spartańska Fundacja na rzecz rozwoju Narodowego Instytutu Geriatrii, Reumatologii i Rehabilitacji w Warszawie.

Golinowska, S. (2021). Potrzeby osób starszych w zakresie zdrowia publicznego, Projekt „Łagodzenie skutków pandemii wśród grup wysokiego ryzyka—osoby 60+" finansowany ze środków Ministerstwa Edukacji i Nauki na podstawie Decyzji Nr 41/WFSN/2021.

Iwagami, M., & Tamiya N. (2019). The long-term care insurance system in Japan: Past, present, and future. MA Journal, 2, 67–69.

Jurek, Ł. (2009). Zmiany stacjonarnej opieki społecznej nad ludźmi starymi w Polsce i wybranych krajach. Uniwersytet Ekonomiczny we Wrocławiu.

Kawałko S. (2014). Istota i zadania współczesnej polityki ochrony zdrowia, Studia Gdańskie. Wizje i rzeczywistość, Vol. 11, 325–338.

Kilian J., Ćwirlej-Sozańska A., Wiśniowska-Szurlej A., Wilmowska-Pietruszyńska A. (2018). System długoterminowej opieki domowej nad osobami starszymi w Polsce i wybranych krajach europejskich, Niepełnosprawność—zagadnienia, problemy, rozwiązania, Vol IV, No. 29, 113-131.

Konstytucja Rzeczypospolitej Polskiej z dnia 2 kwietnia 1997 r. (Dz.U. z 1997 r. Nr 78, poz. 483).

Kuncewicz D., Pabiś M. (2016), Potrzeby osób starszych w zakresie opieki zdrowotnej—konteksty, Pielęgniarstwo XXI Wieku, Vol. 15, No. 4(57), 53–59.

Kułagowska E., Kosińska M., Nowak-Kapusta Z. (2011), Opieka długoterminowa domowa w Polsce, Medycyna Środowiskowa, Vol. 14, No. 2, 64–69.

Lamont M. (2021), Efektywność zespołu terapeutycznego w zakładach opieki długoterminowej, Uniwersytet Medyczny w Lublinie.

Lenio P. (2018), Publicznoprawne źródła finansowania ochrony zdrowia.

Lewandowska-Szweda Z. (2018), Rynek usług opiekuńczych—dynamicznie rozwijający się segment gospodarki, Rynek Pracy, Vol. 3, 25–35.

Łuczak P. (2016). Publiczne i prywatne finansowanie opieki długoterminowej. Przykład Europy Środkowo-Wschodniej, Problemy Polityki Społecznej. Studia i Dyskusje, Vol. 33, No. 2, 35–51.

Minister ds. Polityki Senioralnej (2025). Informacja o sytuacji osób starszych w Polsce za 2023 r., 2024.

Ministerstwo Zdrowia (2025). Ocena opieki długoterminowej w Polsce na podstawie ram oceny przygotowanych przez WHO, World Bank Group, 2024.

Ministerstwo Zdrowia, (2025). Przykłady Międzynarodowych Rozwiązań: Opieka długoterminowa, World Bank Group, 2024.

Ministerstwo Zdrowia (2012), Stan faktyczny i perspektywy rozwoju opieki długoterminowej w Polsce.

Ministerstwo Zdrowia (2021). Zdrowa Przyszłość: Ramy strategiczne rozwoju systemu ochrony zdrowia na lata 2021–2027, z perspektywą do 2030 r.

Mitek A. (2013). Finansowanie i organizacja systemu opieki długoterminowej w Polsce, Studia i Prace Wydziału Nauk Ekonomicznych i Zarządzania, Vol. 34, No. 1, 223–236.

OECD/European Commission. (2024), Health at a Glance: Europe 2024: State of Health in the EU Cycle, OECD Publishing, Paris, doi:https://doi.org/10.1787/b3704e14-en

OECD (2024), Is Care Affordable for Older People?, OECD Health Policy Studies, OECD Publishing, Paris, doi:https://doi.org/10.1787/450ea778-en

OECD (2020), Who Cares? Attracting and Retaining Care Workers for the Elderly, OECD Health Policy Studies, OECD Publishing, Paris, doi:https://doi.org/10.1787/92c0ef68-en

OECD (2023), Beyond Applause? Improving Working Conditions in Long-Term Care, OECD Publishing, Paris, doi:https://doi.org/10.1787/27d33ab3-en

Prędkiewicz P. (2012). Prywatne ubezpieczenia jako źródło finansowania opieki zdrowotnej, Praca doktorska, Uniwersytet Ekonomiczny we Wrocławiu.

Rozporządzenie Ministra Rodziny, Pracy i Polityki Społecznej z dnia 28 sierpnia 2020 r. w sprawie wydawania i cofania zezwoleń na prowadzenie w ramach działalności statutowej placówki zapewniającej całodobową opiekę (Dz. U. poz. 1532).

Shimizutani S. (2014). The Future of Long-term Care in Japan, Asia-Pacific Review, Vol. 21, 88–119.

Stasiak M. & Stasiak J. (2023). Finansowanie ochrony zdrowia w Polsce w kontekście zmian demograficznych, Współczesne problemy gospodarcze - Zarządzanie i finanse sektora publicznego..

Szatur–Jaworska B., Rysz–Kowalczyk B., Imiołczyk B. (2020) Sytuacja Osób Starszych w Polsce–wyzwania i rekomendacje, Biuro Rzecznika Praw Obywatelskich.

Ustawa z dnia 12 marca 2004 r. o pomocy społecznej (t.j. Dz. U. z 2024 r. poz. 1283 z późn. zm.).

Ustawa z dnia 27 sierpnia 2004 r. o świadczeniach opieki zdrowotnej finansowanych ze środków publicznych (t.j. Dz. U. z 2024 r. poz. 146 z późn. zm.).

Long-term Care Insurance in the US

Peter J. Morgan

1 Introduction

This chapter describes the situation of long-term care in the United States (US), including demographic developments and projections of the need for long-term care, public and private insurance schemes, facilities, and caregivers. The demand for long-term care is growing steadily, especially in the cohort aged 85 or older, which suffers most from physical and mental disabilities. Nonetheless, the piecemeal and incomplete nature of the long-term care system and the high costs of treatment in the US mean that the direct burden of such costs on households is very large, especially for middle-income households. The sector faces numerous challenges for long-term sustainability, including inadequate labor supply and demand/supply issues for private long-term care insurance.

Section 1 provides an introduction, section 2 describes developments of aging, health, and the demand for long-term care, section 3 describes the public long-term care insurance system, section 4 the private long-term care insurance system, section 5 the facilities, section 6 the caregivers, and section 7 the major issues, while section 8 concludes.

P. J. Morgan (✉)
Asian Development Bank Institute, Tokyo, Japan
e-mail: pmorgan@adbi.org

H. Lee and G. Nicolini (eds.), *International Comparison of Long-Term Care Insurance Systems*, Contributions to Management Science,
https://doi.org/10.1007/978-981-95-7781-1_4

2 Demographics and Health

2.1 Demographics

The population is gradually aging. The share of the population age 65 and over is expected to rise from 17% in 2022 to 21% in 2030, but the pace will slow thereafter, with the ratio rising gradually to 23% by 2050 thereafter, and the level in 2050 then reaching 82.1 million, an increase of 42% compared with 2022. The share of the population age 85 and over will rise from 2.0% in 2021 to 4.8% by 2050, reflecting the aging of the "baby boomer" generation. This age group is the fastest growing segment of the US population, with an expected increase of 168% between 2022 and 2050, reaching 10.5 million by 2050. Over the same period, the share of the working-age population 18–64 will drop from 61% in 2020 to 59% by 2050 (US Census Bureau, 2023). Roughly a half of population growth in 2020–2050 will be attributable to immigration.

The average life expectancy at birth for men is expected to rise from 77.9 years in 2020 to 82.6 years in 2050, while that for women is expected to rise from 82.4 to 86.2 years (US Census Bureau, 2020).

Thus, the pace of aging in the US is relatively moderate compared with that in many other advanced economies, mainly due to continued substantial rates of immigration. Nonetheless, the population with potential need for long-term care will increase dramatically, especially in the age 85 and over group.

2.2 Developments of Need for Long-term Care

It is estimated that, at age 65, the likelihood of experiencing a LTC event before death is 47 percent for men and 58 percent for women, 51 percent for married individuals, and 54 percent for unmarried individuals. The average duration of care is 3.2 years for men and 4.4 years for women. Married individuals experience an average of 3.6 years of care, whereas unmarried individuals use care for 4.3 years (Braun and Kopecky, 2024). The proportion needing at least five years of care is especially high among those in the lowest income quintile at age 65 (29%) and those reporting fair or poor health at age 65 (25%). Among those who develop a significant disability, the average duration is 5.6 years for women and 5.1 years for men. Of the average 3.2 years that older adults are projected to have a significant disability, they will receive paid care for about 0.8 years, and unpaid caregivers, such as family and friends, will make up most of the difference (Johnson and Dey, 2022).

In the United States, 14 million adults are estimated to need long-term services and support (LTSS), i.e., long-term care, and over half (56%) are individuals aged 65 and older. Given the aging population, the number of those over age 65 with significant disabilities is projected to grow substantially, increasing from 7.6 million in 2022 to almost 14.7 million by 2065. In percentage terms, the share of the older population with significant disabilities is expected to increase from 14% to 16% (Johnson and Dey, 2022).

Most individuals who need LTSS are cared for in their own homes with the assistance of informal caregivers such as family members or friends. An estimated 10.6 million people provide uncompensated care to older adults, and, among those, 30% provide care to individuals aged 85 and older. Moreover, there is an unmet need among older adults who need daily assistance. Analysis of Health and Retirement Study data from 2000 to 2021 found that, among the 8 million older adults who reported dementia or difficulty with one or more daily personal tasks, 3 million reported not receiving assistance (Colello, 2023).

The amount and complexity of care needed per person will also increase, as a result of the increasing number of chronic conditions per person (O'Neill Hayes & Kurtovic, 2020).

2.3 Dementia

The share of older people with dementia is decreasing 1% to 2.5% per year, depending on the time frame and age group examined. But, as the baby boomer population ages, the total number of people with dementia is expected to rise. According to the Alzheimer's Association, in 2024, an estimated 6.9 million Americans aged 65 and above were suffering from Alzheimer's or dementia, about 11% of the total aged population. Around 73% of those people were over the age of 75 years. Dementia is more prevalent at older ages. About 5% of adults ages 65 to 74 have Alzheimer's or dementia, compared with 13.2% of adults ages 44 to 75 and 33% of adults age 85 and over. Women are slightly more likely to have dementia than men (Alzheimer's Association, 2024).

If current demographic and health trends continue, almost 9 million Americans could have dementia by 2030 and over 11 million by 2040 (Alzheimer's Association 2024). This mainly reflects the rapid increase in the number of people ages 85 and over.

3 Income and Cost of Long-term Care

Estimates of the total costs of long-term care vary depending on the assumptions made and the services included. In 2022, the Kaiser Family Foundation (KFF) estimated that the US spent about $415 billion (1.6% of GDP and 9.2% of total health expenditures) on formal long-term support services (LTSS), based on calculations using annual National Health Expenditure data. Spending on home and community-based services was $284 billion and the remaining $131 billion was spent on institutional

Table 1 US median annual cost of long-term care, 2023

Type of Care	Cost
In-Home Care	
Home Maker Services	$68,640
Home Health Aide	$75,504
Community and Assisted Living	
Adult Day Health Care	$24,696
Assisted Living Facility	$64,200
Nursing Home Facility	
Semi-Private Room	$104,028
Private Room	$116,796

Source Genworth Financial, Inc. (2024)

LTSS such as nursing facility care (KFF, 2024a).[1] It is estimated that in 2030 LTC costs will more than double and could reach between $1.3 trillion and $2.5 trillion (O'Neill Hayes & Kurtovic, 2020)

In 2023, the median annual costs of care in the U.S. were estimated to be $68,640 for full-time homemaker services (people who help with instrumental activities of daily living (IADLs) such as preparing meals, managing medication, self-finance, and housekeeping), $75,504 for full-time home health aide care which assists with activities of daily living (ADLs) such as mobility, feeding, dressing, personal hygiene, continence, and toileting, $116,800 for a private room in a nursing home, and $288,288 for round-the-clock home health aide services (see Table 1) (Genworth Financial, Inc., 2024; KFF, 2024a).

Gruber and McGarry (2023) estimate that the imputed costs of informal home-based care in 2018 ranged between $86 billion and $151 billion, about 25%–40% of formal expenditures, depending on the imputed value of leisure time lost due to care giving. Other estimates are even larger. Johnson and Dey (2022) estimate that, among people receiving unpaid family care, the average value of care reaches $204,000, more than the value of all paid LTSS.

The Department of Health and Human Services estimates that an average American turning 65 today who needs to pay for long-term care will incur $245,500 in future undiscounted LTSS costs, with families paying for over one-third of that themselves (Table 2). A person aged 65 currently is estimated to have a 56% probability of requiring LTSS sometime during their life (Johnson and Dey 2022). The largest payer is Medicaid, 42% of the total, followed by out-of-pocket expenses, 38%, while the share covered by private insurance is very small at only 5%. Public funds overall

[1] Estimates of the costs of long-term care vary depending on various assumptions, primarily the treatment of costs covered by Medicare and the costs of post-acute care in LTC facilities. Normally, Medicare only covers costs related to medical treatment, not long-term custodial care. For example, Sengupta, et al. (2022) and Lendon, et al (2024) analyze the costs of post-acute care and long-term care together, which tends to increase the overall cost estimates and the amount covered by Medicare.

Table 2 Projected average sum of LTSS Expenditures from age 65 through death for adults who turn 65 in 2021–2025 and pay for LTSS, by payer and setting

	All Settings		Community-based*		Nursing Facility	
Payer	US$	% of Total	US$	% of Total	US$	% of Total
Public	139,700	57	52,500	46	87,200	67
Medicaid	102,900	42	35,500	31	67,400	52
Other Public	36,800	15	17,000	15	19,800	15
Private	105,700	43	62,200	54	43,500	33
Out-of-Pocket	93,500	38	52,800	46	40,700	31
Private Insurance	12,200	5	9,400	8	2,800	2
All Payers	245,400	100	114,700	100	130,700	100

Source Johnson and Dey (2022)
Notes Estimates are reported in 2020 inflation-adjusted dollars. Residential care is included in community-based care, not nursing-facility care. Nursing home and residential care prices are adjusted for wage inflation; home care prices grow with the average of wage and price inflation. Components do not always sum to totals because of rounding.
*Includes residential facilities

cover 46% of community-based costs and 67% of nursing facility costs (Johnson and Dey 2022).

Only a fraction of US households would be able to bear the average out-of-pocket costs of $93,500 without a severe financial burden. In 2018, half of US households at age 65 or over had annual income lower than $35,000 and total wealth of less than $217,000, and 25% had income of less than $21,000 and wealth of less than $57,000 (Gruber and McGarry, 2023).

People with lower incomes tend to have more of their costs covered by Medicaid and pay less out of pocket. Although Medicaid is used by older adults throughout the age-65 income distribution, it primarily serves those in the bottom 40% of the income distribution. People with lower incomes and wealth also tend to be less healthy and have more issues with ADLs.

4 Public Long-term Care Insurance Systems in the US

There is no general public long-term care insurance program in the US. Nevertheless, with the enactment of Titles XVIII (Medicare) and XIX (Medicaid) of the Social Security Act in 1965, public financing for post-acute or rehabilitative care and long-term services and support (LTSS) in long-term care facilities (LTCFs) became part of the U.S. public health care delivery system. Over time, states and the federal government became the largest payers of LTSS. For a detailed history of federal government support for LTSS see Colello (2023).

Medicare is the main public health insurance program for individuals over age 65, but it is oriented primarily to cover acute conditions, not chronic illness or disability. Medicare does not cover nursing home stays longer than 100 days, and individuals must shoulder a substantial copayment on the portion of the stay beyond 20 days. One exception is for hospice care. If a physician has provided a patient with a prognosis of under six months to live, Medicare will cover hospice care. In 2021, hospices served over 1.7 million Medicare beneficiaries, averaging 92.1 days of care per person (Consumer Affairs, 2024).

The Medicaid system provides long-term care insurance for persons with low income and assets. Unlike Medicare, Medicaid will provide indefinite coverage for a variety of needs, including custodial care. Medicaid is the primary national payer for long-term care services. Medicaid allows for the coverage of these services through several vehicles and over a range of settings, ranging from institutional care to community-based long-term services and supports. The system covers children, adults, and seniors who need long-term care services because of disabling conditions and chronic illnesses (Medicaid, 2024).

Medicaid annual spending per person was nearly nine times higher for people who used LTSS than for those who did not use LTSS ($38,769 vs. $4,480), with particularly high spending for people who used institutional LTSS ($47,279) (KFF, 2024).

However, Medicaid only provides coverage after an individual has exhausted their private LTC insurance benefits, spent down most of their assets (equity in a home is exempt or deferred in some cases), and exhausted Social Security and other retirement income (Cohen, 2016). Although Medicaid guarantees placement in nursing home care for those who qualify in terms of health and income eligibility, access to home care varies by state and is not guaranteed. There are often waiting lists to receive such care. However, various steps are being taken to increase access to home care under various Medicaid waiver programs.

4.1 Medicaid Long-term Care Programs and Eligibility

There are three types of Medicaid programs that cover long-term care for seniors aged 65 and over: Nursing Home Medicaid, Home and Community Based Services (HCBS) Waivers, and Aged, Blind and Disabled (ABD) Medicaid. Regardless of the type of program, all of them consider two major factors, financial need and medical need, but they vary for each program. Eligibility is complicated because the requirements are updated annually or biannually, and they vary depending on the state of residence, marital status, and whether the spouse is also applying.

Three factors are considered when determining if an applicant qualifies financially for Medicaid Long Term Care: 1) income, 2) assets and 3) the value of home equity. Each of the three types of Medicaid Long Term Care program has different values for these limits. Furthermore, the limits vary depending on whether an applicant is married or single and if one or both spouses are applying for Medicaid assistance.

A general guideline is that the monthly income limit to qualify for Medicaid is between 100% and 300% of the federal poverty level. For 2024, the federal poverty income number is $943 per month, and 300% of that is $2,829 per month (Medicaid, 2024).

Regarding assets, in most cases in 2024, single Medicaid Long Term Care applicants are permitted assets valued up to $2,000 and married couples with both spouses applying are permitted a combined value of $3,000 or $4,000. However, this varies by state.

Regarding the value of home equity, in most cases and in most states, the home's equity value will not be counted toward the asset limit if it is under the home equity interest limit for that state. Home equity interest is the portion of the home's value that the applicant owns less any outstanding mortgage or debt. The home interest limit in most states in 2024 is either $713,000 or $1,071,000, depending on the average real estate prices in that state (Medicaid 2024).

Nursing Home Medicaid and HCBS Waivers both require a Nursing Facility Level of Care (NFLOC). The definition and measurement of NFLOC vary by state. In most cases, the level of care need is determined by assessing the applicant's mental and physical health, and their need for skilled nursing or rehabilitative care. An important part of determining NFLOC is an assessment of the individual's ability to independently complete the five activities of daily living (ADLs): mobility, bathing, dressing, eating and toileting. The inability to perform two or three ADLs is generally considered to be a strong indicator of the need for NFLOC, but this is not uniform across states. A medical doctor is usually required to review and approve the NFLOC assessment.

ABD Medicaid only requires that a person be over age 65 and blind or disabled. No specific medical need is required to be approved for the program. However, to apply for specific benefits or long-term care services, they must demonstrate a need for the long-term care services they are applying for (Medicaidlongtermcare.gov, 2024).

4.2 *Nursing Home Care Versus Home and Community-based Care*

During the 1970s, the U.S. Department of Health, Education and Welfare (HEW, now the Department of Health and Human Services) considered alternatives to nursing home care through various federal research and demonstration efforts. These efforts were undertaken not only to find ways to offset the high cost of nursing facility care but also to respond to older adults and individuals with disabilities who desired to remain in their homes and in community-based settings rather than in institutions. In 1981, Congress took significant legislative action to expand HCBS when it authorized the Medicaid Section 1915(c) of the Social Security Act (SSA), Home and Community-Based Services (HCBS) Waiver Program (Colello 2023).

Before 1981, many of the nonskilled personal care and supportive services needed by chronically impaired persons to remain in the community were not covered under Medicaid state plans. With approved HCBS waiver programs, states were allowed to waive certain Medicaid state plan requirements to enable them to cover a wide variety of nonmedical, social, and supportive services designed to assist individuals with independent living (Colello, 2023). As a result, there has been a major shift of Medicaid funding from nursing homes to home and community care, as the share of Medicaid funding for the latter rose from 1% in 1981 to 56% in 2018 (Gruber and McGarry, 2023).

Funding

In 2020 it was estimated that 5.6 million people used Medicaid long-term support services (LTSS), of which 4.0 million (72%) used only HCBS, 1.4 million (24%) used only institutional care, and 0.2 million used both (4%). That year, Medicaid spending—including LTSS and other services such as hospital care and prescription drugs—for the 5.6 million enrollees who used Medicaid LTSS, amounted to $217 billion. (KFF, 2024b).

Medicare is financed by both a dedicated payroll tax and by general government funds. Medicaid is financed jointly by the federal and state governments but administered by the individual states. The federal government specifies certain parameters of the program, but eligibility criteria for long-term care—including income limits, asset limits, and care needs—differ across states.

The Penn Wharton Budget Model predicts that expenditures on LTC by Medicaid, the main public insurer, will double from 0.62 percent of GDP in 2022 to 1.25 percent of GDP by 2050 (He, 2022).

5 Private Long-term Care Insurance

5.1 Products

Private long-term care insurance has been available in the US for over 30 years. Early versions of this insurance were called nursing home insurance because policies only covered care provided in nursing homes, primarily skilled facilities. In the late 1970s and early 1980s only a small number of insurance companies provided such coverage. At that time LTC expenditures were less than $20 billion but were growing rapidly. By 1980, expenditures had risen to $30 billion, and expenditures on LTC exceeded $225 billion by 2016. By the end of the 1990s, more than 100 insurers were selling LTC insurance products, although a relatively small number of companies—less than a dozen—accounted for more than 80% of sales in both the individual and group market (Nordman, 2016).

In the early 1990s, most insurers began providing more comprehensive policies covering care in a variety of settings, including at home. While early policies set the home care benefit as a percentage of the nursing home benefit—typically 50%—more recent policies are integrated in terms of their benefit payments. That means individuals have access to a "pool of benefits" which can be used to reimburse the costs of services once they are determined to be eligible for benefits. The eligibility threshold is in line with federal Health Insurance Portability and Accountability standards—having two or more limitations in activities of daily living or having a severe cognitive impairment (Cohen, 2016).

The high cost of LTC insurance has also led insurers to develop a combination of or hybrid products which combine life insurance or annuities with LTC insurance. Such policies can pay out if LTC is needed, but, if not needed, there is still a death benefit or annuity payout. If an individual uses some, but not all, of LTC benefits, the remainder would be payable as a death benefit. Thus, one of the principal appeals of combination products is that there is still a return on the money invested in the premiums even if LTC is never needed (Cohen, 2016). As a result, these linked-benefit products have become more popular, with in-force policies numbering 600,000 in 2019 and growing annually (Colello, 2023).

Less than 1 percent of employers offered LTC insurance to their employees in 2016, and only 5 to 7 percent of employees enrolled (O'Neill Haley and Kurtovic, 2020).

5.2 *LTC Insurance Market*

Given the high probability of a costly LTC event, as described above, there is high potential demand for long-term care insurance (LTCI). However, according to the National Association of Insurance Commissioners (2023), only 5.1 million individuals in the US owned an LTCI policy in 2022, less than 10% of the population age 65 and over. Moreover, the number of policy holders has actually been declining since 2012 (Braun and Kopecky, 2024). Private long-term care insurance is estimated to cover only 5% of total formal long-term care expenditures (Table 2).

There are a number of reasons for this stagnation. There is widespread lack of knowledge about the limited coverage of Medicare for LTC, premiums for LTCI policies are higher than those for life insurance products, representative LTCI policies offer incomplete coverage against expected losses, and denial rates of applicants by private insurers are high (Braun and Kopecky, 2024).

5.3 *Supply-side Issues*

As required by state insurance laws, private LTC insurance policies were always sold as guaranteed renewable—they could only be cancelled for non-payment of premium—and with fixed premiums. While the premium charged varied by age at the time of purchase, once an individual purchased a policy, the premium was designed (although never guaranteed) to be unchanged for life. Almost all policies reimbursed the actual costs of care up to a daily benefit maximum (Nordman, 2016).

The unchanging level of LTC insurance premiums poses unique challenges to insurers. Insurers can only adjust premiums subject to regulatory approval if their actual cost experience diverges from their pricing assumptions. Most insurers' LTC insurance policies issued before the mid-2000s have seen such adverse experience relative to their original pricing assumptions. Rising claims, lower mortality and lower than expected lapses have led to higher prices which are often unaffordable to a large segment of the potentially affected population. In addition, a number of insurers have left the market, leaving only a relatively few insurers to provide such products (Nordman, 2016).

As a result, the number of insurers offering LTC products has been steadily declining. As of 2014, there were fewer than 15 stand-alone LTC insurance options, down from 125 in 2000. The premiums for these types of insurance plans are typically based on the applicant's health status, and insurers may deny coverage if the applicant is not healthy enough. In 2019, more than half of applicants aged 75 or older and 44 percent of applicants aged 70–74 were denied coverage (O'Neill Haley and Kurtovic, 2020).

5.4 Government Supports for Private LTC Insurance

Federal policymakers have sought to promote private LTSS financing in several ways: by making the purchase of private LTCI more accessible and attractive to consumers through the Medicaid Partnership Program; by providing certain tax benefits and consumer protections for the purchase of private LTCI; and by establishing the Federal Long-Term Care Insurance Program (FLTCIP) for federal workers, retirees, and certain qualified relatives. Policymakers have also established ways for individuals with disabilities and their families to save for LTSS expenses through Achieving a Better Life Experience (ABLE) accounts, which are a type of tax-favored savings account for individuals with qualifying disabilities (Colello, 2023).

In the late 1980s, several state Medicaid programs began to collaborate with private long-term care insurance (LTCI) companies to "create a bridge between Medicaid and private insurance for LTSS." The Partnership Program allows individuals who purchase a private LTCI policy to qualify for Medicaid covered-LTSS without meeting the same Medicaid financial eligibility rules regarding asset limits that other Medicaid LTSS applicants must meet, as long as they meet other Medicaid eligibility criteria. 72 Generally, Partnership Program policyholders would seek Medicaid for extended coverage of LTSS after their private LTCI benefits have been exhausted (Colello, 2023).

Federal law provides tax benefits and minimum consumer protection standards for purchasers of "tax-qualified" LTCI policies, as authorized by the Health Insurance Portability and Accountability Act of 1996 (HIPAA, P.L. 104–191). These provisions are established in the Internal Revenue Code (26 U.S.C. §7702B). Most traditional

LTCI policies sold after enactment of HIPAA are tax-qualified policies. Linked-benefit LTCI policies with a separately identifiable premium component can also qualify for tax benefits (Colello, 2023).

Federal employees, including retirees, and certain relatives are eligible to enroll in the Federal Long Term Care Insurance Program. This program offers comprehensive LTC insurance, including room and board at nursing homes and assisted living facilities and home care services. Roughly 268,000 people are currently enrolled (O'Neill Haley and Kurtovic, 2020).

6 Long-term Care Facilities

There are about 66,600 regulated long-term care facilities in the U.S., according to the National Center for Health Statistics. Together, these institutions serve about 6.9 million individuals. Over the next 10 years, the number of residents in each of these facilities is expected to grow sharply. If trends hold up, the number of nursing home residents could increase by over 75% to 2.3 million residents by 2030 (Consumer Affairs, 2024).

There are five major categories of long-term care options for individuals depending on the needed level of support. Dementia patients are found in all levels of long-term care facilities. The share of Alzheimer's patients is as follows: adult day care centers, 28%; home health care, 36%; residential facilities, 34%; nursing homes, 58%; and hospices, 24% (Consumer Affairs, 2024).

Adult day services centers: These centers provide professional programs designed for individuals to receive supervised care in a group setting with structured activities. Some centers provide personal care, transportation, medication management and meals.

Home health: Home health aides provide professional services for individuals who need personal care attention in one's home to assist with an illness or injury.

Residential care communities: Also known as assisted living communities, these facilities provide a supported environment for individuals who may no longer be able to live safely on their own, providing personal care and health services.

Nursing homes: These facilities provide more medical care and supervision than residential care communities. Nursing homes provide personal care assistance, medication, therapies and rehabilitation, and on-site nursing care 24 hours a day.

Hospice centers: These centers specialize in providing medical care, pain management and emotional support to individuals in the final stages of an incurable illness and their families.

Table 3 summarizes the main statistics on long-term care facilities and services. Three million individuals utilized home health care, representing 43.8% of the total number of individuals participating in long-term health care services. Individuals residing at nursing homes and residential care communities totaled 2.1 million, 30.9% of the total number of individuals utilizing long-term care facilities in 2020 (Consumer Affairs, 2024). Most facilities are for-profit, except for the majority of

Table 3 Long-term care facilities and services, 2020

	No. of facilities	No. served ('000)	Caregiver Staff ('000)	Share for-profit (%)	Share Medicaid registered (%)
Nursing homes	15,300	1,295	660.0	70.3	95.4
Assisted living	30,600	819	376.4	79.2	46.9
Home care agency	11,400	2,978	135.3	82.0	78.9
Adult day care center	4,100	237	17.6	42.3	74.9
Hospices	5,200	1,535	90.5	66.4	--
Total	66,600	6,864	1,279.8	74.4	66.8

Source Lendon et al. (2024), Sengupta et al. (2022)
Note '-'Not available

adult day care centers. The majority of facilities in most categories are registered with Medicaid, except assisted living, where the share is only 46.9%.

6.1 Nursing Homes

Skilled nursing facilities are residential health facilities that provide nursing, rehabilitation, and related services. As of 2020, there were over 15,300 nursing homes in the U.S., containing almost 1.7 million beds. With 50 million individuals aged 65 or older, this amounts to three beds per 100 elderly persons and about 25 beds per 100 persons age 85 or older. On average, 80 percent of these beds are occupied. This occupancy rate has fallen from 90% in 1993 as a result of the shift toward home care rather than institutional care in order to reduce costs and provide care closer to home (Gruber and McGarry, 2023).

The U.S. skilled nursing facility market size was valued at USD 179.0 billion in 2022 and is projected to expand at a compound annual growth rate (CAGR) of 3.43% from 2023 to 2030. Skilled nursing facilities (SNFs) provide high-quality care services at a much lower cost than hospitals. About 70% are for-profit, 25% are non-profit, and 5% are government-run (Grand View Research, Inc., 2024a).

6.2 Assisted Living Residences

Assisted living provides senior residents with long-term housing and care in a community setting. Assisted living communities typically offer a homelike setting with individual apartments or rooms for residents, prepared meals and housekeeping or laundry services. Such facilities provide assistance with various ADLs, but, unlike nursing homes, they do not provide 24-hour nursing or medical care. Continuing Care Retirement Communities (CCRCs) cover a vast array of housing arrangements from low-cost efficiency apartments to luxury condominiums and single-family houses. Most communities include housing owned by the Continuing Care Provider on centralized grounds referred to as a campus. Continuing care communities frequently are part of a skilled nursing facility, an assisted living facility, or personal care home. It has become the dominant option for seniors with support needs.

There are over 30,600 operating assisted living facilities, with nearly 1.2 million licensed beds and an average capacity utilization rate of 80%. The average size is 39 units or beds. More than 818,000 seniors live in assisted living communities, about 88% of all senior residential care community residents.

CCRCs typically charge an entrance fee ranging from several thousand dollars to $1 million in addition to monthly rent. The entrance fee pays for onsite skilled nursing facility or memory care required over the course of the person's residence (Hipp, 2024).

The average age of an assisted living facility resident is 87. The minimum age for qualifying to live in an assisted living facility varies from 62 to 65. Most individuals enter assisted living facilities between the ages of 75 and 85. About 70% of residents are female. The median stay in assisted living communities in 2023 was 22 months (Samuels, 2023).

Fewer than 50% of assisted living facilities are Medicaid certified, and even those rarely accept Medicaid without additional payments. As a result, only about 18% of assisted living residents depend on Medicaid. Other residents are considered to be upper-middle or upper-income adults (Samuels, 2023).

In 2019, 42% of residents were reported to have Alzheimer's disease or other types of dementia. To provide treatment for such residents, about 18% of assisted living facilities provide secure and separate environments for "memory care" and another 11% specialize in dementia patients (National Center for Assisted Living, 2024).

The US assisted living facility market size was estimated at $91.8 billion in 2022 and is expected to increase at a compound annual rate of 5.3%. More than 80% of assisted living communities are for-profit. Non-profits tend to have higher occupancy rates but fewer amenities than for-profit ones.

6.3 Adult Day Care Centers

Adult day care centers and programs provide a safe, secure setting for older adults who need supervision during the day or who would benefit from additional social engagement outside their home. They provide a supervised community setting for older adults with dementia and other health conditions that prevent them from being home alone safely during the day. Programs usually include activities for mental and physical stimulation, such as games, exercises, art and more.

There are more than 7,500 adult day care centers in the U.S. that provide services to older adults, according to the National Adult Day Services Association (NADSA). For participants, adult day care programs provide social interaction, mental stimulation, physical activities, and nutritious meals. Some offer health services as well (Hipp, 2024b).

Adult day care costs typically range from $25 to more than $100 a day, depending on services provided, the location, and the type of federal or state program reimbursement the adult day care center might receive. Reimbursement programs that might pay for adult day care include some state Medicaid programs and the Adult Day Health Care program offered by the U.S. Department of Veterans Affairs.

6.4 Home Care

Formal home care is delivered both by agencies specializing in this business as well as by independent caregivers hired directly by care recipients. The U.S. home healthcare services market size was valued at USD 95.45 billion in 2023 and is projected to grow from USD 100.95 billion in 2024 to USD 176.30 billion by 2032, exhibiting a CAGR of 7.2% during the forecast period (2024–2032) (Forbes, 2024).

In 2020 almost 3 million people were cared for by home care workers from approximately 11,400 agencies. Over 80 percent of these agencies are for-profit, although many of their patients are covered by Medicare or Medicaid which have strict limits on rates and the number and type of visits (Lendon et al., 2024).

6.5 Hospices

Hospices provide end-of-life services to such individuals and focus on improving quality of life through palliative care. In 2020, 1.5 million Medicare recipients in the U.S. received hospice care at 5,200 facilities. Medicare spent approximately $20.9 billion on these services. The U.S. hospice market size was estimated at USD 37.9 billion in 2023 and is expected to reach USD 65.0 billion by 2030, growing at a CAGR of 8.07% from 2024 to 2030 (Grand View Research, Inc., 2024b). Growth can be attributed to the growing geriatric population and the increasing prevalence of chronic disorders amid this demographic. The rising demand for end-of-life care for chronic disorders, such as cancer, dementia, and cardiovascular disease, drives the growth of the industry.

Based on diagnosis, the dementia segment held the largest market share of 25.2% in 2023 and is expected to maintain its dominance in the future.

Table 4 Percent distribution of nursing and social work full-time equivalent employees, by sector and staff type: 2018

Type of facility, %	Social worker	Aide	Licensed practical nurse	Registered nurse
Nursing homes	1.8	62.8	23.3	12.1
Assisted living	1.2	70.0	14.1	14.7
Home care agency	2.6	24.7	21.3	51.5
Adult day care center	9.3	55.6	8.6	26.6
Hospices	11.3	31.6	8.7	48.4

Source Sengupta et al. (2022)

7 Care providers and Caregivers

Gruber and McGarry (2023) estimate that there are 1.9 million people in the United States providing formal help with ADLs or IADLs to those aged 65 or older; 800,000 of these are providing help to those 85 years old or older. This amounts to 3.7 helpers per 100 persons ages 65 or older, and 12.6 per 100 persons ages 85 or older. A much larger population of individuals provide informal care. In 2018 approximately 10.6 million people were estimated to be providing informal care to the elderly, and of these 30 percent were providing care to those 85 years old or older.

All long-term care facilities and agencies employ workers with varying levels of skills—with employees classified as aides, licensed practical nurses, registered nurses, and social workers. Table 4 shows the breakdown of each kind of employee by type of facility. Somewhat surprisingly, the share of licensed practical nurses and registered nurses is not particularly high in nursing homes. By far, home care agencies have the highest share of registered nurses.

Formal home care providers have relatively little schooling, with almost one-fifth having no high school degree and only one-tenth having a college degree or higher. In contrast, informal home care is provided by a much more highly educated population. Formal caregivers are also more racially diverse than informal caregivers, with approximately two-thirds being non-white or Hispanic compared to only one-third of informal caregivers. Roughly one-third of informal care is delivered by spouses. The second most common relationship for informal caregivers is daughters, while sons provide only half as large a share (Gruber and McGarry, 2023).

8 Issues

The long-term care system in the US faces many serious problems, reflecting the lack of a comprehensive national system, the high costs of care, the steadily rising demand for such care, inadequate staffing, and inadequate private insurance coverage. If one includes both formal out-of-pocket costs and imputed costs of informal care, the bulk of the burden of long-term care is borne directly by individual families. Many households face the unenviable choices of either bankrupting themselves to qualify for Medicaid, bearing high out-of-pocket costs, or sticking with informal care.

In addition to cost concerns, a major criticism of the nursing home industry in the United States is the quality of care. In 2016, nearly 45 percent of facilities were cited as deficient in infection control, 40 percent were lacking in food sanitation, 34 percent in the general quality of care, and 25 percent cited the unnecessary use of drugs (Harrington et al., 2018).

The relationship between the for-profit status of a nursing home and the quality of care is an important issue. A recent influential study found that nursing home mortality is significantly higher for those institutions owned by large private companies while non-profit nursing homes typically perform better on this measure (Gupta et al., 2023; GAO, 2020).

Nursing homes face widespread problems of inadequate staffing and high turnover. According to a survey, approximately 77% of nursing homes face moderate to high levels of staffing shortages, and 95% of nursing homes report experiencing difficulty in hiring staff. The biggest obstacles for providers in recruiting new staff are their current financial situations and lack of interested or qualified candidates. More than half of nursing homes report that they are operating at a loss, and 45% of nursing homes say they can't sustain operations at the current pace for more than one year. In particular, many report that it will be very difficult to meet new staffing requirement standards of a minimum of 3.48 hours per resident issued by the Biden administration in 2024 (American Health Care Association, 2023).

Turnover across the LTC sector is estimated to range from 45 to 66 percent. It is reported that one in four nursing assistants and one in five home health aides are actively looking for another job. One in two workers leave jobs in home care within 12 months. Annual certified nursing assistant turnover is at 97 percent, registered nurse turnover is at 52.5 percent, and overall staff turnover is at 69 percent. Much of the problem is due to low wages in the sector (O'Neill Haley and Kurtovic, 2022).

Recruiting and retaining registered nurses (RNs) in nursing homes is challenging because nursing homes generally offer nurses lower wages than they would earn in other health care roles. For example, in 2020, the annual mean wage for RNs in nursing homes ($72,090) was approximately $10,000 (roughly 12 percent) less than that of RNs employed in acute-care hospitals ($81,680) and approximately $17,000 (nearly 20 percent) less than for RNs employed in outpatient care settings ($89,300) (National Academies of Sciences, Engineering, and Medicine, 2022). Furthermore, the nursing home environment is often not conducive to supporting the professional practice and development of RNs. The mean hourly wage in 2020 for nursing assistants in nursing homes was $15.41, and the mean annual wage was $32,050. The bottom quartile of nursing assistants earned less than $26,650 annually, and the bottom 10 percent earn less than $22,750 (National Academies of Sciences, Engineering, and Medicine, 2022).

The COVID-19 pandemic had a severe impact on long-term care workers due to the high incidence of cases among patients. In 2020 during the midst of the COVID-19 pandemic, nursing home workers saw one of the highest death rates among all occupations. The direct-care workforce is likely to experience high rates of burnout, though most of the literature on the topic focuses on the rate of burnout among licensed nurses and physicians (National Academies of Sciences, Engineering, and Medicine, 2022).

The stagnant condition and small share of financing of LTC by the private LTC insurance sector (only 5% of total costs) show the need for reform of the sector. The current situation reflects the combined effects of high care costs, high premium costs, high rejection rates of applicants due to adverse selection, and general lack of information on the part of the public about insurance coverage for long-term care. Braun and Kopecky (2024) analyze three options: universal public LTCI, no public LTCI coverage, and a policy that exempts asset holdings from the public insurance asset test on a dollar-for-dollar basis with private LTCI coverage. They find that the third option enhances social welfare and creates a vibrant private LTCI market while preserving the safety net provided by public insurance to low-income individuals.

9 Conclusions

The long-term care system in the US faces many serious problems, reflecting the lack of a comprehensive national system, the high costs of care, the steadily rising demand for such care, inadequate staffing and high turnover, and inadequate private insurance coverage. It faces risks to long-term sustainability on a number of fronts.

The US population is gradually aging, although not as rapidly as those of some other advanced economies due to high levels of immigration. The share of the population age 65 and over is expected to rise from 17% in 2022 to 21% in 2030, but the pace will slow thereafter, with the ratio rising gradually to 23% by 2050 thereafter. The share of the population age 85 and over will rise from 2.0% in 2021 to 4.8% by 2050, reflecting the aging of the "baby boomer" generation. This age group is the fastest growing segment of the US population, with an expected increase of 168% between 2022 and 2050, reaching 10.5 million by 2050.

Given the aging population, the number of those over age 65 with significant disabilities is projected to grow substantially, increasing from 7.6 million to almost 14.7 million by 2065. In percentage terms, the share of the older population with significant disabilities is expected to increase from 14% to 16%

As the baby boomer population ages, the total number of people with dementia is expected to rise. It is estimated that more than 7 million people aged 65 or older had dementia in 2020, or about 12% of the total. If current demographic and health trends continue, almost 9 million Americans could have dementia by 2030 and over 11 million by 2040.

It is estimated that an average American turning 65 today who needs to pay for long-term care will incur $245,500 in future undiscounted LTSS costs, with families paying for over one-third of that themselves. The largest payer is Medicaid, 42% of the total, followed by out-of-pocket expenses, 38%, while the share covered by private insurance is very small at only 5%. Only a fraction of US households would be able to bear the average out-of-pocket costs of $93,500 without severe financial burden. In addition, the annual cost of informally provided long-term care is estimated to range from $86 billion to $151 billion, also imposing a significant burden on households.

Nursing homes and other LTC facilities are chronically understaffed with high turnover rates, reflecting low wages and difficult working conditions. Facilities are trying to increase hiring, but this requires greater funding, which must be provided primarily by Medicaid and other public insurance.

The private long-term care insurance industry plays a surprisingly small role, covering only 5% of formal long-term care costs. Moreover, the share is actually shrinking due to low demand reflecting high premiums and ignorance about coverage on the one hand and diminishing supply due to industry exit and high rates of denial of coverage. The sector is clearly in need of reform.

References

Alzheimer's Association. (2024). 2024 Alzheimer's Disease facts and figures. https://www.alz.org/media/documents/alzheimers-facts-and-figures.pdf

American Health Care Association. (2023). State of the nursing home industry: Survey of 425 nursing home providers highlights persistent staffing and economic crisis: Mid-Year 2023. https://www.ahcancal.org/News-and-Communications/Fact-Sheets/FactSheets/SNF%20Survey%20Mid-Year%202023.pdf

Braun, R. A., and Kopecky, K. (2024). Reforming the US long-term care insurance market. Working Paper No. 24-17. Federal Reserve Bank of Cleveland. https://doi.org/10.26509/frbc-wp-202417

Centers for Medicare & Medicaid Services. (2024). Long term services & supports. https://www.medicaid.gov/medicaid/long-term-services-supports/index.html

Cohen, M. (2016). The state of the long-term care insurance market. In E. Nordman (Ed.), *The state of long-term care insurance: The market, challenges and future innovations*. CIPR Study Series 2016-1. National Association of Insurance Commissioners and Center for Insurance Policy Research. https://content.naic.org/sites/default/files/inline-files/cipr_current_study_160519_ltc_insurance.pdf

Colby, S. and Ortman, J. (2015). Projections of the size and composition of the U.S. population: 2014 to 2060. *Current Population Reports*, P25-1143, U.S. Census Bureau, Washington, DC. https://www.census.gov/content/dam/Census/library/publications/2015/demo/p25-1143.pdf

Colello, K. (2023). Long-term services and supports: History of federal policy and programs. Congressional Research Service. https://crsreports.congress.gov/product/pdf/R/R47881

Consumer Affairs. (2024). Long-term care statistics 2024. https://www.consumeraffairs.com/health/long-term-care-statistics.html

Favreault, M., & Johnson, R. (2021). Projections of risk and needing of long-term services and supports at ages 65 and older. U.S. Department of Health and Human Services, Office of the Assistant Secretary for Planning and Evaluation Office of Behavioral Health, Disability, and Aging Policy. https://aspe.hhs.gov/sites/default/files/private/pdf/265136/LTSSRisk.pdf

Genworth Financial, Inc. (2024). Cost of care. https://www.genworth.com/aging-and-you/finances/cost-of-care

Grand View Research. (2024a). U.S. skilled nursing facility market size, share & trends analysis report by ownership (for-profit, non-profit, government), by type (freestanding, hospital), and segment forecasts, 2023–2030. https://www.grandviewresearch.com/industry-analysis/us-skilled-nursing-facility-market

Grand View Research. (2024b). U.S. hospice market size & trends. https://www.grandviewresearch.com/industry-analysis/us-hospice-market

Gruber, J. and Mc Garry, K. (2023). Long-term care in the United States. NBER Working Paper No. 31881. National Bureau of Economic Research. https://www.nber.org/papers/w31881

Gupta, A., Howell, S. T., Yannelis, C., & Gupta, A. 2023. Owner incentives and performance in healthcare: Private equity investment in nursing homes (No. w28474). National Bureau of Economic Research. https://www.nber.org/papers/w28474

Harrington, C., Carrillo, H., Garfield, R., and Squires, E. (2018). Nursing facilities, staffing, residents and facility deficiencies, 2009 through 2016. Kaiser Family Foundation. https://ltcombudsman.org/uploads/files/library/deficiencies-09-14.pdf

Harris-Kojetin, L., Sengupta, M., Lendon, J.P., Rome, V., Valverde, R. and Caffrey, C. (2019). Long-term care providers and services users in the United States, 2015–2016. National Center for Health Statistics. Vital Health Stat 3(43). https://www.cdc.gov/nchs/data/series/sr_03/sr03_43-508.pdf

He, Y. (2022). Projecting Medicaid's long term care expenditures. Penn Wharton Budget: Blog Post, Healthcare. https://budgetmodel.wharton.upenn.edu/issues/2022/3/9/projectingmedicaids-long-term-care-expenditures

Hipp, D. (2024a). Assisted living statistics and facts in 2024. https://www.forbes.com/health/senior-living/assisted-living-statistics/

Hipp, D. (2024b). What is adult day care? https://www.forbes.com/health/healthy-aging/what-is-adult-day-care/

IBISWorld. (2024). Long term care insurance in the US-Market research report (2013–2028). https://www.ibisworld.com/united-states/market-research-reports/long-term-care-insurance-industry/#IndustryOverview

Johnson, R. and Dey, J. (2022). Long-term services and supports for older Americans: Risks and financing, 2022. ASPE Research Brief Aug. 2022. U.S. Department of Health and Human Services. https://aspe.hhs.gov/sites/default/files/documents/08b8b7825f7bc12d2c79261fd7641c88/ltss-risks-financing-2022.pdf

Kaiser Family Foundation (KFF). (2015). Long-term care in the United States: A timeline. https://www.kff.org/wp-content/uploads/2015/08/8773-long-term-care-in-the-united-states-a-timeline1.pdf#:~:text=This%20timeline%20outlines%20the%20major%20milestones%20in%20LTC,into%20the%20era%20of%20health%20reform%20and%20beyond

Kaiser Family Foundation (KFF). (2024a). 10 things about long-term services and supports (LTSS). https://www.kff.org/medicaid/issue-brief/10-things-about-long-term-services-and-supports-ltss/

Kaiser Family Foundation (KFF). (2024b). How many people use Medicaid long-term services and supports and how much does Medicaid spend on those people? https://www.kff.org/medicaid/issue-brief/how-many-people-use-medicaid-long-term-services-and-supports-and-how-much-does-medicaid-spend-on-those-people/#:~:text=In%202020%2C%20there%20were%205.6%20million%20people%20who,and%200.2%20million%20used%20both%20%284%25%29%20%28Figure%201%29

Lendon, J., et al. (2024). Overview of post-acute and long-term care providers and services users in the United States, 2020. National Health Statistics Reports Number 208. U.S. Centers for Disease Control and Prevention. https://www.cdc.gov/nchs/data/nhsr/nhsr208.pdf

Medicaidlongtermcare.gov. (2024). Overview of eligibility requirements for Medicaid long term care. https://www.medicaidlongtermcare.org/eligibility/overview/

National Academies of Sciences, Engineering, and Medicine. (2022). *The national imperative to improve nursing home quality: Honoring our commitment to residents, families, and staff*. The National Academies Press. 10.17226/26526

National Association of Insurance Commissioners. (2023). Long-term care insurance experience reports for 2022. https://content.naic.org/sites/default/files/publication-ltc-lr-care-experience-report.pdf

National Center for Assisted Living. (2024). Facts & figures. https://www.ahcancal.org/Assisted-Living/Facts-and-Figures/Pages/default.aspx

Nordman, E. (2016). The state of long-term care insurance: The market, challenges and future innovations. CIPR Study Series 2016-1. National Association of Insurance Commissioners and Center for Insurance Policy Research. https://content.naic.org/sites/default/files/inline-files/cipr_current_study_160519_ltc_insurance.pdf

O'Neill-Hayes, T. and Kurtovic, S. (2020). The ballooning costs of long-term care. American Action Forum. https://www.americanactionforum.org/research/the-ballooning-costs-of-long-term-care/#:~:text=By%202030%2C%2024%20million%20Americans%20will%20need%20long-term,the%20increasing%20number%20of%20chronic%20conditions%20per%20person

Pennsylvania Insurance Department. (2024). Continuing care retirement communities FAQs. https://www.insurance.pa.gov/Coverage/ContinuingCare/Pages/ContinuingCareRetirementCommunitiesFAQs.aspx

Population Reference Bureau. (2021). Fact sheet: U.S. dementia trends. https://www.prb.org/resources/fact-sheet-u-s-dementia-trends/

Samuels, C. (2023). Assisted living statistics: Population and facilities. https://www.aplaceformom.com/senior-living-data/articles/assisted-living-statistics#:~:text=Assisted%20living%20is%20a%20multi,Grand%20View%20Research%20market%20data

Sengupta, M., Lendon, J.P., Caffrey, C., Melekin, A. and Singh, P. (2022). Post-acute and long-term care providers and services users in the United States, 2017–2018. National Center for Health Statistics. Vital Health Stat 3(47). https://doi.org/10.15620/cdc:115346.

US Census Bureau. (2020a). Demographic turning points for the United States: Population projections for 2020 to 2060. https://www.census.gov/library/publications/2020/demo/p25-1144.html#:~:text=Beyond%202030%2C%20the%20U.S.%20population%20is%20projected%20to,2060%2C%20crossing%20the%20400%20million%20threshold%20in%202058

US Census Bureau. (2020b). Living longer: Historical and projected life expectancy in the United States, 1960 to 2060. https://www.census.gov/library/publications/2020/demo/p25-1145.html

US Census Bureau. (2015). Projections of the size and composition of the U.S. Population: 2014 to 2060. https://www.census.gov/library/publications/2015/demo/p25-1143.html

US Census Bureau. (2023). Projections by age and sex composition of the population. https://www.census.gov/data/tables/2023/demo/popproj/2023-summary-tables.html

U.S. Government Accountability Office. (2020). https://www.gao.gov/assets/gao-20-576r.pdf

Exploring the Long-Term Care Partnership Program in the United States: Challenges and Lessons from Connecticut

Shangzhu Huang

1 Introduction

1.1 Research Background

The accelerating global aging population has led to increasing demand for Long-Term Care (LTC), which refers to sustained care services for individuals who struggle with independent living due to aging, illness, or disability. These services encompass various forms, including home-based care, community-based care, and institutional care. However, the high costs of LTC impose significant financial burdens on individuals, families, and societies. Establishing sustainable and equitable LTC security systems has become a critical challenge for nations worldwide.

Taking the United States as an example, the public sector has not established a universal public LTC insurance system. Instead, LTC needs are largely addressed through healthcare-linked models (Wu et al., 2022). As shown in Fig. 1, long-term care costs in the United States are currently mainly covered by public policy programs such as Medicaid and Medicare. While federal programs like Medicare and Medicaid provide medical and care support, their coverage and benefits remain insufficient to meet the increasingly complex care needs of the elderly.

As shown in Fig. 2, Medicaid spending on LTC (including home-based and institutional care) has risen significantly in recent years. In 2023, Medicaid expenditures on LTC reached $112.8 billion, accounting for nearly 20% of total Medicaid spending, with $60.4 billion allocated to institutional care (Drew Desilver, 2025). This places a substantial fiscal strain on state budgets.

Notably, while Medicaid offers basic coverage for low-income individuals, its strict income and asset limits force many middle-class elderly to deplete their assets

S. Huang (✉)
Doctoral candidate, Graduate School of Commerce, Waseda University, Tokyo, Japan

H. Lee and G. Nicolini (eds.), *International Comparison of Long-Term Care Insurance Systems*, Contributions to Management Science,
https://doi.org/10.1007/978-981-95-7781-1_5

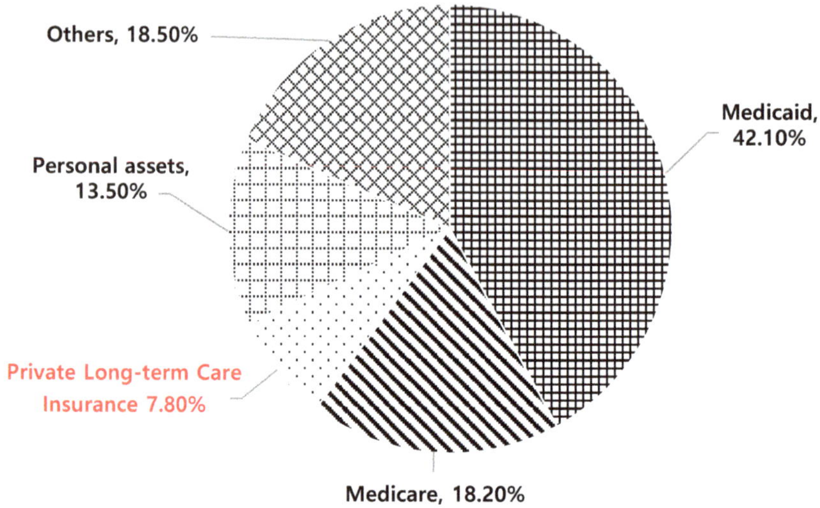

Fig. 1 Cost burden of long-term care insurance for the elderly in the United States in 2022. *Source* Congressional research service (2022)

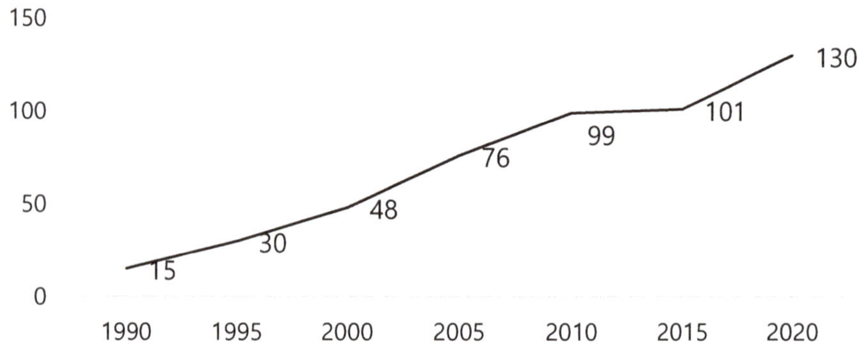

Fig. 2 Inflation adjusted medicaid LTC expenditures 1990–2020 (billions of dollars). *Source* Statista.com (2025)

before qualifying for assistance. This policy design exacerbates rapid asset depletion and intergenerational inequity, raising widespread concerns.

To alleviate fiscal pressures and encourage individuals to prepare for future LTC risks, the U.S. launched the Long-Term Care Partnership Program (LTCPP) in the late 1980s. Its core mechanism combines private LTC insurance with public Medicaid, incorporating an asset-disregard incentive. This allows middle-class participants who purchase qualified LTC insurance to access Medicaid support without exhausting their assets. Initially piloted in four states—Connecticut, California, Indiana, and New York—the program was later expanded nationwide (Greenhalgh-Stanley, 2014).

Connecticut, as the earliest adopter of LTCPP, offers representative policy insights. However, after years of implementation, the program's effectiveness has fallen short of expectations. Challenges include stagnant enrollment, deviations from the original middle-class target group, and limited fiscal relief for public budgets. Thus, a critical analysis of Connecticut's LTCPP is necessary to examine the gap between policy design and real-world needs, prompting a reevaluation of private LTC insurance's role within public welfare systems.

1.2 Research Objectives

Existing literature primarily focuses on empirical studies examining the enrollment rates of private long-term care insurance (LTCI) and its impact on public fiscal expenditures, with limited analysis of the Long-Term Care Partnership Program (LTCPP)'s policy design and implementation outcomes.

Lin and Prince (2013) utilized the staggered adoption of LTCPP across U.S. states to assess its influence on older adults' purchasing behavior for private LTCI. Their findings suggest that LTCPP had a minimal effect on LTCI uptake, and those who enrolled were predominantly high-income individuals, deviating from the program's intended middle-class target group. Supporting this, a U.S. Government Accountability Office (2005) study revealed that more than half of LTCPP enrollees held assets exceeding $350,000, further highlighting the mismatch between policy goals and actual participation.

While prior research has identified this discrepancy in enrollment patterns (wealthy vs. middle-class), the underlying causes remain underexplored. Moreover, most studies analyze factors driving private LTCI adoption without distinguishing between LTCPP and non-partnership LTCI policies. A critical feature of LTCPP—its asset protection mechanism[1]—has not been sufficiently examined to determine whether it serves as a key incentive for middle-class older adults. Furthermore, whether low-income, middle-class, and affluent older adults exhibit divergent long-term care needs remains unresolved.

By examining Connecticut's LTCPP case, this study aims to analyze LTCPP's policy framework and older adults' enrollment motivations and identify operational challenges in the current LTCPP model.

[1] The asset protection mechanism means that individuals participating in the Long - Term Care Partnership Program (LTCPP) are allowed to retain a certain amount of assets when applying for Medicaid assistance for the poor to cover the shortfall after using the insurance benefits provided by the LTCPP.

2 Development and Current Situation of LTCPP in the United States

2.1 Historical Development of LTCPP

To date, the United States has not established a unified public long-term care insurance system. As shown in Table 1, public policies provide the majority of long term care services. Its current long-term care security system is mainly supported by the following three methods. First, Medicare, provided by the federal government, mainly targets short-term medical care services[2] for the elderly. Medicare Plan A covers medical care services within 100 days after hospitalization. Plan B is an insurance for outpatient services and only compensates for the costs of temporary professional care provided at home or in designated facilities within 14 days after discharge (Wu, 2022). Therefore, Medicare's coverage for long-term care is very limited. Second, Medicaid provides a certain degree of long-term care support for low-income groups,[3] but it has strict income and asset restrictions. Third, individuals bear the care costs through personal payments, pensions, personal savings, family resources, or by purchasing private long-term care insurance.

According to a report by the Marceno and Llamas (2025), the total expenditure on long-term care services in the United States amounts to approximately $415 billion, of which Medicaid bears more than half. This has become a significant financial burden for each state. At the same time, medical care costs continue to rise. According to statistics from the Nursing Home Abuse Center (2021) and Genworth (2023a, 2023b), the average annual cost of nursing home care in the United States reaches up to $100,000, and the average annual cost for basic living support services is also about $38,500. In contrast, in 2022, the average annual income of people aged 65 and above in the United States was $47,060, and the median was only $24,190 (Pension Right Center, 2023). The average annual income from Social Security benefits that retirees rely on in 2025 is approximately $23,712 (Social Security, 2025). These figures indicate that it is difficult for most elderly people to afford long-term care services with their own property and savings alone.

[2] Medicare is a federal government public program that provides medical security to elderly people aged 65 and above and young people with physical disabilities regardless of their income. However, Medicare mainly focuses on short - term medical services within 100 days. Therefore, its role as a funding source for long-term care services for the elderly is limited. Medicare is divided into four plans: A, B, C, and D. Among them, Plan A and B are called basic medical insurance. Plan C is known as the "Medicare Advantage Plan", and Plan D is known as "Prescription Drug Coverage". Specifically, Plan A includes services such as inpatient costs, professional nursing and rehabilitation services, hospice care, and home healthcare. Plan B covers services provided by doctors and other medical providers, outpatient consultations, durable medical equipment, and some preventive services. Plan C and D are insurance plans provided by private enterprises and insurance companies based on basic medical insurance and are not included in the scope of social security.

[3] Medicaid is a public insurance program provided to low-income families, who must be below the federal poverty line or have lost most of their assets by paying for health care.

Table 1 Public share of long-term care service costs in the United States

Item	Medicare	Medicaid
Eligibility	Mainly for those over 65 years of age, or young people with specific disabilities.	Mainly for low-income groups
Coverage	Mainly short-term medical expenses	Varies by states but generally includes: Medical services, ophthalmic and dental services, mental health services, rehabilitation, nursing services, maternal and child health services, and other services (such as nutritional guidance, medical equipment, etc.)

Note Data synthesized from reference materials

Moreover, Medicaid applicants must meet a very low asset threshold[4] to be eligible, and many middle-class people can only apply after "spending out their assets through self-payment." Such a system design not only undermines the security of personal assets but also brings about significant social inequality.

Against this background, the proposal of LTCPP aims to break the dual structure of "the wealthy pay out of pocket and the poor rely on Medicaid." It encourages the middle-class to purchase private long-term care insurance to ensure their future needs and thereby reduce the financial burden on Medicaid.

2.2 Current Status and Basic Framework of LTCPP

LTCPP is an incentive program for LTCI jointly promoted by state governments and insurance companies. It was first proposed and funded by the Robert Wood Johnson Foundation in 1987 and piloted in California, Connecticut, New York, and Indiana. Its main objective is to encourage residents to purchase eligible LTCI so that they can pay for part or all of the long-term care costs with insurance benefits when the need arises. At the same time, LTCPP promises that if policyholders exhaust their LTCI benefits and need to apply for Medicaid, their assets can be exempted from Medicaid reimbursement and receive certain protection.

After 2005, based on the federal government's Deficit Reduction Act (DRA), states were allowed to independently decide whether to establish LTCPP, and this

[4] Medicaid provides a minimum level of long-term care services. To prevent moral hazard among the elderly, each state has established a strict eligibility review process for recipients, including medical qualification assessment as well as means testing for individual income and assets. Specifically, the income threshold is set at 75% to 100% of the Federal Poverty Level (FPL), which, as of 2024, corresponds to an annual income of approximately $11,295 to $15,060 for an individual. The asset limit is generally $2000 for an individual and $3000 for a couple, although some states, such as Connecticut, impose even stricter limits—for example, $1600 for an individual.

program gradually spread across the country. Inspired by the successful cases of LTCPP, more and more states have joined the program and made adjustments and improvements according to their respective situations.

The core components of the LTCPP consist of several aspects: state-certified long-term care insurance, Medicaid eligibility, and an asset protection mechanism.

Participants are required to enroll in long-term care insurance that complies with the regulations set by their state government. These insurance policies typically include a specific benefit period, benefit amount, and coverage scope. Once the long-term care insurance benefits are exhausted, participants can apply for Medicaid. During the asset evaluation process, a portion of their assets may be exempted. The specific amount of asset exemption is directly linked to the amount of benefits received from long-term care insurance. LTCPP does not change the fundamental eligibility criteria for Medicaid. Even after the exemption is applied, participants must still meet Medicaid's income and asset thresholds.

What distinguishes LTCPP from general LTCI is its core mechanism of asset protection. Individuals who participate in the program and purchase a designated LTCI policy can, after receiving benefits from the insurance, apply for Medicaid if further long-term care is needed. In this case, assets equivalent to the amount of benefits received from the LTCI are exempted from the Medicaid asset test. For example, if an elderly person receives $30,000 in insurance benefits through LTCPP, they can exclude that same amount from their personal assets when applying for Medicaid. This mechanism allows policyholders to retain a portion of their assets when receiving Medicaid assistance, thereby preventing the liquidation of family wealth.

As shown in Table 2, States can classify LTCPP into the following two types according to the differences in asset-protection methods. The first is the Dollar-for-Dollar model, which means assets equivalent to the insurance benefit amount are exempted. The other is the Total Asset model, by which all assets are retained under specific conditions.

Moreover, to prevent abuse of the program, most states have set eligibility criteria for LTCPP insurance. For example, according to the reports issued by the Connecticut Office of Policy and Management and Genworth, Connecticut requires a minimum daily benefit of $325, a monthly benefit of $9885, and a lifetime benefit of at least $124,100 Genworth (2023a, 2023b).

Table 2 Classification of "asset protection"

Type	Core rule	Representative state	Target group
Total asset	Maintaining all assets under specific conditions	New York, Indiana, etc.	Wealthy layer (high insurance materials are necessary)
Dollar-for-Dollar	Insurance benefit amount = asset exemption amount	Connecticut, California, etc.	Middle-tier and medium-to-high asset groups (highly flexible)

Note Data synthesized from reference materials

3 Analysis of the Case in Connecticut

3.1 Overview of Connecticut's LTCPP

As the first state in the United States to implement the LTCPP, Connecticut officially launched this program in 1992. Through a public-private cooperation mechanism, it aims to encourage middle-class residents to purchase LTCI, relieve the burden on public finances, and enhance individuals' autonomy in old-age security. Connecticut adopts the "Dollar-for-Dollar" model, where the total compensation amount received by the policyholder from a private insurance company is equivalent to the amount of personal assets exempted when applying for Medicaid.

Connecticut has set relatively high thresholds for policies in its LTCPP. According to the state government's official website, the specific requirements are as follows.

The insurance must be certified by the state government. According to the official guidance provided by the Connecticut state government under its LTCPP policy, in Connecticut, there is no upper limit on the lifetime maximum benefit of a LTCPP insurance policy. Generally, policyholders can choose a lifetime maximum benefit ranging from $40,000 to $1,000,000 or even opt for an unlimited benefit. However, the state has established a minimum coverage requirement: the lifetime benefit must be at least $124,100. Policyholders can select a high-value coverage amount based on their personal needs and financial situation but must meet this minimum threshold. In addition, the current minimum daily benefit is $334 per day for nursing facility care and $167 per day for home care.

According to the Connecticut Partnership for Long-Term Care Policy Certification Standards, the insurance policy must provide coverage for at least three years of long-term care services, including home-based care, institutional care, and community-based care. Furthermore, the insurance must be issued by a company registered in the state of Connecticut; policies purchased from out-of-state providers are not eligible for Partnership certification (Connecticut Office of Policy and Management, 2024).

Furthermore, according to official guidance from the Partnership for Long-Term Care, the assets exempted when applying for Medicaid do not need to be repaid later and are not included in the estate recovery[5] procedures. This mechanism significantly enhances the motivation of middle-and high-income groups to enroll in the program, ensuring the sustainability of assets in old age and supporting the intergenerational transfer of family wealth.

[5] Medicaid is a government-funded medical insurance program mainly targeting low-income individuals and people with disabilities. To maintain the sustainability of the program, some states have the right to recover from the beneficiary's estate the medical expenses paid by Medicaid throughout their lifetime after the beneficiary's death. Usually, estate recovery mainly targets the following services: Nursing Facility Services, Home and Community - Based Services, Hospital Services, and Prescription Drugs.

3.2 Current Operation Status

The implementation of the LTCPP has, to some extent, promoted the development of the LTCI market. By providing asset protection, the LTCPP has alleviated individuals' concerns when purchasing LTCI and enhanced their willingness to enroll. However, due to factors such as the pricing of LTCI, the scope of coverage, and market promotion, the promoting effect of the LTCPP on the LTCI market remains limited.

Despite the clear original intention of the system design, the actual operation of Connecticut's LTCPP shows an obvious deviation. Table 3 shows that the number of LTCPP enrollees in the state has been increasing gradually, but it has shown a tendency to stagnate or decline in the 2020s. Moreover, the number of people who applied for Medicaid after enrolling in the LTCPP is less than 1% of the total number of enrollees. The proportion of those who actually received LTCPP insurance benefits is less than 7%, and the proportion of those who applied for Medicaid after using the LTCPP is less than 1%. It is possible that those who enrolled in the LTCPP do not actually need Medicaid.

As shown in Table 4, based on the report in 2022, among the cumulative LTCPP enrollees from 1992 to 2021, more than 50% held assets worth over $350,000, far exceeding the median household asset value of the entire state. About half of the enrollees had a monthly income exceeding $5000, and most of them came from families with good economic conditions.

This data shows that the users of Connecticut's LTCPP are mainly concentrated among the wealthy, and the middle-class group targeted by the original policy has not actively participated. In other words, the system has shown limited effectiveness in encouraging the participation of the target group.

Table 3 Participation in LTC insurance partnership programme of Connecticut (before 2022) (by person)

Year	Partnership policies ever purchased (since program's establishment)	Persons who ever received LTCI benefit	Total purchaser who received Medicaid
As of 2017	59,804	3389	211
As of 2018	59,968	3829	247
As of 2019	60,116	4351	269
As of 2020	60,242	4828	323
As of 2021	60,596	5190	326

Source State of Connecticut, Office of Policy and Management (2018, 2019, 2020, 2021, 2022)

Table 4 Income and assets at time of purchase of connecticut

Year	Average monthly household income	Percentage	Total assets (besides home and car)	Percentage
As of 2003	Less than $2500	57%	Less than $50,000	19%
			$50,000–199,999	17%
	$2500–4999	14%	$200,000–349,999	17%
	$5000+	14%	$350,000+	48%
As of 2021	Less than $2500	17%	Less than $50,000	10%
			$50,000–199,999	24%
	$2500–4999	35%	$200,000–349,999	20%
	$5000+	49%	$350,000+	45%

*Due to rounding, figures may not total to 100%. *Sources* Julie Stone-Axelrad (2005), Medicaid's Long-Term Care Insurance Partnership Program; The Connecticut Partnership for Long-term Care, A Progress Report to the General Assembly, January 2022

3.3 Nursing Care Needs and the Supply of LTCPP

As shown in Table 5, the data shows that almost all participants in LTCPP in Connecticut have chosen insurance plans that cover both "institutional care" and "home-based care." This indicates that the elderly population prefers to receive services in a familiar environment.

Moreover, Table 6 shows that most participants live with their spouses, reflecting that the family support network still plays a crucial role in elderly care. This trend also suggests that the current global long-term care system is evolving towards the integration of a three-tier structure of "home-community-institution."

Besides, 37% of policyholders stated that their primary motivation for purchasing the insurance was asset inheritance—to avoid asset recovery by Medicaid and to leave their assets as an inheritance according to the report in 2022.

Table 5 Type of policy purchased

Service Type	Percentage
Nursing Home & Home Care Coverage	100%
Nursing home only coverage	0%

*Due to rounding, figures may not total to 100%.*Sources* The Connecticut Partnership for Long-term care, A Progress Report to the General Assembly, January 2022

Table 6 Living arrangements

Living Arrangements	Percentage
Living with spouse	76%
Living alone	16%
Living with children/relatives/other	10%
Children living with me	6%

*Due to rounding, figures may not total to 100%
**Not mutually exclusive.*Sources* The Connecticut Partnership for Long-term Care, A Progress Report to the General Assembly, January 2022

4 Problems of the LTCPP

4.1 Problems in the Operation of LTCPP

4.1.1 The Effect of Alleviating the Burden on Public Finance Is Limited

One of the key policy objectives of the LTCPP is to reduce the financial burden on Medicaid. The government aims to encourage some individuals to cover long-term care expenses through private insurance benefits, thereby decreasing their reliance on Medicaid. In theory, if more people use private insurance to meet their care needs, government spending on low-income populations would gradually decline. However, in practice, the program has shown limited effectiveness in alleviating fiscal pressure.

As of 2022, the enrollment rate in private long-term care insurance across the United States remains below 10% (Clifford Pendell, 2022), significantly lower than the coverage levels seen in countries like Germany and Japan. Moreover, most LTCPP policyholders belong to the affluent class, who are already less likely to depend on Medicaid. A large portion of middle-and lower-income families are not covered by the LTCPP, and their long-term care costs still rely heavily on personal savings and Medicaid. As previously mentioned, only a very small percentage—less than 1%—ultimately apply for Medicaid, and among those who exhaust their insurance benefits, only a tiny fraction continue to require long-term care. This suggests that the program has not achieved the expected large-scale substitution effect for Medicaid.

Even though the LTCPP is technically viable, without supportive measures such as premium subsidies, tax incentives, and strengthened public trust, it remains difficult to attract a large number of middle-class families to participate, making the goal of reducing the financial burden on Medicaid difficult to realize.

Furthermore, the LTCPP may lead to inequitable allocation of Medicaid resources, as only those who can afford and purchase long-term care insurance are entitled to asset protection. Individuals who cannot afford such insurance are excluded from this benefit.

4.1.2 Lack of System Sustainability and Market Attractiveness

In recent years, the LTCI market in the United States has faced multiple serious challenges. Many insurance companies have been forced to withdraw from the market due to factors such as high claim ratios, policy uncertainties, and interest rate spread losses. For example, in 2021, New York State officially announced the suspension of the sales of LTCPP-related products. The background includes the need to increase large-scale reserves due to stricter regulatory requirements, the setting of claim limits, the shrinking market size caused by the stagnant growth of the number of policyholders, and the increase in operating costs. Moreover, the low general awareness of LTCI, high insurance premiums, and long waiting periods have reduced the willingness to purchase.

As shown by the data mentioned earlier, although Connecticut continues to operate the program, the number of new policies sold has declined year by year, indicating that the system is difficult to sustain without dynamic adjustments and innovative incentives.

4.2 Mismatch Between the Needs and Supply of LTC

4.2.1 Deviation Between the System Goals and Actual Participants

One of the main goals of the LTCPP is to protect family assets and prevent the depletion of household wealth due to long-term care expenses. Research has shown that LTCPP has achieved this goal to a certain extent. By offering asset protection, LTCPP enables policyholders to retain part of their assets while receiving Medicaid support, thereby improving their quality of life.

However, for several reasons, LTCPP's effectiveness in protecting middle-class assets remains limited. On one hand, the relatively high entry thresholds for LTCPP insurance products—such as a daily benefit amount of over $325 and a minimum lifetime benefit—result in high premiums, making it unaffordable for low-income individuals and lower-middle-class families. LTCPP was originally designed to target the "elderly middle-class population," with the aim of encouraging them to purchase insurance through asset protection incentives, thereby easing the financial burden on Medicaid. However, data from Connecticut's implementation indicates that the program's participants are mainly concentrated in the upper-middle class and affluent groups. This deviates significantly from the policy's original intent.

Only those with considerable assets have a strong incentive to take advantage of the asset disregard mechanism. As a result, although the policy was aimed at the middle class, the incentive structure disproportionately benefits high-income individuals, effectively transforming what was intended as middle-class asset protection into a tax-preferential benefit for the wealthy. This has led to an unequal distribution of social resources.

Furthermore, a study by Lin and Prince (2013) pointed out that the promotion of LTCPP had minimal influence on the general public's willingness to purchase long-term care insurance. Those who responded positively to the policy were mostly individuals who already intended to purchase insurance, indicating that the policy had limited additional incentive effects. This, in turn, highlights the program's limitations in expanding insurance coverage.

4.2.2 Moral Hazard of the "Asset Protection" Mechanism

The original purpose of "asset protection" is to prevent the liquidation of the basic property of policyholders in their later life and to avoid their falling into poverty due to LTC expenses. However, recent data from Connecticut shows that approximately 37% of participants are using the LTCPP as an "asset inheritance tool." By purchasing insurance, they legally retain assets that should originally be allocated to LTC and transfer their inheritances.

This phenomenon highlights the "moral hazard" potentially existing in the system design. On the one hand, insurance products are being used for wealth protection rather than risk coverage. On the other hand, public resources are indirectly used to safeguard the property of wealthy families, which may undermine social fairness.

If this trend continues to expand, the LTCPP may transform from a "risk-protection" mechanism into a "tax-arbitrage" tool, which could go against the original spirit of the program.

5 Conclusions and Policy Recommendations

5.1 Conclusions

In this chapter, taking Connecticut as a case study, we systematically organized the institutional background, policy objectives, and actual operation status of the LTCPP in the United States, and focused on analyzing the contradictions and challenges in the institutional design and implementation process. The research results are as follows:

First, as a public-private partnership mechanism, the LTCPP indeed shows innovation in its institutional design. In particular, through the "asset protection" mechanism, it has enhanced the willingness of some people to purchase private LTCI and provided an institutional path for alleviating the financial pressure on Medicaid and protecting individuals' property.

Second, the implementation experience in Connecticut reveals an obvious deviation. Although the policy objectives were originally set for the middle-class, the actual participants are concentrated in the high-income group. The coverage rate of private insurance remains low, and the effect of reducing the burden on public finance is not significant. At the same time, the "asset protection" mechanism has caused moral hazard in practice and is being used by some wealthy families for the purpose of asset inheritance.

Third, the effectiveness of LTCPP is shaped by both its internal institutional logic and the structure of supply and demand in the insurance market. The integration with private insurance inevitably results in high entry thresholds and expensive premiums. In the absence of effective subsidy mechanisms, most middle-and lower-income groups are excluded from participation, leaving only a small portion of wealthy individuals able to benefit. This limited enrollment further undermines the long-term sustainability of the program.

In summary, the actual operation of LTCPP exposes various issues related to equity and sustainability in public-private care systems. Its limitations in realizing its original policy intentions call for serious reflection and further investigation.

5.2 Policy Recommendations

To enhance the effectiveness of the Long-Term Care Partnership Program (LTCPP) and improve the overall long-term care system, several policy recommendations are proposed. First, to increase accessibility for middle-income groups, the government should lower policy entry thresholds, reduce initial premiums, and offer financial incentives such as tax deductions or subsidies. These measures would help ensure that the LTCPP better serves its originally intended target population. Additionally, the asset disregard mechanism should be regulated by setting reasonable caps and time limits to prevent its misuse as a tool for wealth transfer. The exempted assets should be limited to essential living needs rather than enabling the accumulation of significant inheritances.

Furthermore, the government should strengthen coordination with insurance providers to develop long-term care products tailored to the diverse needs of different income groups. In particular, there should be an emphasis on promoting insurance models that integrate home-based care with community support services. Such developments could help revitalize the private insurance market and make LTCPP more inclusive and sustainable in the long term.

5.3 Future Directions

The world is currently facing the growing challenges of an aging population and the weakening of family caregiving capacity, making the development of long-term care systems a key direction in social security reforms across countries. Although the Long-Term Care Partnership Program has its limitations, its core approach—using asset protection to encourage individual responsibility and leveraging private insurance to reduce the burden on public finances—remains a valuable model worth referencing.

In designing long-term care systems, it is worth exploring diversified financing mechanisms that gradually encourage private sector participation in service provision. This would allow for the combined efforts of public support, private insurance, and individual responsibility, thereby reducing the pressure on any single party to bear long-term care risks. At the same time, to ensure equity within the system, it is important to guard against policies that disproportionately benefit high-income groups and to strengthen foundational protections for low-and middle-income populations.

References

Congressional Research Service. (2022, June 15). Who pays for long-term services and supports? (Congressional Research Service In Focus Report No. IF10343). https://fas.org/sgp/crs/misc/IF10343.pdf

Connecticut Office of Policy and Management. (2024). The Connecticut Partnership for Long-Term Care: A Progress Report to the General Assembly. State of Connecticut. https://portal.ct.gov/-/media/opm/hhs/ltc/annrpt---jan-2024_submitted.pdf

Drew Desilver. (2025). What the data says about Medicaid. https://www.pewresearch.org/short-reads/2025/06/24/what-the-data-says-about-medicaid/

Genworth. (2023a). Genworth releases cost of care survey results for 2023: Twenty years of tracking long-term care costs. https://investor.genworth.com/news-events/press-releases/detail/972/genworth-releases-cost-of-care-survey-results-for-2023

Genworth. (2023b). 2024 partnership minimum benefit requirements for CA, CT, IN, and NY. https://meritins.com/wp-content/uploads/Partnership_Min_Requirements.pdf

Greenhalgh-Stanley, N. (2014). Can the government incentivize the purchase of private long-term care insurance? Evidence from the long-term care partnership program. *Applied Economics Letters*, *21*(8), 541–544.

Lin, H. and Prince J. (2013). The impact of the partnership long-term care insurance program on private coverage and Medicaid expenditures. *Journal of Health Economics*, *32*(6), 1205–1213.

Marceno, L., & Llamas, A. (2025, March 25). Medicaid cuts could jeopardize access to critical long-term care services for people with disabilities and older adults. To the Point (blog). The Commonwealth Fund. https://www.commonwealthfund.org/blog/2025/medicaid-cuts-could-jeopardize-access-critical-long-term-care-services-people

Nursing Home Abuse Center. (2021). Facts and statistics about U.S. nursing home. https://www.nursinghomeabusecenter.org/informative/facts-statistics-nursing-homes/

Pendell, C. (2022). Long-term care statistics 2022. https://www.jrcinsurancegroup.com/long-term-care-statistics/

Pension Right Center. (2023). Income of today's older adults. https://pensionrights.org/resource/income-of-todays-older-adults/

Social Security. (2025). https://www.ssa.gov/faqs/en/questions/KA-01903.html

State of Connecticut, Office of Policy and Management. (2018). The Connecticut partnership for long-term care, a progress report to the general assembly, January 2018. https://cslib.contentdm.oclc.org/digital/collection/p128501coll2/id/540622/

State of Connecticut, Office of Policy and Management. (2019). The Connecticut partnership for long-term care, a progress report to the general assembly, January 2019. https://portal.ct.gov/-/media/opm/hhs/ltc/annrpt-jan-2019.pdf

State of Connecticut, Office of Policy and Management. (2020). The Connecticut partnership for long-term care, a progress report to the general assembly, January 2020. https://portal.ct.gov/-/media/opm/hhs/ltc/annrpt-jan-2020.pdf

State of Connecticut, Office of Policy and Management. (2021). The Connecticut partnership for long-term care, a progress report to the general assembly, January 2021. https://portal.ct.gov/-/media/opm/hhs/ltc/annrpt--jan-2021/annrpt--jan-2021.pdf
State of Connecticut, Office of Policy and Management. (2022). The Connecticut partnership for long-term care, a progress report to the general assembly, January 2022. https://portal.ct.gov/-/media/opm/hhs/ltc/annrpt--jan-2022.pdf
Statista.com. (2025). Medicaid long-term care services expenditures in the United States from FY 1990 to FY 2022. https://www.statista.com/statistics/245415/medicaid-spending-on-long-term-care-services-in-the-us-since-1990/
Stone-Axelrad, J. (2005). Medicaid's long-term care insurance partnership program. https://www.everycrsreport.com/files/20050121_RL32610_a6320a2b5a8d5600c5c3cb26bcc3e6f26e409419.pdf
U.S. Government Accountability Office. (2005). Overview of the long-term care partnership program. https://www.gao.gov/products/gao-05-1021r
Wu Yiwen (2022). *Changqi hulibaoxian zhidugouian de Zhongguo jinlu* [The Development Path of China's Long-Term Care Insurance System]. Zhongguo caizheng jingji chubanshe.

Role of the Public and Private Sectors of Long-Term Care Insurance in Japan

Hongmu Lee

1 Introduction

Aging is a global phenomenon, and Japan has one of the highest rates of aging in the world, because of declining birthrates and an increasing life expectancy. The population of Japan was approximately 120 million as of the end of March 2023. Of this population, 29.1%, or 36 million, were 65 years of age or older.

The percentages of the elderly in major countries are shown in Fig. 1.

As shown in Fig. 2, Japan's population of people aged 100 and over is also increasing rapidly.

Of the population aged 65 and over, approximately seven million need long-term care, as shown in Fig. 3.

The numbers in Fig. 3 show that the number of people has increased to more than three times the two million recorded in 2000, when the public long-term care insurance system was introduced.

As shown in Fig. 4, dementia increases rapidly with age, with over 50% of people aged 85 and older suffering from dementia.

As shown in Table 1, dementia accounts for 18.1% of the causes of long-term care needs among the elderly.as shown in the following table.

The purpose of this chapter is to analyze how public and private long-term care insurance in Japan plays its role against dementia and to identify its problems.

H. Lee (✉)
Professor of Risk Management and Insurance, School of Business, Waseda University, Tokyo, Japan
e-mail: hmlee@waseda.jp

H. Lee and G. Nicolini (eds.), *International Comparison of Long-Term Care Insurance Systems*, Contributions to Management Science,
https://doi.org/10.1007/978-981-95-7781-1_6

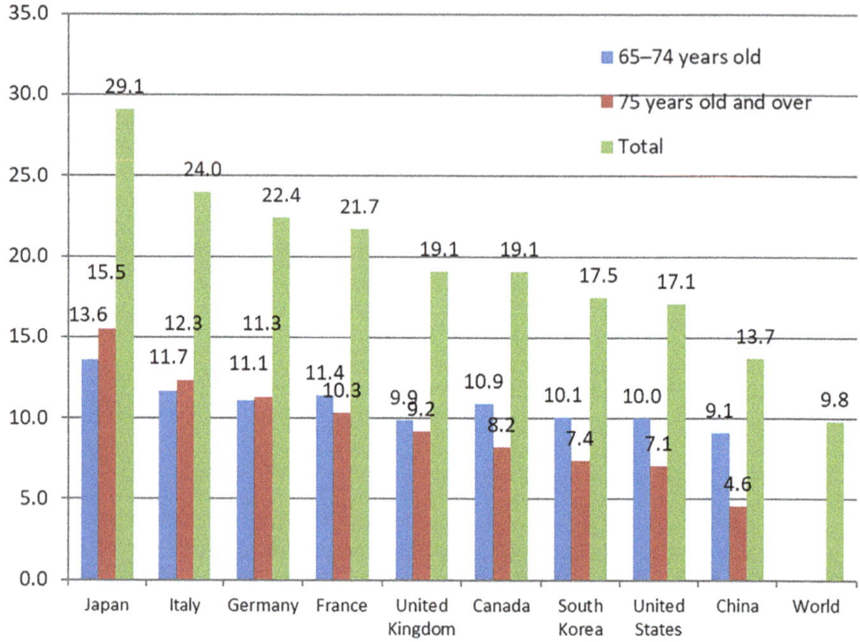

Fig. 1 Percentage of older adults in major countries (2022). *Source* Compiled from Ministry of Health, Labor and Welfare statistics of Japan, etc.

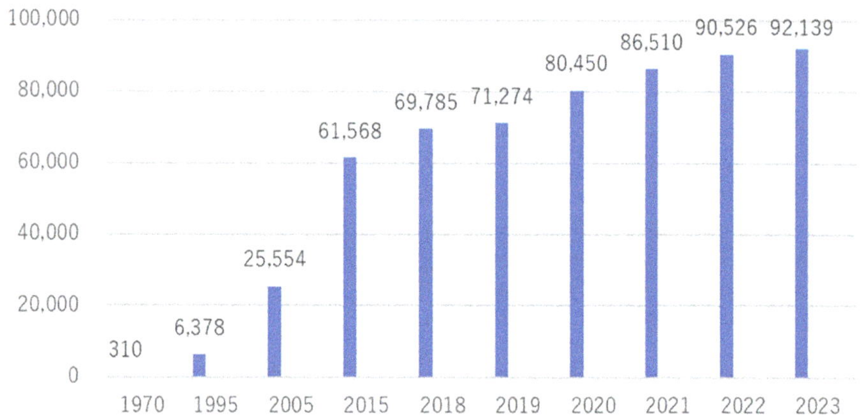

Fig. 2 Number of people aged 100 or older. *Source* Compiled from Ministry of Health, Labor and Welfare statistics of Japan, etc.

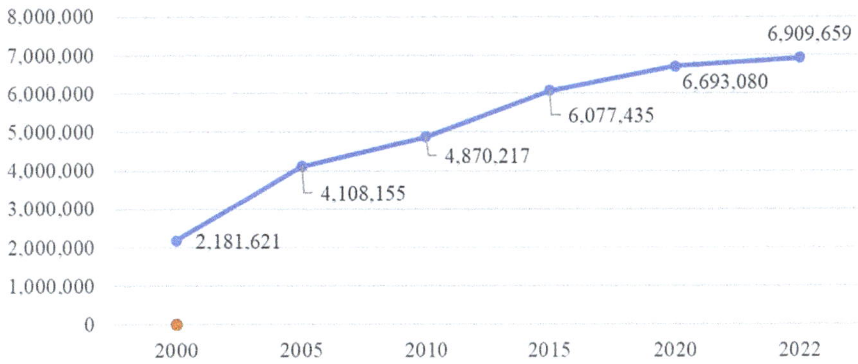

Fig. 3 Number of people certified as needing long-term care (needed assistance). *Source* Ministry of Health, Labor, and Welfare, 2022 White Paper on Health, Labor, and Welfare of Japan

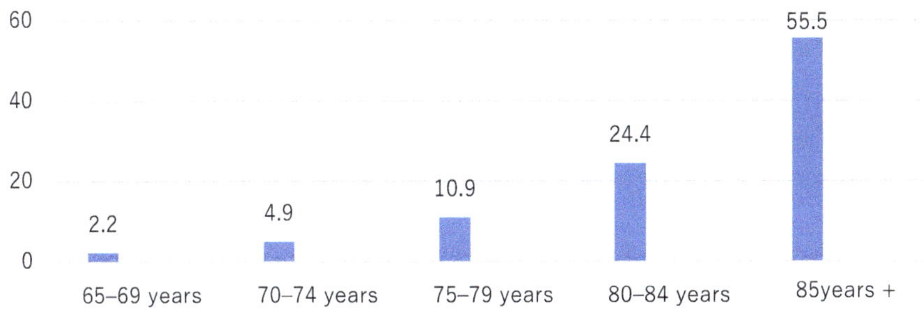

Fig. 4 Percentage of people with dementia (by Age) (%). *Source* Ministry of Health, Labor and Welfare of Japan

Table 1 Causes of long-term care for people 65 years of age or older in need of long-term care

(Unit: %)	Cerebrovascular Disease (Stroke)	Cardiac Disease (Heart Disease)	Arthritic Disease	Dementia	Fractures and Falls	Weakness due to Old Age	Others
Total number	15.0	4.7	11.0	18.1	13.0	13.3	25.0
Male	24.5	6.3	4.6	14.4	5.8	11.3	33.2
Female	10.3	3.9	14.2	19.9	16.5	14.3	21.0

Source Cabinet Office of Japan, 2022 White Paper on the Elderly, 2022 edition

2 Types and Symptoms of Dementia

As shown in Fig. 5, the most common cause of dementia in the elderly is Alzheimer's disease at 67.6%, followed by vascular dementia at 19.5%.

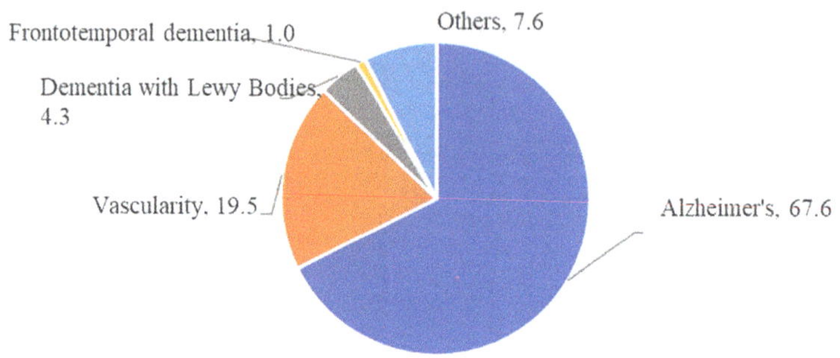

Fig. 5 Type of dementia (%). *Source* Ministry of Health, Labor, and Welfare of Japan, 「Enhancement of Dementia Response Capability (August 30, 2023)

As shown in Fig. 6, symptoms of dementia include core symptoms and BPSD (Behavioral and Psychological Symptoms of Dementia).

Core symptoms refer to impairments in cognitive function, not the mental function of the brain. Core symptoms are commonly found in people with dementia. BPSD, on the other hand, is a combination of psychiatric symptoms such as depression and delusions, and behavioral disorders. This BPSD manifests differently in different people. Thus, it is difficult to quantify long-term care time needed for BPSD.

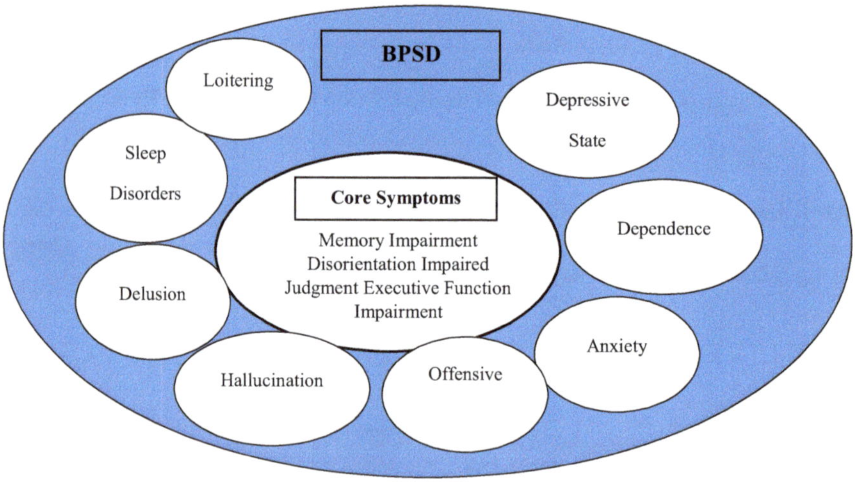

Fig. 6 Symptoms of dementia(%). *Source* Created by the author

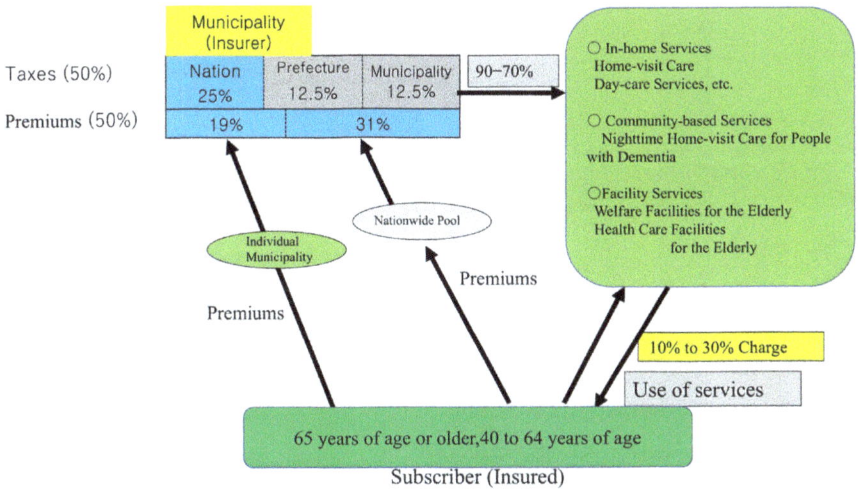

Fig. 7 Structure of public long-term care insurance. *Source* Ministry of Health, Labor and Welfare of Japan

3 Public Long-Term Care Insurance and Dementia

3.1 Structure of Public Long-Term Care Insurance

When receiving public long-term care insurance services, users pay from 10% to 30% of the cost as copayment, depending on their income. The costs excluding the user's copayment are covered 50% by taxes and 50% by subscribers' insurance premiums, as shown in Fig. 7.

Public long-term care insurance premiums are to be paid by all residents from age 40 to the time of death. In principle, people 65 years of age or older are eligible for long-term care services when they are certified as needing long-term care or support, regardless of the cause.

However, long-term care services are also provided to subscribers aged 40 to 64 if the cause of the long-term care required is one of the 16 specified diseases[1] recognized as physical and mental changes due to aging.

Public long-term care insurance differs from medical insurance in that it requires prior certification of the long-term care grade by the municipality. The grade determines the long-term care insurance services that can be used.

The procedure for using public long-term care insurance is as shown in Fig. 8.

To use public long-term care insurance, the following procedures must be followed. ① The user (or his/her family) applies to the municipality for certification of the need for long-term care. ② An on-site survey is conducted for certification, and an attending physician's written opinion is prepared. ③ The certification is made

[1] Long-Term Care Insurance Law Enforcement Order Article 2

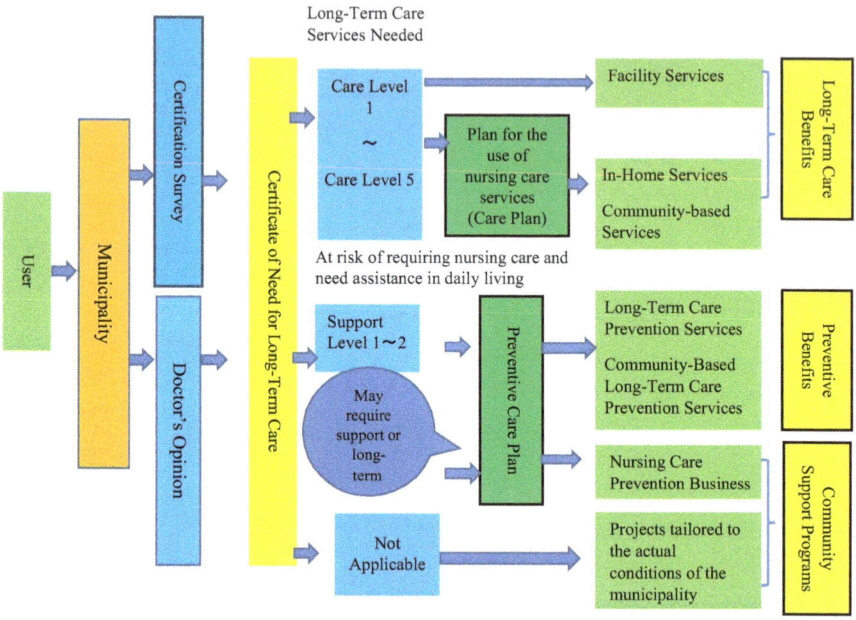

Fig. 8 Procedures for using public long-term care insurance. *Source* Ministry of Health, Labor, and Welfare of Japan

based on the examination judgment. ④ A long-term care (long-term care prevention) service plan is prepared. ⑤ The user starts using long-term care services.

Long-term care certification in public long-term care insurance determines the grade of care depending on the amount of time the symptoms require care. The computer's initial assessment is based on the physician's diagnostic opinion and evaluation of 79 items, as shown in Fig. 9.

The required standard care time is measured across five domains, as shown in Table 2.

Behavioral and Psychological Symptoms of Dementia (BPSD), which is considered a problematic behavior in dementia, is one measurement area.

Long-term care certification is classified into seven levels according to the degree of care required, as shown in Table 3, with a budget and services allocated for each level.

3.2 *Services of Public Long-Term Care Insurance*

Public long-term care insurance services are classified into home-based services, facility-based services, and community-based services, as shown in Fig. 10.

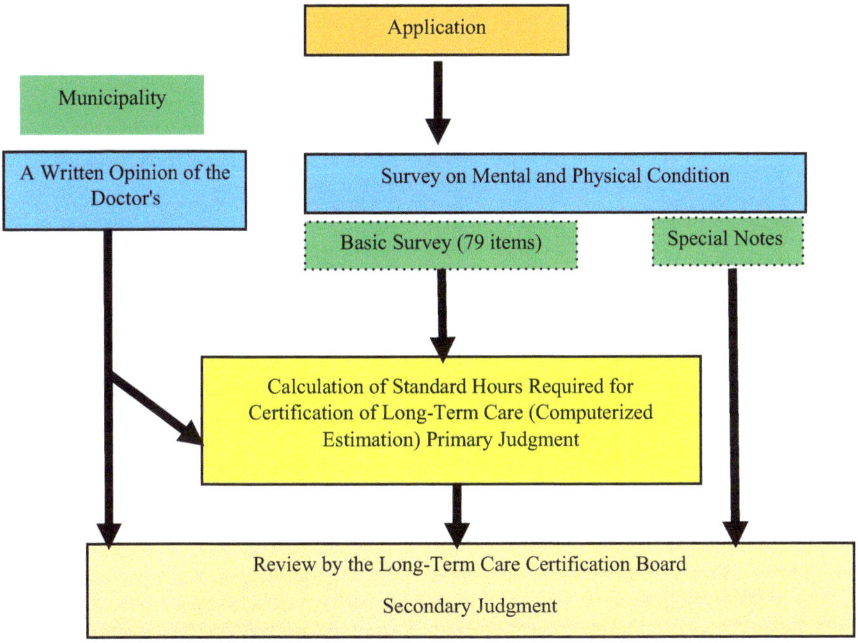

Fig. 9 How public long-term care insurance certifies need for long-term care. *Source* Ministry of Health, Labor and Welfare of Japan

Table 2 Classification of standard hours of care required

Classification	Contents
Direct living support	Care for bathing, exhaustion, meals, etc.
Indirect living support	Household chores such as laundry, cleaning, etc.
Problem behavior (BPSD)	Searching for wandering, cleaning up after filthy behavior, etc
Functional training-related activities	Functional training such as walking training, daily living training, etc.
Medical-related actions	Assist in medical treatment, such as administration of infusions, treatment of bedsores, etc.

Source Ministry of Health, Labor and Welfare of Japan

In-home services are long-term care services that allow people requiring long-term care or support to receive services while still living in their current residence. In-home services are categorized into home-visit services, day-care services, and short-term residential services. In home-visit services, service providers visit people requiring long-term care or support who live at home and provide daily living support such as shopping and cleaning, care for meals and elimination, nursing care such as health management and hygiene instruction, and rehabilitation and bathing services.

Table 3 Standard hours for certification of need for long-term care

Classification	Contents
Support level 1	A condition recognized as equivalent to a certified care level requiring 25 minutes or more but less than 32 minutes of care.
Support level 2 Care level 1	A condition recognized as equivalent to a certified care level requiring 32 minutes or more but less than 50 minutes of care.
Care level 2	A condition recognized as requiring 50 minutes or more but less than 70 minutes of care, or equivalent to this standard
Care level 3	A condition recognized as requiring 70 minutes or more but less than 90 minutes of care, or equivalent to this standard
Care level 4	A condition recognized as requiring 90 minutes or more but less than 110 minutes of care, or equivalent to this standard
Care level 5	A condition recognized as requiring 110 minutes or more of care certification standard time or equivalent

Source Ministry of Health, Labor and Welfare of Japan of Japan

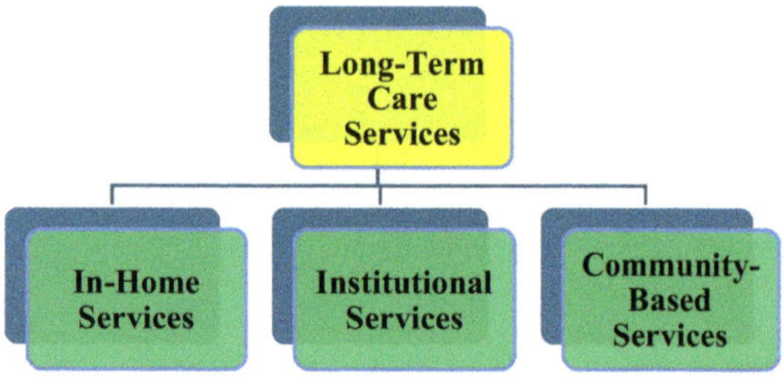

Fig. 10 Types of long-term care services. *Source* Ministry of Health, Labor and Welfare of Japan

Day-care service is a care service in which people requiring nursing care or support who live at home spend the daytime at a facility as a commuter, and receive nursing care such as meals and elimination, nursing care such as health management and hygiene guidance, and rehabilitation and bathing services. Short-term residential care service is a care service in which people requiring long-term care or support are admitted to a facility for a certain period and are provided with nursing care such as meals and elimination, nursing care such as health management and hygiene guidance, and rehabilitation and bathing services.

Institutional services are provided in welfare facilities for the elderly requiring long-term care (special nursing home for the elderly), health care facilities, and integrated facilities that provide both medical and long-term care. In the past, admission was limited to those requiring nursing care 1 or higher, but as of August 2015, in principle, admission is now limited to those requiring nursing care 3 or higher.

Welfare facilities for the elderly mainly provide daily living care such as meals, elimination, and bathing, whereas health care facilities provide long-term care and rehabilitation services focusing on care and rehabilitation. There are two types of integrated medical and long-term care facilities: Type I and Type II. Type I is a facility whose facility standards are equivalent to those of medical care beds and is designed to accept people whose physical condition is likely to change suddenly. Type II has the same facility standards as those for elderly people and is intended for residents who require less nursing care and medical care than Type I and whose condition is stable.

Community-based services are long-term care services established in 2006. It is an intermediate concept between in-home services and facility services, combining in-home services, day-care services, and residential services. Service centers for community-based services are designated by municipalities and are available only to those who have a certificate of residence in the area. In community-based services, the size of the facility is kept small so that users can spend their time in a home-like atmosphere (Lee, 2021). This is due to the increasing number of elderly people living alone and those with dementia. Dementia day-care services are specialized day-care services for people with dementia to live comfortably and safely in their own neighborhoods.

In the community-based services, group homes are facilities that are exclusively for elderly people who have developed dementia. Group homes are facilities for elderly people with dementia who are certified as requiring support level 2 or higher and who have a certificate of residence in the same municipality as the facility. Group homes are characterized by the fact that each unit consists of five to nine residents, who share household chores such as cooking and cleaning. In group homes, people who need assistance can use dementia care facilities.

The initial cost of a group home requires an upfront or security deposit. Food and housing costs in group homes have traditionally been borne entirely by the residents. If a resident becomes bedridden and requires medical treatment after moving in, he/she will be transferred to another facility where medical treatment is available.

The Community Comprehensive Support Center is a "comprehensive consultation service" established by the municipality and staffed with public health nurses, social workers,[2] and chief long-term care support specialists to provide residents with the assistance they need to maintain their health and stabilize their lives through a three-professional team approach. Through this, the facility aims to provide comprehensive support for the improvement of their health and welfare.[3] Municipalities are in charge of establishing community comprehensive support centers, which also provide the following rights protection: protection against economic exploitation and fraud through the use of the adult guardianship system, and response to, prevention of, and early detection of abuse. An adult guardianship system is a system in which an adult guardian manages the person's property and enters into contracts on behalf

[2] The main tasks of social workers include counselling and supporting the elderly, the disabled and the needy, as well as liaising with relevant agencies. However, social workers in Japan have several different job categories, with different targets and workplaces, and therefore different job descriptions. Social workers who work in special nursing homes and private homes for the elderly are known as lifestyle consultants. On the other hand, those working in 'long-term care health facilities for the elderly' are called support counsellors. Residents of long-term care healthcare facilities for the elderly are intended to return home, and support consultants also play a role in helping residents return to their own homes.

[3] Article 115–46, Paragraph 1 of the Long-Term Care Insurance Law

of a person who has become incapable of making decisions due to dementia or other causes.

There are two types of adult guardianship systems: the "legal guardianship system" and the "voluntary guardianship system." In the legal guardianship system, the adult guardian is selected by the family court. If there is a relative, the relative is elected as the guardian. On the other hand, if the person has no relatives or if there is a risk that a relative may cause problems, a lawyer, judicial scrivener, or social worker is selected. Voluntary guardianship is a system that allows people to choose their own adult guardian while they still have cognitive ability. As in the legal guardianship system, it is possible to choose a guardian from relatives, lawyers, judicial scriveners, etc. According to the Supreme Court of Japan, in 2021 dementia accounted for 63.7% of the causes of initiation of the adult guardianship system. In addition, long-term care insurance contracts account for 13.6% of the motives for applying for adult guardianship.

3.3 Number of Certified Long-Term Care Recipients and Long-Term Care Facilities

The number of individuals certified as requiring nursing care (or support) (as of March 31, 2023) is shown in Table 4.

The total number of Category 1 insured persons were 35,845,134 as of March 31, 2023. Of these, approximately 19%, or 6,814,344 people, were certified as requiring long-term care. It can be observed that the number of people certified for long-term care increases with increasing age.

The trend in the capacity of nursing care facilities is shown in Fig. 11.

Overall, the capacity of long-term care facilities is increasing, especially the capacity of Toll Homes for the Elderly. This is partly due to the fact that public long-term care facilities are not fully equipped to meet the needs of the elderly but also due to the fact that the demands of the elderly are becoming more diverse. In other words, the number of elderly people who want to stay in high-end facilities is also increasing.

3.4 Users' Cost of Public Care Insurance Services

Public long-term care insurance covers the limit of the approved grade. Within this range, users are responsible for 10% to 30% of the service cost as a co-payment, depending on their income. If the amount exceeds this limit, the full amount is borne by the user.

The monthly maximum amount by care grade is as shown in Table 5.

covers

Table 4 Number of people certified as needing long-term care (support) as of March 31, 2023

Classification		Support Level 1	Support Level 2	Care Level 1	Care Level 2	Care Level 3	Care Level 4	Care Level 5	Total
Category 1		972,852	940,039	1,424,784	1,133,865	901,502	869,867	571,435	6,814,344
	Aged 65–69	29,732	32,048	37,510	35,857	25,065	23,264	19,702	203,178
	Aged 70–74	80,321	80,053	97,481	86,254	62,056	56,927	43,531	506,623
	Aged 75–79	148,992	134,407	174,619	134,226	95,915	87,720	64,011	839,890
	Aged 80–84	267,352	225,635	319,021	221,735	160,347	144,979	98,455	1,437,524
	Aged 85–89	282,120	268,741	419,071	306,597	233,682	214,810	138,166	1,863,187
	Aged 90+	164,335	199,155	377,082	349,196	324,437	342,167	207,570	1,963,942
Category 2		11,970	19,457	21,259	26,544	18,573	16,316	15,914	130,033
Total		984,822	959,469	1,446,043	1,160,409	920,075	886,183	587,349	6,944,377

Source Cabinet Office of Japan: Japanese Government Statistics

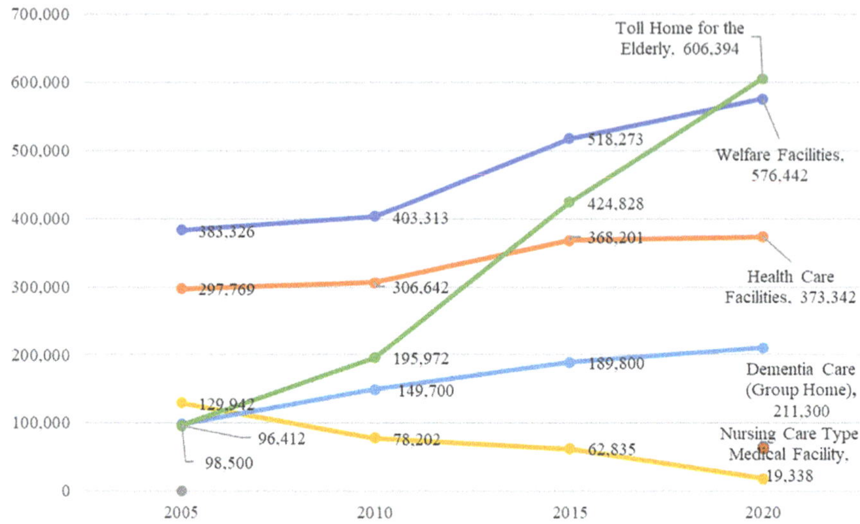

Fig. 11 Trend of capacity of long-term care facilities. *Source* Cabinet Office of Japan

Table 5 Monthly limit by long-term care grade (revised October 2019)

Long-Term Care Grade	Usage Limits (Yen)
Support level 1	50,320
Support level 2	105,310
Care level 1	167,650
Care level 2	197,050
Care level 3	270,480
Care level 4	309,380
Care level 5	362,170

Source Ministry of Health, Labor and Welfare of Japan

When using long-term care insurance in-home services, the maximum amount of service costs to be covered by insurance is determined according to the grade of long-term care required.

The scope of coverage for public long-term care insurance for care services is as shown in Fig. 12.

The question is whether public and private pensions can pay the user's share of the cost. This is where private long-term care insurance needs to play a role.

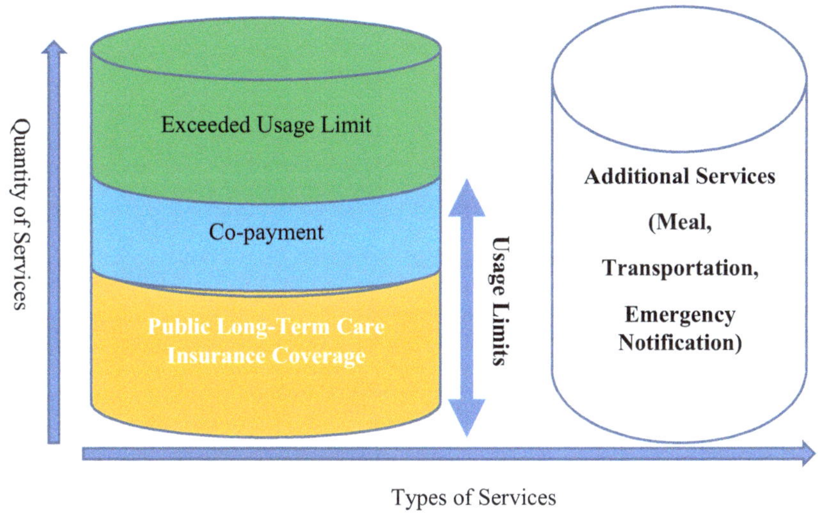

Fig. 12 Public long-term care insurance coverage for long-term care services. *Source* Author

4 Private Long-Term Care Insurance and Dementia

The difference between healthy life expectancy and average life expectancy is one measure of the duration of long-term care services required. This is because it is the period of time during which a person is not healthy and requires long-term care services.

Figure 13 shows men's healthy life expectancy and average life expectancy.

Figure 14 shows women's healthy life expectancy and average life expectancy.

The average "unhealthy period" in 2019 is 8.73 years for men and 12.06 years for women. As can be seen in the graph above, women have a longer life expectancy than men, but they also require a longer period of long-term care services.

As shown in Fig. 15, the cost of long-term care gradually increases from the initial stage through to the end-of-life stage, while public pension benefits remain a fixed amount (Lee, 2022).

Long-term care costs consist of physical care, daily living assistance, and monitoring (Lee, 2021). These long-term care costs include more long-term care supplies and services in the mid-term stage than in the initial stage, as well as more hospitalization costs. Furthermore, in the final phase, the cost of accommodation at the facility is added to the intermediate costs, in addition to the increased medical costs.

When an elderly person develops dementia, in addition to the issue of care costs, financial institutions freeze their accounts, and they cannot receive insurance benefits. Therefore, it is necessary to take action in the case of dementia, such as designating an insurance beneficiary or adult guardian to receive private long-term care insurance.

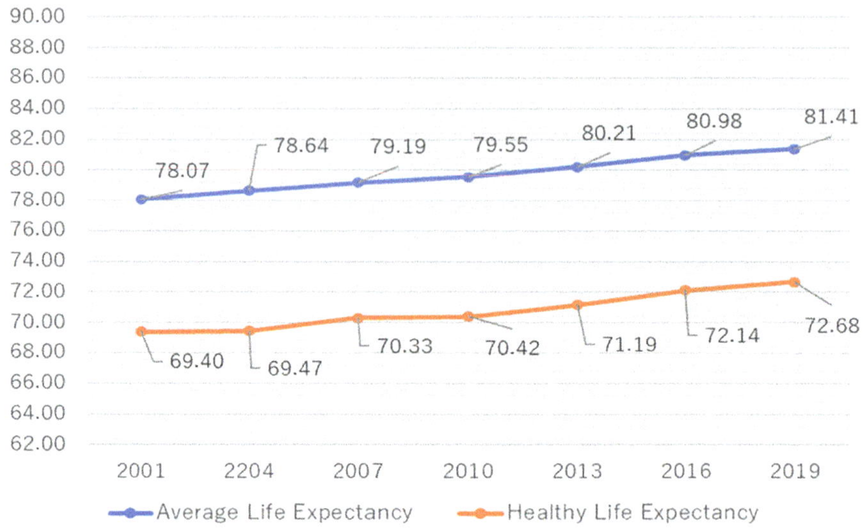

Fig. 13 Healthy life expectancy and average life expectancy (male). *Source* Ministry of Health, Labor, and Welfare of Japan

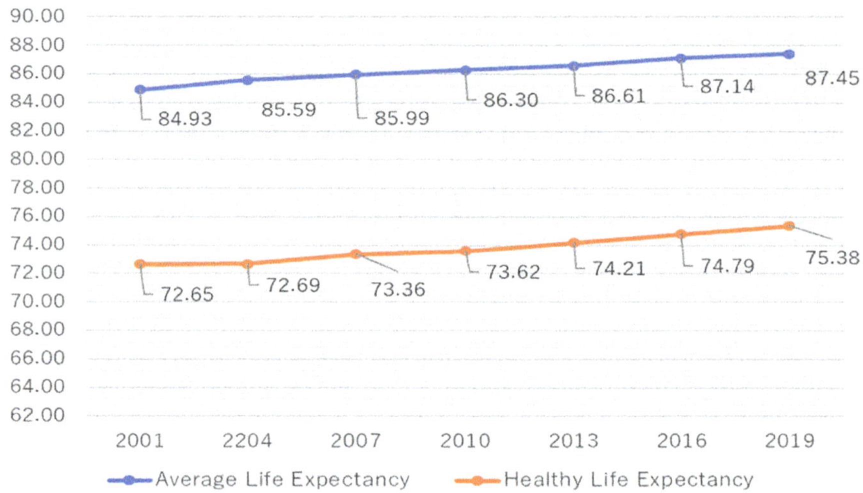

Fig. 14 Healthy life expectancy and average life expectancy (female). *Source* Ministry of Health, Labor, and Welfare of Japan

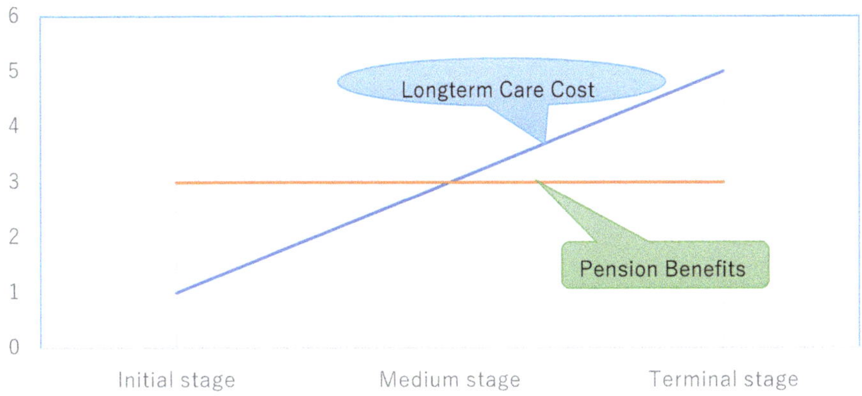

Fig. 15 Long-term care costs and pension benefits. *Source* Author

5 Conclusion

Dementia among the elderly is increasing rapidly with the aging of the population in Japan. This dementia also presents a number of problems for the identification of the grade of care required by public insurance. This is because, although certification of the grade of care required is based on the time needed to provide care, BPSD is difficult to quantify among the symptoms of dementia. In Japan, community-based services are provided to address this dementia. This is to enable older people with dementia to live in their own familiar neighborhoods.

In addition, public long-term care insurance sets a limit for each grade of care required, and in addition to the co-payment amount, the amount spent in excess of this limit is fully borne by the user. Furthermore, any additional services to those covered by the public long-term care insurance are to be paid for in full by the user. In addition, the cost of long-term care is characterized by an increase toward the mid-term and final stages rather than the initial stages. The role of private long-term care insurance is required to cope with this user burden. Furthermore, if an elderly person develops dementia, financial institutions will freeze their accounts, so it is necessary to decide when they are healthy how to receive and use the private long-term care insurance proceeds or to make use of adult guardianship schemes.

Institutional services are also increasingly in demand, with public facilities being less expensive, but with demand for more upscale facilities.

Acknowledgements This work was supported by JSPS KAKENHI Grant (Grant-in-Aid for Scientific Research (C) · 22K01563) from the Japan Society for the Promotion of Science.

References

Lee, H. (2021). *Personnel risk management and insurance*. Hakueisha.

Lee, H. (2022). *Retirement income security in Japan: An overview of the public and private pension system. International comparison of pension systems: An investigation from consumers' viewpoint*. Springer.

Private Long-Term Care Insurance in Japan

Akio Hoshino

1 Analysis of Public and Private Long-Term Care Insurance (LTCI)

1.1 Comparison of the Structure of Public and Private Long-Term Care Insurance

(As detailed in Part 1, Chapter 2) Japan's public long-term care insurance is universal, requiring all residents aged 40 and above to participate. The insureds in public long-term care insurance are residents of each municipality aged 40 years or older who are registered in the Basic Resident Registry, regardless of nationality. Insured individuals are divided into Category 1 (40–65 years) and Category 2 (65 years and above) according to age. The coverages are different between Categories 1 and 2.

The public long-term care insurance system was introduced in 2000 under the Long-Term Care Insurance Law. While the central government (the Ministry of Health, Welfare, and Labour) oversees the national system, local governments, such as municipalities, manage its operations.

The three key concepts of the public LTCI system are stated in the government's propositions as follows.[1]

[1] Translated by the author from"Kaigohoken Seido no Gaiyou Reiwa 3 Nen 5 gatsu Kosei Rodosho Rojin Hokenkyoku" or Outlines of Long-Term-Care-Insurance System May 2021 Health and Welfare Bureau for the Elderly, Ministry of Health, Labour, and Welfare. https://www.mhlw.go.jp/content/000801559.pdf Retrieved 15 July 2025.

A. Hoshino (✉)
School of Commerce, Waseda University, JapanTokyo
e-mail: a.h@waseda.jp

H. Lee and G. Nicolini (eds.), *International Comparison of Long-Term Care Insurance Systems*, Contributions to Management Science,
https://doi.org/10.1007/978-981-95-7781-1_7

A. Support the independence of the elderly: This program not only aims to merely meet the personal needs of the elderly but to also help those requiring nursing care live independently.
B. User-oriented: A system in which users can comprehensively access healthcare and welfare services from various entities according to their choice.
C. Social insurance system: The system is designed as a social insurance model rather than welfare, aiming to visualize the relationship between benefits and contributions.

A notable characteristic of the public LTCI is that it does not provide cash benefits to the insured. Instead, it is designed to offer care services with benefits paid directly to service providers, such as nursing homes and in-home assistance. Services covered by the public LTCI are strictly defined and stipulated in the Long-Term Care Insurance Act, consisting of 54 services in 26 categories. Public LTCI does not pay for other costs such as rehabilitation, daily necessities (e.g., diapers), or meals in nursing homes. The costs not payable by the public LTCI must be paid by the insured.

Public LTCI is designed to encourage the use of professional caregivers rather than reliance on family members. Like any other system, Japan's LTCI has both advantages and disadvantages.

When the public LTCI system was introduced, the care service business for the elderly increased sharply, especially among high-income groups (Tamiya et al. 2011). The study also showed that the average time family caregivers spent providing care decreased considerably following the introduction of the LTCI. This is a clear benefit that Public LTCI has brought to society. However, working hours for family caregivers increased significantly in the high-income group but not in the low- and middle-income groups. Although the public LTCI reduces the workload of family caregivers, it may have had a limited effect on increasing their income. As direct benefits for family caregivers, such as cash, pensions, and workers' compensation, are not available in the LTCI system in Japan (as provided in Germany and other countries), the need for financial benefits remains even when public LTCI plays a primary role.

Given these characteristics of public LTCI, private LTCI is expected to fill the gap between the financial needs of the insured and the benefits of public LTCI. Private LTCI can provide financial support to households with elderly people and their family caregivers, particularly for expenses not covered by public LTCI. Private LTCI is suitable for social interests when designed accordingly and is gaining popularity in Japan.

The primary difference between public and private LTCI is that public LTCI is compulsory, whereas private LTCI is voluntary. Consumers are free to choose whether or what private LTCI products they should purchase. It is an insurance policy marketed similarly to medical insurance, and the Financial Services Agency oversees insurers and their products in the same manner as it does for medical insurance.

As detailed in Sect. 3, private LTCI is provided by both life and non-life insurers, with life insurers being the main providers.

With public LTCI functioning as the primary social long-term care system, private LTCI was designed as a supplement. As stated earlier, the gap between public needs and the benefits of public LTCI lies mainly in providing financial support to caregivers; therefore, most private LTCI products are designed to address this gap.

The Japan Institute of Life Insurance (JILI), a public-interest association, simulated the typical case of a household with a patient at Care Level 3 (Appendix A). In this simulation, the insured person was a 66-year-old male with a disability caused by a prior cerebral infarction who received the following care services: A1: a weekly one-hour visit from a nurse for blood pressure monitoring and advice on preventing the recurrence of cerebral infarction; A2: a weekly 40-min visit by a speech therapist for vocal rehabilitation; B: three one-hour visits per week from a caregiver for physical support with activities such as changing and excretion; C: visits to a daycare facility three days a week for six to seven hours per visit, including assisted bathing. In addition, this case included one-night short stays from Saturday to Sunday in a nursing home twice a week, rental of a wheelchair and a special bed, procurement of a portable toilet, and reforming the house to flatten floor gaps. Short stays are not scheduled for weekends; therefore, the family (typically the wife or daughter) cares for the insured.

In this simulation, the total cost of regular services is JPY 285,880 (USD2030).[2] The public LTCI limit for this case with Care Level 3 was JPY 270,480, which represents a 10% reduction. This means that the excess limit (JPY 28,580–270,480 = 15,400) and 10% of the cost (JPY 270,480 × 10% = 27,048) were left uncovered.

1.2 Comparison of the Roles of Public and Private Long-Term Care Insurance

The Japanese government, the Financial Services Agency, and the Ministry of Health, Welfare, and Labour jointly announced the guiding principles for the roles of public and private LTCIs in a leaflet[3]: "In principle, public insurance operated by the government is compulsory, whereas private insurance operated by insurance companies is voluntary. Because private insurance complements public insurance in some respects, it is important to understand the coverage of public insurance and purchase private insurance as needed." This statement clarifies the roles of public and private LTCIs. Public LTCI is the primary source of coverage for long-term care risks, whereas private LTCI provides supplemental coverage.

As the Ministry of Health, Welfare, and Labour declared in Proposition A in the "three key concepts," the purpose of Public LTCI, at least to some extent, is to change the Japanese public custom that elderly people are dependent. This implies that the families and relatives of the elderly are obligated to take care of them.

Therefore, to understand private LTCI, it is essential to recognize its limitations and shortfalls of public LTCI. Public LTCI has a limitation known as "co-payment"

---

[2] Exchange rate 1 USD = 140.85 JPY (as at 9/16/2024).

[3] https://www.fsa.go.jp/ordinary/insurance_leaflet.pdf Retrieved 22 July 2024 (In Japanese).

(see Part 1, Chapter 2), where insured individuals and their households must bear part of the expense. The benefits to the private insurance sector include this payment.

As discussed in the following sections, private insurance may cover losses from events not associated with public LTCI.

2 Types of Private LTCI

2.1 Background of Life and Non-life Insurance Companies

Before discussing the product characteristics of the Japanese private LTCI, an essential background of the insurance business (summarized below) will help us understand the differences in products.

The Japanese Insurance Business Act establishes two types of licenses: life insurance and non-life insurance (Article 3). A single entity cannot hold both licenses, meaning that an insurance company must operate exclusively as a life insurer or non-life insurer.

However, the law permits insurance-holding companies to own life and non-life insurance subsidiaries. Consequently, many non-life insurance groups and some major life insurance companies have a subsidiary or "group company" operating in the other insurance domain. Both companies can market private LTCI products.

The law allows life and non-life companies to sell LTCI insurance products using two payment types: fixed-amount and reimbursement products. Fixed-amount policies pay fixed insurance proceeds, whereas reimbursement policies pay the costs incurred within the amount insured.

The payment type affects business operations. Generally, life insurers excel in providing fixed-benefit policies, whereas non-life insurers are more familiar with indemnity policies.

The old Insurance Business Act (before revision in 1995) allowed life insurance companies to provide only fixed-amount products and non-life insurance companies to provide only reimbursement products. Although insurers can now sell both fixed-amounts and reimbursements LTCI products, life insurers specialize in the former and non-life insurers specialize in the latter.

Japanese non-life insurers refer to reimbursement products as "Long-term Care Expense Insurance" to distinguish them from fixed-amount products.

2.2 Scopes of LTCI Products

Life and non-life insurance companies offer various LTCI insurance products. Although the concept of insurance products varies, private LTCIs primarily aim to cover expenses that public LTCIs do not sufficiently cover.

a. Fixed-Amount Private LTCI

Fixed-amount LTCI products provide lump-sum benefits, long-term care annuities, or both, upon certification of the need for nursing care. The lump-sum benefit can cover the initial costs of coping with care needs such as electric beds, assistive bathtubs, stair railings, and other home renovations. Annuity payments support daily living expenses and supplement public long-term care insurance by covering co-payments. However, unlike reimbursement LTCI, the benefit or annuity of fixed-amount policies is not linked to actual expenses. Policyholders can use the benefits at their discretion.

Annuity coverage is beneficial and essential for long-term care needs, but premiums for annuities are higher than for lump-sum benefits alone. Thus, private LTCI with annuity coverage is considered full-scale LTCI insurance, whereas lump-sum only products are more manageable and affordable.

b. Reimbursement Private LTCI

Simultaneously, reimbursement-based LTCI products cover actual expenses, while insurance payments are based on care costs. Policyholders must submit certified documentation to the insurer to claim benefits and ensure that the claim corresponds to the expenses. Cost of care typically includes payments to nursing homes, caregivers, and hospitals.

Some policies cover expenses that are not directly related to caregiving. For instance, certain insurance products cover the costs incurred by family members in searching for missing-insured individuals with dementia.

It may also cover liability coverage for damage caused by events, such as when a person causes injury to others in their daily lives or renders trains inoperable by entering railroad tracks. Liability coverage can compensate for damages of up to JPY 100 million.

Reimbursement products often include supplemental fixed-amount benefits.

c. Summary of the Types

In summary, private LTCIs can be categorized by their principal benefits, as shown in Table 1. Some products offer multiple benefits.

Considering the financial needs of long-term elderly care, a lifetime annuity is an ideal form of insurance coverage and is regarded as a fully-fledged and reliable coverage.

Simultaneously, one-time payment products are popular for limiting the burden of premium payments. Section 4 examines typical amounts and premiums for both types.

In addition, there are multiyear non-lifetime annuity products, which are characterized as interim products between lifetime annuities and one-time payments.

d. Conditions of the Payment

There are two typical causes or triggers for benefit payment.

Table 1 Categories of private LTCI by principal benefits

Payment period		Principal benefits		Characteristics
		Fixed amount	Reimbursement	
One-time		Diagnosis benefit	Temporary Expenses (Reform, Wheelchair &c.)	Low premium Covers initial costs Only incidental compensation
Annuities	Multi-years	Yearly annuity payment up to contracted years or age of insured	Expenses for Medical facilities, Nursing homes, and miscellaneous[4] costs up to contracted years	In between the above and the below
	Lifetime	Yearly annuity for lifetime	Expenses for Medical facilities, Nursing homes, and miscellaneous costs for lifetime	Full-fledged High premium

One is care-level certification under the public LTCI. Local governments have the authority to certify care levels based on the opinions of medical doctors. Many private LTCI products link their payment conditions to those of public LTCI.

The alternative is to have independent conditions for the product.

Both conditions are commonly set for a product, requiring customers to meet at least one to be eligible for insurance.

The independent conditions for most private LTCI products are when the patient is bedridden or has dementia. Bedridden status is often defined in the policy closure as the inability of the insured to rise from bed combined with the disability to perform one or more activities of daily living (ADLs). ADLs included bathing, caring for incontinence, dressing, eating, using the toilet, and transferring (e.g., getting in or out of a bed or chair). Policyholders become eligible for benefits when the insured is bedridden and unable to perform ADLs independently.

Dementia is usually defined as a condition in which a medical doctor diagnoses an insured person as having disoriented dementia. Some LTCI products cover not only dementia but also mild cognitive impairment (MCI).

Many insurance products cover both the bedridden and dementia risks, whereas others cover only one of those with lower premiums.

[4] Paid as quasi-fixed-amount.

3 Brief History of Private LTCI in Japan

The first private LTCI insurance product in Japan was introduced in 1985 by Aflac Life Insurance Japan (a group company of the American Family Life Assurance Company in Columbus, US). The company claimed that it offered the first insurance product of its kind worldwide.[5] The product was a whole-life insurance policy with dementia care benefits without dividends (Muhaito chiho kaigo kyufukin tsuki shushinhoken). As the name suggests, it is a whole-life insurance policy, with LTCI riders covering dementia. Following this product, many life insurance companies launched whole-life policies with LTCI riders between 1985 and 1988 (Sakaguchi 1991). A few of these LTCI riders covered dementia, whereas most covered bedridden conditions.

Life company products vary in terms of the causes of claims and payment types. In contrast, companies in the non-life insurance industry launched uniform products in 1988, as discussed in Sect. 5. Although more than a quarter of a century has passed, the main features of non-life private LTCI products remain unchanged.

Private LTCI insurance products were introduced many years before 2000, when the public LTCI began. In its early stages, when an aging society was more of a prospect than reality, the market for private LTCI was limited. However, after the introduction of the public LTCI, public attention to it increased. According to a survey published by the Japan Institute of Life Insurance (JILI), the participation rate for long-term care insurance and long-term care rider policies handled by private life insurance companies, post offices, JA (agricultural cooperatives), prefectural mutual aid associations, and co-ops was 9.5%.[6] This percentage increased from 6.9% in 2004 to 28%. Despite the steady increase in participation rates, the percentage of private LTCI remains low compared with other coverage areas. The above survey showed participation rates of 73.1% for medical insurance, 42.6% for cancer insurance, and 21.7% for private annuities.

4 Typical Products #1 Fixed Amount

This section examines typical fixed-amount private LTCI products and summarizes their characteristics.

Private fixed-amount LTCI products vary in detail; therefore, for simplicity, we first outline the main patterns of significant product characteristics in Table 2 and then present them in Table 3.

Most private fixed-amount LTCI insurance products link the conditions of payment (the event that triggers the insurance benefit) to the care requirement authorization (a five-level graded system) of public LTCI. This has clear advantages for

[5] https://www.aflac.co.jp/corp/profile/development.html Retrieved 22 July 2024.

[6] "Survey on Livelihood Security 2022 <Chart V-19> Long-Term Care Insurance Participation Ratio" Japan Institute of Life Insurance.

Table 2 Significant product characteristics

	Typical case	Variations	Notes
Conditions of payment linked to public LTCI	Care Level 2 or higher (A)	Care Level 3 or higher (B) Care Level 1 or higher (C)	
Alternate conditions of payment for the bedridden	Bedridden and unable to perform two or more of the five ADLs(A)	Five or more disabled ADLs, including walking (B) Combination of six to seven ADLs (C)	Applies to people before age 65 Conditions must stay longer than 180 days
Alternate conditions of payment for dementia	Diagnosed as demented with disorientation by a medical doctor (A)	Three or more disabled ADLs in addition to the left (B) Three or more problematic behaviours in addition to the above (C)	Applies to people before age 65 Conditions must stay longer than 180 days
One-time benefit	Same amount as death benefit (mostly ¥1[7]M to ¥30M) (A)	Half of death benefit (B) Fixed amount (C) Same as the yearly annuity (D)	
Multi-annuities	Contracted yearly amount for 10 years (A)	Contracted yearly amount for five years (B) Amount linked to the Care Level for 10 years (C)	
Lifetime annuities	Contracted yearly amount (A)	Linked to the Care Level (B)	Some products set low yearly amounts, such as ¥60,000 (A*)
Additional benefits	Additional benefit or annuity for severe stage (A)	Smaller benefit or annuity for lighter stage (B)	
Death coverage	Contracted yearly amount for whole life (A)	Amount multiple (5–10) of yearly annuity (B)	
Premium waiver	Same condition as benefit or annuity (A)	Lighter stage (care level 1 or support level 2) (B) Severe disability or Same condition as benefit or annuity (C)	

the insurers. First, it provides objective evaluation criteria and relieves insurers of the burden of judging payment conditions. Second, it is simple and easy for policyholders to understand.

The downside of this payment condition is that the public LTCI provides minimal coverage for individuals younger than 65. If the insured are under 65 and suffer from the same conditions as public LTCI care levels, they will not eligible except for 16 "special diseases," such as ALS and terminal cancers. Excluding care needs for the

[7] ¥ stands for JPY or Japanese Yen.

Table 3 Products of top-selling companies

Company		Asahi		Taiyo	Tokio marine life	Gibraltar
Product #		1	2	3	4	5
Condition linked to public LTCI		B&C	C	A	A	A
Independent conditions for payment	Bedridden	–	–	A	B	C
	Dementia	–	–	A	A	A
One-time benefit		C	–	–	–	B
Multi-year annuity		–	–	–	A or B	–
Lifetime annuity		–	B	A*	A	–
Additional LTC benefits		B	–	–	–	–
Death coverage		–	–	–	–	A
Wavier of premium		B	A	–	–	–
Specific feature			(Care level + 1) times 1/6 of base annuity	Five times of regular annuity in the first year Variable interest	Choice of annuity from lifetime, 10 years and 5 years Total premium less paid annuity will be returned to the policyholder	Death coverage decreases after LTCI payment
Company		Sony	Aflac	Daiichi		Daido
Product #		6	7	8	9	10
Condition linked to public LTCI		A	A	A	A	A / C (by optional rider)
Independent conditions for payment	Bedridden	C	C	A	A	B
	Dementia	C	A	–	–	B
One-time benefit		D	C	A	–	C
Multi-year annuity		–	C	–	A or B	–
Lifetime annuity		A	–	–	A	–
Additional LTC benefits		–	B (by optional rider)	–	–	–
Death coverage		B	–	A	–	–
Wavier of Premium		C	C	A	A	A
Specific feature		Twice of regular annuity in the first year Death coverage decreases after LTCI payment		Same amount for death, LTC and three major diseases (cancer, cerebral stroke, acute myocardial infarction)	Choice of annuity from lifetime, 10 years and 5 years	One-time LTC cover only

younger population may make sense for public LTCI, given budget constraints, but not for private LTCIs.

Most private fixed-amount LTCI insurance products set alternate payment conditions for individuals aged 65 and younger to mitigate this issue. Alternative conditions include being bedridden or having dementia.

Private fixed-amount LTCI is the category of most active insurance product development. As Table 3 illustrates, coverage and payment amounts vary.

To select the best private fixed-amount LTCI, consumers must understand (1) the potential expenses of long-term care when it arises, (2) the coverage provided by public LTCI, and (3) the various products provided by the insurers.

Therefore, consumers must recognize the complexity of choosing the right private LTCI and allocate sufficient time and effort compared with other insurance products.

5 Typical Products #2 Reimbursement

Reimbursement-type private LTCI was introduced by the non-life insurance industry.

Non-life insurance companies developed the Long-term Care Expense Insurance in 1989 through an industry collaboration. The product was identical across all non-life insurance companies.

Long-term Care Expense Insurance is listed on the General Insurance Association of Japan's homepage. However, according to the author's research, all major insurance companies stopped selling new policies between 2000 and 2010 and only keep the in-force policies. Consequently, the industry's total premium income is negative at JPY 3366 Million (surrender refunds exceed premiums).

Non-life insurance does not sell replacements for Long-term Care Expense Insurance and is effectively withdrawn from the private long-term care insurance market.

The non-life insurance industry does not officially disclose their reasons for withdrawing from the private LTCI market; however, some companies announced they have stopped selling these products to simplify their product line-up.

All three major non-life insurance groups—Tokio Marine, MSIG, and Sompo (Mega Three)—have life insurance subsidiaries. All of them decided to rely on life subsidiaries in the medical insurance market, and non-life companies withdrew from the business except for special products for company employees. Therefore, it is natural to assume that they adopted an approach similar to that of private LTCIs. Life insurance subsidiaries of the Mega Three group actively market private LTCIs.

Long-term Care Expense Insurance is more complicated to manage than private fixed-amount LTCIs insurance. First, its payment conditions are not linked to the care requirement authorization (a 5-level graded system) of the public LTCI. Therefore, insurers must make independent payment decisions that may invoke customer objections or complaints.

Second, reimbursement payments are complex. Customers must provide proof of their expenditures and insurers must verify them.

Table 4 Long-term care expense insurance of non-life companies

Company		Non-life companies		
Product #		1 Regular type	2 Bedridden only	3 Dementia only
Condition linked to public LTCI		–	–	–
Independent conditions for payment	Bedridden	B	B	–
	Dementia	One or more disabled ADLs in addition to A	–	One or more disabled ADLs in addition to A
One-time benefit		Initial expenses for (1) nursing care equipment (wheelchairs, nursing care beds, portable bathtubs and heaters, electric air pads, etc.) and (2) remodeling homes		
Multi-year annuity		The same amount as below for years contracted by a rider		
Lifetime annuity		Monthly expenses for (1) medical institutions and nursing homes less public LTCI coverage and (2) amount depending on the dwelling (home, hospital, or Elderly facilities as specified by law)		
Additional LTC benefits		–		
Death coverage		–		
Wavier of premium		A		

Furthermore, the advantage of fixed-amount products is more appealing considering that the role of private LTCI is supplemental to public LTCI, which is designed to cover most caregiving costs.

Table 4 summarizes the characteristics of Long-term Care Expense Insurance in the same format as Table 3.

6 New Products

Many life insurers, including subsidiaries of the Mega Three non-life groups, have launched new products. This is the most active area in the development of insurance products.

Taiyo Life and Sompo Japan Himawari Life introduced new LTCI products in 2018 covering MCI, an early stage of dementia development. The LTCI is based on the belief that reviewing one's lifestyle, exercise habits, and appropriate treatment and prevention can help prevent dementia onset. These insurance products provide preventive benefits (which can be used to implement dementia prevention services provided by companies and medical institutions) to prevent the onset of dementia.

In 2021, Tokio Marine and Nichido Life launched the "Dementia Anshin Plan," insurance that provides preventive services to dementia. A variation in the product provides a premium refund, the amount of which is the total premium paid minus the benefits received.

Tokio Marine and Nichido Fire, one of the non-life Mega Three groups, launched a product that does not cover care expenses but addresses the financial damage that may be incurred by the insured to their family. Coverage includes compensation for search expenses when a person with dementia is missing, driving expenses for transporting a car driven by a person with dementia from the site to their home, cab fares when a person is found in a distant place, personnel expenses when a search is requested from a care provider, detective fees, and personal liability compensation.

Sompo Japan Nippon Koa, also one of the Mega Three, began selling an insurance product that covers nursing expenses borne by children caring for their parents. This product was designed to prevent children from leaving the workforce to care for their parents.

The product is a group insurance policy in which the company is the policyholder and its employees with elderly parents are the insureds.

7 Scale of the Market

According to Hoken–Kenkyusho's Statistics of Life Insurance Business in Japan 2021, the total number of new business cases of fixed-amount private LTCIs sold by life insurers was 363,271. This figure represents standalone LTCI policies and excludes LTCI riders (statistics for riders are not available.)

Compared with the 3,570,858 new policies of medical insurance, private LTCI policies remain small. JILI estimates that 9.5% of households participate in private LTCI.

8 Insurers' LTC Business

In Japan, insurance companies have become significant owners of care providers.

In December 2015, SOMPO Holdings acquired 100% shares of Watami's Nursing Care. Watami is a holding company of the izakaya (Japanese-style pub restaurants) chain and has operated a nursing home business since 2005. Sompo took over the business at a price of JPY 21.0 B and became a major player in the nursing home business. Watami's Nursing Care was renamed SOMPO Care and is now the second largest in the industry with a revenue of JPY 136 B.[8]

Before SOMPO's movement, some insurers were involved in care-providing businesses. For example, Tokio Marine owns Better Life Services, a small company that provides daily care services to local communities.

The next significant development occurred nearly a decade later in June 2024, when Nippon Life and one of its subsidiaries acquired a 99.6% stake in Nichii Holdings, the largest care provider in Japan.

---

[8] From the company's financial statements in March 2023.

According to Nikkei newspaper,[9] Nichii Holdings was held by BCJ-43, which was primarily controlled by Bain Capital Private Equity. Nippon Life acquired BCJ-43 for ¥ 210 B and renamed it Nissay Life Support. Nikkei estimated the revenue of Nichii Holdings' nursing home business to be JPY 160-170B, larger than that of SOMPO Care.

The care provider business has significant growth potential because of Japan's aging society. Currently, a major challenge is the lack of caregivers. Despite the fact that care services are physically and emotionally challenging, the compensation remains close to the minimum wage. The structural difficulty of the industry is that the primary source of revenue, public LTCI, has budget constraints with the prospect of an increasing elderly population and a declining number of young people paying premiums. Increasing caregiver salaries without damaging the public LTCI balance is difficult.

Entrants from the insurance industry could improve this situation. With abundant capital and technological resources, the insurance industry can bring business innovations to care providers to lessen their hard work and enhance their profitability.

Sompo Care has stated the following as one of its management goals:

> It is the creation of 'caregiving of the future' that makes the best use of technology and focuses on what only people can do.

Additionally, the company stated, "Our goal is predictive care… Alongside technology, we will collect and analyse data generated daily in the field to propose interventions and assistance that prevent the deterioration of conditions and support independence. We will also work to improve care management skills and provide appropriate interventions and assistance."

Nippon Life Insurance announced plans to transfer some of its acquired Nichii shares to its subsidiary, Nissay Information Technology (NIT). These three companies cooperate to promote DX in the nursing, medical, and childcare fields.

9 Summary

Private LTCI bridges the gap between the financial needs of the insured and the benefits provided by public LTCI. The first private LTCI insurance product in Japan was introduced in 1985; since then, various products have been introduced. Life insurance companies are the primary providers of private LTCI, focusing on fixed-amount products. However, reimbursement products offered by non-life insurance companies have not been successful. New products are being actively introduced, and their variations are increasing.

Choosing the right private LTCI is a complex issue, and consumers must understand the following: (1) expenses associated with long-term care; (2) coverage of

[9] https://www.nikkei.com/article/DGXZQOUB277AH0X21C23A1000000/ Retrieved 2 March 2026.

public LTCI; and (3) the various products provided by insurers. Therefore, consumers should be aware of this complexity and spend sufficient time and effort researching to make the most appropriate choice for their needs.

Appendix A

[Unauthorized translation of simulation of Care Level 3 by the Japan Institute of Life Insurance (JILI)].

What are the actual costs of long-term care? Long-term care insurance benefits vary depending on whether the patient is at home or in a facility.

There are different types of utilization plans for long-term care services, depending on the user's preference and situation. Some plans mainly use "home services" or "facility services." Depending on their income, the users pay 10% to 30% of the cost.

Which specific examples can be considered for public long-term care insurance home care services? An example of home care services is shown below:

Mr. Takada was certified as requiring three years of home care.

Mr. Takada (66 years old, male) lives with his wife Yoshiko (58 years old). A year ago, Mr. Takada suffered a stroke that left him paralyzed on the right side of his body with a slight speech impediment. He was certified as needing three years of care.

To continue caring for him at home, Yoshiko decided to use home care insurance services to live a comfortable couple life. She consulted with her care manager, informing her that her daughter who lived in a neighboring town would help on weekends. A care plan that considered Yoshiko's rest days was subsequently created.

Mr. Takada's weekly care plan

	Mon	Tue	Wed	Thu	Fri	Sat	Sun
AM	C	B	C	B	C	The daughter and Yoshiko provide care	
PM		A-1		A-2			

A-1 Home Nursing: Weekly, one hour or less per visit. A medical nurse measures blood pressure and advises on preventing the recurrence of cerebral infarction. Nurses were sent from home nursing stations.
A-2 Home Nursing: Weekly, 40 min or less per visit. A speech therapist gives training for speaking.
B: Home Nursing Care: Twice weekly, one hour or less per visit. Physical assistance is provided, such as toileting and changing clothes.

Day-care Rehabilitation: Three times weekly, 6 to 7 h per visit. Bathing assistance is included.

*Others:

Short-term residential care (short stay at health facilities for the elderly): twice a month on Sat-Sun.
Welfare equipment rental: Wheelchairs and special beds for rent.
Specific welfare equipment: Purchase of portable toilet.
House reforming: alterations to eliminate gaps between the entrance approach and inside the house.

Mr. Takada's care expenses.

I. Coverage of Public LTC and own expense (monthly amount).

Items	Unit price	Frequency	Amount
A-1 Home nursing	¥8210	5 times/month	¥41,050
A-2 Home nursing	¥2930	5 times/month	¥14,650
B Home nursing care	¥3960	9 times/month	¥35,640
C Day-care rehabilitation	¥10,140	13 times/month	¥131,820
Short stay*1	¥9430	4 days/month	¥37,720
Welfare equipment rental*2	–	monthly	¥25,000
X Total amount of service			¥285,880
Y Limit of benefit (for Care Level 3)			¥270,480
Z Amount exceeding the limit (X–Y)			¥15,400

	General case (10% co-payment)	High income (20% co-payment)	High income (30% co-payment)
Amount within Limit	¥27,048	¥54,096	¥81,144
High-cost care service benefits*3	¥0	▲¥9696	▲¥36,744
Z Amount exceeding the limit (100% co-payment)	¥15,400	¥15,400	¥15,400
Service outside of public LTC*4	¥17,150	¥17,150	¥17,150
Own expense ①	¥59,598	¥76,950	¥76,950

*1: Use of stand-alone facilities (unitary private rooms)
*2: 70% to 90% of the expense is covered depending on income.
*3: Expenses exceeding the maximum amount are refunded on application as high-cost care service benefits.

*4: Short-stay accommodation and food costs (¥2,500*4 days) and food costs of daycare (¥550*13 days) are not covered by public LTCI.

In addition, various additions and subtractions apply depending on the care provider's system and the nature of use.

II. Other expenses (initial costs) covered by public LTCI

Items	Amount
Specific welfare equipment: Purchase of portable toilet	¥40,000
House reforming: Alterations to eliminate gaps	¥160,000
Total	¥200,000

	General case (10% co-payment)	High income (20% co-payment)	High income (30% co-payment)
Own expense ②	¥20,000	¥40,000	¥60,000

Estimated own expense	General case (10% co-payment)	High income (20% co-payment)	High income (30% co-payment)
Beginning month (① + ②)	¥79,598	¥116,950	¥136,950
Regular month (①)	¥59,598	¥76,950	¥76,950

—Based on the 2021 (2021) long-term care nursing care fees.

The case of 30% co-payment is for households with a taxable income of less than JPY 3.8 million and an annual income of less than approximately JPY 7.7 million. The portion that exceeded JPY 44,400 was reimbursed.

For those aged 65 and over and with high incomes, the co-payment is 20% or 30%.

The co-payment rate for those aged 65 and over (Category 1 insured) is 10% for those with a total income of JPY 1.6 million, 20% for those with a total income of JPY 1.6 million or above, and 30% for those with a total income of JPY 2.2 million or above.

Total income was calculated after deductions for public pensions and before basic and spousal deductions.

The co-payment rate for people aged 40–64 and those exempt from resident tax was 10%, regardless of income.

Reduced co-payment system (high-cost care service)

If the monthly co-payment (10%–30% of the expense) exceeds the limit, the excess amount will be reimbursed as a high-cost care service benefit upon application.

Appendix B

Percentage of people with long-term care insurance and long-term care rider

Percentage of those who purchased private LTCI from the life insurance company, JA (agricultural cooperative), prefectural mutual, cooperative, and similar entities.

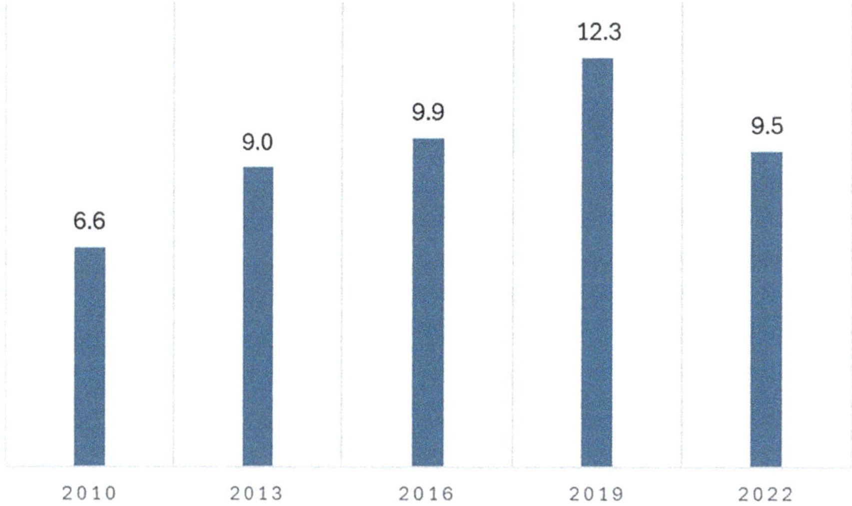

Note The age of those surveyed is 18–79 in 2022 and 18–69 before 2019. Prepared by the author based on the "Survey on Livelihood Security 2022" by Japan Institute of Life Insurance (JILI)

Long-term care insurance and long-term care rider subscription rates (by sex and age)

Percentage of those who purchased private LTCI from the life insurance company, JA (agricultural cooperative), prefectural mutual, cooperative, and similar entities. Prepared by the author based on the "Survey on Livelihood Security 2022" by Japan Institute of Life Insurance (JILI)

Bibliography

Campbell, J. C., & Ikegami, N. (2000). Long-term care insurance comes to Japan. *Health Affairs, 19*(1), 26–39.

Campbell, J. C., Ikegami, N., & Gibson, M. J. (2014). Lessons from public long-term care insurance in Germany and Japan. *Health Affairs, 29*(1), 87. https://doi.org/10.1377/hlthaff.2009.0548

Hashimoto, H., Horiguchi, H., & Matsuda, S. (2010). Micro data analysis of medical and long-term care utilization among the elderly in Japan. *International Journal of Environmental Research and Public Health, 7*(8), 3022–3037.

Iwagami, M., & Tamiya, N. (2019). The long-term care insurance system in Japan: Past, present, and future. *JMA Journal, 2*(1), 67. https://doi.org/10.31662/jmaj.2018-0015

Kongstvedt, P. R. (2020). *Health insurance and managed care* (5th Ed). Jones & Barnet Learning. ISBN: 978-1-284-15209-8

Luk, S. Ching Yuen. (2020). *Aging, long-term care insurance and healthcare finance in Asia.* Routledge ISBN: 978-1-138-06948-0

Noguchi, H., & Shimizutani, S. (2007). Nonprofit/For-profit status and earning differentials in the Japanese at-home elderly care industry: Evidence from micro-level data on home helpers and staff nurses. *Journal of the Japanese and International Economies, 21*(1), 106–120.

Shimizutani, S. (2013). The future of long-term care in Japan. RIETI Discussion Paper Series 13-E-064.

Stevenson, D., Cohen, M., Tell, E., & Burwell, B. (2010). The complementarity of public and private long-term care coverage. *Health Affairs, 29*(1), 96–101. https://doi.org/10.1377/hlthaff.2009.0920

Tamiya, N., Noguchi, H., Nishi, A., et al. (2011). Population aging and wellbeing: Lessons from Japan's long-term care insurance policy. *The Lancet, 378*(9797), 1183–1192.

References (Japanese Only, Romanized)

Kōsei Rōdōshō Rōjin Hokenkyoku [Ministry of Health, Labour and Welfare, Health and Welfare Bureau for the Elderly]. (2021). *Kaigo hoken seido no gaiyō* [Overview of the long-term care insurance system]. https://www.mhlw.go.jp/stf/seisakunitsuite/bunya/hukushi_kaigo/kaigo_koureisha/gaiyo/index.html Retrieved 23 February 2026.

Matsuyoshi, N. (2018). *Hoken gaisha ni okeru kaigo jigyō no tenkai jōkyō nado ni tsuite* [Long-term care business development by insurance companies]. *Kyōsai Sōken Repōto*, 160 (Dec. 2018). JA Kyōsai Research Institute.

RIETI Policy Discussion Paper Series, 16-P-014. Institute of Developing Economies, RIETI.

Sakaguchi, M. (1991). *Minkan kaigo hoken no tenkai to kadai* [Development and issues of private long-term care insurance]. *Osaka Shiritsu Daigaku Seikatsu Kagakubu Kiyo*, **39**.

Suzuki, W. (2016). *Kaigo hoken shikō 15-nen no keiken to tenbō: Fukushi kaiki ka, shijō genri no tettei ka?* [Fifteen years of long-term care insurance: Return to welfare or full market principles?].

Long-Term Care Insurance in South Korea

Soyoung Lim

1 Introduction

The aging of the population in Korea began relatively recently compared to other countries, but the pace of aging is unprecedentedly fast. Korea is expected to enter a super-aged society in 2025, when the proportion of the population aged 65 or older will exceed 20.3%. In addition, the proportion is expected to exceed 34.3% in 2040 (Statistics Korea 2024). The population of the elderly aged 75 or older, whose demand for care increases due to the acceleration of the aging rate and the extension of life expectancy, is also expected to continue to increase. In Korea, where one-third of the total population will be aged 65 or older, it is inevitable that there will be great concern about the direction in which long-term care insurance should proceed in the future.

Due to rapid aging in Korea, the number of elderly people who need long-term care due to old age, dementia, and stroke has increased rapidly. In addition, care by family members has weakened due to the nuclear family and the increase in women's social participation. Accordingly, the government established a public elderly care security system in the early stage of aging to relieve the people's anxiety about old age and reduce the burden of support for elderly care homes. In order to provide specialized and diverse services centered on the choice of the general public, long-term care insurance was introduced in 2008 as the fifth social insurance system.

The long-term care insurance system is a social insurance system that provides services to support physical activities and household activities for the elderly who have difficulty performing daily life activities on their own due to old age (65 years or older) or geriatric diseases, thereby reducing the burden on the elderly and their

S. Lim (✉)
Assistant Professor of Risk Management and Insurance, School of Commerce, Waseda University, Tokyo, Japan
e-mail: sylim@waseda.jp

H. Lee and G. Nicolini (eds.), *International Comparison of Long-Term Care Insurance Systems*, Contributions to Management Science,
https://doi.org/10.1007/978-981-95-7781-1_8

families (Article 1 of the Long-Term Care Insurance Act). Currently, subscription to the long-term care insurance in Korea is mandatory by law, and those who are enrolled in health insurance are automatically enrolled in long-term care insurance. Korea collects long-term care insurance premiums and health insurance premiums together, and long-term care insurance premiums are 6.55% of health insurance premiums.

This chapter examines the structure, current status, and necessity of long-term care insurance in Korea, and identifies challenges for future directions.

2 Structure of Public Long-Term Care Insurance

2.1 Management and Operation System of Long-Term Care Insurance

The Ministry of Health and Welfare oversees the long-term care insurance business and plays a role in establishing and coordinating the basic long-term care plan. The National Health Insurance Service (NHIS), as an insurer, performs the roles of managing the qualifications of long-term care insurance subscribers and their dependents and medical aid beneficiaries, imposing and collecting long-term care insurance premiums and managing finances, investigating applicants, operating the rating committee and determining long-term care grades, managing and evaluating long-term care benefits, verifying the content of long-term care benefits provided, geriatric disease prevention projects, and investigating, researching, and promoting long-term care projects. Long-term care institutions are established and designated in accordance with the Elderly Welfare Act and the Elderly Long-Term Care Insurance Act. They sign contracts with recipients and provide long-term care benefits and bill the National Health Insurance Service (NHIS) for the cost of long-term care benefits provided to recipients. Finally, local governments establish and implement detailed implementation plans according to the basic long-term care plan and carry out geriatric disease prevention projects. They also have the authority to establish and designate long-term care institutions. Figure 1 shows the management and operation system of long-term care insurance.

2.2 Scope and Application

The application target of our country's long-term care insurance system is the entire population in accordance with the principle of universalism. According to the social insurance method, the insured are the same as the insured for the national health insurance, and the recipients of long-term care benefits are "elderly people aged 65 or older or citizens under 65 who have dementia, cerebrovascular disease, Parkinson's

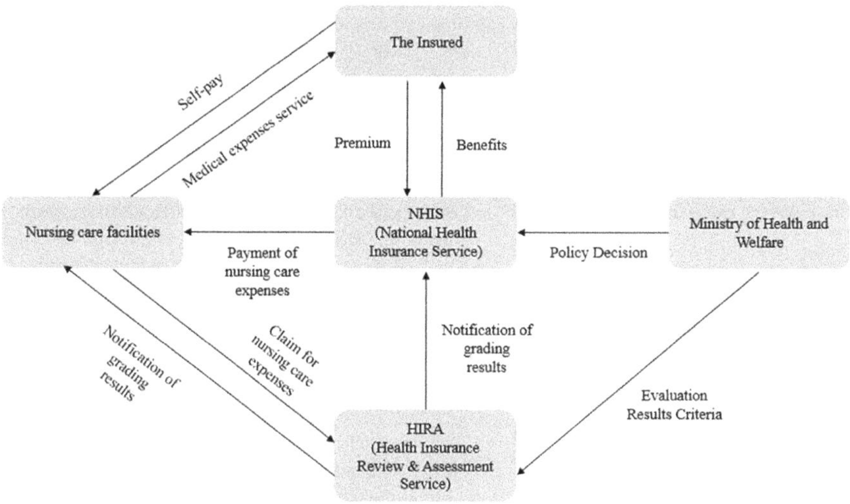

Fig. 1 Management and operation system of long-term care insurance. *Source* Written by the author with reference to NHIS

disease, or other geriatric diseases and are recognized as having difficulty performing daily life on their own for more than 6 months, and those who have been assessed according to the grade assessment criteria stipulated by the presidential decree, such as mental and physical condition and the degree of need for long-term care." As such, the long-term care insurance system is fundamentally for the elderly and can be seen as a system to prepare for the demand for elderly care services in an aging society in the future. In addition, medical aid beneficiaries under the Medical Aid Act are also included among the subjects of this Act (Park, 2022).

In other words, the system applies to all citizens, and those eligible for long-term care are senior citizens aged 65 or older and those under 65 but with geriatric diseases who have difficulty living on their own for more than 6 months and who have been graded by the Long-Term Care Grade Assessment Committee. Table 1 shows the classification of the target of the Long-Term Care Insurance System and the scope of the target.

2.3 Nursing Level

Anyone who wishes to use long-term care services at a long-term care facility must be recognized as eligible for use by the National Health Insurance Service (NHIS). Figure 2 shows the process for recognition of eligibility for long-term care insurance.

In accordance with the level of "care grade" stipulated by this recognition, the available services and upper limits of benefits in long-term care insurance are stipulated. This is a characteristic of long-term care insurance. The background to this is

Table 1 Applicable target of long-term care insurance system

Category	Scope of application
Those eligible for the Long-Term Care Insurance	All Korean citizens The insured of Long-Term Care Insurance and dependents (the same as the health insurance) + recipients of medical benefit
Those paying the contributions	Among the insured of National Health Insurance, the contributions of the employee insured and the self-employed insured are to be calculated under the contributions system of the National Health Insurance
Those applying for long-term care assessment	Those eligible for Long-Term Care Insurance elderly over 65 or those under 65 with geriatric diseases
Those assessed for long-term care	Of those who have applied for Long-Term Care Insurance and with difficulty taking care of daily life alone for more than six months assessed as needing long-term care by the Long-Term Care Grading Committee

Source Written by the author with reference to NHIS

Fig. 2 Procedure for recognition of eligibility for long-term care insurance. *Source* Written by the author

that, unlike medical care that has a treatment goal, care is characterized by targeting the irreversible thing of increasing age. In other words, it is difficult to objectively recognize the input standard for care services, and in public insurance, it is necessary to draw an upper limit when providing care (Kang et al., 2019).

Applicants are those aged 65 or older or those under 65 who have difficulty moving due to geriatric diseases. Applicants who wish to use the long-term care insurance must submit an application for long-term care recognition, a doctor's opinion if under 65, and the agent's ID if a family member applies on their behalf to the National Health Insurance Service (NHIS).

Once the application for long-term care recognition is received, the Corporation conducts an on-site investigation of the applicant according to the questionnaire and calculates the long-term care recognition score based on the investigation results. The investigation areas include physical function, cognitive function, behavioral changes, nursing treatment, and rehabilitation. If the Long-Term Care Grade Determination Committee, established at the city, county, and district level, determines that it is difficult for the individual to perform daily life activities on one's own for a period of 6 months or longer based on the investigation results—an application form, doctor's opinion, and other materials necessary for deliberation—then the applicant

Table 2 Grading criteria

Grade	Status	Long-Term Care Assessment Evaluation
Garde 1	A person with mental and physical disabilities completely dependent on the help of another person to take care of daily life	Over 95
Garde 2	A person with mental and physical disabilities in partial need of the help of another person to take care of daily life	Between 75 and 95
Garde 3	A person with mental and physical disabilities in partial need of the help of another person to take care of daily life	Between 60 and 75
Garde 4	A person with mental and physical disabilities in partial need of the help of another person to take care of daily life	Between 51 and 60
Garde 5	A person with dementia	Between 45 and 51
Long-term Care Grade Cognitive Assistant	A person with dementia	Under 45

Source Written by the author with reference to NHIS

will be deemed eligible for long-term care benefits (recipients) according to the grade determination criteria.

Korea currently divides long-term care into 5 levels and cognitive support levels. Generally, levels 1 and 2 can use facility services, while levels 3, 4, 5 and cognitive support levels can use home services. The cognitive support level is a level that has been implemented since 2018 to prevent and manage increasing dementia (elderly disease) at a national level. Table 2 shows the criteria for determining the level.

2.4 *Nursing Care Benefits and Services*

Long-term care insurance premiums are borne by long-term care insurance premiums and the state (local government), and the recipients themselves bear a portion. State support includes 20% of the estimated long-term care insurance premium and the long-term care benefit cost burden for medical aid recipients (state and local government portion) as well as the state burden of long-term care insurance premiums for civil servants and teachers. The self-payment portion is a system in which the recipient also bears a portion of the benefit cost. In the case of general recipients, they bear 20% of facility benefits and 15% of home care benefits. National basic livelihood recipients do not have to bear a self-payment portion, and medical aid recipients and those subject to reduced adaptation have their self-payment portion reduced by 50%.

In Korea, long-term care insurance benefits are divided into three categories: "home care benefits," "facility benefits," and "special cash benefits". Table 3 shows the types and contents of services for each long-term care insurance benefit.

There are four types of home care benefits: "Home-Visit Service," "Day and Night Care," "Short-term Care," and "Other in-home Benefits (Welfare Equipment)." Here, "Home-Visit Service" is the most basic service of long-term care services and includes three types: "Home-Visit Care," "Home-Visit Bath," and "Home-Visit Nursing." "Home-Visit Care" is a service where a service provider visits the recipient to provide physical activity support (excretion, eating) and daily living support (cooking, laundry, cleaning). "Home-Visit Bath" is a service where a long-term care worker visits the recipient's home in a vehicle equipped with bathing equipment to provide bathing. "Home-Visit Nursing" is a service where nurses, etc. provide health care under the direction of a doctor.

"Day and Night Care" is a service that protects the recipient at a long-term care facility for a certain period of time during the day. It is a benefit that protects the recipient at a long-term care facility for a certain period of time during the day and provides support for physical activities and education and training to maintain and improve mental and physical functions. It mainly supports moving services, bathing, meal service, nursing, functional recovery training, dementia management, etc.

Table 3 Service and benefits of long-term care insurance

Category	Service Type	Contents
Home Care Benefits	Home-Visit Care	A caregiver visits the recipient's home and helps with daily life such as bathing, using the toilet, cooking, and cleaning.
	Day and Night Care	Provides education and training to maintain and improve physical and mental functions, such as bathing, eating, and nursing, protecting recipients in long-term care facilities for a certain period of time during the day
	Short-term Care	Long-term care benefit of providing recipients with care in a facility for a certain period within the scope decided by the Ministry of Health and Welfare to support their physical activity and provide training and education in order to help them maintain and improve their mental and physical functions
	Other in-home Benefits (Welfare Equipment)	Purchase or rent equipment necessary to support the recipient's daily life and physical activities, such as wheelchairs, beds, and portable toilets, at a low price.
Facility Benefits	Admission to Aged Care Facility	Long-term admission to Aged Care Facility (excluding hospital) to provide meals, nursing care, and other conveniences necessary for daily life

Source Written by the author with reference to NHIS

"Short-term Care" protects the recipient at a long-term care facility for a period of up to 15 days per month and provides support for physical activities and education and training to maintain and improve mental and physical functions. It can be used for up to 15 days per month and up to two times per year only in cases where there is no family to care for the recipient due to family travel, hospital treatment, etc. In this case, activities such as bathing service, meal service, nursing service, and functional recovery training are supported.

"Other in-home benefits (welfare equipment)" is a service that provides various welfare equipment such as wheelchairs. Welfare equipment benefits are benefits provided to purchase or rent equipment necessary for daily life or physical activities for elderly long-term care insurance beneficiaries who have difficulty in daily life due to decline in physical and mental functions. Benefits are provided to beneficiaries of the Elderly Long-Term Care Protection Act (grades 1 to 5) through purchase or rental.

"Facility Benefits" provides both home care and facility admission services. It refers to long-term care benefits that allow service recipients (users) recognized by the National Health Insurance Corporation to stay in a facility for a long period of time to provide physical activity support, daily living support, and education and training to maintain and improve physical and mental functions. There are two types of facilities that provide Facility Benefits: "Aged Care Facility" and "Senior Congregate Housing."

There are services such as family care expenses, special care expenses, and nursing hospital care expenses as special cash benefits, but only family care expenses are actually implemented. Family care expenses are cash benefits paid in cases where long-term care facilities are severely lacking in areas such as islands and remote areas, and therefore care is inevitably received from family members. The National Health Insurance Service (NHIS) pays 150,000 won per month regardless of the level of need for long-term care services.

3 Finances of Public Long-Term Care Insurance

3.1 Financial Composition

The Long-Term Care Insurance Act for in Korea is not a pure form of social insurance but rather a hybrid system that includes government subsidies (taxes) and insurance premiums for social insurance subscribers. In other words, the cost of care benefits and operation of the long-term care insurance system is designed to be covered by government burdens (taxes), insurance premiums for subscribers, and out-of-pocket expenses. Table 4 shows the financial structure of the long-term care insurance system in Korea.

In Korea, users of the benefit service must bear a portion of the cost. The self-payment is 15% of the benefit cost for home care benefits and 20% for facility

Table 4 Financial composition of Korea's long-term care insurance system

Category	Contents
Public Sector	Tax (30%): The government provides NHIS with an amount equivalent to 20% of the expected long-term care insurance premium income for the current year within the budget
Premium	National Health Insurance Enrollees Health insurance contribution x $\frac{\textit{Long-term care insurance contribution rate}\ (0.9082\%)}{\textit{Health insurance contribution rate}\ (7.09\%)}$
Out-of-pocket expenses	Home care benefits: 15% of long-term care benefits costs Facility Benefits: 20% of long-term care benefits costs

Source Written by the author with reference to NHIS

benefits. Those entitled to benefits under the National Basic Livelihood Security Act are exempt from the self-payment. In addition, a system for reducing the recipient's burden (40–60% of the self-payment) is in operation for low-income earners and those whose income has decreased due to natural disasters.

3.2 *Long-Term Care Insurance Premium Rates and National Support*

Since 2013, as the expenditure growth rate has been faster than the insurance premium growth rate, the long-term care insurance premium rate began to increase from 6.55% in 2017 to 7.38% in 2018, and will approximately double in five years to 12.27% in 2022. Since long-term care insurance premiums are linked to health insurance premium rates, they are automatically increased when health insurance premium rates increase, so insurance premium income naturally increases along with the annual increase in health insurance premium rates (Lee et al., 2022). However, due to the increase in long-term care insurance expenditures, the long-term care insurance premium rate is also increasing every year at a greater rate than the increase in health insurance premium rates. Table 5 below shows the changes in health insurance premium rates and long-term care insurance premium rates from 2008 to 2022.

The long-term care insurance premium rate can be increased by revising the Enforcement Decree of the Long-Term Care Insurance Act after deliberation by the Long-Term Care Committee. The procedure for increasing the long-term care insurance premium rate is similar to the procedure for increasing the health insurance premium rate, as it is determined by presidential decree after deliberation by the Health Insurance Policy Deliberation Committee (Nam, 2024). However, unlike the procedure for increasing the health insurance premium rate, which is set by law to determine the health insurance premium rate at an upper limit of 8%, there is no upper limit range for the long-term care insurance premium rate. Unlike medical services used by all age groups, services used by the elderly who are recognized as

Table 5 Changes in national health insurance premium rates and long-term care insurance premium rates

Year	National Health Insurance Premium Rate	Long-Term Care Insurance Premium Rate
2008	5.08	4.05
2009	5.08	4.78
2010	5.33	6.55
2011	5.64	6.55
2012	5.80	6.55
2013	5.89	6.55
2014	5.99	6.55
2015	6.07	6.55
2016	6.12	6.55
2017	6.12	6.55
2018	6.24	7.38
2019	6.46	8.51
2020	6.67	10.25
2021	6.86	11.52
2022	6.99	12.27

Source Ministry of Health and Welfare

needing care and nursing are borne by all age groups, so it can be seen that there is also an issue of intergenerational equity.

On the other hand, since national treasury support is calculated based on the expected insurance premium income, the national treasury support rate has usually been below 20% after the insurance premium income has been confirmed, but the proportion of national treasury support compared to post-insurance premium income has also increased from 18% in 2019 to approximately 20% in 2020, up to the statutory rate. In addition to the statutory national treasury support, the long-term care costs of medical aid recipients and the management and operation costs of long-term care insurance are to be shared by the state and local governments, but as the long-term care insurance benefit costs of medical aid recipients increase, the medical aid burden is also rapidly increasing.

3.3 Financial Trends of Long-Term Care Insurance

The fiscal balance of long-term care insurance continues to deteriorate as the increase in the demand for care has been accompanied by a rapid increase in the cost of benefits, which has exceeded the level of premium increases. Table 6 shows the financial trend of long-term care insurance.

Table 6 Long-term care insurance financing trends (Unit: Billion KRW, %)

Category		2008	2010	2012	2014	2016	2018	2020
Revenue	Premium	4,770	18,316	23,697	27,047	30,916	39,245	63,568
	Public funding	1,207	3,323	4,152	5,033	5,525	7,107	12,414
	Health care co-payments	2,661	9,704	7,018	8,025	9,761	14,347	19,463
	Etc.	51	434	750	1,381	1,095	833	692
	Total (A)	8,690	28,777	35,614	41,486	47,297	61,533	96,138
Costs	Insurance benefit expenses	4,314	24,153	27,328	35,984	44,204	64,652	90,858
	Administrative and operating expenses	1,079	1,441	1,663	1,977	2,164	2,502	3,039
	Etc.	156	297	382	536	858	855	798
	Total (B)	5,549	25,891	29,373	38,497	47,227	68,008	94,695
Gross Profit Ratio (B/A) (%)		64	90	83	93	100	111	99
Accumulated reserves		230	3,082	11,258	12,855	17,038	17,685	4,136

Source National Health Insurance Service (NHIS)

The total balance sheet ratio (cost/revenue) of long-term care insurance finances was 63.9% when it was introduced in 2008, but it began to show a net deficit of 108.7% in 2017, and the deficit finances increased to 109.1% in 2019. Although the total balance sheet ratio improved to 98.5% in 2020, this is due to the increase in health insurance premium rates and long-term care insurance premium rates, the use of accumulated reserves, and the expansion of national treasury support, so there is still uncertainty about the sustainability of future finances.

4 Facilities for Public Long-Term Care Insurance

4.1 Status of Long-Term Care Facilities

Table 7 shows the status of long-term care facilities by facility benefits and home care benefits.

Table 8 shows the status of the number of institutions by type of home care benefit from 2020 to 2024. This is the status of each type of benefit provided by home care benefit institutions.

Table 7 Number of institutions of long-term care insurance

Year	Total	Number of Institutions Providing Facility Benefits	Number of Institutions Providing Home Care Benefits
2020	25,383 (100%)	5,762 (22.7%)	19,621 (77.3%)
2021	26,547 (100%)	5,988 (22.60%)	20,559 (77.40%)
2022	27,484 (100%)	6,150 (22.40%)	21,334 (77.60%)
2023	28,366 (100%)	6,269 (22.10%)	22,097 (77.90%)
2024	28,985 (100%)	6,310 (21.80%)	22,675 (78.20%)

Source National Health Insurance Service (NHIS)

Table 8 Number of institutions providing home care benefits by type

Year	Total	Home-Visit Care	Home-Visit Bath	Home-Visit Nursing	Day and Night Care	Short-term Care	Welfare Equipment
2020	33,948 (100%)	15,412 (45.40%)	11,086 (32.70%)	774 (2.30%)	4,587 (13.50%)	148 (0.40%)	1,941 (5.70%)
2021	35,444 (100%)	16,214 (45.70%)	11,506 (32.50%)	801 (2.30%)	4,832 (13.60%)	137 (0.40%)	1,954 (5.50%)
2022	36,660 (100%)	16,850 (46.00%)	11,789 (32.20%)	828 (2.30%)	5,090 (13.80%)	126 (0.30%)	1,977 (5.40%)
2023	37,518 (100%)	17,475 (46.60%)	11,799 (31.40%)	830 (2.20%)	5,235 (14.00%)	108 (0.30%)	2,071 (5.50%)
2024	38,306 (100%)	17,969 (46.90%)	11,905 (31.10%)	838 (2.20%)	5,395 (14.10%)	100 (0.20%)	2,099 (5.50%)

Source National Health Insurance Service (NHIS)

4.2 *Home Care Provider*

Long-term care facilities are institutions that have the facilities and personnel necessary for long-term care, as prescribed by the Ministry of Health and Welfare Ordinance, and are designated by the mayor of the city, province, county, or district with jurisdiction. Home care benefit providers are institutions that provide benefits such as Home-Visit Care, Home-Visit Nursing, and welfare equipment.

Table 9 Facility benefits provider type

	Aged Care Facility	Senior Congregate Housing
Size	10 or more residents	More than five residents or less than nine residents
Facility	· Medical and nurses' stations · Bedrooms, restrooms, sinks, and baths · Physical (occupational) therapy rooms, program rooms · Dining and kitchen areas, emergency preparedness facilities · Dementia rooms	· Bedroom, toilet, and sink (bath) room · Physical (occupational) therapy or program rooms · Dining rooms and kitchens
	· Separate male and female rooms for co-ed facilities · No more than four people per dormitory bedroom	
Manpower	· Physician or nurse (nurse practitioner): one for every 25 residents (one for 10 or fewer residents) · One physical (occupational) therapist · Nursing assistant: one for every 2.5 residents	· One of a physician, nurse (nurse practitioner), or physical (occupational) therapist · Nurse aide: One for every three residents

Source Written by the author with reference to NHIS

4.3 Facility Benefits Provider

There are two types of facilities that provide Facility Benefits: "Aged Care Facility" and "Senior Congregate Housing." The difference between the two facilities is their size. Aged Care Facility refers to a facility with a capacity of 10 or more people, while Senior Congregate Housing refers to a facility with a capacity of five to nine people. In addition, Aged Care Facility is also divided into facilities with a capacity of 30 or more people and facilities with a capacity of 10 to 29 people. Aged Care Facility provides both daily living support and physical activity support regardless of its size. Table 9 shows a comparison of the types of Facility Benefits providers.

4.4 Aged Care Facility Admission Target

The target of admission to the Aged Care Facility varies depending on the care level. First, for grades 1–2, those with a care recognition score of 75 or higher are eligible. Second, for grades 3–4, those who wish to enter the facility are eligible if the grade assessment committee determines that at least one of the following reasons applies: difficulty in receiving care from family members of the same household; poor living conditions making facility admission inevitable; and mental and physical conditions making it impossible to use home care benefits. Third, for grade 5, those who wish to enter the facility are eligible if the grade assessment committee determines that at least one of the following reasons applies and the dementia-related documents are judged to have a certain score or higher: difficulty in receiving care from family members of the same household; and poor living conditions making facility admission inevitable.

5 Conclusion

Due to the acceleration of the aging rate and the extension of life expectancy, the elderly population aged 75 or older, whose demand for care is increasing, is also expected to continue to increase. Currently, Korea is about to enter a super-aged society as the baby boomer generation enters old age, and various changes in the care environment are expected due to the improvement of the service expectations of the new elderly generation. In addition, considering the high prevalence of dementia in Korea, the demand and financial expenditures for the elderly care sector, including long-term care insurance, are expected to continue to increase in the future.

The pace of long-term care insurance benefit expenditures, which shows an annual growth rate of 10–20% or more, is expected to accelerate in the future considering factors such as the increase in the elderly population, the increase in demand for care, and the increase in fees to improve service quality. Accordingly, the need to expand government support by 20% of insurance premiums is expected to exist in the future, and the need to improve the sustainability of long-term care insurance is growing.

References

Kang, E.-N., Lee, Y.-G., Lim, J.-M., Joo, B.-H., & Bae, H.-W. (2019). *2019 Long-term care survey*. Ministry of Health and Welfare, Korea Institute for Health and Social Affairs.

Lee, Y.-K., Lee, S.-H., Kang, E.-N., Kim, S.-J., Nam-Gung, E.-H., Choi, Y.-J. (2022). 2022 Long-Term Care Survey. Sejong: Ministry of Health and Welfare, Korea Institute for Health and Social Affairs.

Nam, H.-J. (2024). The role and policy direction of long-term care insurance for the elderly in a super-aging society. Health and Welfare Forum.

National Health Insurance Corporation, Long-term Care Insurance Statistical Yearbook.

Park, K.-D. (2022). Comparative study on long-term care insurance in Korea and Japan-Focused on local government. *Journal of Local Administration, 19*(2), 75–95.

Statistics Korea. (2024). Future population projections, 2072, major population indicators (sex ratio, population growth rate, population structure, dependency ratio, etc.) nationwide. https://kosis.kr/statHtml/statHtml.do?orgId=101&tblId=DT_1BPA002&conn_path=I2

The Roles of the Private Long-Term Care Market—Focusing on Comparison of Japan and Korea

Seungho Hwang

1 Introduction

1.1 Aging Population

According to the standards set by the UN, when the proportion of elderly people aged 65 and over in the total population reaches 7%, it is called an aging society, and when it reaches 14% and 20%, it is called an aged society and a super-aging society. Table 1 shows that Japan became an aging society in 1970 and a super-aged society in 2005, and the entire baby boomer generation (Dankai-sedai: born in 1947–1949) in 2025 will be in the late stages of aging. South Korea entered an aging society 30 years later than Japan, but the population of baby boomers (born in 1955–1963) began to become the elderly, over the age of 65, in 2021 and is expected to peak at 52% of the elderly population in 2030. A comparison of the current aging of Japan and South Korea can be summarized as shown in the Table 1.

Figure 1 shows that the aging rate in South Korea has gradually increased, rising to 15.6% in 2020, and although the aging rate in South Korea is still at a lower level than Japan's 28.9%, the declining birthrate and aging population are faster than in Japan.

Over the past 10 years, the number of people aged 65 and over in South Korea has increased by an average of 4.2% per year, and the rate of aging has been twice as fast as that of Japan (2.1%). The aging rate of South Korea is expected to surpass Japan's in 2045, with 37.3% compared to 36.8% as in the figure.

S. Hwang (✉)
Graduate School of Commerce, Waseda University, Tokyo, Japan
e-mail: seunghohwang@akane.waseda.jp

H. Lee and G. Nicolini (eds.), *International Comparison of Long-Term Care Insurance Systems*, Contributions to Management Science,
https://doi.org/10.1007/978-981-95-7781-1_9

Table 1 Comparison of Japan and South Korea aging population

Items	Japan	South Korea	Gap
Population	124.35 million (Oct. 2023)	51.73 million (Dec. 2013)	n/a
Older than age 65	36.23 million (29.1%, Oct. 2023)	9.44 million (18.2%, Dec.2013)	n/a
Aging society	1970 (7.1%)	2000 (7.2%)	30 years
Aged society	1994 (14.1%)	2017 (14.2%)	23 years
Super-aging society	2005 (20.1%)	2026 (21.1%)	21 years

Source Statistics Bureau, Ministry of Internal Affairs and Communications of Japan (e-STAT)[1] and Korean Statistical Information Service (KOSIS)[2]

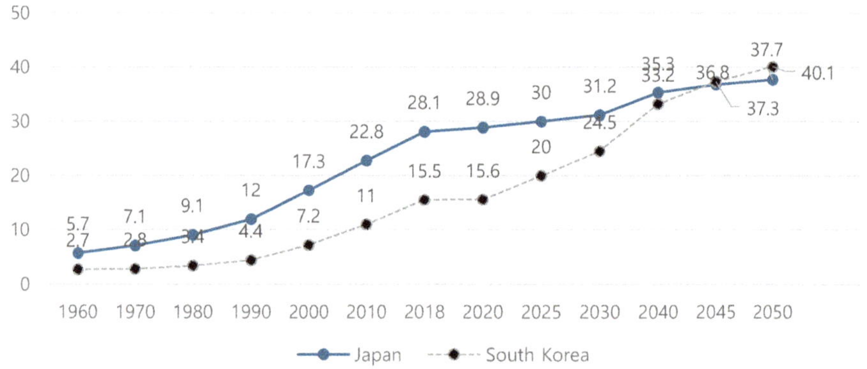

Fig. 1 Trend in the aging rate in Japan and South Korea. *Source* From e-STAT and KOSIS website

1.2 Comparison of Public LTC Insurance in Japan and South Korea

The long-term care (LTC) insurance system in Japan was introduced in 2000, modeled on the German LTC insurance system because of the need to control the problem of elderly care due to the rapid increase in life expectancy, the need to eliminate social hospitalization, and the increase in medical expenses for the elderly. In 2008, South Korea started a LTC insurance system for the elderly with reference to Japan's LTC insurance system. A comparison of these systems is summarized in Table 2.

The above table shows that Japan has been active in community-based management of each municipality, operation by care managers, and the entry of private corporations from the beginning, while South Korea has achieved good results in terms of supply through nationwide management by the National Health Insurance

[1] Homepage: https://www.stat.go.jp/, https://www.e-stat.go.jp/en.

[2] Homepage: https://kosis.kr.

Table 2 Public LTC insurance systems in Japan and South Korea

Items	Japan	South Korea
Eligibility	• Category 1st insured: over 65: 35.88 million (Jan. 2024) • Category 2nd insured: 40–64: 41.93 million people (2019)	• Residents of Korea (no age limit) • 52.97 million people with medical coverage, 9.86 million people aged 65 and over (2023)
Number of beneficiaries	• 1st insured: 6.94 million (18.3%) (2024) • 2nd insured: 130,000 (0.3%) • 5.6% of the total population, 19.1% of those aged 65 and over (total papulation based on Oct. 2023)	• Approx. 1.10 million (as of June 2023) • 2.1% of the total population • 11.1% of those aged 65 and over
Benefit conditions	• Those who have been certified as requiring LTC or support (in principle, they are 65 years old or older, but those aged 40–64 who have been certified as requiring LTC or support due to a specific disease can also receive benefits)	• Persons who have been certified for LTC (those aged 65 years or older, but also those under the age of 65 who have diseases and have been certified for LTC)
Financial resources	• 1st insured premium: 23% • 2nd insured premium: 27% • Public Expenses (National and Local Governments): 50%	• Premium: 67.1% • Government Treasury Assistance: 19.6% (in principle: 20%) • Others: 13.3%
How to collect insurance premiums	• 1st insured: Collected from pension • 2nd insured: Collected from medical insurance premiums	• Collected in conjunction with health insurance premiums
Insurance rates	• 1st insured: 6,225 yen (9th term from 2024) • 2nd insured: 6,276 yen • Health Insurance Association: 1.73% of income • Employees are split evenly with the employer	• The rate of medical care in the public × 12.95% • 0.91% of income (2024) • * Employees are split evenly with the employer
Type of benefit	• Benefit in kind	• Primarily benefit in kind
Maximum benefit amount	• Upper limit according to the degree of care required	• There is an upper limit according to the LTC grade
Self-payment	• Flat-rate contribution (10%, but 20% or 30% for high-income, 100% self-payment for exceeding the maximum amount) * There is an upper limit on the amount of self-payment according to income	• Fixed-rate contribution (15% for home benefits, 20% for facility benefits. 100% self-payment for exceeding the maximum amount)
Where to apply	• Municipality	• National Health Insurance Service

(continued)

Table 2 (continued)

Items	Japan	South Korea
Certification standards	• Municipal Care Accreditation Review Board	• National Health Insurance Service
Accreditation criteria	• In need of nursing and assistant Division (seven divisions) • *Assistance required two categories + nursing care required five categories	• LTC grade (six categories) • *5 level + dementia support level
Care management	• The care manager creates a care plan • (Users can also create their own care plans)	• The National Health Insurance Service prepares a standard LTC usage plan

Source Federation of Health Insurance Societies (2020)

Service and the overcrowding of small facilities by individuals but has brought problems such as cost fraud and low quality of services. There is a need to strengthen facility supervision and the entry of large private corporations.

The Ministry of Health, Labor and Welfare (MHLW) of Japan revised its LTC system for the eighth phase in 2021 and is focusing on supporting the construction of comprehensive support systems for municipalities that respond to the increasingly complex and complex support needs of local residents and promoting the development of medical and nursing care data infrastructure.

2 Limitations of Public LTC Insurance

2.1 Limitations of Public LTC Insurance in Japan

2.1.1 Rapid Increase of People Certified as Requiring LTC

In the third revision of LTC insurance, from 2006, a regional comprehensive support center was established, and benefits for those in need of support were made into LTC preventive benefits, a regional comprehensive support center was established, and LTC preventive care management was implemented by the regional comprehensive support center, LTC prevention business. Policies that emphasize LTC prevention, such as the implementation of community support projects such as comprehensive support projects, have been added. Using the number of LTC insurance beneficiaries as a criterion for certified persons, the number of people in need of LTC (in need of support) increased from 2.18 million in 2000 at the time of introduction to 6.79 million in January 2021, an increase of more than three times over this 20-year period as shown in the Fig. 2.

The number of people certified as requiring long-term care and support as of the end of February 2024 is estimated to be 7.07 million. Based on the trend of the above

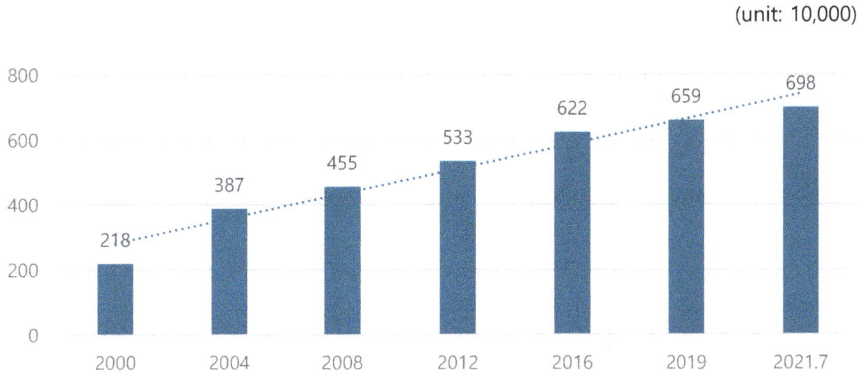

Fig. 2 Trend in the number of people certified as requiring LTC in Japan (unit: 10,000). *Source* Summary from the LTC Business Status Report by MHLW

figure, MHLW estimated that the number of people certified as requiring long-term care will peak around 2040 at 9.88 million.

Some of the preventive care services used by people with moderate to mild need of LTC and dementia have been transferred to municipalities, and both the number of users and LTC insurance premiums are decreasing. The number of people aged 65 and over is expected to reach 36.77 million in 2025 and peak in 2042 (39.35 million). In particular, it is estimated that by 2025, all the "baby boomers" will be 75 years old or older, and the population of the elderly will reach 21.8 million. In addition, the proportion of the total population aged 75 and over is expected to increase and exceed 25% by 2055.

2.1.2 Limitations of LTC Insurance Finances

According to a survey by MHLW, the total cost of LTC insurance in 2019 was 10,509.5 billion yen, an increase of 3.5% from the previous year, and by service, LTC services were 10.2457 trillion yen and preventive care services were 263.8 billion yen. According to the Ministry of Finance (MOF), in the 2021 budget, the cost of LTC insurance will be about 12.8 trillion yen (total cost basis[3]: 13.4 trillion yen). It is expected that the burden of public expenses—6.5 trillion yen (50.2%), 2nd category premium: 2.9 trillion yen (22.4%), the 1st category premium: 2.6 trillion yen (20.1%), self-payment burden: 0.9 trillion yen (7.2%)—will increase, and in 2025, the monthly premium for the 1st category will have to be raised from an average of about 5,900 yen in 2018 to about 7,200 yen in 2025 and about 9,200 yen in 2040.

[3] From 2006, the total cost of LTC insurance will be budgeted by adding the cost of community support projects. Regional support project expenses increased from 0.1 trillion yen in 2006 to 0.6 billion yen in 2021.

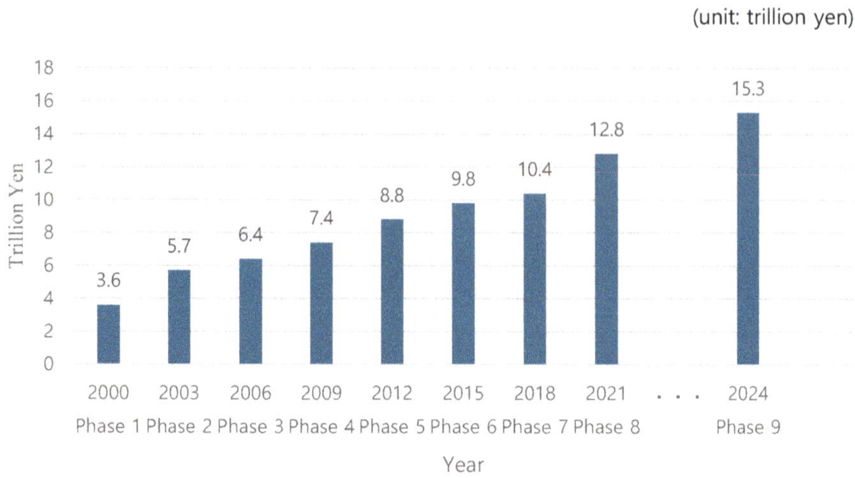

Fig. 3 Trend in LTC insurance benefits in Japan (unit: trillion yen). *Source* MOF (2021)

The benefits of LTC insurance are also expected to rise to 15.3 trillion yen in 2025 as per the Fig. 3 (MOF 2021).

As shown in the figure above, the 9th phase will begin in 2024. Japan formulates a LTC insurance business plan with one three-year term (one five-year term until fiscal year 2005) and reviews it every three years. Insurance premiums are set every three years to maintain fiscal balance throughout the three-year period based on the estimated amount of service costs stipulated in the business plan, and LTC insurance premiums are expected to rise due to the progress of the aging population.

2.2 *Limitations of Public LTC Insurance in South Korea*

2.2.1 Rapid Increase of Certified People and LTC Micro-Facilities

Since 2018, the South Korean government has been offering a "certified support grade" for elderly people with mild dementia symptoms and offers programs to slow the progression of dementia. As of June 2020, there were 8.28 million elderly people (15.7% aging rate) and 1.63 million people aged 80 and over (3.1% of the total population), but since the aging rate is faster than Japan, the aging rate of South Korea is expected to be the highest in the world after 2050. The number of people eligible for LTC insurance benefits for the elderly (65 and over) was 772,000 in 2019, an increase of 15.1% from the previous year (9.6% of health insurance subscribers aged 65 years and older). The increase in the elderly (65 and over) population and the transition of the number of people certified for long-term care insurance for the elderly are shown in the Fig. 4.

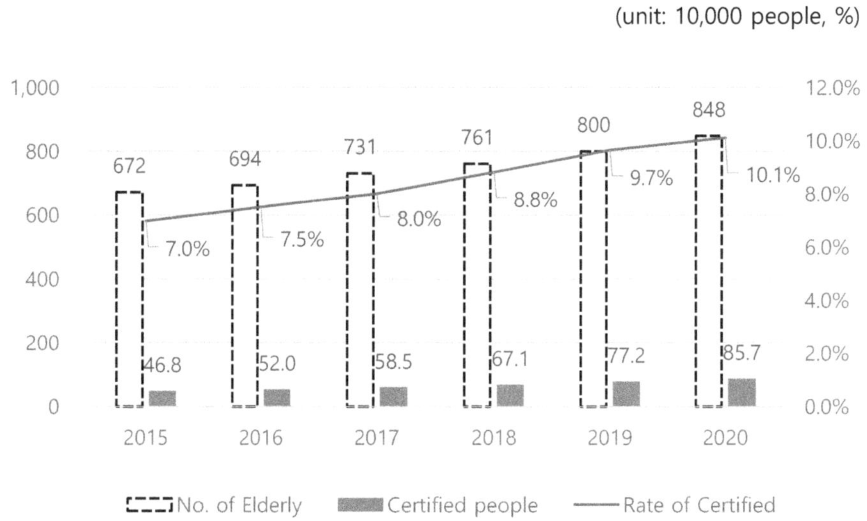

Fig. 4 Trend of people certified as requiring LTC in South Korea (unit: 10,000 people, %). *Source* NHIS (2021), Statistical annual report

Based on the trend in the figure above, the number of people receiving LTC benefits in 2022 was 1.01 million, exceeding 1 million for the first time. The LTC insurance premium rate for 2024 has been determined to be 0.9182% of income. In 2024, the average monthly premium per subscriber household was expected to be 16,860 won. In 2024, LTC fees were expected to increase by an average of 2.92%. With the increase in life expectancy and the increase in the number of elderly people in later life, the demand for LTC services is expected to continue to increase, and the number of people certified for LTC care is expected to increase to about 1.45 million by 2027 (NHIS 2023).

According to National Health Insurance Service (NHIS) of South Korea, the number of designated LTC institutions is on the rise, in home care services, with an increase of 21.5% and a 4.2% increase in the number of nursing facilities in 2019. The trend of the number of home service facilities can be seen in the Fig. 5.

However, the supply is falling short of the increase in demand for LTC. By 2022, there was an anticipated shortage of 875 nursing homes and 515 day and night shelters. In 2019, 72.7% of nursing homes were sole proprietors, 25.2% were corporations, and 2.1% were public pension facilities, with 69% of small businesses with fewer than 30 employees. It is also a severe problem that the operation of such a small facility, as well as the inadequate safety management of the facility, frequently results in cases of accounting fraud by individual proprietors. Although the number of facilities has increased rapidly, the low quality of services is also an issue that needs to be improved, and it is necessary to expand the number of designated institutions centered on corporations.

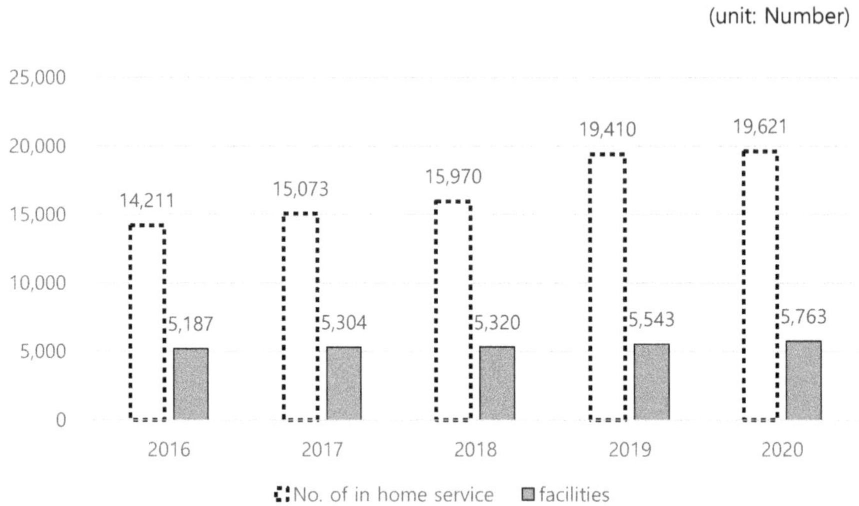

Fig. 5 Trend of LTC facilities for the elderly in South Korea (unit: Number). *Source* NHIS (2021), Statistical annual report

Such a rapid aging of the population has exposed the limitations of the current public LTC insurance system, and it has become necessary to take a new policy for insurance companies and major private corporations to enter the LTC market.

2.2.2 Limitations of LTC Insurance Finances

The benefits of LTC insurance increased from 458.5 billion won in 2008 to 9.5 trillion won in 2020, increasing at an average annual rate of 29.4%, and the growth of expenditure accelerated, and since 2016, the fiscal has turned into the balance deficit, with the cumulative reserve in 2020 at 400 billion won and the government is currently considering whether to increase premiums or finance with tax.

The accumulated reserve fund is also decreasing, which is red financially. In addition to forecasting the demand for LTC insurance for the elderly and examining the ability to continue to provide benefits based on this, long-term care insurance for the elderly as social insurance will promote health promotion and stable living for the elderly in cooperation with private insurance. As a social insurance system, the function of long-term care insurance will be established and jointly examine the possibility of sharing roles with private insurance. In light of the aging trend and the expansion of welfare finances, there is a need for cooperation between the public and private sectors.

In 2008, premium income from geriatric care insurance was 372.3 billion won, but in 2020 it was 6.5 trillion won, an increase of about 17 times. In 2008, the government support was 118.1 billion won, but by 2020 it was 1.2 trillion won, a ten-time increase.

The government support is 20% of the premium income stipulated by law, but the government must comply with the statutory standards for state support.

The self-payment ratio for using LTC services in Japan was set at 10% for both home care and facilities while in South Korea this was 15% for home care and 20% for facility services. In this way, South Korea has set a higher self-payment rate for service use than Japan. It is thought to be based on the Korean government's fiscal management policy of "minimizing of fiscal expenditures" (Kim 2021a, b).

South Korea's LTC insurance budget was only 0.31% of GDP in 2017, compared to Japan's total LTC insurance cost of 1.76% of GDP in 2017. The South Korean government's low fiscal expenditure is likely to be a factor in lowering the wages and treatment levels of workers working in nursing care facilities for the elderly (KIM 2020a, b).

To improve the finances of the LTC insurance system and to improve the fiscal procurement system are required to combine social insurance and taxation. It is necessary to improve health insurance premiums and self-payment rates, and to comply with state support. In particular, the management of fraudulent claims by micro-companies is of note; in 2015, 774 nursing homes were caught claiming fraudulent LTC benefits. There is an urgent need for a multifaceted review of the problems such as improving the quality of low-wage care workers and services, the state of financing, the lack and distortion of information, and the lack of ties between local governments and NHIS (Ahn and Park 2019).

3 Development of the Private LTC Market

3.1 Development of the Private LTC Market in Japan

In 2000, LTC insurance for the elderly was introduced. The private LTC business subsequently expanded from the actual 3.6 trillion yen; according to industry trends, the performance of the LTC industry in Japan in 2020 was 1,033.8 billion yen, with a growth rate of 6.8% and a profit margin of 2.9%.

This is a reorganization from initially small to now centered on large operators, with growth prospects due to increased qualitative and quantitative demand, increased care for the elderly, a decrease in family services, and an increase in demand for social services. It is estimated that there will be a shortage of 370,000 nursing care workers in 2025 as all the "baby boomers" will be in the late elderly category; the government enforced a new status of residence, "Specified Skilled Worker," from April 2019, while the LTC industry has begun to accept foreign human resources.

Since the enactment of the LTC Insurance Act in 2000, the number of entrants from other industries has increased, and competition has intensified due to acquisitions and the launch of new businesses. Mitsubishi Residences, Nomura Real Estate Holdings, Mitsui Fudosan Residential, and Asahi Kasei have also entered the LTC industry and are working to capture demand for housing such as rental housing for seniors and

Table 3 LTC industry sales ranking (2020) in Japan (Unit: 100 million yen, %)

Rank	Company name	Sales	Share (%)
1	Nichii Gakukan	1,537	14.9
2	Sompo holdings	1,384	13.4
3	Benesse HD	1,238	12
4	Tsukui	932	9
5	SECOM	716	6.9
6	Graduate HD	607	5.9
7	Unimat retirement	585	5.7
8	Cent care HD	459	4.4
9	Solast	447	4.3
10	Care 21	339	3.3

Source Summary from Industry Trends website

housing for the elderly with services. In 2020, Mitsubishi Corporation and ALSOK formed a capital and business alliance in the nursing care business. HITOWA HD, an LTC facility company, has started a travel business for residents of nursing care facilities, has also started a "VR grave visit" service using VR technology, and is embarking on earning revenue outside of insurance. In Japan, where the population is aging, demand in the nursing care industry is expected to expand. It is expected that large companies will continue to acquire small and medium-sized enterprises in the future.

The Table 3 shows the top 10 listed companies in terms of consolidated sales in the nursing care business in the fiscal year ending in March 2020. Companies in the LTC industry provide not only nursing care services but also housekeeping services, indicating that they are familiar with the needs of users.

In February 2024, the sales ranking of the LTC industry was as follows: 1st, Nichii Gakukan has sales of 267.3 billion yen; 2nd, Sompo Holdings has sales of 136.6 billion yen; while Nichii Gakukan showed sales with a 1.7-times increase in a four-year period. Sales in the LTC industry reached the 11 trillion-yen level in 2023, an increase of 250.8 billion yen from the previous year. Nursing care services alone exceeded 10 trillion yen, and preventive care services increased by 3.4% to 279.7 billion yen.

The examples of Japan's large-scale LTC business can be summarized as shown in the Table 4.

As shown in the Table 4, the current status of the LTC business of major companies is summarized as follows. Nichii Gakukan was a long-established company in the nursing care industry founded in 1968 before it was delisted in November 2020 through MBO (management buyout). Tsukui, ranked fourth, also accepted a takeover by an investment fund and delisted in June 2021. Nichii Gakukan's inheritance tax measures and Tsukui's management concerns during the Corona disaster are said to be the reasons for accepting the acquisition and delisting. Benesse Care is also involved in the operation of nursery schools and after-school clubs, and the sales

Table 4 Cases of major corporation's LTC business in Japan

Company	Business
Nichii Gakukan[4]	• Started a medical-related business in 1968 • Started an LTC business centered on home care in 1996 • Has expanded its business domains in line with the progress of globalization, including medical and nursing care, healthcare business, childcare, education, and therapy business, and is developing diversified businesses • Total sales were 300 billion yen, while LTC-related sales accounted for 150 million yen, and the LTC industry ranked first with a market share of 14.9% in 2020; the LTC operating profit margin has reached 10.3% • With approximately 1,800 locations in 47 prefectures nationwide, the company provides "total LTC services" ranging from home care to residential care services
HITOWA holdings Co., Ltd[5]	• A company that operates LTC, childcare, and education both inside and outside the group • Developing a "comprehensive life support service" that supports all families and their lives throughout their lives, from childhood to old age, and continues to provide services that support all families and their lives
Benesse holdings[6]	• Operating its business on five axes, including nursing care and childcare, which is the second pillar of its business, Berlitz language education, and others
Solast[7]	• Solast is committed to improving the skills and career support of all those involved in "medical administration," "nursing care services," and "childcare services," as well as these services • SOLAST is a pioneer in medical office work, founded as Japan's first medical office educational institution. Since then, the company has expanded its business domains to include medical-related contract services, nursing care services, and childcare services, and has approximately 30,000 employees nationwide engaged in the fields of medical care, nursing care, and childcare
Anbis holdings Co., Ltd[8]	• Mainly operating businesses related to the LTC business, and is engaged in the welfare services for persons with disabilities (in-home care and others), a consulting business, and other ancillary businesses

(continued)

[4] Nichii Gakukan website: https://www.nichiigakkan.co.jp/.

[5] HITOWA Holdings website: https://www.hitowa.com/.

[6] Benesse Holdings website: https://www.benesse-hd.co.jp/ja/index.html.

[7] Solast website: https://www.solasto.co.jp/.

[8] Anvis Holdings Co., Ltd. Website: https://www.amvis.com/company/profile/.

Table 4 (continued)

Company	Business
Tsukui[9]	• Since the launch of welfare services in 1983 has been focusing on securing and training personnel and has been working to strengthen its service network through the initiative-taking opening of offices • More than 21,200 employees and the total number of offices for all businesses reached 700 in March 2020
SECOM[10]	• In 1983, SECOM aimed to build a "social system industry," focusing on the security business, disaster prevention business, medical business, insurance business, and geospatial information service business • SECOM Medical System, engaged in BPO and ICT businesses, is engaged in the medical business and provides medical services ranging from "medical care" to "nursing care" and "health and prevention" to protect the health of loved ones
ALSOK nursing care[11]	• ALSOK strives to "review and improve the content of services" on a daily basis, focuses on "securing and developing human resources who will be responsible for high-quality nursing care services," and strengthens nursing care capabilities through "digitalization that leads to service sophistication and operational efficiency" and "multidisciplinary collaboration that contributes to community-based comprehensive care." • In 2020, the company was working to become a "high-quality nursing care service base that coexists with the community." • Total sales of 469.9 billion yen, of which sales in the nursing care business were 4.0 billion yen and 8.6% of total

Source Summary from website of each company

figures for most nursing care companies are those for the medical business, which includes services such as home medical care, hospital management support, and network medical care, and not for the nursing care division alone.

3.2 Development of the Private LTC Market in in South Korea

According to the "Annual Report on Long-term Care Insurance for the Elderly 2020" published by the NHIS, the number of registered LTC facilities as of 2020 reached 25,384. This is an increase of 30.86% from four years ago in 2016 (19,398 locations), and the number of employees in nursing homes was recorded as 503,983, an increase of 46.40% in just four years, compared to 344,242 in 2016. Among them, 450,000 were recuperating guardians, followed by social workers at 30,000. The number of people certified for LTC insurance was 858,000, and health insurance premiums increased significantly. In 2020, the annual beneficiaries (self-payment + public

[9] TSUKUI Holdings website: https://tsukui-hd.co.jp.

[10] SECOM website: https://www.secom.co.jp/.

[11] ALSOK website: https://www.alsok.co.jp/.

contribution) for LTC insurance were 98,248 trillion won, an increase of 14.7% from the same period last year. The annual beneficiaries were 810,000, and the average monthly benefit per person was 1.32 million won. However, 72.7% of the 875 nursing homes were individuals, and it is also true that there are still problems with micro-independent businesses that are not managed and supervised, such as fraudulent receipt of benefits and low-quality facility environments and services. Major corporations that provide nursing care services have not yet actively entered the market. The reasons for this are uncertainty about profitability and lack of management knowledge related to the medical care service business.

Compared to major countries, the overall number of beds in South Korea is slightly higher than the average for the OECD 31 countries, but the number of beds per 1,000 people aged 65 and over is low compared to other countries. This indicates the lack of facilities and the need to improve the infrastructure to meet the quality of care services, such as increasing the number of wards and beds in consideration of privacy (Kang & Kim 2019).

4 Development of Insurer's LTC Business

4.1 Development of Insurer's LTC Business in Japan

4.1.1 LTC Insurance Products of Insurance Companies

The differences of LTC insurance between public and insurance companies are that public LTC insurance provides a "benefit in kind" and LTC insurance of insurance companies provides a "cash benefit," while the "LTC status" that is a requirement to receive benefits is different. The LTC requirements of insurance companies have their own standards set forth in the terms and conditions. Recently, there has been an increase in the number of products linked to the certification of LTC required by public LTC insurance, but the degree of LTC required varies depending on the product.

Unlike public LTC insurance, insurer's LTC insurance can be contracted even under the age of 40. In addition, there are no age restrictions like public LTC insurance. Public LTC insurance is insured by people over the age of 40, and the subscriber pays the premium for the rest of his life, while the LTC insurance of insurance companies pays the premium for the period specified in the contract, and if the insurance premium is paid during the premium payment period and the benefit is received, the premium is generally exempt from payment for products that continue to be contracted after that.

Private LTC insurance in Japan has been on the market since before 2000, and with the introduction of LTC insurance, LTC services have become more systematic, and the means of securing funds have been secured. In the relationship between LTC insurance and services, private LTC insurance functions as a complement to public

Table 5 The ratio of individual insurance of life insurance companies in Japan

Types	Number of policies	Ratio (%)	Premiums	Ratio (%)	Average claims (1,000 yen)
Individual	190,249,912	100.00	815,763,086	100.00	4,287
1. Death Insurance	158,711,784	83.42	698,542,601	85.63	4,401
2. Mixed life and death	21,404,597	11.25	106,563,064	13.06	4,978
LTC insurance	11,099,734	5.83	37,508,976	4.60	3,379
Term LTC insurance	176,663	0.09	1,334,431	0.16	7,553
3. Endowment	10,133,531	5.33	10,657,421	1.31	1,051
Pension	20,788,505	100.00	101,796,208	100.00	4,896

Source Life Insurance Association of Japan

LTC insurance. With the deregulation of insurance in the third sector such as LTC insurance in Japan, subsidiaries of birth and grandchildren insurance companies can sell from January 2001. According to a fact-finding survey conducted by the Japan Life Insurance Culture Center (2018), the participation rate of LTC insurance and LTC riders in Japan in 2018 was 14.1%, and in 2006–2018 (12 years) it was about 15% (13.7–16.1%), but the reality is that the ratio of the number of individual insurance policies and premiums of life insurance companies is still low, as shown in Table 5.

Japan is experiencing a full-fledged aging population and is introducing new products and services to the market one after another with an eye on the "super-aging future," which is said to be the era of the 100-year lifespan. Some of these trends are shown in the Table 6 (Maeda 2019).

New products and services that look ahead to the 100-year life era in the super-aging future, which is also called the 100-year life era, have been introduced to the market one after another, and the Table 6 can be summarized as products and services that provide peace of mind until the end of life, such as products that respond to anxiety about the risk of longevity, products that respond to anxiety about dementia, and products that support health and prevention (Maeda 2019).

The percentage of LTC insurance and riders by households in was 16.7% (14.1% in the previous survey), an increase of 2.6 % points in 2021 as the Table 7. By household member, the number of heads of households was 13.6% and that of spouses was 8.5%, an increase of 3.1 % points for heads of households.

According to Life Insurance Culture Center (2021), the household coverage rate of dementia insurance and dementia riders[12] among households enrolled in private health insurance (excluding Japan Post Insurance) is 6.6%. By household member, 5.2% were heads of households and 3.3% were spouses.

[12] LTCI (rider) does not include a lump-sum payment or pension that allows the individual to receive a lump-sum payment or pension when they are in need of LTC for a period of time other than for dementia.

Table 6 Trends of products and services responding to an aging society in Japan

Year	Insurers	Products
Longevity risk products (Tontine Annuity Insurance)		
2016	Japan life	• Nissay longevity survival insurance (Low surrender value type) (Gran age)
2017	Dai-ichi life	• New personal annuity insurance for longevity
	Japan post life	• Longevity support insurance (Longevity happiness)
2018	Solar LIFE	• Insurance suite best (100-year-old pension)
Dementia risk products (dementia insurance)		
2016	Solar life	• Whole life insurance for dementia treatment
	Asahi life	• Anshin nursing care dementia insurance
2018	Solar life	• Sunflower dementia insurance prevention insurance
	Fukoku life	• Anshin nursing care dementia insurance care double (special contract)
	Sompo Japan	• Link Cross
	Japan Koa Himawari Life	• Dementia insurance that protects your smile
	Tokio Marine & Nichido Fire	• Dementia safety plan
	Sompo Japan Koa	• The power of parents and children
	Dai-ichi life	• Easy notice dementia insurance
2019	Mitsui Sumitomo	• Dementia Kobe model (dementia accident relief system)
Providing peace of mind until the end (family trust, life support)		
2015	Sumitomo Mitsui trust bank	• Security-type trusts
2016	Mitsubishi UFJ trust and banking	• Mirai no Mamori
2017	Mizuho trust and banking	• Choice of peace of mind trust
2018	Meiji Yasuda life	• Family function service (Gran Age Star)
Products that support health prevention (health promotion insurance)		
2018	Sumitomo life	• Vitality
2019	Meiji Yasuda life	• Best style health cashback

Source Maeda (2019)

Table 7 Trend of ratio of LTC insurance (riders) in private insurance in Japan (unit: %)

Year	Household	Head of household	Spouse
2021	16.7	13.6	8.5
2018	14.1	10.5	7.8
2015	15.3	11.8	7.9
2012	14.2	10.8	7.6
2009	13.7	11.1	6.2

Source Life Insurance Culture Center (2021)

Table 8 Cases of LTC business of insurers in Japan (2018)

Parent company	Company name	Home	Facility (Number of beds)
Sompo	Sompo care[13]	686	25,500
Tokio Marine	Better life[14]	80	605
Sumitomo Mitsui	CareNet[15]	6	223
Aioi Nissay Dowa	Fureai do life service[16]	4	–
Japan life insurance	Nissay Seirei health and welfare foundation[17]	3	760
Meiji Yasuda life insurance	San venus[18]	n/a	137
Sony insurance	Life care design[19]	n/a	196

Note based in Oct. 2018
Source Kang & Kim (2019)

4.1.2 LTC Business of Insurers

Insurance companies involved in the LTC business include non-life insurance companies such as Sompo Holdings, Tokio Marine Holdings, and Mitsui Sumitomo, as well as insurance groups of life insurance companies such as AII Nissay, Japan Life, and Meiji Yasuda Life. The in-home care business of insurance companies includes home-visit nursing care, day and night care, and home care support, while the institutional care business includes services such as fee-based nursing homes, home services for the elderly, low-burden elderly homes, group homes, and long-term care health facilities. In particular, insurance companies engage in the nursing home business, with high profits and high self-payment rates.

According to a 2012 survey by Mizuho Corporate Bank, the market size for the elderly is expected to reach 101.3 trillion yen by 2025, up from 62.9 trillion yen in 2007, and the nursing care industry alone is expected to reach 15.2 trillion yen. Therefore, the Japan insurance industry predicted the growth of the nursing care business as a "fourth core business" that could generate new revenues for the insurance industry in the future.

The Table 8 shows the summary of the situation in 2018 when Japan insurance companies were entering the nursing care business.

From the Table 8, the LTC services of leading insurance companies, such as Sompo Care and Tokio Marine Better Life Services (BLS), are summarized as follows.

[13] https://www.sompocare.com/.
[14] https://www.tnbls.co.jp/.
[15] http://www.msk-carenet.com/docs.
[16] https://www.fureai-do.co.jp/index.html.
[17] https://www.nissay-seirei.org/.
[18] https://www.sunvenus.co.jp/.
[19] https://www.lifecaredesign.co.jp/.

(561) Examples of Sompo Care

In the case of Sompo Care (a subsidiary of Sompo Holdings) in 2012, Somp entered the LTC industry with our investment in Cedar. In 2015, Sompo acquired Watami's nursing care business. The following year, in 2016, it became a subsidiary of Message, a major fee-based home company, and in 2018, it merged four nursing care companies under its umbrella, and in 2017, it grew to become the second largest company in its sector and achieved a return to profitability. The transition of the actual results is shown in Fig. 6. By establishing a system to provide all services such as nursing care facilities, day and night protection, and home-visit care, it formulated group medical insurance and LTC support plans to synergize with core business, provided nursing care services to employees, and integrated the management knowledge of large companies into the LTC business. The figure below shows the changes in sales and profits of Sompo Care since 2016.

Sompo Care's sales in fiscal year 2023 reached 16.756 billion yen, and it operates approximately 470 facilities nationwide, including approximately 300 nursing homes and residential-type fee-based nursing homes, approximately 150 serviced homes for the elderly, and 20 group homes.

The business overview of Sompo Care as of 2021 is summarized in the Table 9.

Looking at the LTC insurance and senior care business strategy from the 2021 Sompo Holdings New Medium-Term Management Plan, in addition to expanding the number of users, Sompo will develop a solution business for nursing care providers with RDP (Real Data Platform) as the key while supporting many elderly people as a nursing care operator and achieving both overwhelming quality and productivity. Sompo aims to commercialize initiatives to support active seniors.

(2) Examples of Tokio Marine Holdings Better Life Services (BLS)

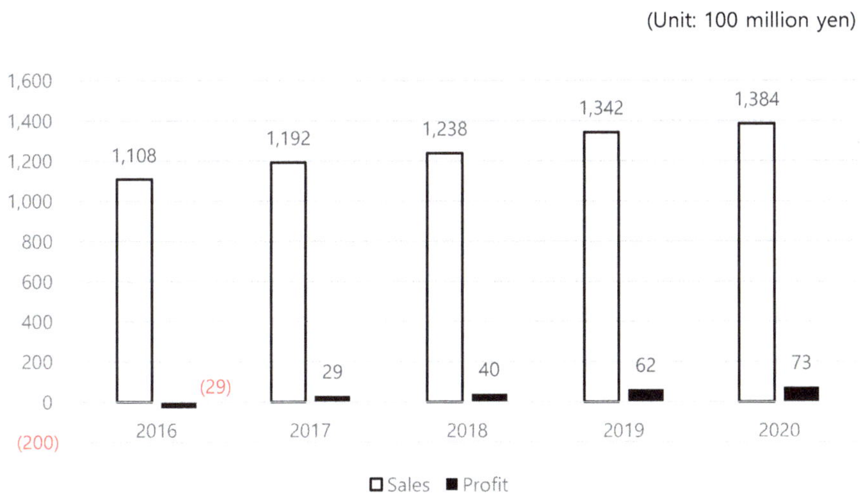

Fig. 6 Sompo Care business results (as of March 2021) (Unit: 100 million yen). *Source* Sompo Holdings (2021)

Table 9 Overview of Sompo care (as of March 2021)

Items	Number
Number of employees	23,611
Sales	¥131.8 billion
Number of senior living rooms	Approx. 27,000 rooms
Nursing homes	307
Serviced senior housing	145 Buildings
In-home services	561 Establishments

Source Sompo Holdings (2021)

Table 10 Services of better life services (BLS)

Service Items	Substance
Home visit	• Operating 40 nursing care centers, according to the nursing care plan the care recipient can live at home. Providing living support (cleaning, meal preparation, proxy purchase) services
Fee-based nursing care housing facility (Hilldemor/Hütte)	• Residential facilities for the elderly (D-Festa)—residential facilities that are occupied by LTC consumers
Contract management	• In 2016, BLS was commissioned by Daiwa House Group, a major residential construction company, to operate two service-based senior housing operations, providing operations and visiting services to diversify its revenue streams
Nursing care solution service	• Expert care counseling for policyholders

Source TMNF Better Life Service Homepage[20]

Better Life Services (BLS), a subsidiary of Tokio Marine Holdings, provides custom services in the LTC business and provides services by lifelong health level with various staffing arrangements. The specific details of these services are summarized in the Table 10.

As shown in the Table 10, Tokio Marine and Nichido Better Life Service Co., Ltd. (BLS) is a comprehensive nursing care company of the Tokio Marine Group, established in 1996 with the aim of providing high-quality nursing care services. The company's business is summarized under brands such as "Mizutama Nursing Care Station," which provides in-home care bases, fee-based nursing homes for the elderly, housing for the elderly with services, and solution services for companies and corporations.

[20] https://www.tnbls.co.jp/.

4.1.3 Challenges of Insurer's LTC Business

Japan is characterized by paying half of tax revenues and half of social insurance premiums and responding to long-term care services through the introduction of market mechanisms and the promotion of privatization. Therefore, the private sector, especially the insurance industry, appears to play a key role in cooperation with the public sector through its active participation in the long-term care business. Due to the merger of existing small businesses, it is considered a more successful entity than other industries, mainly because it provides long-term care services to insurance companies. In particular, the involvement of Japanese insurance companies in the fee-based nursing home business is a good example of a company that generates profitability with consumers who want to receive superior quality services. As the phenomenon of mergers in the nursing care business continues, it is expected that the size of the business entity will increase.

There is a synergistic effect on the insurance industry for insurance companies by linking related businesses with long-term care insurance products. In particular, Japanese insurance companies provide insurance products and long-term care services through their subsidiaries and long-term care companies, especially the development of new long-term care insurance facilities that combine medical management with pre-mortem care functions and living facility functions, and the development of incentive-type insurance products that pay premiums when nursing care conditions are improved. As a result, synergistic effects are expected among insurance companies, and cost savings are expected for consumers (Kang and Kim 2019).

Regarding the basic guidelines of the LTC Insurance Department of Japan in February 2020, in the 8th period (FY2021-FY2023), based on the goals and specific measures in the 7th Plan, it is necessary to take a medium- to long-term view of the elderly population and the needs of LTC services, keeping in mind the development of a community-based comprehensive care system aiming for 2025 and 2040, when the number of working generations will decline sharply.

4.2 Development of Insurer's LTC Business in South Korea

4.2.1 Insurer's LTC Insurance Products

The LTC insurance products of insurance companies can be assembled with special provisions on how to pay premiums, the scope and method of insurance prohibition, and other products. LTC insurance products developed in the U.S. and EU countries include pre-established LTC insurance, mutual fund-type LTC insurance, lump-sum annuity insurance, home-backed LTC insurance, annuity-linked LTC insurance, and home care limited insurance products.

Public and private LTC insurance differ in many ways as seen in the Table 11, such as the law of evidence, the timing of introduction, the governing body, the obligation to join, eligibility, and eligibility. Private LTC insurance serves as a complement to public LTC insurance. There are differences such as private LTC insurance paid in the form of in-kind benefits, while public insurance is paid as fixed-amount insurance. The comparison of public insurance and insurance companies' LTC insurance can be summarized as shown in the Table 11.

As shown in the Table 11, LTC products provided by insurance companies are voluntary, and the contents of the payment vary depending on the terms of the policy, so it can be seen that it is difficult to enrol. In addition, it can be difficult to choose between insurance companies because it can take a long time to pay out insurance claims, and the coverage and conditions offered by each insurance company are different.

According to the 2020 financial results of the Life Insurance Association, the income premiums of long-term care insurance of life insurance companies are still only 0.78% of the total premiums, as shown in the Table 12.

There is a limit to public LTC insurance for the elderly which can be strengthened at an early stage by reforming the accumulation method, but it is necessary to

Table 11 Comparison of LTC insurance between public and private of South Korea

Items	Public LTC insurance	Private LTC insurance
Law	Long-term care insurance for the elderly	Health law
Start year	2008	2003
Insurer	National health insurance service	Insurance company
Obligation	Compulsory enrolment	Voluntary enrolment
The insured	All health insured persons	Certified standards by each insurer
Eligibility	The elderly over 65 years of age or only under 65 years of age who has dementia, Alzheimer's disease	Eligibility requirements under the diagnosis of severe dementia and disability during the policy
Claim	Obtain a long-term care grade and receive medical care services	The reason for payment is in the terms and conditions of policy
Method of payment	Facility benefits, in-home benefits	Lump-sum payment (diagnosis benefit), pension (nursing care)

Source Kang and Kim (2019)

Table 12 Life insurance premiums of South Korea in 2020

Items	Premiums (millions of yen)	Ratio (%)
Total	714,818,452	n/a
General	516,694,564	72.28%
Individual	511,603,902	n/a
Long-term care	**5,556,839**	**0.78%**
Organization	5,090,662	n/a
Special	198,123,888	27.72%

Source Life Insurance Association (2021)

Table 13 LTC business of insurers in South Korea

Parent company	Company	Business
Hana financial	Hana care center	• In 2009, the Hana Care Center was established • Size: 99 insured, 54 staff • Services: ① Medical care by contract doctors, 24-h specialized nursing services; ② Rehabilitation (physical therapy, UNIT home care, external walking; ③ Healthcare (blood pressure, pulse, body temperature, respiration, blood sugar, weight); ④ Personal hygiene (bathing, dentures)
KB general	KB gold life care	• In 2016, KB gold life care was established • Operating one sanatorium and two day-and-night shelters and is currently building a second sanatorium store • Size: 132 hospitalized, 82 staff (day-and-night shelters: 49 and 21 staffs)
Samsung life	Samsung county nursing home[21]	• In 2001, based on the Welfare Act for the Elderly, Samsung Noble Counting Nursing Home was established • LTC insurance beneficiaries are eligible for admission
Samsung F&M	n/a	• In 2021, signed an investment agreement with HMC Network, which operates the caregiver matching service platform "Care Country," in order to pre-empt the nursing care market, and in addition to forming a business alliance

Source Cho (2021)

consider how to consolidate the obligations of some of the current LTC insurance for insured persons by replacing the private LTC insurance that they have been entrusted with in advance with LTC insurance for the elderly. If private LTC insurance can be introduced, it will be possible to reduce the burden on descendants of future intergenerational transfers when insured persons under private LTC insurance enrol in public LTC insurance (Kim 2020a, b).

4.2.2 LTC Business of Insurers

Some insurance companies and other financial institutions have recently entered the nursing care service industry. The reason major companies are not active is due to uncertainty about profitability and lack of relevant knowledge. The Table 13 summarizes the companies and business contents of Korean insurance companies that are in the LTC business.

From the Table 13, the LTC services of leading insurance companies, such as "Samsung Noble County" and "KB Gold Life Care," are summarized as follows.

A. Case of Samsung Noble County

[21] From homepage of samsungnc.com.

Samsung Noble County was founded in 2001 by the Samsung Life Insurance Foundation and is a facility that combines a residential welfare facility for the elderly (nursing home) and a medical welfare facility for the elderly (elderly care facility) that complies with the Elderly Welfare Law. Samsung Noble County Nursing Home is a long-term care facility for the elderly. As of 2021, there are 555 nursing homes where elderly people who do not have any problems with their daily lives are admitted, and 174 beds are used for elderly people with significant physical and mental disabilities due to geriatric diseases. The contract rate is 100% and the occupancy rate is 99%.

A special nursing home for the elderly can be moved into if one of the two people is 60 years old or older as of the scheduled move-in date, and in the case of a married couple, if one of the two people is 60 years old or older.

The average age of nursing home residents was 72 years old when the clinic opened in 2001, but as of 2020 it has increased to 85 years old. At the beginning, the amount of pensioners was about 10%, and now it has increased to 17%.

Nursing homes are open to people aged 65 and over who need assistance with daily activities due to senile illnesses such as dementia and stroke. A security deposit must be paid for the use of residential and other facilities. The deposit will be fully refunded upon discharge. Monthly living expenses are billed on a sliding scale according to the level of medical care, and consumables, medical expenses, and food expenses (540,000 won for 90 meals per person) are billed separately. The monthly living expenses for one room are 605–7.84 million won (100 million won move-in deposit), 4.42–5.19 million won (70 million won move-in deposit) for 2 bedrooms, and 400–4.2 million won for 4-person rooms (50 million won for move-in deposit).

Those who enter Samsung Noble County are not eligible to receive long-term care insurance benefits for the elderly, because in the case of an elderly care facility with a capacity of 30 or more, the company who set up the facility must own the land and building of the facility, but Samsung Noble County Nursing Home operates under a lease agreement.

As of 2020, the average age of nursing home residents was 86 years old, and the prevalent diseases were dementia (86%), stroke (35%), Parkinson's disease, and the nervous system (44%) (CHO 2021).

B. Case of KB Gold Life Care

The KB Group will prioritize the expansion of LTC facilities in the city center, which has a demand that will lead to improved regulations, and will prioritize Seoul, the metropolitan area, and regional large cities where the supply is insufficient and the rate of increase in the number of elderly people is higher than the demand for facilities for the elderly in Seoul. To this end, we will promote the improvement of capabilities in business processes, service processes, and operational systems, through collaboration with leading overseas companies, and grow as a specialized business operator. In addition, based on our operational capabilities through the nursing care facility system, we are building a network within the Group and outside the Group, providing welfare services for the elderly in the latter stages of health, while improving the safety and convenience of living for the elderly, and creating the effect of providing high-quality housing for the next generation without further housing construction. Home welfare services for the elderly are used by healthy elderly people to relieve discomfort and anxiety in their lives at the pre-care stage, and the use of residential welfare facilities for the elderly has the effect of slowing down the progress of aging and delaying the entry of nursing homes to the maximum. As a long-term expected effect, the expansion of housing welfare facilities for the elderly will improve the safety of housing and convenience for the elderly, provide high-quality housing to the next generation without further housing construction, stabilize housing for the elderly, and solve the housing problem of the younger generation, which is difficult to deal with due to the shortage of urban housing when housing for the elderly is excellent in locations such as large cities. Further housing construction will no longer be necessary. In order to respond to the life cycle journey of the elderly, a total senior care system for healthcare housing and welfare services for the elderly leads to long-term care services. Therefore, as an improvement to the subsidiary of the financial group, such as KB General, the establishment of private facilities is permitted to use land and buildings owned by others for private facilities that meet the specific requirements of the area stipulated in the special clause on the installation of facilities. It proposes to the Financial Services Commission that new regulatory improvements are needed to allow private capital and firms to enter the market while maintaining the purpose of regulation (Cho 2021). The status of KB Gold Care Life is summarized in the Table 14.

In order to take the businesses summarized in the Table 14 one step further, KB Golden Life Care and Sompo Care signed a memorandum of understanding (MOU) in 2023 to operate the infrastructure of the nursing care industry, develop related products and services, and share capabilities. Through this business alliance,

Table 14 Summary of KB gold care life

Item	Contents
Establishment	• November 2016
Business	• Elderly medical welfare facilities, homebound elderly welfare facilities, and elderly residential welfare facilities
Capital	• 26 billion
Parent company	• KB general insurance company
Number of employees	• 212
Vision	• Contributing to a society that guarantees a happy old age for all citizens through care services that provide peace of mind and hope
Mission	• A company that provides the care services that the public trusts the most
Business direction	• Expansion of urban medical care service business in demand in line with deregulation • Based on the medical care service business, we will build a network inside and outside the Group to provide housing welfare services for the elderly. There is no need to build additional housing in consideration of housing safety and convenience for the elderly

Source KB Gold Life Care (2021)

KB Financial Group will provide high-quality nursing care services by sharing the capabilities of Sompo Holdings in the "infrastructure management of the nursing care service industry" and "development of nursing care products and services" that Sompo Holdings has accumulated in Korea. In particular, KB Golden Life Care, the Group's nursing care subsidiary, plans to collaborate with Sompo Care in the field of "digital technology" to collect data based on IoT (Internet of Things) and provide nursing care services tailored to customers. Sompo Holdings is also aiming to enter the Korean LTC industry market directly and indirectly through its collaboration with KB Financial.

4.2.3 Development of LTC Business of Insurers

Since the introduction of the long-term care insurance system in 2008, silver-related demand has increased due to the aging of the population and other factors, from about 3 trillion won in 2012 to about 10 trillion won (up 16.6%) in 2020.

According to a symposium by Financial Service Committee (FSC) in 2021, LTC services are classified as senior-friendly products according to the Senior-friendly Industry Promotion Act and its implementation order from 2006. The Korea Health Industry Promotion Agency estimated that the "old-age affinity market size (excluding the financial industry)" increased from 27.4 trillion won in 2012 to 39.3 trillion won in 2015, an increase of 43% in three years. In addition, the affinity market for the elderly is expected to grow at an annual rate of 13.1% from 2015 to 2020 and reach about 72.8 trillion won (5.5% of GDP) in 2020.

In South Korea, public health data has been available to insurance companies since 2021, and to fulfill that purpose, insurance companies have been able to develop dedicated products for the elderly and the sick, as well as provide healthcare-related flat form services through deregulation. They can capture the healthcare market in a variety of ways, including establishing subsidiaries, introducing and expanding their own applications, and strategic alliances. Market research firm Global Market Site predicted that the global digital healthcare market would reach 600 trillion won by 2025, growing by an average of 29.6% annually from 130 trillion won in 2020 (Kim 2021a, b).

New ways to link housing pensions and LTC have recently been discussed abroad. The combination of home annuity and LTC insurance has the advantage of reducing the risk of adverse selection, reducing the burden of insurance premiums, and expanding new markets (Kim 2021a, b).

As South Korea's aging population accelerates, interest in LTC insurance is increasing and it is necessary to diversify the composition of insurance coverage like other countries. The U.K. should consider offering a lifetime annuity that can be enclosed to LTC insurance beneficiaries, the U.S. selling LTC annuities with a LTC rider added to the annuity, and Germany selling cash and in-kind benefits as annuities based on a detailed classification of insurance benefits (Jung and Kown 2021).

From the 2021 Financial Services Committee (FSC) symposium, in order to make inroads into the medical care service business of insurance companies, the first problem of the medical care market was evaluated as follows. Inadequate linkages between private insurance products such as LTC dementia insurance and LTC services, as well as restrictions on credit contributions, are factors that limit the entry of insurance companies into the medical care service business. Insurance companies are playing a significant role in the medical care service business through system improvement, such as (1) increased private investment in elderly care facilities, (2) revitalization of cooperation between the medical care service business and financial and insurance products, (3) providing investment incentives for insurance companies, and (4) using the Insurance Training Institute to train medical care specialists.

The report shows that the expected effects of insurance companies entering the nursing care service business include strengthening the role of social security for the elderly, discovering new businesses for insurance companies in the future, and having a positive impact on employment opportunities. In particular, when insurance companies combine healthcare, insurance, and medical care services, they are expected to provide life-cycle customized services such as (1) advanced management of health risks through healthcare, (2) coverage of disease treatment costs through insurance products, and (3) support for the living of the elderly through LTC services.

LTC insurance can be used as a source of funding for LTC services, which is the main positive reason for insurance participation in the long-term care business, indicating a strong link between LTC insurance and LTC services. The role of LTC is also important, but there are still issues to be raised: on the demand side, nursing care and medical needs are complex, the service field is unclear, nursing care awareness is low, and demand is not properly expressed, and on the supply side, there is market uncertainty due to high initial investment costs, large management risks, high reputational risk, difficulty in human resource management, and policy fluctuations. The reform of laws and institutions could be considered the market (Kang and Kim 2019).

As an insurance industry, it is necessary to formulate a management strategy with the nursing care industry as a new growth force, based on the forecast that the LTC market is expected to expand and that the number of users of LTC services will increase by 2.5 times by 2050 compared to 2018 (4.5 times at the level of developed countries).

5 Conclusion

Both and South Korea will be affected by the situation of the rapid increase in the number of elderly people and the increased risk of longevity. It could lead to a surge in demand for LTC insurance services for the elderly. Japan's baby boomer generation reached the late elderly stage in 2025. South Korea predicts that the baby boomer generation will peak in 2030 as they become the late elderly.

In South Korea, LTC insurance, which was introduced in 2008, is funded by the financial resources of LTC services, but the cost of LTC is increasing amid the rapid aging of the population, and it is difficult to meet the demand for high-quality LTC services. However, there is a need for qualitative improvement of current nursing care facilities.

As directions for the privatization of LTC services, the LTC systems have been realized against the background of private-sector commercialization in both countries. The challenges faced by both countries are how to strategically overcome the limitations of the LTC system (lack of service supply and the fragility of user rights). The problem of fraud by business operators was serious in the beginning in South Korea, while in Japan there was a system introduced and managed in which the principle of competition was operated under strong government control. South Korea and Japan indicated that in terms of protecting and supporting the elderly, while South Korea was in the initial stages of direct management of LTC services, Japan was systematically supporting the elderly through active government supervision and care management to control the quality of operators and services.

In addition, regarding the challenges of private LTC in Japan and South Korea, South Korea needs to actively intervene with the government's direct control system to address the maximum oversupply and excessive competition among suppliers in the LTC services market. In addition, the introduction of care management in Japan requires cooperation with service users, insurers, and businesses to find ways to ensure service quality and strengthen active government oversight. Second, the common challenge between Japan and South Korea is that many for-profit companies have entered the nursing care service market, and systematic measures are needed to improve problems such as deteriorating working conditions and a shortage of caregivers (for example, the widespread use of certification systems for nursing care human resource training programs implemented by local governments in Japan).

Although the roles of LTC businesses by insurance companies are important, it is difficult to provide high-quality LTC services due to these constraints, so complementary policies are necessary to create a market environment.

References

Korean References

Ahn, M., & Park, J. (2019). *Examining the problems and improvement measures of the elderly care insurance system*. Transactions of the Korean Content Society.

Cho, Y. (2021). *Comparison of Japan-Korea long-term care service supply systems and the case of insurance companies*. KIRI.

Jung, C., & Kown, O. (2021). *Cases and implications of overseas nursing insurance linked pension insurance*. KIRI Aging Review Ishu Analysis.

Kang, S., & Kim, H. (2019). *The current status of long-term care services for the elderly and the role of insurance companies*. KIRI.

Kim, T. (2021a). *Why insurance companies decided to provide healthcare services as a new business for the future*. Hankyung Business.

Kim, Y. (2021b). *Overseas housing pension and long-term care collaborative product discussion*. KIRI Report Global Issue.

Kim, Y. (2020a). *The elderly's long-term medical care and protection of the elderly need to be given a plan for the sharing of the role.* KIRI.

Japanese References

Federation of Health Insurance Societies. (2020). *International comparative survey on public long-term care systems.*
Kim, M.-J. (2020b). *Current status and challenges of the long-term care insurance system for the elderly in Korea.* Nissay Research Institute Report.
Life Insurance Culture Center. (2021). *Nationwide survey on life insurance.*
Maeda, N. (2019). *Latest trends in the insurance and finance industry: Looking ahead to the 100-year life era.* NLI Research Institute Report, July 2019.
Ministry of Finance. (2021) *Social Security, (References) April 2021.*
Ministry of Health, Labor and Welfare Bureau for the Elderly. (2021). *Overview of the long-term care insurance system May 2021.*
Ministry of Health, Labor and Welfare. (2021). *Long-term care insurance business status report.*
National Health Insurance Service. (NHIS). (2021, 2023). Homepage. https://www.nhis.or.kr/nhis/together/wbhaec06300m01.do
SOMPO Holdings. (2021). *New medium-term management plan.*

Websites

Industry Trends. (n.d.). gyokai-search.com/3-kaigo.htm.
Ministry of Health and Welfare. (n.d.). www.mohw.go.kr/
Ministry of Health, Labour, and Welfare statistics. (n.d.). www.mhlw.go.jp/toukei/
Korean Statistical Information Service (KOSIS). (n.d.). Homepage. https://kosis.kr/
Statistics Bureau of Japan. (n.d.). Homepage. https://www.stat.go.jp/, https://www.e-stat.go.jp

Social Long Term Care Insurance in China

Chao Lu

1 The Current Aging Problem in China

It is generally regarded that when the proportion of elderly people aged 60 or above reaches 10% (or aged 65 or above reaches 7%) of the total population in a country or region, it means that the country or region concerned has become an aging society, while an aged or hyper-aged society is formed as the proportion of elderly people increases to 14% or 20%.

According to the seventh national census data in 2020 published by the National Bureau of Statistics, the share of the elderly populations aged over 60 and 65 in China were 18.7% and 13.5%, respectively, while the total fertility rate stood at 1.3 births per woman over a lifetime, far below the replacement level (2.1 children per woman) and the international warning line of 1.5. The United Nations predicted that by 2025, the proportion of people aged 65 and above in China would rise to around 14% of the total population. There will be one elderly person in every four Chinese people by 2045 in contrast with the continuously declined fertility over decades.

Table 1 summarizes China's fertility rate, mortality rate, and natural growth rate every five years from 1990 to 2020. Both in terms of the fertility rate and aging trend, the significant downward trend of the natural growth rate of the population suggests an optimistic outlook for the population development. Besides, the annual birth population in 2022 was 9.56 million (with a fertility rate of 6.77‰) and the death population was 10.41 million (with a mortality rate of 7.37‰). That is, the natural population growth rate was −0.60%, marking the first negative population growth in China since the year 1962.

In comparison to many developed countries and areas, which took nearly one century to transition from an aging society to a hyper-aged society, such an aging

C. Lu (✉)
Faculty of Economics, Hangzhou Normal University, Hangzhou, China
e-mail: wasedalu@163.com

H. Lee and G. Nicolini (eds.), *International Comparison of Long-Term Care Insurance Systems*, Contributions to Management Science,
https://doi.org/10.1007/978-981-95-7781-1_10

Table 1 Fertility rate, mortality rate and natural growth rate in China (1990–2020)

	1990	1995	2000	2005	2010	2015	2020
Fertility rate	21.06	17.12	14.03	12.40	11.90	11.99	8.52
Mortality rate	6.67	6.57	6.45	6.51	7.11	7.07	7.07
Growth rate	14.39	10.55	7.58	5.89	4.79	4.93	1.45

(Unit: %)
Source China statistical yearbook 2023, China Bureau of Statistics

process will be shortened to 35 years in China. As shown in Table 2, the share of the elderly population in mainland China has been increasing and has rapidly exceeded the world average since 2000. Correspondingly, Fig. 1 suggests that the old-age dependency ratio in China has been steadily increasing in the past 30 years. In 2020, nearly one out of five persons (19.7%) are older than the working ages (≥ 65-year-old), among whom many are dependent on others for support and survival.

Moreover, population challenges in China are also characterized by the features of rapid development, large scale, increasing poverty, and disability along with the aging issues. Thus, pension security and elderly care service system have become

Table 2 Proportion of aging population

	Age	1990	1995	2000	2005	2010	2015	2020
China	≥60	8.1	9.1	10.1	11.1	12.8	15.6	17.8
	≥65	5.3	6.0	6.9	7.8	8.6	10.0	12.6
Worldwide	≥60	9.1	9.5	9.9	10.3	11.1	12.3	13.5
	≥65	6.1	6.5	6.9	7.3	7.7	8.3	9.4

(Unit: %)
Source The 2022 revision of world population prospects

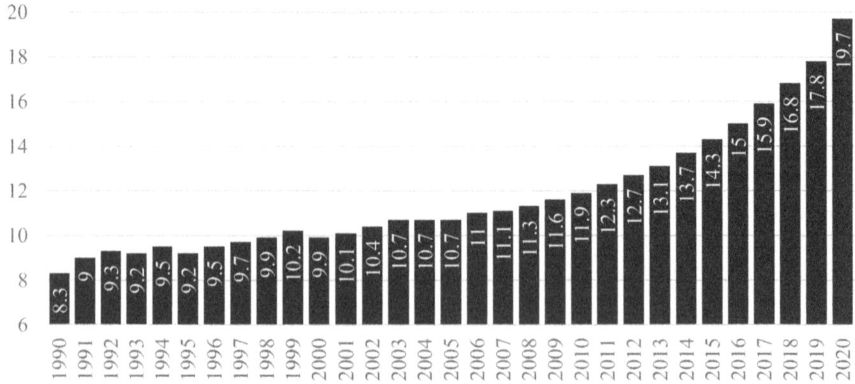

Fig. 1 Changes in old-age dependency ratio (%). *Source* China statistical yearbook 2023, China Bureau of Statistics

important factors that will significantly affect social development. According to the *Report on the Development of China's Aging Industry* published by the China Aging Science Research Center, as of the end of 2022, the number of persons aged 60 or over in China reached 280 million, of which approximately 44 million were elderly with disabilities or invisible disabilities who require different levels of medical care and long-term care (LTC) services. The needs for special care and services for disabled individuals are increasing against the backdrop of an increasingly aging population.

According to the data provided by the National Health Service Survey, the self-assessment health status of the elderly (2013) is summarized in Table 3. Among the four aspects of disability in walking, hearing, speaking, and vision, visual impairment is the most severe problem (25.2%), followed by hearing problems (23.8%). Compared to urban areas, elderly people with disabilities in rural areas of China are under more difficult situations, while the economically disadvantaged central and western regions are experiencing more serious challenges in comparison with the relatively developed eastern regions.

With the sharp increase in the demand for elderly care, the shortage of care services and the rise in nursing costs have begun to add an economic burden to the elderly people in various countries. Those states that took the lead in the aging society have been strengthening their efforts to explore and plan the daily lives of and medical security for the elderly population since then. As a result, long-term care insurance that adapts to the unique contexts and conditions of each country has emerged.

Long-term care insurance (LTCI), which is a social security system that provides services or financial support regarding basic living and medical care for individuals who have physical or mental disabilities due to aging, illness and so forth, is an important guarantee to meet the LTC needs of the increasing elderly population.

However, the overall coverage of LTCI is still at a relatively low level from a global perspective. Different with the traditional social insurance programs that mainly paid in cash, LTCI usually provides various actual services with forms of both at-home and institutional. Nevertheless, due to the short history and low coverage, work on LTCI is still in the early phases of exploration. Since LTC is strongly dependent on the service supply system, the care services have long been more regarded as the responsibility of the respective families and therefore should be provided by their younger generations or relatives. With the acceleration of population aging and changes in family structure, traditional modes of household health care have become unsustainable. Alternatively, LTC is gradually becoming an important part of the social security system.

In this context, the Fifth Plenary Session of the 18th CPC Central Committee in 2015 addressed that China should establish the LTCI system to meet the essential needs of aging problem. On June 27, 2016, the Ministry of Human Resources and Social Security issued the *Guiding Opinions on Pilot Implementation of the Long-term Care Insurance System* (hereafter referred to as *Guiding Opinions No. 1*), deploying to launch the pilot program in 15 cities and designating Jilin and Shandong, two northern provinces of China, as key regions for special focus. The 2019 Government Work Report then proposed to continue expanding the pilot of the LTCI policy nationwide. Subsequently, on September 16, 2020, the *Guiding Opinions on*

Table 3 Disability status of elderly population in both urban and rural areas

Disability		Total	Urban areas				Rural areas			
			Subtotal	Eastern Region	Central Region	West Region	Subtotal	Eastern Region	Central Region	West Region
Walking	Prolonged bed rest	3.3	3.4	2.8	3.9	3.5	3.2	2.9	3.6	3.0
	Unable to walk independently	2.0	1.9	1.5	2.0	2.3	2.1	1.9	2.3	2.1
	Unable to go out alone	6.8	6.4	6.5	5.5	7.3	7.3	6.1	6.9	9.0
Hearing	Hard to hear clearly	5.6	4.9	4.3	5.5	5.2	6.4	6.0	6.5	6.8
	Need to raise voice	18.2	16.1	14.0	14.7	20.1	20.5	18.1	21.7	21.9
Speaking	Have difficulty	10.7	11.2	8.9	12.2	13.1	10.1	8.8	11.4	10.3
Vision	Moderate difficulty	21.5	18.4	15.2	17.8	23.2	24.9	23.7	25.6	25.5
	Severe difficulty	3.7	3.4	2.8	3.3	4.3	4.0	3.5	4.2	4.4

(Unit: %)

Source Analysis report on the fifth national health service survey, China Union Medical University Press, 2015

Expanding the Pilot Program of the Long-term Care Insurance System (hereafter referred to as *Guiding Opinions No. 2*) were released by the National Healthcare Security Administration (NHSA) and the Ministry of Finance (MOF), in which 14 additional cities were added to the original pilot list. As of the end of December 2023, the LTCI in China already covered 49 cities and 170 million elderly people. The cumulative number of recipients had exceeded two million, with about 65 billion RMB expenditure in the special-purpose fund. In addition, in order to standardize the pilot work of the LTCI, as well as to better protect the legitimate rights and interests of old persons, NHSA and MOF jointly issued the *Management Measures for the Evaluation of Disability Level of Long-term Care Insurance (Trial)* at the end of 2023. The unified principles and fundamental requirements are clarified under the provisions of such a regulation, which aims at promoting the high-quality development of the pilot work through more standardized management.

Generally, understanding the LTCI in China can not only help to understand the formation and development of LTC in developing countries but also provide theoretical guidance for improving LTCI under different models and promoting the healthy development of the care service market and the elderly-care-related industries.

2 Pilot Implementation of China's LTCI System

Population growth at older ages in China is driven by lower mortality and increased survival, while an upward shift in the population age distribution is caused by a sustained drop in the fertility level. Especially since the inauguration of the policy of reform and opening up, which contributes to a significant transformation both economically and socially, the attendant increasing mobility of labor has led to shrinking household size and ineffective functioning of traditional family elderly care. Countries with aging populations should take steps such as improving the sustainability of social security and pension systems by establishing universal health care and LTC systems, to adapt the public conditions to the growing ratio of older persons.

The experience of developed countries and regions demonstrates that the LTC requirement from the elderly is firmly guaranteed by both sound LTC services and insurance systems. Establishing a solid LTCI framework is a crucial component for China to deal with the growing challenges posed by the rapid demographic transition toward population aging.

The LTCI system usually covers both social insurance and commercial insurance. The former is country-led mandatory insurance with universal coverage, providing protection for insured and retired individuals who have been in a state of long-term disability to alleviate their living and medical expenses. The latter is a commercial insurance product developed by insurance institutions, which improves and supplements social LTC services to meet the diversified needs of the general public.

Although the main objective is to socialize the responsibility of LTC to benefit elderly persons nationwide, LTCI in China is still in the pilot stage at present. Basically, the premiums are co-paid by the urban residents with basic medical insurance for urban employees and companies they worked for, while in some cities those who have participated in the basic medical insurance for urban residents are also covered in the LTCI system.

This chapter mainly focuses on China's social LTCI. The overview of pilot cities, the operating status of representative cities, and the current problems will be evaluated and analyzed comprehensively in the remaining sections.

2.1 Spatial Layout of the Pilot Cities

To cope with the upcoming peak of the aging population and growing demand for elderly care services, the Chinese government has launched a pilot project for pretesting the LTCI system. The first batch of 15 pilot cities published by the Ministry of Human Resources and Social Security in 2016, marking the beginning of official promotion of LTCI in China, covered 14 out of 34 provinces and autonomous regions in China. The pilot located across China included two cities in the north-eastern region (Qiqihar and Changchun), seven cities in the eastern region (Chengde, Qingdao, Nantong, Suzhou, Shanghai, Ningbo, and Guangzhou), three cities in the central region (Jingmen, Anqing, and Shangrao), and three cities in the western region (Shihezi, Chengdu, and Chongqing). Table 4 shows the location information with regard to different pilot cities, along with the respective proportions (in percentage) of the elderly population aged 65 or above before the implementation year of the pilot program.

Most of the pilot cities adopted the government-led social LTCI, which is an operational management process managed and handled by the government. Every urban resident covered in the basic medical insurance for urban employees pays an LTCI premium. The implementation process completed independently by the respective local governments has strength in mutual assistance, wide range of coverage, and capacity. Professional insurance institutions such as commercial insurance companies are not allowed to participate throughout the project.

Other cities (e.g., Chengde, Shangrao and Chengdu), though minor, see their local governments opt to participate in an indirect way. Through tenders or purchasing particular services from commercial insurance institutions, the governments are responsible for selecting the most suitable partner(s) and integrated management. This mode improves the efficiency of LTCI and thus reduces stress on the government by making full use of professional service and experience.

In light of the achievements and failures of the start-up phase, the geographical scope has been further expanded with 14 new cities added to the pilot list in 2020. The second batch of pilot cities includes one in the north-eastern region (Panjin in Liaoning Province), three in the eastern region (Shijingshan District in Beijing, Tianjin, Fuzhou in Fujian Province), three in the central region (Jincheng

Table 4 Location information and degree of aging about the first 15 pilot cities (2015)

Order	Region	Province	Pilot city	Proportion of 65+ population
1	Northeast	Heilongjiang	Qiqihar	10.84
2		Jilin	Changchun	10.91
3	East	Hebei	Chengde	10.17
4		Shandong	Qingdao	11.66
5		Jiangsu	Nantong	12.69
6			Suzhou	12.69
7			Shanghai	12.82
8		Zhejiang	Ningbo	11.27
9		Guangdong	Guangzhou	7.37
10	Center	Hubei	Jingmen	11.23
11		Anhui	Anqing	11.18
12		Jiangxi	Shangrao	9.06
13	West	Xinjiang	Shihezi	7.13
14		Sichuan	Chengdu	12.94
15			Chongqing	13.29
16	National average			10.47

Source China statistical yearbook 2016, China Bureau of Statistics

in Shanxi Province, Kaifeng in Henan Province, Xiangtan in Hunan Province), and seven in the western region (Urumqi in Xinjiang, Hohhot in Inner Mongolia, Gannan Tibetan Autonomous Prefecture in Gansu Province, Hanzhong in Shaanxi Province, Qianxinan Buyi and Miao Autonomous Prefecture in Guizhou Province, Kunming in Yunnan Province, and Nanning in Guangxi Province).

Additionally, compared with the overall average of 10.47%, which is the share of the elderly population aged 65 or over in China, approximately half of the pilot cities have a higher proportion and the other half are lower when taking all the 29 pilot cities into consideration. The pilot cities are mainly distributed in economically developed eastern regions. These regions have relatively sufficient medical and care conditions, which are more conducive to the establishing and testing of the LTCI system. Therefore, the selection of pilot cities is the result of comprehensive consideration after balancing various factors such as economic development and aging level.

2.2 *Financing and Payment of the Pilot Cities*

As of the end of December 2018, the first batch of pilot cities for the LTCI system had all been launched and implemented, among which 13 pilot cities had started paying benefits, and about 49,000 eligible recipients had received the LTC services. During the pilot period, it is vital to create an effective financing and payment environment to guarantee the smooth implementation of LTCI. In response to varying local situations, each pilot city has adopted different approaches for receiving and releasing the LTCI funds. Considering the short duration of the second batch of pilot cities, this section mainly focuses on the financing and payment mechanisms regarding the first 15 pilot cities.

2.2.1 Financing

The LTCI pilots are financially supported by diversified channels for the fee, such as transfer of funds, government subsidies, personal wages, employing unit payments, medical insurance fund transfers, public welfare funds of a welfare lottery, and social donations. Among them, the transfer of basic medical insurance pooling funds is the main source of capital and is contained in the LTCI funds with respect to all pilot cities. The composition of LTCI funds generally includes the following four types:

1. Single-channel: Composed of only one type of fund. Representative cities: Shanghai, Ningbo, and Guangzhou.
2. Dual-channel: Composed of two types of funds. Representative cities: Qiqihar, Changchun, Suzhou, Anqing, and Chongqing.
3. Triple-channel: Composed of three types of funds. Representative cities: Chengde, Nantong, Jingmen, Shangrao, and Shihezi.
4. Quad-channel: Composed of four types. Representative cities: Qingdao and Chengdu.

The LTCI fund is usually generated through quota-based, proportion-based, and mixed ways. Specifically, the quota system requires the insured to pay a fixed amount of premium, and the total insurance expenditure is estimated and distributed evenly to each insured person without considering the income gap. In contrast, the premiums are paid in accordance with the prescribed share percentage in the proportion system, where the total salary per capita disposable income or basic medical insurance premium over the previous year can be regarded as the payment base. The mixed system is a combination of quota and proportion systems, which adopts different payment methods for different groups of people.

The respective characteristics of the three financing methods are summarized and compared in Table 5. The funding level of LTCI in China is currently influenced by various factors such as the economic development circumstances of each pilot city and the scope of LTCI coverage. Overall, the funding level is relatively low and still needs to be improved (e.g., the standard for the quota system is only RMB30–150, and for the proportion system is not higher than 0.5% of the transferred account funds).

In addition, to encourage more residents to participate in the LTCI as early as possible and pay the premium continuously, Jingmen City has also implemented a special incentive mechanism, which links the payment period to the level of benefits: (a) for people who have accumulated paid fees over a period more than 15 years,

Table 5 Summary and comparison of financing approaches

Financing approach	Quota system	Proportion system	Mixed system
Characteristics	The payment amount varies among different cities, mostly around RMB100.	The total salary/ per capita disposable income/ basic medical insurance premium over the previous year can be regarded as the payment base.	Different payment methods are implemented for different groups of people.
Advantages	The calculation is simple and easy to apply universally.	The principles of mutual assistance and mechanism of redistribution are reflected by considering the economic factors of the insured.	Flexible in the use of financing as it combines the advantages of both quota and proportion systems
Disadvantages	May not maximize resource allocation and utilization	The calculations involved are relatively complex.	The calculations for resource allocation and payment are relatively complex.
Representative cities	Qiqihar, Nantong, Suzhou, Ningbo, Guangzhou, Anqing, Shangrao, Shihezi, Chongqing	Chengde, Shanghai, Jingmen, Chengdu	Changchun, Qingdao

the insurance level will be increased by 4%; (b) for people who have paid fees more than 30 years, the insurance level will be increased by 6%; (c) for people who have paid fees more than 45 years, the insurance level will be increased by 8%; and (d) for people who have paid fees more than 60 years, the insurance level will be increased by 10%.

2.2.2 Payment

Everyone aged 60 or over and covered in the LTCI is eligible for benefits if he/she is in a state of long-term disability. As it is still in the early stages, the LTCI project concentrates primarily on alleviating economic problems for the severely disabled elderly who are in critical need of basic living and medical care. At present, long-term disability status is generally assessed by the Barthel Index for Activities of Daily Living (ADL), in which 10 items closely related to daily living activities are taken into consideration. In this Index, full marks represent the status of complete self-independence. A total score below 40 out of a possible 100 is normally classified as severe disability, while scores in the ranges of 41–60 and 61–99 are moderate and mild disabilities, respectively. Cities such as Suzhou, Shanghai, and Chengdu have developed their own assessment standards based on local care needs and service supply capabilities. During the pilot phase, the main beneficiaries of LTCI were older persons with severe disabilities. Meanwhile, certain adjustments have also been made to adapt to specific circumstances. Based on the classification of disability levels, the scope of protection varies in different cities that is broadly categorized into the following four types:

1. Only elderly individuals with severe disabilities are considered as eligible recipients. The requirements for receiving benefits are as follows: being bedridden for at least six months due to illness; disability or other reasons; and complete inability to take care of themselves after having become physically stable. Representative cities: Chengde, Jingmen, Anqing and Shihezi.
2. Older persons with severe and moderate disabilities are eligible to apply for premiums. Representative cities: Changchun, Qingdao, Nantong and Suzhou.
3. Both physical and mental disabilities are included in the insurance coverage. Representative cities: Qingdao and Shangrao.
4. Priority is given to disabled elderly people aged 60 or above. Representative cities: Shanghai and Guangzhou.

Notice that the mental disability here refers in particular to Alzheimer's disease, a progressive neurodegenerative disorder that causes decline in cognition and functional abilities. This disease is the most common form of dementia; either medical diagnosis results from professional institutions or synthetic judgment based on internationally recognized standards and clinical manifestations can be taken as an assessment basis.

The possible forms of payment provided by LTCI include financial compensation and actual services. The former gives financial support by the government payments for the fees (e.g., United States), while the latter provides care services from suppliers in the LTC market (e.g., Japan). In reality, a combination of the two forms is to be found more frequently.

LTCI is designed to cover the long-term services in a variety of settings including institutional care, community care, and home care. The institutional care covers services from professional institutions such as chronic-care hospitals and nursing homes, aiming to provide comprehensive services to the insured. Community care mainly includes day services and short-stay services, under which recipients can reside at home and receive partial institutional care. Home care includes various services such as visiting nurses and housekeeping, which provides physical therapy, treatment, daily supportive services etc.

These three modes for elderly care are recognized by most of the pilot cities. Specially, caregivers for home care should come from a partner or designated institution. A few cities have further relaxed restrictions on the scope of caregivers to relatives and neighbors. The eligible services to apply for insurance payments in the respective pilot cities are as follows:

1. Services from care institutions only. Representative city: Changchun.
2. Institutional and at-home services (nursing homes are not included). Representative cities: Guangzhou, Chengdu, and Chongqing.
3. Institutional and at-home services (including nursing homes). Representative cities: Qiqihar, Chengde, Qingdao, Nantong, Suzhou, Shanghai, Ningbo, Shangrao, and Shihezi.

4. Institutional, communal, and at-home services (including nursing homes). Representative cities: Jingmen and Anqing.

In most pilot cities, the amount of insurance payment is set to be proportional to the actual care expenses, while taking into account the minimum and maximum payment standards. Minor versions adopt a fixed payment method, so that the payment amount will not be affected by the actual care expenses.

Guiding Opinions No. 1 requires the differentiated insurance policies based on the levels of care demand, the forms of service provision, and the insured objects. This is manifested in diversity in payment ratios, payment limits, and payment quotas. For LTC expenses that meet the assessment criteria, the specific payment ratio can be determined by the local governments of pilot cities, with the overall ratio of insurance benefits payments being controlled at around the level of 70%.

According to practical application, the minimum and maximum payment ratios of basic medical insurance for urban employees are 50% and 90%, respectively. The limit standard for severely disabled elderly persons is RMB 20–170 yuan per day. Evidently, there are significant differences in terms of the payment standards among different cities, due to the combined factors such as local economic level, development needs, policy orientation, and service supply.

2.3 Current Status of LTCI Operation in Pilot Cities

Qingdao, located in the eastern Shandong Province of China, is the earliest city in China to implement the LTCI. As early as July 1, 2012, Qingdao has already issued the *Opinions on Establishing a Long-term Medical Care Insurance System (Trial)*, taking the lead in initiating the pilot work to reimburse certain long-term medical care expenses for medical insurance insured personnel. Thanks to such an attempt, Qingdao won the Best Practice Award for Innovation from the Chinese government in 2015. Later in the same year, rural districts were further included in the scope of LTCI coverage. In 2016, Qingdao was formally selected as one of the first 15 pilot cities by the Chinese government. The LTCI system in Qingdao not only focuses on protecting the basic care needs of aging people with severe physical or mental disabilities but also provides training and guidance on functional maintenance for the elderly with moderate and mild disabilities, and even for the at-risk population to delay their symptoms.

Throughout the operation and development process of LTCI, Qingdao is a representative sample among the first 15 pilot cities. For these reasons, this section will take Qingdao City as an example to introduce and analyze the implementation background, the system construction, the operational status, the policy effects, and other aspects of LTCI in pilot areas.

2.3.1 Implementation Background

In China, Qingdao was one of the first cities to step into the population aging stage. The share of the elderly population aged 60 or above in Qingdao had already exceeded 10% as early as 1987, which was 13 years ahead of the national average. Moreover, according to the Seventh National Population Census of China given in Table 6, the number of elderly people aged 60 or above in Qingdao reached 2.04 million and the aging rate had rapidly increased to 20.28% as of November 1, 2020. This rate had climbed by 5.53% when comparing to the data of the previous census conducted in 2010. It is noticeable that the elderly population aged 65 or above grew rapidly by 3.94%. Regarding all 10 districts under the jurisdiction of Qingdao City, the proportion of elderly people aged 65 or above exceeded 7%, among which four districts were even higher than 15%. It is thus clear that the increasingly aging population is becoming a critical challenge for the future development of Qingdao.

In contrast with the swift growth rate of older population, the fertility level has fallen markedly over recent decades. As the age distribution has been shifting toward older ages, the traditional care mode that mainly relies on family members will be difficult to sustain. According to incomplete statistics, there are approximately 100,000 elderly people with physical or mental disabilities in Qingdao. Besides, the household size has also been gradually shrinking from 2.79 (sixth census) to 2.55 (seventh census) people per household. It is difficult to guarantee the basic living standards and quality of life of the elderly once the disabling symptoms appear. Thus, how to provide appropriate service guarantees for the elderly is an important issue to be resolved without delay for the Qingdao Municipal Government.

On a positive note, hospital beds and medical staff have significantly increased in recent years as a consequence of the rapid expansion of hospitals at all levels in the city. The number of practicing physicians (including assistants) for every thousand people has increased from 2.32 (sixth census) to 3.94 (seventh census). In the meantime, the basic medical insurance base for urban employees, which depends on the average monthly salary of the employee in the previous year, is 11% (9% paid by employers and 2% paid by individuals) in Qingdao. Such a ratio is higher than 8%, the proportion fixed by the Chinese government. In general, the medical insurance system in Qingdao provides relatively sufficient financial support for the LTCI project.

Table 6 Age structure of the population in Qingdao (2020)

Ages	Number of people	Ratio
0–14	1552097	15.41%
15–59	6476976	64.31%
60 or above 65 or above	2042649 1429813	20.28% 14.20%
Total	10071722	100.00%

Source Bulletin of the seventh national census of Qingdao City (No.4), Qingdao Government Affairs Website

Moreover, before the implementation of the LTCI pilot work, some elderly people with medical insurance chose to be hospitalized for long periods in order to save on the LTC costs, resulting in a great waste of medical resources. On the other hand, enormous economic pressure and practical difficulties cannot be avoided for elderly people with disabilities who have no basic medical insurance. In this context, for the purpose of alleviating the shortage of hospital resources and solving the LTC problems from different population groups, Qingdao has begun its exploration of LTCI system.

2.3.2 System Construction

Before launching the LTCI policy in 2012, Qingdao had issued a series of relevant guidance documents, in which both institutional and at-home are encouraged to meet the objectives of carrying out better services for disabled elderly persons, as well as establishing the LTCI system by initially integrating medical care into the framework of medical insurance.

With the operation of the *Opinions on Establishing a Long-term Medical Care Insurance System (Trial)* in 2012, the LTCI system was official implemented in Qingdao. In the early stages of the implementation, the scope of insured persons only covered residents with basic medical insurance for urban employees or basic medical insurance for urban residents. The former with higher payment standards serves urban residents who are employed by a company, while the latter with lower payment standards are for non-working groups. The LTCI was then divided into the employee care insurance and the resident care insurance. Afterwards, in 2015, the *Management Measures for Long term Medical Care* was promulgated to further incorporate the rural residents who participated in new rural cooperative medical insurance into the coverage of LTCI. Since then, the LTCI system has achieved full coverage in both urban and rural areas.

With the deployment and operation of pilot cities nationwide, Qingdao was selected as one of the first pilot cities for LTCI in 2016. Elderly people aged 60 or over with severe Alzheimer's disease were further included in the insurance coverage in the following year. In 2018, considering the diversified demands of elderly people from households of different income levels, care suppliers were required to give sufficient consideration to the actual needs of disabled elderly individuals, which should be ensured by the fair and reasonable allocation of resources. The objective is to provide timely, continuous, and integrated services including health and basic living care, functional maintenance, hospice care, end-of-life care, spiritual comfort and other care services for insured persons.

(1) Funds.

The LTCI funds in Qingdao are managed at the municipal level and are raised with a dynamic adjustment mechanism following three principles—expenditure in line with income, balance between income and expenditure, and a small operating surplus. LTCI funds should not be used to pay for medical insurance, occupational injury insurance, maternity insurance, or other care expenses that should be borne by third parties in accordance with the law. The funds for employees and non-employees should be managed separately under the respective financial special accounts for specific purposes. Specifically, the LTCI funds for employees are mainly raised through three channels: transfer of basic medical insurance funds, withholding from personal medical insurance accounts, and financial subsidies. The specific financing strategies are as follows:

1. Transfer from the pooling fund of basic medical insurance for urban employees at the level of 0.5% on a monthly basis
2. Transfer from the personal account of basic medical insurance for urban employees at the level of 0.2% on a monthly basis
3. Subsidized by the government with a fixed amount of RMB 30
4. One-time allocation of the balance remaining (no more than 20%) of basic medical insurance at the end of the calendar year in accordance with the Measures for the Qingdao Social Medical Insurances (Order No. 235 announced by the Qingdao Municipal People's Government).
5. Social donations are accepted.

In terms of population groups belonging to the basic medical insurance for urban residents, the funds are raised by transferring from the pooling fund of basic medical insurance for urban residents at the level of no more than 10%. Resident individuals do not pay the premiums for the time being.

(2) Forms of Care.

At present, a "4 + 3" mode is practically implemented in Qingdao. That is, for elderly people with complete or severe disabilities, there are four types of care services are available for each option:

1. Specialized care: health care provided by institutions that are qualified for specialized medical care services
2. Nursing care: health care provided by institutions that are qualified for medical and nursing care services
3. Home care: health care provided by caregivers from care institutions through home visits over the long-term
4. Short-stay care: health care provided by caregivers from care institutions through home visits periodically

Besides, for elderly individuals with severe dementia (in particular Alzheimer's disease), there are three types of care services provided by health care professionals available for each option:

1. Long-term care: providing uninterrupted long-term and full-time care services
2. Daytime care: providing daytime care services
3. Short-term care: providing short-term care services for a cumulative period of up to 60 days in a natural year

In most cases, during the period of LTC, other social medical insurance benefits such as hospitalization, receiving medical treatment in other locations, outpatient major illness, and accidental injury should not be entitled simultaneously.

(3) Participants.

Every resident who pays the basic medical insurance premium automatically participates in the LTCI without extra registration procedures. Qingdao has drafted preferential policies protecting insured persons aged 60 and older with severe disabilities, especially for those who have been bedridden for a long time, unable to take care of themselves for more than six months due to aging, illness, disability and other reasons. Before applying for LTCI benefits, a level assessment of care needs must be conducted.

The different needs for care are divided into levels 0–5, which are six categories from the mildest support required level to the most severe care level. Level 0 indicates a good overall health condition, while Level 1, Levels 2–3, and Levels 4–5 correspond to mild, moderate, and severe disabilities, respectively. When the acceptable levels (Levels 3–5) are reached, an applicant should also meet the following conditions to be an eligible recipient:

1. For those applying for specialized care services, the result of assessment should reach Level 5, with the total payment from medical insurance pooling funds and care insurance funds exceeding RMB 5000 over the past 12 months, and meanwhile satisfy any of the following circumstances:

   (a) External drainage tubes such as tracheal cannula, bile duct drainage tube, fistula tube, and deep vein catheterization are required to be retained for a long time due to the state of illness (nasogastric tubes and catheters are excluded).
   (b) Coma, total body paralysis, hemiplegia, paraplegia caused by neurological diseases or trauma, with muscle strength of both lower limb or unilateral upper and lower limb at level 0.
   (c) Other conditions for specialized care recognized by social security agencies.

2. For those applying for nursing care and home care services, the result of assessment should reach at least Level 3, with the total payment from medical insurance pooling funds and care insurance funds exceeding RMB 3000 over the past 12 months (or exceeding RMB 5000 over the past 24 months), and meanwhile satisfy any of the following circumstances:

   (a) Have the following chronic diseases or conditions: stroke sequelae (at least one lower limb muscle strength at Levels 0 – III), Parkinson's disease (severe), late stage of rheumatoid arthritis (severe multi-joint deformity) or other serious chronic osteoarthropathy that affects daily living activities, vegetative state, cachexia.
   (b) External drainage tubes such as stomach tube and urinary catheter are required to be retained for a long time due to the state of illness.

   (c) Long-standing non-union of fractures accompanied by chronic serious diseases.
   (d) Long-term coma, total body paralysis, or paraplegia caused by various reasons.
   (e) Other conditions for specialized care recognized by social security agencies.

3. For those applying for short-stay services, the result of assessment should reach at least Level 3.

Regarding the elderly who suffer from severe mental disabilities (Alzheimer's and vascular dementia) and are unable to take care of themselves, assessment results issued by designated institutions are required to be eligible for LTC benefits according to the *Pilot opinions on incorporating elderly people with severe mental disabilities into the long-term care insurance coverage and implementing "dementia zone" management* (Qingdao Municipal Bureau of Human Resources and Social Security [2016] No. 27). The care needs are categorized into five levels, and the eligible insured persons are entitled to apply for the corresponding level of insurance benefits based on their own conditions.

During the application process, the applicants' relevant materials such as medical records and social security cards must be submitted to any of the designated authorities by the applicants or their family members in advance. After a preliminary screening, standard-compliant applications are then transferred to the assessment body for further evaluation. The assessment body will assign professional staff to conduct on-site investigations (household survey) and comprehensive assessments, on the basis of which a *Qingdao Long-term Care Needs Level Assessment Results Notification* will be fed back to the applicants eventually.

(4) Care Contents.

The insured employees who paid a higher basic medical insurance premium can benefit from both medical care and basic living care. By contrast, only a medical care benefit can be applied for by the insured residents.

Medical care mainly includes maintenance therapy, examination and testing, and the use of drugs and consumables. The policy stipulates that all designated care institutions must standardize the use of drugs, consumables, and service items, whilst priority should be given to essential drugs, conventional consumables, and service items. In the case that: a) drugs, consumables, diagnostic, and therapeutic items beyond the prescribed scope are used out of necessity; b) special care services are provided or prescribed time for home care services is exceeded, and formal confirmation of acceptance (signature) is required by the elderly persons insured or their family members. Any related expenses incurred without the agreement of the insured or their family members shall be borne by the designated care institutions.

The eligible costs incurred in respect of care services shall be paid by the LTCI funds under the system of the quota lump sum settlement. The specific settlement standards are as follows:

1. Specialized care: RMB 210 per day for tertiary hospitals, RMB 180 per day for secondary hospitals. Specially, for patients with tracheostomy, the settlement standard is RMB 300 per day.
2. Nursing care: RMB 65 per day.
3. Home care: RMB 50 per day.
4. Short-stay care: RMB 2500 per year for insured employees, RMB 2200 per year for adult residents belonging to the payment of Tier 1, minors, and college students, and RMB 1500 per year for adult residents belonging to the payment of Tier 2.
5. Care for severe mental disabilities: RMB 65 per day for long-term and short-term care, RMB 50 per day for daytime care.

Institutional services including specialized care, nursing care and care for severe mental disabilities, are able to provide comprehensive basic care services according to the actual needs of the insured. Different benefits can be received as the assessment results of recipients vary:

1. The basic living care expenses incurred by recipients with assessment care need levels 3–5 are subject to a monthly payment limit of RMB 660 (¥22/day), RMB 1050 (¥35/day), and RMB 1500 (¥50/day), in which 10% of the total fees are paid by the recipients themselves.
2. The basic living care expenses incurred by recipients with severe mental disabilities of levels 1–5, corresponding to a monthly payment limit of RMB 1500 (¥50/day) for long-term and short-term care and RMB 750 (¥25/day) for daytime care, in which 10% of the total fees are paid by the recipients themselves.

Similarly, in terms of home care services, different living care benefits are provided based on the assessment level. Applicants with assessments levels 3, 4 and 5 are entitled to receive basic living care services up to 3, 5 and 7 hours per week, respectively. The care expenses incurred are paid according to the standard of RMB 50 per hour (including 10% at their own expenses). The focus of home care services with a total of 60 specific service items is mainly on providing professional support that cannot be completed independently by the family caregivers. The specific service content and time can be determined by recipients or their family members in consultation with the designated care service institutions according to their actual needs. Any expenses incurred beyond the service time and content specified in the document shall be borne by the recipients themselves. Additionally, those who apply for medical care benefits only (without basic living care services) are required to have a nurse visiting at least once a week and a doctor visiting at least once a month to master the recipients' situation in time.

(5) Reimbursement.

The reimbursement ratio varies depending on the insured's basic medical insurance contribution base. For medical care expenses incurred that accord with the regulations, the reimbursement ratio for insured employees is 90%, for adult residents belonging to the payment of Tier 1, minors, and college students it is 80%, and for adult residents belonging to the payment of Tier 2 it is 70%.[1] Expenses such as consultation fees, treatment fees, and medical consumables incurred during the short-stay period shall be paid by the LTCI fund according to the above-mentioned standards. Expenses for drugs, examinations and testing shall be settled through basic medical insurance in accordance with the relevant regulations of outpatient major illness.

The designated care institutions should handle intermediate settlements with insured people every three months. For other reasons such as the changes in recipients' physical condition that terminate the care services, timely settlement should be made to ensure the effectiveness of the process. The amount settled must be consistent with the actual expenses. The insured people will be required to charge fees that should be borne by individuals according to regulations. After the settlement, the designated care institutions will issue invoices and print out the *Qingdao Long-term Care Insurance Settlement Form*, which should be confirmed and signed by the insured or their family members. The designated care institutions are obligated to issue the receipt for medical care fees/medical expenses and basic living care fees/home care fees to the insured or their family members, on which the total amount, the item details of the fees, the overall payment amount, and personal payment amount should be specified clearly.

2.3.3 Policy Effects and Operational Status

With the continuous adjustment and optimization, Qingdao's LTCI has become the longest running LTCI project among all the pilot cities in China. During the period of 2012–2021, the LTCI system in Qingdao developed from its initial stage to cover 9.09 million insured employees and residents. Meanwhile, the number of beneficiaries increased from 8000 to 17,000, with the cumulative payment funds increasing from RMB 45 million to RMB 3.5 billion. Correspondingly, suppliers in the LTC market also expanded rapidly, with the number of care institutions from 143 to 978.

In the development process of care institutions, the LTCI system has also become an important bridge for medical care resources moving towards economically underdeveloped regions. Compared to urban residents, elderly people in rural areas have more urgent demands for access to care services. To a certain extent, the implementation of LTCI enables rural elderly people to receive more abundant medical resources.

Nevertheless, the care institutions (especially professional institutions with medical care licenses) are currently still in short supply. Despite the rapid growth of care service institutions in Qingdao, LTCI is far from fully covered. To this end,

[1] The payment standards for unemployed residents who participated in basic medical insurance for urban residents (2024 edition) are as follows: RMB 462 per year for adult residents belonging to the payment of Tier 1; RMB 395 per year for adult residents belonging to the payment of Tier 2; RMB 395 per year for minors; and RMB 150 per year for college students.

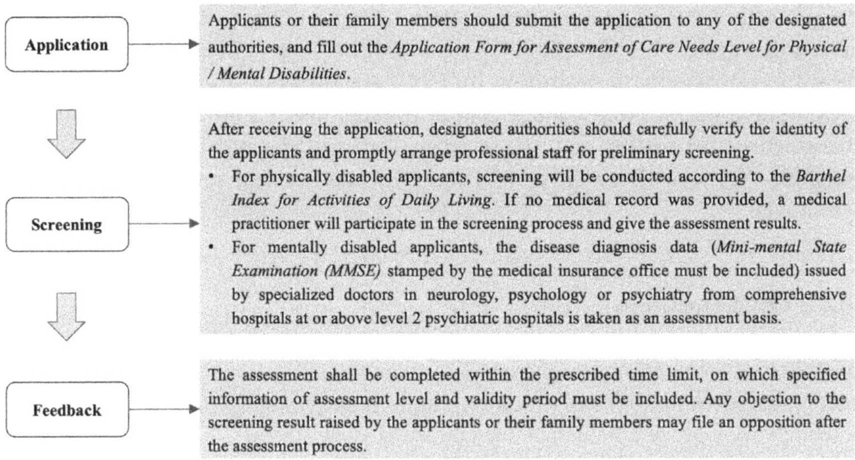

Fig. 2 Application procedures for LTCI in Qingdao

three service forms including home care, institutional care, and daytime care have been designed to alleviate the supply pressure through more flexible ways.

In addition to the inadequate service supply, the shortage of caregivers is more severe. According to relative data, the proportion of licensed caregivers is less than 10%. The majority of caregivers working for care institutions are concentrated at the ages of 40–50 with a low educational level and are mostly from rural areas. As a result, the lack of training and experience is almost inevitable at the moment. Thus, how to deal with the problem of professionalism is one of the key tasks for Qingdao to develop a robust LTCI system in the next stage.

In the actual operation process, the following procedures for application should be undertaken by the insured party before receiving benefits (Fig. 2):

In the practice of the LTCI system, Qingdao has taken the lead in introducing commercial insurance companies to be involved in handling management. In the beginning, the commercial insurance companies only dispatched employees to participate in the joint office work. After several years of operation, the commercial insurance companies gradually took on more functions which involved accepting applications, assessing disability levels, settling expenses and supervising service quality.

In addition, continued regulatory efforts such as strict assessment for eligibility of the insured persons, a strict institutional qualification entrance system, intelligent supervision, standardized management, and third-party handling mode are important prerequisites to ensuring the smooth operation of LTCI.

These regulatory mechanisms are completed through multisectoral collaboration. Specifically, the medical insurance department is responsible for supervising and managing the LTCI system. The medical security agencies are responsible for financing, paying, and managing LTCI funds. The civil affairs department is responsible for industry management and system connection work. The finance department is responsible for fund guarantee and supervision. The human resources and social security department is responsible for vocational training, skill improvement, salary and employment subsidy protection for LTCI practitioners. The health department is responsible for industry management of relevant institutions and providing technical guidance for medical and care services. The insurance regulatory department is responsible for supervising the service quality of participating commercial insurance institutions.

2.3.4 Open Questions

As a pilot city, even though Qingdao has accumulated a wealth of experience and made remarkable progress in promoting high-quality development of LTCI policy, there are still some practical problems awaiting to be solved.

Firstly, there is insufficient sustainability regarding the sources of insurance funds. At present, the LTCI funds in Qingdao mainly come from the basic medical insurance funds and government subsidies. However, the growing concentration of the aging population will disrupt the balance between income and expenditure of pooling funds from basic medical insurance. Fiscal expenditure of local governments may struggle to keep pace with the expansion of the disabled population and the increase of LTC costs. Moreover, the diversified financing methods introduced previously may not be suitable with respect to all regions in Qingdao (especially in low- and lower-middle-income districts) due to different levels of economic development and financing capabilities.

Secondly, there is a shortage of care institutions and professional caregivers. The existing number of care institutions in Qingdao cannot fully cover the entire elderly population that is in need of LTC despite the rapid development of the care services market. The main beneficiaries of LTCI so far are still limited to elderly persons aged 60 or above with severe physical or mental disabilities. Those with moderate and mild disabilities that also need LTC are excluded from eligibility for benefits. Besides, expenses for basic living care are not covered, particularly regarding basic medical insurance for urban residents. That is, compared to the city residents who are paying basic medical insurance premiums for urban employees, unemployed residents in a more disadvantaged position in terms of economic ability and social status can only get lesser reimbursements for LTCI, which also reflects the lack of fairness during the redistribution process.

Thirdly, there is an absence of systematic policy support. At the current stage, complementary policies concerning measures to encourage and guide more social forces to participate in the LTC market have not been introduced yet. Considering the shortage of healthcare practitioners, it is necessary for the government and relevant institutions to take steps to improve the salary and benefits of caregivers, and to combine LTC services with emerging technologies such as the Internet of Things (LoT) and artificial intelligence (AI).

Last but not least, the establishment of effective monitoring mechanisms is premature. The inadequate integration of services caused by the scattered distribution of home care service leads to significant regulatory costs. The privacy and security of service characteristics, along with the long period of benefits payments, also bring regulatory inconvenience to the management of LTCI funds. Moreover, the simple content of assessment standards for disability levels that blurs the boundaries between different levels will also limit the regulatory capacities. For these reasons, more focus and concentration should be given to the standardization of assessment and regulation for LTCI.

In response to these problems, how to take measures in the aspects of funds, services, systems, and regulations to adapt to social development and meet public needs has become an important challenge that Qingdao and other pilot cities need to face and solve in the near future.

3 Comprehensive Evaluation and Nationwide Popularization

Accompanied by the continuous exploration of pilot areas, the construction of system criteria and the coverage of benefits has also gradually improved, which has consequently reduced the financial burden and family pressure for elderly individuals suffering from disabilities. With the accumulation of practical experience during the pilot work, a solid foundation has been laid for establishing the LTCI nationwide.

It is pertinent to point out that the economic development level and population structure of pilot cities determine the intensity of the LTCI policies, and the policy intensity will in turn affect the economic development of the respective cities. Taking the interaction between socioeconomic development and population structure into account, timely adjustment of policy intensity is an important means to ensure the effectiveness of running the LTCI.

The implementation and optimization of the LTCI system have enabled elderly people with disabilities to receive professional care services and improve their quality of life. Accordingly, the efficiency of medical resource allocation has also been increased, which drives the development of the LTC market and expands the labor demand. Nevertheless, China's social LTCI system is still in its early stages, and many shortcomings associated with coverage, financing, services, and compensation remain to be addressed. This section will analyze the achievements and existing problems of China's LTCI system, then discuss the feasible path from pilot to popularization, and conclude with policy recommendations.

3.1 Comprehensive Evaluation of Pilot Work

According to data released by the National Healthcare Security Administration in 2024, the number of insured individuals that have participated in the LTCI has exceeded 176 million, among which more than 2.25 million disabled elderly individuals have received benefits, reducing care expenses by RMB 14,000 per capita per year. The LTCI system in China has begun to show its effectiveness of its protection function. The positive impacts of the pilot work mainly include the following aspects:

First of all, the economic and care burden on the elderly and their families are remarkably reduced. The disabilities of elderly people usually share the characteristics of being long-term, randomness, irreversibility, and significant economic loss. LTCI can meet such actual care needs of disabled elderly people by providing various services from daily care to end-of-life care and help elderly people with disabilities to overcome their difficulties related to the access to health care based on the insurance principles of risk-sharing and co-funding. In addition, since social care has a substitution effect on care provided by family members, the increase in social care supply will significantly reduce the time spent by the family members, which may also allow more potential labor to be released.

Besides, medical resources are significantly optimized and stresses on basic medical insurance are mitigated. The implementation of the LTCI has provided additional options for elderly people being reimbursed for medical expenses through long-term hospitalization, allowing the limited medical resources to be more fully utilized. Moreover, as options are given to elderly people to choose between different care services based on their own physical or mental situations, an environment of healthy competition between hospitals and care institutions will be cultivated, which in turn promotes the long-term development of the elderly care system and its related industries.

Moreover, the pilot work also contributes to employment creation and industrial upgrading. As the service supply side, care institutions have advantages in terms of providing professional services for the elderly, alleviating their loneliness, and forming scale effects in order to lower the costs effectively. As the labor demand side, care institutions also provide numerous job opportunities for caregivers. Through improving service quality and efficiency, LTCI may be expected to realize the potential needs of elderly people into actual service supply. Such a process will contribute to drive the development of the LTC market and promote industry upgrading under the industry competition and monitoring mechanisms, during which new economic growth points will be formed gradually.

Although China's social LTCI has developed rapidly with the support of various government policies in recent years, there is still a significant gap when comparing to the average level of developed countries. At present, LTCI operates independently only in the respective pilot cities that have not yet established a mature system or made clear provisions about the overall framework, which results in a lack of effectiveness while implementing the LTCI system on a larger scale. Considering the current difficulties in flexibly responding to care needs in different situations, there are still many practical issues that need to be addressed in the nationwide implementation of social LTCI.

First, there is the existence of mismatches between supply and demand in care services market. Compared to the increasing demand for LTC among elderly people in

China, the services provided by suppliers are at a relatively low level both in quantity and quality. According to the seventh national census data in 2020, the population of elderly people aged 60 or above in China has exceeded 260 million, of which over 40 million were elderly with disabilities or invisible disabilities requiring different levels of medical care and LTC services, indicating that approximately one in every six elderly people is less likely to successfully carry out activities of daily living. By contrast, as of the end of 2020, there were 4.9 million registered beds in care institutions, while the number of elderly persons using these is only 2.2 million. The high vacancy rate (over 50%) implies the coexistence of mismatch between supply and demand and the low occupancy rate of care institutions, which also demonstrates a serious structural imbalance between social care services and actual demand. This problem not only fails to meet the care needs of the elderly but also restricts the sustainable development of care institutions.

Second, there is an unreasonable allocation of LTC services. The facilities for elderly care service have significant urban-rural and regional differences. The overall number and quality of institutions are characterized by rural areas far exceeding urban areas and eastern regions far exceeding western regions. Public and private care institutions are two different service suppliers that LTCI normally offers. At present, China's LTCI mainly focuses on the former. The development of the latter, however, is fairly slow and uneven in level due to inadequate financial support and uncertain market environment. The insufficient service capabilities and management difficulties remain pervasive issues that limit the expanding of LTC institutions, resulting in difficulties in meeting market demand in terms of scale, structure, as well as efficiency of care services. To protect the income and profit to the maximum extent, some care institutions tend to serve high-end clients, while LTC services for the higher age groups with disabilities and low income are usually hard to carry out in practice due to high risks. Related studies have shown that over one-third of care institutions strictly limit their recipients to elderly people with daily living ability and exclude those with disabilities or invisible disabilities. Such unequal health output indicates a greater actual gap in LTC service supply than the theoretical estimates.

Third, there is limited scope of protection and unclear definition of care level. Currently, the population insured by LTCI is only those people who are paying premiums to basic medical insurance for urban employees in most of the pilot cities, and therefore the number of people qualified for receiving the LTCI services is relatively small. This phenomenon deviates from the original intention of designing the LCTI system, which may further widen the urban-rural gap in the long run. In addition, controversies over specific issues such as the coverage of the insurance, the assessment levels, and the regulations on the charging standards remain to be clearly defined.

Overall, China is still at the early stage of exploring the LTCI system. Despite some progress, there are many practical issues such as unfair system design, insufficient care facilities, shortage of funds and human resources, uneven distribution of institutions, and low service quality which remain to be settled. As the growing care needs cannot be met on many occasions, it is necessary to further clarify the policy directions and continuously improve the service system in order to build a more flexible and suitable LTCI system for China's national conditions.

3.2 Implementation Path for Nationwide Popularization

The pilot system is a unique policy test in China's governance practice, which is a localized decision-making and implementation activity carried out within a certain space scope to verify the correctness and feasibility of policy proposals, as well as to obtain specific details of policies.

To cope with the complex and dynamic economic environment, the "pilot first" approach objective to gradually explore the feasibility of the application of a specific policy has been implemented over periods of economic construction and development in China. LTCI is carried out through such a strategy, with the aim of repeatedly testing and continuously improving the system in pilot cities before the superior government works out an overall comprehensive LTCI system. A key benefit of the pilot project is the ability to incorporate the experience and suggestions from the grassroots into national policies, thereby minimizing the risks and costs of the following nationwide implementation. According to the promotion process of the pilot system, universal access to the LTCI system in China mainly comprises four stages: early exploration, first batch of the pilot project, expansion of the pilot project, and nationwide popularization.

Phase 1: Early exploration and preparation of the system (2012–2016). LTCI was only initially and roughly attempted on a modest scale. For example, Qingdao and Shanghai were pioneers in establishing medical care plans for disabled elderly individuals in 2012 and 2013, respectively. In the following years, the content and scope of such plans have been continuously promoted and improved, which provide preliminary reference for the practice of LTCI pilot projects.

Phase 2: Launch of the pilot project in the first batch of 15 Chinese cities (2016–2020). The issue of *Guiding Opinions No. 1* by the Ministry of Human Resources and Social Security in 2016 marked the start of the second phase in the process of the LTCI system. In addition to the designated 15 cities in the guidance, this project was also actively practiced in some other regions such as Haidian District in Beijing, Weifang City in Shandong Province, and Nanjing City in Jiangsu Province. This stage of pilot work was projected to take three to five years to conduct preliminary exploration and to improve the social recognition of the LTCI system to enhance the national awareness of insurance participation.

Phase 3: Expansion of the pilot work (2020–). In September 2020, the *Guiding Opinions No. 2* were jointly released by the National Healthcare Security Administration and the Ministry of Finance, where 14 new cities were added to the original pilot list. Replicable and promotable experiences can be drawn by comprehensively evaluating and summarizing both achievements and mistakes from the previous stages.

Considering the actual situations with respect to various regions, systematic optimization and adjustment will be carried out to fully leverage the guidance and reference role of pilot cities.

Phase 4: National promotion and popularization. At the National Healthcare Security Work Conference held on January 9, 2024, the National Healthcare Security Administration pointed out that the establishment of the LTCI system should proceed steadily in accordance with the decisions and deployments of the Party Central Committee and China's State Council. After accumulating sufficient experience in the aspects of financing, servicing, reimbursement, and regulation, LTCI as an important system for security for the elderly is expected to be promoted across the country in the near future.

3.3 Policy Recommendations

In spite of efforts undertaken by the Chinese government for continuously establishing and enhancing a standards-based and flexible LTCI scheme, there is still a long way to go to achieve the goal of national implementation. Drawing upon the pilot experience, more emphasis should be put on the following aspects when formulating the specific policies in order to ensure the smooth and effective promotion of the LTCI system.

(1) Establishment of multi-channel and sustainable financing mechanisms.

In consistence with the mainstream of the international financing mechanism, the funding strategy of LTCI in China is based on the pay-as-you-go approach that only provides funds to cover current year costs without consideration of the accumulated future costs, for the purpose of constructing dynamic funding standards that are adaptable to the level of care services. Almost all the pilot cities have adopted the basic medical insurance funds as the main resource of LTCI funds, which, however, makes it difficult to maintain sustainability and may put additional strain on the basic medical insurance system with the deepening of the aging tendency.

Therefore, it is necessary to build a more diversified financing mechanism to ensure the sustainable development of the LTCI system. During the pilot phase, various sources such as government subsidies, personal wages, employing unit payments, lottery profits, and social donations feature in the financial supportive measures for LTCI. The fund's contribution, however, is still predominated by the transfer of basic medical insurance pooling funds. Further refinement and amendment are essential regarding the funding sources in the future stage of national promotion.

(2) Explicit consideration of the insurance coverage and beneficiaries.

As a part of the social security system, LTCI requires social members to jointly share the risk of loss spent on the care for disabled elderly people. In the long run, LTCI is projected to achieve the ultimate goal of universal inclusion, during which more targeted approaches based on scientific assessments should be effectively formulated and implemented in a co-ordinated manner. The insurance coverage can first cover urban employees before expanding to unemployed urban residents. Then, as sufficient experience accumulates from different groups in practice, more beneficiaries from rural areas can be accommodated in the system, so as to ultimately achieve the goal of full coverage in China.

On the other hand, the definition of eligible beneficiaries should be taken as the first issue that needs to be clarified while starting up the LTCI system. In the initial stage of the pilot program, only elderly individuals aged 60 or above with severe physical disabilities are eligible to apply to receive the premium. For further development, consideration should also be given to elderly people suffering from moderate physical disabilities as well as severe mental disabilities. As the policies related to LTCI continue to mature, the scope of care services planning should incorporate a broader population with the coverage progressively extended to those who are under the age of 60 with diseases recognized by law.

(3) Development of sound standards for assessment.

The regulations with respect to forms, content, institutions, and level recognition of LTC services are still relatively rough at the present stage, and thus formally identified standards with clear and quantifiable indicators are urgently required for long-term consideration. Only a few cities so far have developed specific rules to define the LTCI services based on different levels of disabilities, while most pilot cities simply adopt the Barthel Index for Activities of Daily Living as the assessment criteria for identifying.

In the future process of policy construction for LTCI, a complete set of standardized disability assessment tools that can be uniformly used nationwide should be developed in the light of practical research. It is a relatively effective method to build on international experience and success, which will enable China to keep pace with international standards efficiently. Based on the fairness and rationality of the system, by fully using China's advantages in the fields of the internet and other technology industries, more detailed and scientific care plans that taking national circumstances into account are expected to be designed to adapt to different care needs.

(4) Standardization of benefits payments.

In most pilot cities, the service items of LTCI are only briefly listed without specifying the content and standards. Besides, the overall guidance is to focus on basic living and medical care expenses closely related to basic livelihood for elderly individuals aged 60 or over with severe disabilities, whereas it becomes vague in the respective cities when referring to the specific definition and payment standards regarding different forms of care. In order to fully protect the rights and interests of the insured persons, as well as to develop a sound LTC service industry, it is recommended that the government establish a nationwide unified catalog to clearly regulate the scope of fund payments. Meanwhile, moderate adjustments on such a basis should be allowed in practice considering the actual situations varies in different regions.

Additionally, inspiring the elderly to focus more on home care services is an effective means of alleviating the payment pressure caused by the increase in institutional care expenses and improving the efficiency of fund utilization. Moreover, unnecessary steps can be avoided in many cases by drawing upon development practices and experiences abroad. For example, by learning from Japan's preventive care services for elderly individuals with mild or potential disabilities, the rapid growth of the elderly with moderate or severe disabilities will be mitigated to a large extent.

(5) Construction of professional care service institutions and talent management system.

The insufficient supply capacity of care services is a common problem for States during the process of establishing the LTCI system. Since the development of the LTCI system and the care service market is synergistic and complementary, the government should encourage the participation of private care institutions by providing them with tax and cost incentives to mobilize social forces to the full under strictly control of market access, which will eventually achieve the target of creating a healthy environment for LTC service market.

In addition to care institutions, the shortage of caregivers also affects the supply of services in a direct way. Currently, caregivers in China usually have the characteristics of high average age and not being skilled enough to meet professional care needs. In this regard, corresponding policies such as emphasizing talent cultivation, improving professional skills and establishing a certification system for caregivers should be introduced to create a more high-quality talent system.

(6) Strengthening of regulation and risk management.

Only with effective risk management can the LTCI system achieve the expected social policy goals and subsequently promote the innovative development of LTC services and related emerging industries. Some practical problems such as insufficient regulatory resources and inadequate regulation, however, have been discovered in many pilot cities. Therefore, how to improve the regulatory system and realize the social security function of LTCI will be an important task in the future course of generalization.

In response to the common issues of adverse selection and moral hazard between insured persons and service suppliers, as well as fund management risks in the insurance department, it is necessary to verify the authenticity of the respective applications before paying the LTCI benefits, while a sound regulatory mechanism should be established to better master the use of funds by financial institutions.

In addition, a comprehensive supporting scheme incorporating the legal system, social insurance agencies, and commercial insurance that is optimized from the top-level design also plays an important role in promoting the long-term stable development of the LTCI system. Generally, it can be foreseen that China's LTCI system will become a representative reference model for other developing countries in the near future.

Reference

Qingdao Municipal Bureau of Human Resources and Social Security. (2016). Pilot Opinions on Incorporating Elderly People with Severe Mental Disabilities into the Long-term Care Insurance Coverage and Implementing "Dementia Zone" Management (Qingdao Municipal Bureau of Human Resources and Social Security [2016] No. 27).

Long-Term Care Insurance in Malaysia and the Role of the Public and Private Sectors

Mohamad Fazli Sabri, Husniyah Abd. Rahim, and Maheswaran Periasamy

1 Long-Term Care Situation

Long-term care-giving is a service designed for individuals who are unable to care for themselves and require long-term assistance from caregivers. This type of care-giving spans across all generations and is typically provided by family members or relatives who take care of elders or individuals with chronic illnesses or other limitations in self-care. This traditional form of long-term care-giving is often referred to as informal long-term care-giving and has been practised for many years. The elderly or senior citizens are defined as individuals aged 60 years and above which is in line with the definition given by the World Assembly on Aging 1982 in Vienna. This age range is a stage of life that is particularly susceptible to chronic diseases, making proper long-term care essential.

Informal long-term care-giving has progressively become less popular among potential caregivers due to socio-demographic changes and a preference for less co-residence. Consequently, the concept of formal long-term care has emerged, providing professional caregivers and additional facilities and services for more effective elderly care. When dealing with self-care disability, caregivers' tasks are categorized based on the elders' functional needs (Hamdy and Md Yusuf 2018). Activities of Daily Living (ADL) encompass fundamental tasks such as bathing, dressing, using the toilet, transferring, continence, and feeding. Additionally, there is another category beyond ADLs: Instrumental Activities of Daily Living (IADL). While some individuals may be independent in ADLs, they might require assistance in community-related tasks like cooking, housework, laundry, shopping, or medication management. The long-term care system in Malaysia is fragmented due to separate health and social care systems, as well as a divide between publicly and

M. F. Sabri (✉) · H. Abd. Rahim · M. Periasamy
Faculty of Human Ecology, Universiti Putra Malaysia, Serdang, Malaysia
e-mail: fazli@upm.edu.my

H. Lee and G. Nicolini (eds.), *International Comparison of Long-Term Care Insurance Systems*, Contributions to Management Science,
https://doi.org/10.1007/978-981-95-7781-1_11

privately funded care. This fragmentation can pose challenges in providing comprehensive and coordinated long-term care services. Services offered encompass various components, including healthcare, accommodation, meals, and assistance with daily tasks for older people.

In Malaysia, long-term care policies are overseen by the Ministry of Health (MOH) and the Ministry of Women, Family, and Community Development. The MOH manages two key policies: the National Health Policy for Older Persons 2011 and the Plan of Action for Older Persons Health Services 2008 (revised in 2017/2018). Additionally, the Ministry of Women, Family, and Community Development provides welfare and social support for older persons based on the National Policy and Plan of Action for Older Persons (2011–2020). These services include financial assistance, public institutions for independent and bed-ridden older individuals, home visits by volunteers (HomeHelp), and transportation services (United Nations, 2018).

To regulate private care facilities, the Ministry of Health introduced the Private Aged Healthcare Facilities and Services (PAHFAS) Bill in 2017. Although it was passed by Parliament, its implementation is pending the drafting and adoption of regulations. Previously, private care facilities for senior citizens operated under the Care Centers Act 1993 enforced by the Social Welfare Department. The PAHFAS Act 2017 aims to set higher standards for long-term and health care delivery to older persons. Admissions to government care facilities can be voluntary or through court orders for destitute individuals. Certain legislation, such as the Mental Health Act 2001, allows for the detention of persons with mental disorders by court order or medical officers.

In cases of abuse, neglect, or maltreatment of older persons referred to the Social Welfare Department, the District Social Welfare Officer manages these cases according to the provisions under the Domestic Violence Act 1994. The Department offers support by assisting needy older individuals in filing police reports and, if necessary, applying for court orders. Additionally, they provide a secure and safe place to stay and counselling services. The Malaysian Social Protection Council, established in 2016, reviews and formulates a comprehensive social protection system in Malaysia, including provisions for older persons.

In 2023, the demographics of Malaysia were characterized by a population of 16,810,000 women and 17,735,000 men, resulting in a ratio of 1,055 men per 1,000 women. The share of the Malaysian population aged over 65 years was 8.0 percent (2,767,055) in 2023, representing an increase compared to the previous year's 7.5 percent (as shown in Fig. 1). The data from 2012 to 2023 in Fig. 1 displays a gradual increase in the share of the population older than 65 years in Malaysia, rising from 5.4 percent to 8.0 percent. This trend indicates that the aging elderly population is growing year by year. Malaysia is currently grappling with the prospect of an aging population. These ratios of people older than 65 could be the potential of those requiring long-term care which shows a gradual increase in the ratios from 2012 to 2023.

An aging population is defined as one in which individuals aged 65 years and older constitute at least 15 percent of the total population (Statista Research Department,

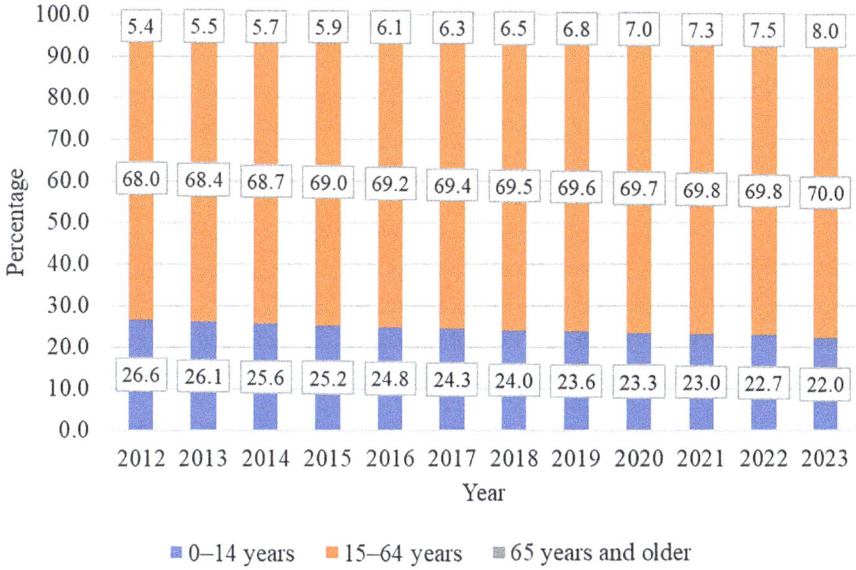

Fig. 1 Age structure from 2012 to 2023 for Malaysia. *Source* Department of Statistics Malaysia (2024a, b)

2023). According to statistical data, this 15 percent threshold will be surpassed by 2030. This figure is projected to increase to 23.1 percent by 2050, primarily due to advancements in medical treatments that have led to an increase in life expectancy. Over the past decade, Malaysia's age structure has undergone a transformation: the proportion of the population between 0 and 14 years has steadily declined from 26.6 percent in 2012 to 22.0 percent in 2023, while the opposite trend holds true for those aged 65 and older (Department of Statistics Malaysia, 2024a, b). The average age of the Malaysian population reflects this shift, projected to reach 34.1 years in 2030, up from 28.5 years in 2014. Figure 1 on the age structure of Malaysians witnessed the shrinking of the youngsters as compared to the elderly. Long-term care is projected to increase according to the increase in the average age of the Malaysian population and the increase in the proportion of those aged 65 and older.

Malaysia faces challenges in preparing for its rapidly aging population. A survey revealed that over 70 percent of Malaysian respondents believe it is the duty of the young to care for the elderly, placing the burden on a shrinking base of young people (Statista Research Department, 2023). Existing issues, such as a lack of professional caregivers, affordable care, and elderly-friendly housing, need prompt attention to ensure the country is ready for its aging citizens.

Adding to the burden of old age care, the number of older adults suffering from dementia is expected to nearly triple over the next 30 years in Malaysia. Due to the nature of the disease, many dementia patients would progress toward the severe stage of dementia within years, which in turn, will take up more of the healthcare system. Psychiatric and behavioural problems, functional impairments, and dependency on others would surface (Lai et al. 2022). There may be memory decline, language impairment, and the depletion of socialization skills and physical abilities that affect the ability to perform daily activities.

The Alzheimer's Disease Foundation estimated 204,000 to 264,000 individuals (8.5% to 11%) were living with dementia in 2020. In 2022, approximately 260,000 older adults in Malaysia, or around 8.5 percent of the population, were estimated to be living with dementia, according to the World Health Organisation (2022). It is projected to increase 312 percent by 2050, reaching 637,500 to 825,000 cases. Globally, dementia has a disproportionate impact on women. In Malaysia, the female-to-male ratio is 1:69. This trend is influenced by women's longer life expectancy and their higher representation among older adults. Dementia, which causes memory deterioration, impairs thinking and affects daily activities, is a major cause of disability among the elderly. People with dementia, who require medical attention and a safe environment, may need care beyond the traditional aged-care facilities in the form of community housing.

The demand for senior living facilities in Malaysia is increasing as the population is aging. The growing aging population and the declining younger population also contribute to the need for more structured senior care facilities in Malaysia. The facilities can be classified as one for independent living and the other for assisted living (Lee 2021). Those seniors who do not require assistance for daily activities can have independent living facilities; however, the facilities also include services such as dining, housekeeping, and social programs. As for assisted living, those that require medical treatment usually cannot live independently. Many affordable private long-term elderly care facilities are operating at full occupancy rate. Well-planned long-term care facilities for the elderly have to be set up for a better conducive aging environment. In summary, Malaysia is experiencing a demographic shift that involves increasing numbers of elderly people, which can be attributed to the increase in life expectancy. This aging population imposes a burden on healthcare systems and social security programs; nevertheless, it offers potential growth in the economy due to the increasing development of companies providing facilities and care for the elderly.

2 History

The mean household income in Malaysia exhibited a small increase before 2010, rising from RM3,011 in 2002 to RM4,025 in 2009, according to the Department of Statistics Malaysia (2024a, b). Subsequently, the trend saw a larger increase, reaching RM5,000 in 2012 and further rising to RM8,479 in 2022. As income increases, it is expected that spending on necessities will also rise. Additionally, households tend to allocate more of their income toward regular spending on non-necessities and may explore new spending that will benefit them in the long run. The impact of time series data on family takaful, income, and health-related costs in Malaysia is illustrated in Fig. 2. Notably, health expenditure has gradually increased alongside household

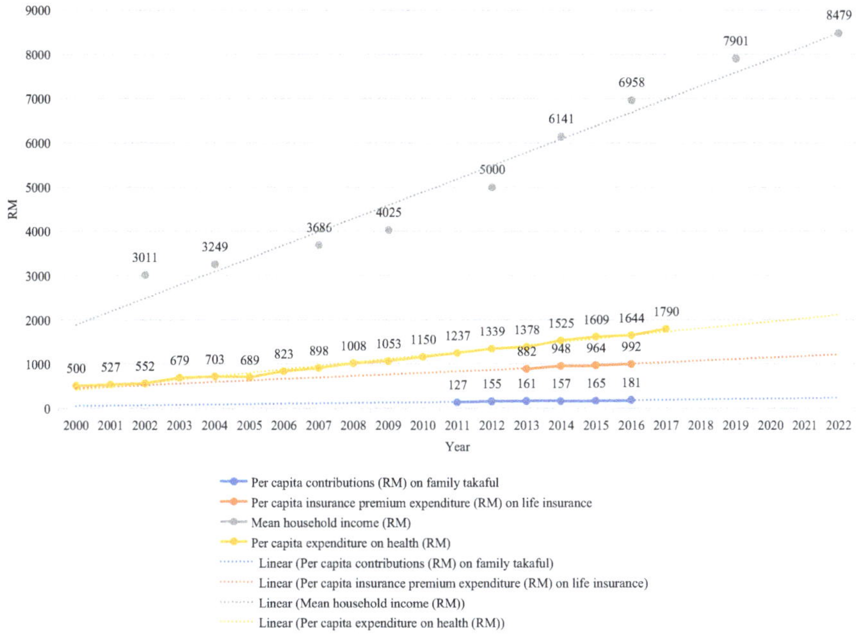

Fig. 2 Impact of time series on family takaful, life insurance, income, and expenditure on health. *Source* Bank Negara Malaysia (2024a, b), Department of Statistics Malaysia (2024a, b) and Malaysia National Health Accounts (2019)

income. Specifically, per capita health spending tripled from RM552 in 2002 to RM1,790 in 2017. In 2002, health spending accounted for 18.3 percent of household income, rising to 24.0 percent by 2016. Over time, historical health spending aligns with income growth, reflecting the greater purchasing power associated with higher earnings.

Contributions on family takaful in 2016 was 2.6 percent from household income while the insurance premium expenditure in 2016 was 14.3 percent. This reflects that the spending on Islamic risk management products was much lower than for conventional insurance. Muslim residents seem to be less prepared to mitigate risks as compared to their counterparts, moreover for their future self. Between 2013 and 2016, as the mean household income for Malaysians increased, their contributions to family takaful and insurance premium expenditure on life insurance showed only a slight increment. Specifically, per capita contributions to family takaful rose from RM882 in 2013 to RM992 in 2016, representing an increment of RM110 over three years. Similarly, per capita insurance premium expenditure on life insurance increased from RM127 in 2011 to RM181 in 2016, which corresponds to a RM54 increment over the five years. These may show individuals' lack of awareness of their financial needs and the risks that they may face in the long run especially during their old age.

2.1 Income and Long-Term Care Costs

As elderly individuals age, their sources of income tend to diminish. Upon retirement, most people earn significantly less, typically around the age of 60. Meanwhile, the cost of living for older individuals increases due to factors such as deteriorating health. Those who have saved adequately for their old age can manage, but many unprepared individuals struggle to maintain a pleasant lifestyle during their later years. The healthcare costs for elderly Malaysians on average are: community-dwelling elderly individuals bear approximately RM426.50 per year; outpatient care costs are around RM141.24; while inpatient care costs were RM2,527 in 2018 (Koris et al. 2019). These costs have increased over the years due to the inflation rate and the impact from COVID-19. Additionally, indirect costs such as transportation and caregiving contribute to the financial burden. The longer life expectancy which has increased over the years to 76.4 years of age in 2023 (Fig. 3), from 72.8 years of age in 2000 and from 65.7 years of age in 1975, would add to the cost of financing for older age.

For nursing homes, costs vary based on factors like location, facilities, and required care level (Batumalai 2020). Starting from 2023, nursing home costs in Malaysia range from RM2,500 to RM6,000 per month. According to iMoney, semi-independent elderly individuals who require minimal assistance and hire domestic workers spend around RM3,100 per month. Alternatively, elderly people needing specialized care may choose to reside in nursing homes or care centers. Managed-Care studies indicate that basic facilities in Kuala Lumpur and Selangor nursing

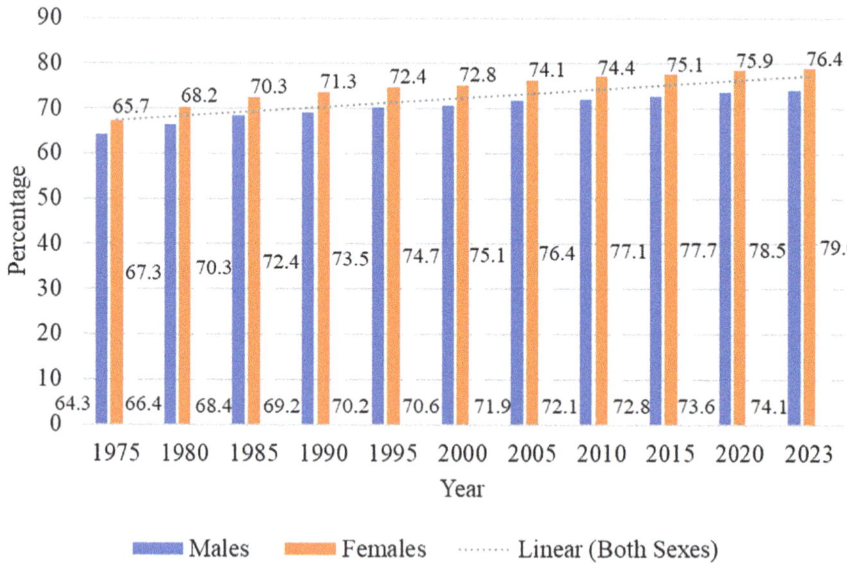

Fig. 3 Life expectancy in Malaysia from 1975 to 2023. *Source* Department of Statistics Malaysia (2024a, b)

homes and care centers cost between RM1,200 and RM3,500 per month, with prices increasing as elderly needs escalate. Adding to this is the cost due to dementia which is significant. The costs include medical services, support, and daily care. Projections indicate that the number of older adults with dementia will continue to rise as discussed earlier (World Health Organisation 2022).

3 Private Long-Term Care Insurance

3.1 History

The Life Insurance Association of Malaysia (LIAM) stated that the average incident rate, which refers to the percentage of insured individuals who go to the hospital in any given year, across the entire population, is approximately 10 to 12 percent (Pillai 2023). However, as individuals reach the age of 75 or older, this rate significantly increases to around 50 percent. When examining other societies, it becomes evident that this issue is not solely a concern for Bank Negara (the central bank of Malaysia); rather, it is a government matter. Addressing this challenge requires government intervention because no commercial entity can propose a viable solution. Unfortunately, the recently passed Health White Paper does not provide a concrete solution. Instead, it outlines a strategic review of the health system's readiness to meet the future needs of an aging population over the next 15 years. This review will consider factors such as service demand, facilities, human resources, technology, and funding. Additionally, it will explore options for expanding benefit packages and contribution schemes to include long-term care.

The Malaysian government is planning to introduce the Senior Citizens Bill in Parliament in 2024, which aims to address elderly care. However, the government seems to place the responsibility for elderly care on families rather than proposing widespread social care provision or subsidizing private facilities. Managing healthcare for an aging population requires a holistic approach beyond the central bank's purview. The issue of medical insurance for seniors remains significant, especially when considering the incident rates. Insurers find it commercially not viable to underwrite or maintain coverage for individuals aged 75, 80, or 85 years old.

Thus, the elderly care insurance is not feasible for insurers due to high payouts. In Malaysia, long-term care is prohibitively expensive for insurers. While life insurance becomes more affordable as people live longer, the cost of insuring long-term care rises significantly due to the prevalence of health issues among Malaysians in old age. Over the past few decades, life expectancy has increased (Fig. 3) but so has the likelihood of illness during the final years of life. Consequently, insuring against long-term care expenses becomes financially challenging. Although there are methods to mitigate costs, it is unlikely that a comprehensive solution enabling insurers to cover the full expenses of nursing homes and elder care will emerge in the near future.

3.2 Current Status

In 2023, the life insurance industry continued to perform well, displaying a double-digit growth of 11.6 per cent in new business total premiums. Life insurance remains a crucial aspect of financial planning for Malaysians, with a projected market volume of US$15.12 billion in 2024, according to the Life Insurance Association of Malaysia (2023). The growth was driven by strong performance in group policies and investment-linked policies. Group policies recorded a growth of 14.5 percent to RM5.1 billion, while investment-linked policies saw a growth of 13.6 percent to RM6.2 billion.

For Malaysia, some of the life insurance products include medical treatment with home nursing care for a limited time such as for a maximum of 180 days in their lifetime and coverage until the age of 100 (RinggitPlus 2024). Thus, the demand on life insurance is presented to reflect part of the insurance that will be considered as insurance for old age care. The income from life insurance premiums purchased in Malaysia increased from 2017 to 2023 from 33.05 billion to 42.06 billion Malaysian ringgit as shown in Fig. 4. In 2023, life insurance companies in Malaysia witnessed the total premium income rise to approximately 42.06 billion Malaysian ringgit, marking an increase from the previous year. This reflected the increasing demand for life insurance products among Malaysians. The increasing awareness of financial protection among the Malaysian population has led to a surge in demand for life insurance in the market.

The Family Takaful fund assets also increased from RM14,377 million in 2011 to RM23,200 million in 2016 as displayed in Fig. 5. Similarly, Fig. 6 shows the increase in per capita contributions on Family Takaful from RM127.3 in 2011 to RM181.2 in 2016. The increase of 61 percent for Family Takaful fund assets and the increase of 42 percent for per capita contributions on Family Takaful shows the increase in demand for Shariah insurance products.

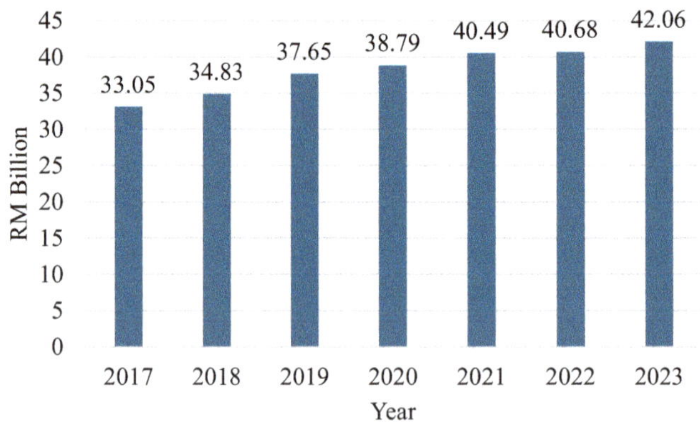

Fig. 4 Income from life insurance premium from 2017 to 2023. *Source* Statista Research Department (2024)

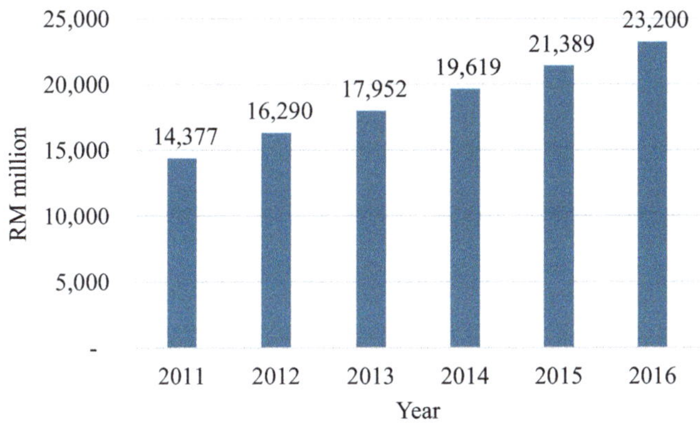

Fig. 5 Family takaful fund assets. *Source* Bank Negara Malaysia (2024b)

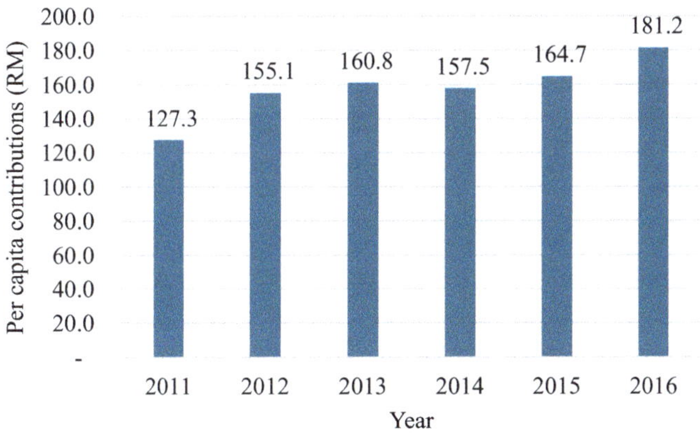

Fig. 6 Per capita contributions (RM) on Family takaful. *Source* Bank Negara Malaysia (2024b)

3.3 Insurance Products

The life expectancy for Malaysians in 2023 was 76.4 years of age and it has been increasing over the years. Malaysians on average are expected to live near to 80 years of age, thus they may be more interested in purchasing insurance products that have a coverage period until at least 80 years of age. Some of the insurance products that would cover old age care until at least 79 years of age are listed in Table 1. Allianz HealthInsured and FWD Insurance Medi First which has a coverage period of up to 100 years old are among the highest in the annual coverage of RM5 million and are without lifetime limit. Manulife ManuHealth Elite Medical Card and AIA A-Plus Health Medical Card also have a coverage period of up to either 99 or 100 years of age but with lower annual coverage of RM2.2 million and RM2 million respectively.

Table 1 Insurance products in Malaysia

No	Insurance Product	Coverage Period	Annual Coverage	Lifetime Limit
1	Allianz HealthInsured	Up to 100 years old	RM5 million	No limit
2	FWD Insurance Medi First	Up to 100 years old	RM5 million	No limit
3	Manulife ManuHealth Elite Medical Card	Up to 99 years old	RM2.2 million	No limit
4	AIA A-Plus Health Medical Card	Up to 100 years old	RM2 million	No limit
5	Prudential PRUMillion Med Medical Card	Up to 80 years old	RM2 million	Not applicable
6	Takaful Kaotim Medikad	Up to 85 years old	RM1.1 million	-
7	Tokio Marine iHealth + Medical Card	Up to 90 years old	Not applicable	RM3 million
8	Manulife ManuEZ-Med Medical Card	Up to 99 years old	RM250,000	RM2.5 million
9	Great Eastern Smart Medic Medical Card	Up to 79 years old	RM200,000	RM2 million
10	AIA A-Life Medik Famili Medical Card	Up to 100 years old	RM150,000	No limit

Source RinggitPlus (2024)

Other insurance products that offer quite a high annual coverage are Manulife ManuHealth Elite Medical Card, AIA A-Plus Health Medical Card, PRUMillion Med Medical Card and Takaful Kaotim Medikad exceeding RM1 million. Many of the insurance products have no lifetime limit for the coverage amount such as Allianz HealthInsured, FWD Insurance Medi First, Manulife ManuHealth Elite Medical Card, and AIA A-Plus Health Medical Card among those that have annual coverage of at least RM2 million. Another product is the AIA A-Life Medik Famili Medical Card having no lifetime period with a lower annual coverage of RM150,000.

The Tokio Marine iHealth + Medical Card, Manulife ManuEZ-Med Medical Card, and Great Eastern Smart Medic Medical Card have a lifetime limit for hospital claims ranging from RM2 million to RM3 million. Individuals prefer insurance products that have no lifetime limit, longer coverage period, and high annual coverage. However, they have to bear the high cost of premium or contribution and it depends on their affordability.

3.4 Insurance Benefits

Insurance plans are offered with various benefits for the welfare of policy holders and to attract potential prospects as they contribute to long-term income for the insurers. As for the customers, purchasing the policies earlier would reduce the spending on mitigating their risks. Depending on individuals' willingness to pay for the premium or contribution, wise decisions have to be made to enjoy the benefits in the long run and until old age. The insurance products discussed below are on their benefits specifically other than the nursing care facilities, which is discussed in the following section.

The Allianz HealthInsured insurance plan includes outpatient kidney dialysis and cancer treatment. It also offers comprehensive medical coverage with no overall lifetime limit and a high overall annual limit of up to RM5 million. This plan includes a unique full COVID-19 coverage for Category 3, 4, and 5, as well as Allianz Care@Home services for medical-assisted attention at home. Category 3 are those having symptoms with lung infection, Category 4 are those appearing as symptomatic with lung infection and needing oxygen supplementation, and Category 5 are critical patients with multiple organ complications. Additionally, it provides extensive cancer coverage, access to genomic testing, and extended outpatient cancer treatment. The plan also features flexible deductible options and an all-in-one medical card to streamline admission and discharge processes. HealthInsured even protects preborn children from as early as 13 weeks into pregnancy, with guaranteed renewable coverage up to 100 years of age.

The FWD Insurance Medi First provides coverage for various medical expenses. These include pre-hospitalization diagnostic tests, surgical fees, consultations before hospitalization, medication, treatment, hospital services, supplies, day care surgery, anaesthetist fees, post-hospitalisation treatment, outpatient benefits, outpatient cancer treatment, and organ transplants. Additionally, it covers emergency accidental outpatient treatment, medical evacuation, and repatriation up to USD250,000 per lifetime. The policy is also claimable for emergency dental treatment including follow-up care for up to 30 days. Eligible policyholders can receive a cash allowance at government hospitals ranging from RM80 to RM200 daily, with a maximum of 200 days per year. Furthermore, insured individuals are entitled to the child guardian benefit to attend to their hospitalized child, which provides quite a high coverage from RM75 up to RM250 for a maximum hospital stay of 200 days per year.

The Manulife ManuHealth Elite Medical Card provides a comprehensive range of benefits. These include pre-hospitalization diagnostic tests, surgical fees, pre-hospitalization consultations, hospital supplies, anaesthetist fees, and post-hospitalization treatments. Additionally, the card covers day surgery, emergency accidental outpatient treatment, medical evacuation, and repatriation services. The policy holder is entitled to a cash allowance at government hospitals, ranging from RM50 to RM100 per day for up to 60 days. Additionally, the policy includes an insured child guardian benefit, providing RM50 to RM100 per day for up to 120 days per policy year. A unique second medical opinion is claimable up to RM2,000 per policy year on selected plans only.

The A-Plus Health Medical Card insurance plan by AIA provides coverage for pre-hospitalization diagnostic tests, surgical fees, pre-hospitalization consultations, medication, and treatment, as well as hospital services and supplies. The plan also covers day care surgery, anaesthetist fees, and post-hospitalization treatment. Emergency accidental outpatient treatment is covered, along with pregnancy complications up to RM10,000 per lifetime. Medical evacuation and repatriation are covered per event up to USD1 million. Additionally, the plan includes emergency dental treatment, an insured child guardian benefit, and intra-ocular lens coverage up to RM7,000 per lifetime. Traditional medical treatment is covered within 150 days after hospitalization. A coverage on cosmetic treatment is subject to the plan and the total amount available in the health wallet.

The Prudential PRUMillion Med Medical Card offers comprehensive coverage for individuals, including benefits such as pre-hospitalization diagnostic tests within 60 days before hospitalization, and coverage for surgical fees. It also includes medication and treatment ranging from RM2,000 to RM5,000, hospital services and supplies, anaesthetist fees, and operating theater fees. Post-hospitalization treatment is covered within 90 days after discharge. The plan provides coverage for organ transplants, day surgery, and emergency accidental outpatient treatment ranging from RM4,000 to RM10,000 per accident. Additionally, it covers intra-ocular lenses up to RM6,000 per lifetime.

Another insurance plan, Kaotim Medikad, offers comprehensive coverage that includes inpatient and daycare surgical benefits, anaesthetist fees, hospital supplies and services, and day surgery. It provides a daily cash allowance of RM100 for hospital stays at government hospitals, with no limit on the number of days. Outpatient benefits include coverage for pre-hospitalization expenses within 60 days before hospitalization, post-hospitalization treatment within 90 days after discharge, and emergency accidental outpatient treatment.

The Tokio Marine iHealth + Medical Card provides coverage for pre-hospitalization diagnostic tests within 30 days before hospitalization, as well as surgical fees, including post-surgery care for up to 90 days. It covers pre-hospitalization consultations within 30 days before hospitalization, hospital services and supplies, and anaesthetist fees. Post-hospitalization treatment is covered within 90 days after discharge. Organ transplant coverage is available up to RM60,000 once per lifetime. The plan also includes day surgery and emergency accidental outpatient treatment ranging from RM1,000 to RM4,000 per accident within 24 h. Funeral benefits are provided up to RM5,000, except for Plan 1 and Plan 2. Additionally, there is a cash allowance at government hospitals ranging from RM50 to RM200 per disability, with a maximum of 150 days.

Manulife ManuEZ-Med Medical Card is an insurance plan that provides comprehensive coverage for various medical expenses. It includes pre-hospitalization coverage for diagnostic tests, surgical fees, and consultations within 60 days prior to hospitalization. During hospitalization, it covers hospital services and supplies, as well as anaesthetist fees. Post-hospitalisation treatment is also covered. Other benefits include day surgery, emergency accidental outpatient treatment up to RM1,000 per injury, and medical evacuation and repatriation up to RM100,000 per lifetime. The plan also provides medical assistance services and a cash allowance at government hospitals of up to RM50 per day.

The Great Eastern Smart Medic Medical Card provides coverage with various co-insurance requirements. Pre-hospitalization diagnostic tests and pre-hospitalization consultations are subject to a 10 per cent co-insurance within 60 days before hospitalization. Surgical fees, hospital services and supplies, and anaesthetist fees each have a 10 per cent co-insurance, with a maximum coverage of RM500. Post-hospitalization treatment is subject to a 10 per cent co-insurance within 90 days of discharge. Day surgery also has a 10 per cent co-insurance, with a maximum of RM500. Emergency accidental outpatient treatment is covered up to RM8,000 depending on the plan type. Accidental death benefits range from RM10,000 to RM20,000. Additionally, there is a cash allowance of RM50 per day for government hospital stays, up to 120 days a year.

The AIA A-Life Medik Famili Medical Card covers pre-hospitalization diagnostic tests, surgical fees, and pre-hospitalization consultations. It also includes hospital services and supplies, anaesthetist fees, and post-hospitalization treatment. Outpatient kidney dialysis treatment is covered up to RM300,000 per lifetime. Additionally, the plan provides coverage for day surgery, emergency accidental outpatient treatment, and medical evacuation and repatriation up to USD1 million. Emergency dental treatment and an insured child guardian benefit are also included.

3.5 *Relationship with Nursing Care Facilities*

For senior citizens in Malaysia, there are insurance options that can help cover medical expenses and nursing care facilities. Medical cards offer coverage for hospitalization fees, surgical procedures, outpatient treatments, medications and other healthcare services, and are subject to a limited age coverage. Some nursing care facilities may not be applicable to the elderly such as claims for costs incurred during confinement. Certain medical cards provide coverage for nursing care services within the home setting. While critical illness coverage doesn't specifically target nursing care, it does offer financial protection in the event of severe health conditions. Regrettably, comprehensive insurance plans specifically designed for nursing homes and elder care are not currently feasible in the Malaysian market (Pillai 2023).

Some of the insurance plans that cover up to at least 80 years of age include home nursing care or nursing care facilities. One of these is the Allianz HealthInsured insurance plan that also includes Allianz Care@Home services for medical-assisted attention at home. Allianz Care@Home is an exclusive home monitoring service provided by medical care professionals in Malaysia. It offers medical-assisted attention for qualified illnesses at home. Qualified illnesses covered are dengue with the medical teams monitoring and treating dengue patients at home, especially those who do not develop severe symptoms, gastroenteritis, cellulitis, and COVID-19 (Category 3, 4 & 5). There will be home visits by doctors and nurses to provide treatment, therapy, and support. Home nursing care is offered for a maximum of 180 days in one's lifetime.

The FWD Insurance Medi First plan offers home nursing care as charged, with coverage for a maximum of 180 days per lifetime. It provides room and board expenses ranging from RM150 to RM500. Intensive Care Unit (ICU) services are covered for a maximum of 100 days per year. The plan also includes coverage for ambulance fees, operating theater fees, and outpatient kidney dialysis treatment. In-hospital physician visits are covered with a limit of two visits per day. Outpatient benefits include radiotherapy, chemotherapy, targeted therapy, hormonal therapy, and immunotherapy, as well as physiotherapy up to RM5,000. Additionally, outpatient benefits cover chiropractic, acupuncture, chiropody, homeopathy, and osteopathy, which are available within 150 days following hospital discharge, depending on the chosen plan.

The Manulife ManuHealth Elite Medical Card provides home nursing care ranging from RM500 to RM1,000 per disability per policy year. It also covers in-hospital physician visits, Intensive Care Unit (ICU) services, outpatient kidney dialysis treatment, stroke treatment, and therapies including speech, occupational, and physical therapy. Additionally, the card includes coverage for operating theater fees, ambulance fees, and room and board expenses ranging from RM150 to RM250 for unlimited days of hospitalization. Outpatient cancer treatment, including radiotherapy and chemotherapy, is covered, as well as outpatient stroke treatment, which includes speech, occupational, and physical therapy.

The A-Plus Health Medical Card by AIA provides claims on home nursing care for a larger amount ranging from RM3,000 to RM10,000, up to 180 days per lifetime including coverage for outpatient kidney dialysis, cancer treatment, and stroke treatment. Outpatient cancer treatment and kidney dialysis treatment are claimable up to RM1,000,000 per lifetime for each treatment. Outpatient stroke treatment is subject to the plan and the total amount available in the health wallet. Room and board expenses range from RM150 to RM500, with coverage up to 150 days per disability. The plan also includes claims on Intensive Care Unit (ICU) services as charged, operating theater fees, and in-hospital physician visits, limited to a maximum of two visits per day.

Prudential PRUMillion Med Medical Card offers several benefits, including post-hospitalization care for up to 365 days. It provides up to RM500 per day for up to 120 days for room and board. Post-hospitalization benefits also encompass extended outpatient rehabilitation treatments, such as physiotherapy up to RM14,000 per year, and alternative therapies, after hospital discharge for serious conditions. It covers in-hospital physician and specialist visits, which are limited to two visits per day. This Prudential medical card also provides home nursing care for up to 180 days over a lifetime. Additionally, it covers operating theater expenses and Intensive Care Unit stays for a maximum of 60 days per disability as well as outpatient kidney dialysis, dengue fever treatment, and cancer treatment.

Takaful Kaotim Medikad provides coverage for daily hospital room and board with no limit on the number of days, up to RM200 per day. It covers Intensive Care Unit (ICU) stays for a maximum of 60 days per disability. The plan also includes coverage for operating theatre expenses, as well as outpatient cancer treatment and outpatient kidney dialysis treatment.

The Tokio Marine iHealth + Medical Card provides coverage for Intensive Care Unit (ICU) stays for up to 60 days per disability. It covers operating theater fees and room and board expenses ranging from RM100 to RM600 which is among the highest, up to 150 days per disability. In-hospital physician visits are covered as charged, with a maximum of two visits per day. The card also includes coverage for outpatient kidney dialysis treatment, outpatient cancer treatment, ambulance fees, and home nursing care which ranges from RM100 to RM250 and is covered for up to 150 days per policy year. Outpatient cancer treatment includes consultation, examination tests, and prescribed take-home drugs.

The ManuEZ-Med medical card from Manulife Malaysia covers various outpatient treatments, including kidney dialysis, cancer treatment, and care for dengue fever. Additionally, it provides coverage for room and board expenses ranging from RM150 to RM250 per day, as well as fees related to intensive care units (ICUs), operating theaters, in-hospital physician visits, and ambulance services.

The Great Eastern Smart Medic Medical Card provides coverage for room and board expenses ranging from RM100 to RM400 per day, up to a maximum of 180 days per year. It also covers Intensive Care Unit (ICU) stays for up to 180 days per year which is among the longest stay claimable. Operating theater fees are subject to 10 percent co-insurance, with a maximum coverage of RM500. In-hospital physician visits are also subject to 10 percent co-insurance, with a maximum of two visits per day. Outpatient cancer treatment, outpatient kidney dialysis treatment, and organ transplant are covered with 10 percent co-insurance, up to RM500. Ambulance fees are subject to a 10 percent co-insurance, with a maximum coverage of RM500, while hospital accommodation is covered for up to 180 days.

The AIA A-Life Medik Famili Medical Card provides comprehensive medical coverage. It includes in-hospital physician visits, with a maximum of two visits per day. Room and board expenses are covered up to RM150 per day and this hospital accommodation is claimable for up to 150 days. Additionally, outpatient cancer treatment is available once per lifetime, and physiotherapy is covered. The plan extends coverage for intensive care unit (ICU) stays for up to 150 days per year that is considerably long as compared to other products. Operating theater fees are included, and home nursing care is provided for a maximum of 180 days per lifetime.

3.6 Problems and Issues

Private long-term care insurance faces various problems and issues as follows. The issues are affordability of the insurance plan, eligibility of the potential policy holder, the coverage limitation, and increase of premium throughout the enforcement of the insurance plan. In terms of affordability, the long-term care insurance plan can be priced highly. Premiums can be expensive, especially for those having health issues, and typically it will increase as one gets older. Long-term care insurance can be used to pay for long-term care like nursing homes, hospice care, adult day care, and getting assistance with activities of daily living, such as bathing, dressing, and eating.

Another issue is eligibility to purchase the insurance plan where someone may find him or herself not eligible for coverage. Individuals with pre-existing conditions or health problems may have difficulty finding suitable long-term care insurance or may face hefty long-term care insurance costs. Rejection in applying a suitable insurance plan may result in having no insurance policy to cover the risks.

The coverage limitations posed another issue in obtaining long-term care insurance. The insurance plan may not cover everything an aging person requires. They may have to purchase more than one insurance policy to include several types of coverage leading to paying a high premium or contribution in total. Some important aspects of coverage for old people may not be available at all.

The potential increase of premiums would add to the problem for policy holders. Insurers may raise premiums on existing customers due to underestimating claims and overestimating investments. Long-term care insurance costs may differ based on multiple factors. Usually, the long-term care rates are not being set earlier and can increase as one ages. It may factor in the future inflation rate in the price which increases long-term care coverage amounts based on an annual percentage.

4 Long-Term Care Facilities

4.1 Public Facilities

(1) History

In Malaysia, the provision of long-term care services for older individuals has evolved over time. Traditional informal care and historically witnessed elderly care was primarily provided through informal caregiving within families and communities. Family members and relatives took on the responsibility of caring for their elders, especially those with chronic illnesses or disabilities. These informal caregivers assisted with fundamental tasks known as Activities of Daily Living (ADL), including bathing, dressing, using the toilet, transferring, continence, and feeding (Hamdy and Md Yusuf 2018). Later, there was a shift towards formal long-term care as socio-demographic changes occurred and co-residence became less common, and as the demand for formal long-term care services thus increased.

The Malaysian government recognized this need and implemented the National Policy for the Elderly in 1995, followed by the National Policy for Older Persons in 2011 under the Ministry of Women, Family and Community Development (Asrulsani et al. 2023). The overarching goal of the National Policy for Older Persons is to enhance the well-being of older individuals. This policy works in conjunction with the National Health Policy for Older Persons 2008 under the Ministry of Health. One of the seven strategies highlighted under this policy provides a continuum of health care services for the elderly. Both policies empower individuals, families, and communities by providing elderly-friendly services and creating enabling environments to enhance well-being in old age.

Each policy is accompanied by a plan of action namely the Plan of Action for Older Persons Health Services 2008 (revised in 2017/2018) and the Plan of Action for the Older Persons (2011–2020). The National Family Policy with a comprehensive set of action plans for the years 2010 until 2020 assists in continuously advocating family values across generations. The policy aims to develop prosperous, healthy, and resilient families, ensuring social stability. As a result, it promotes informal long-term care by family members. To enhance further elderly services in Malaysia, the 2011–2015 Department of Social Welfare's Transformation Plan established the Elderly Division. This division is dedicated to the well-being of senior citizens, with responsibilities that encompass planning, executing, and overseeing programs and activities related to elderly individuals, including addressing their challenges and issues. The division is further organized into four branches.

The Institutional Services branch oversees the operation, administration, and financial management of public facilities for the elderly. Specifically, it focuses on the initiation and development of physical facilities, including day care centers and nursing homes. The Elders Empowerment branch is primarily responsible for welfare programs and activities for the elderly, encompassing spiritual and religious programs both within institutions and in the community, apart from managing a life-long learning program for the elders. Meanwhile, the Elders Social Support branch manages additional support programs and facilities, such as providing special seats in public transport and designated parking lots. On the other hand, the National Advisory and Consultative Council for Older Persons focuses on preparing for old age and promoting intergenerational solidarity. The Minister of Women, Family and Social Development as one of the council members is expected to assist the government in formulating proper responses to address the challenges posed by the aging population.

As part of the policy, various institutional care centers, including Seri Kenangan Home, Ehsan Home, 1Malaysia Family Care, and Home Help Services, offer support to older people. Hence, public long-term care facilities were established to cater to older individuals who lacked immediate family support. These facilities aim to address various components of long-term care, including healthcare, accommodation, meals, and daily assistance. A range of services is offered, including home-based care and institutional care, such as welfare (financial) assistance, public institutions for independent and bed-ridden older persons, home visits by volunteers (HomeHelp), and transportation services.

The goal is to ensure that these facilities effectively meet the long-term care needs of Malaysian elders based on their Activity of Daily Living (ADL) and Instrumental Activity of Daily Living (IADL) requirements. In summary, Malaysia has made strides in formalizing long-term care services, recognizing the importance of supporting older individuals who may not have family caregivers. These efforts contribute to enhancing the quality of life for seniors in need of assistance. While acknowledging that the government has been proactive in providing long-term care services to the aged population over the past two decades, it is also important to note that the current resources and services are still insufficient to meet the needs of the aging population.

A council was established in 1990 which actively promotes the welfare and social well-being of senior citizens known as the National Council of Senior Citizens Organisations, Malaysia (NASCOM). It is a not-for-profit federation of senior citizens organizations with affiliates throughout Malaysia. The council operates independently and is not directly under any specific ministry or agency. Its mission is to advocate for the development of policies and services aimed at enhancing the quality of life and well-being of older persons in Malaysia. NASCOM's objectives include encouraging and supporting senior citizens, empowering them to maintain their place in mainstream society and lead fulfilling lives. Additionally, NASCOM recognizes and appreciates the invaluable contributions of senior citizens to the nation, upholds Asian family values of love and respect for elders, fosters improved understanding and communication between the younger generation and senior citizens, generates community interest, support, and participation in organizing programs and activities for the benefit of senior citizens, coordinates the activities of various senior citizen organizations across Malaysia, and encourages the establishment of senior citizen organizations throughout the country. In conjunction with Malaysia introducing palliative care services in 1995, the Ministry of Health developed and published the Palliative Care Services: Operational Policy in 2010. Palliative care is the care for residents with serious health conditions. Previously, private care facilities for senior citizens were governed by the Care Centers Act 1993 enforced by the Social Welfare Department.

Community-Based Services

Community-based services are provided under the Ministry of Women, Family, and Community Development, in collaboration with voluntary welfare organizations that receive financial assistance from the government. These organizations offer various support services for older individuals facing unfortunate circumstances. However, the number of older persons in need exceeds the available support. Consequently, the government may need to allocate additional resources to address the growing number of older individuals in Malaysia.

The Silver Hair Program encourages active aging by promoting physical fitness, mental health, and social engagement among seniors. It includes fitness classes, workshops, and community events. The National Council of Senior Citizens Organizations (NACSCOM) collaborates with government agencies to advocate for the rights and welfare of senior citizens (Chung et al. 2020). They work on policy development, awareness campaigns, and community outreach. The 1Malaysia Elderly Health Screening Program (1MEHSP) focuses on preventive health measures for seniors, providing free health screenings to detect and manage common health conditions such as diabetes, hypertension, and cholesterol levels. Additionally, Community-Based Rehabilitation Centers offer rehabilitation services for elderly individuals who require physical therapy, occupational therapy, or speech therapy, aiming to improve their quality of life.

(2) Types and Operators

Under the Ministry of Women, Family, and Community Development, there are five types of facilities available for long-term care. Those are the Senior Citizen Activity

Centers, Senior Citizens Care Unit Program, Respite Care, Home Help Services, and Senior Citizen Club. The Department of Social Welfare in each state plays a crucial role in providing welfare aid to citizens. These institutions are responsible for administering various welfare programs and services across the country, including long-term care.

Senior Citizen Activity Centers serve as community hubs where elderly individuals actively participate in daily activities. These centers offer a diverse range of services, including social support and developmental programs, through strategic collaboration between the Ministry of Women, Family, and Community Development, other government agencies, and non-governmental organizations (NGOs). The Senior Citizen Activity Centers initiative has several key objectives. These include expanding facilities to enhance the well-being and development of senior citizens, fostering appreciation by creating a space where seniors feel valued through sharing their experiences and expertise, encouraging participation and collaboration among various stakeholders, providing alternatives for low-income senior citizens, and enhancing the overall quality of life for seniors. Senior Citizen Activity Centers offer a variety of activities and programs, including religious programs, recreational activities, therapy and rehabilitation, health talks, and relevant training or courses. Seniors interested in becoming Senior Citizen Activity Centers members can register at a nearby center without any fees. Additionally, the Senior Citizens Central Database and Senior Citizen Activity Centers empowerment were planned under the 12th Malaysia Plan, while the Senior Citizen Action Plan is periodically reviewed to ensure the continuity of a sustainable National Senior Citizen Policy.

The Senior Citizens Care Unit Program offers transportation facilities and services to elderly individuals who reside alone or with families unable to afford medical care at hospitals or clinics under the Department of Social Welfare. These facilities and services enable them to access health screening and treatment at either government or private sector hospitals or health clinics. Its objectives are to provide transportation facilities for senior citizens and enable them to access health screening and treatment at hospitals and health clinics. Additionally, the unit collaborates with the Welfare Voluntary Organisation to assist underprivileged elderly individuals who struggle with managing their daily lives. Furthermore, the unit strives to enhance senior citizens' accessibility to public facilities, particularly medical services, while also offering support to seniors with physical and mental disabilities in seeking necessary treatments and services.

Respite Care at Seri Kenangan Homes provides an alternative service for caregivers and guardians, allowing them to temporarily place elderly individuals in an institution. This service is essential due to job demands outside the district or country, or any other reason that necessitates placing the elderly in the institution. Within this framework, Respite Care services encompass comprehensive care and protection for senior citizens, including the management and provision of necessities such as food, health, and accommodation. Another accommodation for elderly, Ehsan Homes, also serves the same function as Seri Kenangan Homes. Nevertheless, it is limited to only older people who are chronically ill and unable to take care of themselves.

The Home Help Services program provides essential support to senior citizens, particularly those who live alone and lack family members' presence at home. This program serves as a social outreach service, where dedicated case workers proactively visit senior citizens, eliminating the need for them to actively seek assistance. The Home Help Services Program relies on volunteers who offer social support to the elderly and disabled within their homes. Additionally, the program aims to foster more structured and effective voluntarism within the community. By engaging volunteers through the Home Help Program, the community empowerment process is streamlined, promoting shared development and well-being. This approach aligns with the government's commitment to enhancing community services and fostering social integration among local residents. The Home Help Program, initiated as part of the NBOS7 (National Blue Ocean Strategy 7) - 1Malaysia Family Care initiative, was launched in July 2012 through a strategic collaboration between the Department of Social Welfare, the Ministry of Health Malaysia (MOH), and the Welfare Voluntary Organisation.

The Senior Citizen Club, an initiative aimed at promoting community and non-governmental organizations (NGO) involvement in senior care, operates under the umbrella of the Master Health Clinic throughout Malaysia. These clubs offer a variety of services and activities designed to improve the well-being and quality of life for older individuals.

(3) Operational Status

Throughout Malaysia, there are currently 143 Senior Citizen Activity Centers in 2024 as compared to 132 activity centers for older people in 2020, with an increase of 11 activity centers (Department of Social Welfare 2024). Table 2 displays the distribution of Senior Citizen Activity Centers according to states in Malaysia. In general, states with a larger number of residents have more centers of public facilities for long-term care. Table 2 displays the number of Senior Citizen Activity Centers by states in Malaysia. The Senior Citizen Activity Centers are places where elderly individuals engage in daily activities within their community. These centers provide a range of services, including social support and developmental programs, through strategic collaboration between the Ministry of Women, Family, and Community Development, other government agencies, NGOs, and the Department of Social Welfare. Various activities and programs are available at Senior Citizen Activity Centers, including religious programs, recreational activities, therapy and rehabilitation, health talks, and relevant training or courses.

More Senior Citizen Activity Centers nationwide will be created in facing the challenges of an aging nation by 2030 and targeting the establishment of a Senior Citizen Activity Center in every parliamentary constituency across the country to encourage active aging among Malaysians. Strategic cooperation with government-linked companies to assist the government in providing services to the elderly involves government agencies, the corporate sector, private companies, non-governmental agencies, and individuals, to implement corporate social responsibility programs for the elderly.

Table 2 Senior citizen activity centers by states

State	Senior citizen activity centers
Johor	16
Selangor	17
Sarawak	13
Sabah	16
Kelantan	11
Kedah	12
Pahang	12
Kuala Lumpur	10
Terengganu	6
Negeri Sembilan	6
Pulau Pinang	6
Melaka	6
Perak	7
Perlis	3
Labuan	1
Putrajaya	1
Total	143

Source Department of Social Welfare Portal (2024)

The Senior Citizen Care Unit Program currently operates nine vehicles stationed in several states across Peninsular Malaysia. This service is provided free of charge to seniors. To avail of this service, seniors can contact the Senior Citizen Activity Center or Rumah Sejahtera. These nine Senior Citizen Care Unit Program vehicles are stationed in the following Peninsular Malaysia states: Perlis, Kedah, Selangor, Melaka, Johor, Pahang (with two vehicles), Terengganu, and Kelantan.

Respite care services at Seri Kenangan Homes and Ehsan Homes cater to senior citizens and caregivers. Eligibility criteria for senior citizens include being aged 60 years and above, which encompasses spouses, siblings, parents, aunts/uncles, grandparents, and their siblings. Additionally, they must be free from contagious diseases and capable of self-care. To qualify, individuals must be Malaysian citizens or permanent residents. Caregivers, whether they are family members (such as children, siblings, grandchildren, or spouses) of the senior citizen, or non-family caregivers (such as foster families or friends), must be Malaysian citizens. The placement period for both senior citizens and caregivers can vary, ranging from a minimum of one day (one hour to 24 hours) up to a maximum of 30 days, subject to approval by the Director-General of Social Welfare.

Seri Kenangan Home is established to assist senior citizens without close relatives and provides a peaceful and dignified living environment with proper medical care and security. The institutional life also encourages social networking among the elderly within their age group. Additionally, life in the institution promotes "active aging" through activities both within and outside its premises. Those seeking shelter support can apply for admission by contacting the Department of Social Welfare (District Office), where a Social District Officer conducts an in-depth investigation and provides a comprehensive report for consideration by the Director General. As of now, there are 10 existing Seri Kenangan Homes across Malaysia. However, due to increasing numbers of senior citizens and the country's aging population, the capacity of these existing homes is no longer sufficient.

Ehsan Home was established to provide care, treatment, and protection to elderly individuals who are sick, homeless, and without heirs. The goal is to create a comfortable and safe environment for them. It offers various services and facilities, including care and protection, guidance and counselling, physiotherapy, religious guidance, recreation, job recovery, and medical treatment. There are two Ehsan Home facilities directly managed by the Department of Social Welfare: Ehsan Home Dungun in Terengganu and Ehsan Home Kuala Kubu Bahru in Selangor. To be eligible for admission, individuals must meet certain criteria, such as being Malaysian, lacking self-care ability, having no heir or guardian, being diagnosed with contagious diseases, having no income, being authorized by a Government Medical Officer as a destitute patient, and not having a psychiatric illness. Admission applications are voluntary and follow the guidelines outlined in the Home Patient Management Regulations of 1978.

The institution facilities for respite care include specialized accommodation equipped with basic amenities, basic medical services and treatments provided at the institution's clinic, regular health check-ups and essential medication administered by community nurses, advanced medical treatment and examinations available at nearby government health clinics and hospitals if necessary, facilities for physiotherapy and assistive devices managed by trained Medical Rehabilitation Officers (if needed and approved by the family), a prayer room accommodating up to 200 congregants at a time with various religious activities and programs, fully managed laundry services by institution staff, and a recreation room for socializing and leisure activities with other residents and visitors. Application for respite care services can be made at the District Social Welfare Office nearest to them.

The implementation of the Home Help Services Programme meets four main criteria of NBOS which are low cost, high impact, rapid execution, and sustainability to ensure that these services truly benefit the target group in line with the principles of value for money. Managed by the Community Division under the Department of Social Welfare, this program not only provides social support services to clients, but it is also a rehabilitation, care, and client integration service performed by volunteers in the community. Through the implementation of this program, it can reduce the entry of senior citizens and disabled people to government, private, and NGO welfare institutions as well as support the efforts of the Department of Social Welfare in the success of the Deinstitutionalization (DI) program. Home assistance is a program that offers support services to the elderly and disabled, particularly those who reside alone or with family members in under-served and underprivileged households. It involves trained volunteers who provide social companionship through social outreach, guided by the principles of voluntarism and the concept of virtue as a shared responsibility.

The welfare volunteers offer a range of assistance services tailored to individual needs. These services include preparing food and drinks, assisting with self-care tasks (such as bathing, nail-cutting, and hair combing), providing companionship, organizing leisure activities, maintaining living spaces, handling laundry, managing financial transactions (including withdrawing money from the bank and paying bills), offering qualified physiotherapy, training caregivers in care techniques, promoting healthy lifestyles, accompanying seniors and individuals with disabilities to medical appointments, ensuring proper medication administration, and providing any other necessary support. For additional information, please reach out to the Community Division within the Community Development Branch.

As of 2017, there are 233 Senior Citizen Clubs under the Master Health Clinic throughout Malaysia. The Family Health Development Division Portal under the Ministry of Health Malaysia provides more information regarding this club. Senior clubs typically offer a range of services to enhance the well-being and quality of life for older adults. These services include social interaction, health and wellness programs, educational workshops, counselling and support, community engagement, transportation assistance, and advocacy and empowerment initiatives.

(4) Profit

Since the services and programs are offered by the Department of Social Welfare under the Women, Family, and Community Development Ministry, and also under the Ministry of Health, there is no fee charged to the seniors in need. Most of the services under the Department of Social Welfare are performed with the assistance from volunteers in providing those services. Seniors interested in becoming Senior Citizen Activity Centers members can register at a nearby center without any fees.

4.2 Private Facilities

(1) History

In 2017, Malaysia operated at least 310 private homes that benefited over 7,000 older individuals, according to the Ministry of Women, Family, and Community Development. During the same period, there were 1,019 private facilities scattered across the country (Chung et al. 2020). There were 400 private care centers for older people listed under the ministry in 2024. These private facilities, although more widespread, tend to be costlier and cater primarily to urban and higher-income residents. They operate on a profit-making basis, but the exact number of high-income households receiving services from private care centers remains unknown. Malaysia may need approximately 2,000 registered elderly care centers by 2030 to meet the demands of its aging population and to ensure consistent operational standards across the country (Advance Care Planning 2018).

Private corporations also offer similar services, requiring residents to pay monthly fees for care and support. Additionally, some non-governmental organizations provide limited charitable services, although their reach may not be widespread. Free institutions, which admit healthy and self-manageable elderly individuals, offer minimal care and supervision. For those requiring frequent supervision and long-term care, private for-profit care institutions become essential. The government permits private firms to participate in supplying care services to older persons under the Care Centers Act 1993.

(2) Type and Operators

In Malaysia, private elderly facilities address a range of needs and preferences among the elderly population. Some of these facilities provide multiple services at a single location. The primary types of private elderly facilities include care centers, day care centers, rehabilitation centers, nursing homes, home care services, and retirement homes.

Care centers can offer services for both long-term stays for elderly, spanning several months or years, and short-term stays, known as respite care. These centers provide accommodation, meals, and essential care services for the elderly. They are staffed by trained professionals who offer medical assistance, administer medications, and help with daily activities. Respite care provides short-term stay options, giving family members peace of mind when temporarily leaving their elderly at the centers. This type of care offers temporary relief for both the caregiver and the person being cared for. Such care centers include IG Care, Golden Roots Elder Care Center, My Aged Care, and Genesis Life Care.

Day care centers provide care and activities for the elderly during the day, allowing them to return home each evening. These centers offer social activities, meals, and some level of medical care. They are intended for elderly individuals who struggle to manage independently at home or who feel isolated. Day care centers enable family members to fulfil other commitments, such as work and family responsibilities. Day care center operators include MyAgeingCares (Universiti Putra Malaysia), Harvestars Elderly Day Care Home, and Golden Mansion Care Center, as well as Komune Care.

Rehabilitation centers provide a range of services including physical therapy, stroke therapy, occupational therapy, and various other rehabilitation treatments. They assist seniors in recovering from injuries, surgeries, or illnesses and are crucial for maintaining mobility and enhancing overall well-being. Notable examples of such centers in Malaysia include Well Rehabilitation Center, Rehabilitation Center for the Elderly (RICE), and Promenade Care Center.

In Malaysia, nursing homes generally offer a broad range of facilities and services to cater to the needs of their elderly residents. These include 24-h nursing care, physiotherapy and occupational therapy, as well as social and recreational activities and assistance with daily living tasks. The homes also provide access to various medical specialists, such as doctors, nurses, and dietitians. Additionally, nursing homes in Malaysia offer diverse accommodation options, from private rooms to shared apartments, allowing residents to select the level of privacy and independence that best suits their preferences. Some facilities also create a safe and supportive environment for older adults who can no longer live independently. Furthermore, many nursing homes also offer specialized care for residents with dementia or Alzheimer's disease. This can include memory training, counselling, and support for caregivers.

Hospice and palliative care are also available in nursing homes. Hospice care is designed for individuals with terminal illnesses who prioritize comfort and quality of life over curative treatments. This specialized care focuses on providing relief from pain and improving overall well-being rather than pursuing aggressive treatments. On the other hand, palliative care is intended for anyone with a serious illness, regardless of whether they are at the end of life, and aims to alleviate symptoms and support quality of life. Nursing homes offering these services can vary significantly in terms of the care provided, amenities, and costs. Families typically select facilities based on their elderly relatives' specific needs and preferences. Examples of such nursing homes include TLC Nursing Home, Mediskill Nursing Center Sdn. Bhd., and Lions Nursing Home.

Private home care services offer in-home caregivers who assist the elderly with activities of daily living (ADLs), such as showering and medical escorts, as well as address medical needs and provide companionship, enabling seniors to stay in their own homes. These services also include medical support like physiotherapy, occupational therapy, and nursing care. Examples of home care providers are Homage Homecare, Alpro Homecare, and Senioracare Sdn. Bhd.

Retirement homes can be categorized into independent living communities and assisted living facilities. Independent living communities offer a lifestyle with minimal assistance, providing accommodation and basic amenities without extensive medical care. Examples of such homes include Sunshine Retirement Home, Senior Living @ Taman Tun, and Happy Retirement Home.

Assisted living facilities offer support with daily activities such as bathing, dressing, and medication management, while still allowing residents more independence than nursing homes. They provide a higher level of care than independent living communities but less intensive care compared to nursing homes. These facilities aim to create a secure and comfortable environment for seniors. Examples of assisted living facilities include Lotus Care Premium Assisted Living, Assunta Hospital Senior Living, and Kulai Heritage Care Home.

Upscale retirement villages are available offering high-end amenities, such as gourmet dining, recreational activities, and luxurious living accommodations. They may provide varying levels of care depending on the needs of the residents. Those operating in Malaysia are GreenAcres Retirement Home, Eden-on-the-Park, and Millennia Village.

(3) Operational Status

As of 2024, there were 400 private homes operated in Malaysia listed on the Ministry of Women, Family and Community Development's website. The number had increased since 2017 when there were 310 private homes operating in Malaysia which benefited more than 7,000 older persons. Table 3 provides the number of private care centers for older persons based on states. Similar to the public facilities for long-term care, private care homes in the states are larger due to the higher population.

Table 3 Private care center for older persons based on states

State	Private care center for older persons listed under the ministry
Selangor	98
Perak	89
Johor	65
Federal Territory of Kuala Lumpur	31
Negeri Sembilan	28
Pulau Pinang	28
Melaka	19
Kedah	11
Pahang	11
Sabah	7
Kelantan	4
Sarawak	3
Perlis	3
Terengganu	2
Federal Territory of Labuan	1
Federal Territory of Putrajaya	0
Total	400

Source Department of Social Welfare Portal (2024)

Selangor, Malaysia's most populous state, also boasts the largest economy in terms of gross domestic product (GDP) of 25.9 percent in 2023, with a population of 7.341 million (Department of Statistics Malaysia 2024a, b). This was followed by the Federal Territory of Kuala Lumpur (15.9 percent), Johor (9.5 percent), Sarawak (9.1 percent), Penang (7.4 percent), and Sabah (5.3 percent) for Malaysia's 2023 GDP. The second and third places in private care centers for older people after Selangor were Perak and Johor with 89 and 65 care centers respectively. Though Sarawak contributed the third most to Malaysia's 2023 GDP, the activities from private care centers for older people may not be a significant contribution to the GDP as there are only three care centers in the state.

Figure 7 exhibits the number of private care centers for older people listed by the Ministry of Women, Family and Community Development in comparison with the population of each state in Malaysia. The listed private care centers are provided not in tandem with the population of each state, reflecting a large market in states with high populations but lack of private care centers. Those are Sabah, Sarawak, Kedah, Kelantan, Pahang, and Terengganu which have less than 12 private care centers and as low as three centers. Nevertheless, the demand needs to be studied as the residents in these states may prefer the traditional way of aging in their own homes and the costs may hinder them to obtain the private care center services. There may also be unregistered private care centers operating at large. The elderly or their family

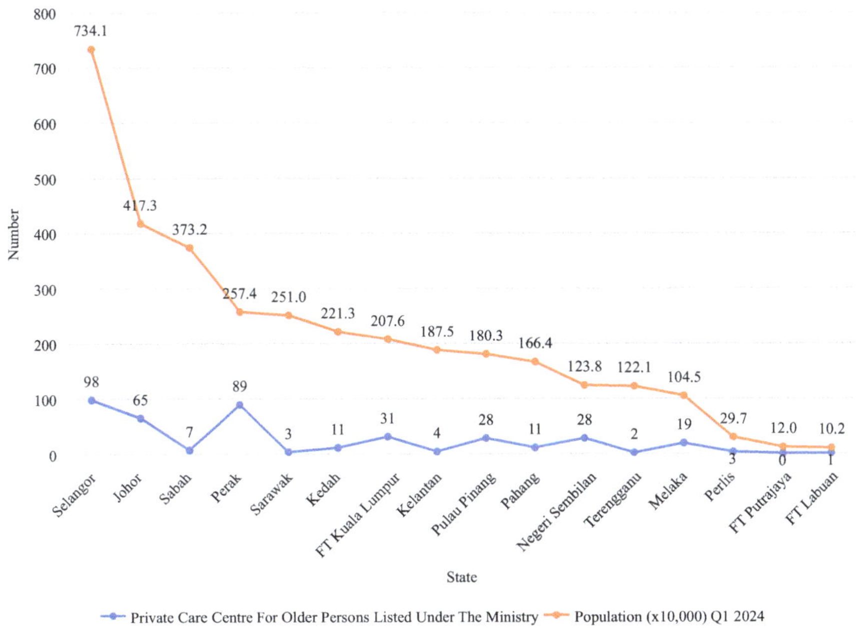

Fig. 7 Private care center and population of states in Malaysia. *Source* Department of Social Welfare Portal & Department of Statistics Malaysia (2024a, b)

members may also prefer free services offered by centers operated under the ministry. However, the centers under the ministry usually operate at full occupancy.

Federal Territory Putrajaya was the latest state established in 2001 with the highest average household income of RM13,473 in 2022, which was higher than the national average of RM8,479 (Department of Statistics Malaysia 2024a, b). Currently, there is no registered private care center in Putrajaya owing to its younger population as compared to other states. The median age in Putrajaya is approximately 25.8 years, while the median age for Malaysia as a whole is 30.8 years. Thus, Putrajaya posed an opportunity to set-up a private care center in the near future suitable to the lifestyle of the residents.

(4) Profit

The operation of private facilities for old age care was intended to be profit-making as opposed to the public facilities or non-governmental agencies' services. The standard of services offered varies and thus a benchmark on the price is not possible. However, some possible prices for old age care are presented which are assumed to surpass the costs of delivering those services to enable profit making. In 2016, the reported cost for basic care services in a semi-private room ranged from RM1,200 to RM2,600, while a private room cost between RM2,650 and RM3,500 as compared to a current rate of RM3,900 monthly (refer to the discussion below).

The information provided on the care centers and nursing homes websites as of July 2024 stated that daily living care is charged as low as RM30 for a duration of one hour by local certified caregivers, while nursing care is as low as RM36 for one hour extended by local licensed nurses. For elderly individuals that require home therapy, the charge is as low as RM135 per hour. Hiring a private nurse in Malaysia costs approximately RM50 to RM80 per day and other services are offered in packages to help ensure affordability. Such costs are for private nurses who are registered nurses holding a valid Annual Practising Certificate with the Malaysian Nursing Board and who have at least two years of ward experience.

One nursing home offering services including medical care and personal hygiene management had a price of RM130 for eight hours for a private nurse, while for services including basic check-ups and simple medical treatment such as wound care and feeding tube insertion the price can start from RM100 per visit. The charge will increase accordingly to the care needed by old-age customers. In the case of providing skilled nursing and assisted living facilities, including weekly doctor's visits, the price starts from RM1,800 a month.

In terms of nursing homes that offer medical treatment, the cost of facilities varies based on the health and physical condition of potential residents. For instance, one nursing home charges RM2,000 per month for six to eight bedded wards where patients can walk and eat with minimal supervision. The highest rate for this type of ward in this nursing home is RM2,600 for bedridden patients without bed sores. Additionally, small single rooms are priced as low as RM3,900 per month for patients who can walk and eat independently. On the high end, large single rooms cost RM5,900 per month for patients requiring intensive nursing care and physiotherapy. Day-care services are available at RM150 per day, and short-term stays have a daily rate of RM250 with a minimum stay of 10 days. Doctors conduct a medical assessment upon admission, which costs RM460, with an additional charge of RM200 for facilities like dressing, oxygen, suctioning, and emergency calls. Thus, depending on the level of care and medical treatment required by the elderly, such pricing for elderly care services is made to ensure the business is profitable.

5 Nursing Care Providers

5.1 Current Status

Generally, aged care living in Malaysia can be divided into two categories, namely the nursing homes and old folks' homes. As of 31 December 2019, only 21 nursing homes (775 beds) were licensed by the Ministry of Health and the number was the same in 2022. To ensure that the minimum standard of care is delivered to the elderly in these centers, private nursing homes were regulated under Act 586 Private Healthcare Facilities and Services Act 1998. Later, the Private Aged Healthcare Facilities and Service Act 2018 (Act 802) was passed by the Parliament on 29 November 2017 and came into force on 29 March 2018. The new Act replaces the Private Healthcare Facilities and Services Act 1998 [Act 586] which regulates private nursing homes as well as the Department of Social Welfare—Care Center Act [Act 506] which regulates care centers. If the center is registered with the Department of Social Welfare, it is deemed to be licensed under 802.

Table 4 exhibits the list of licensed nursing homes in Malaysia as of May 2022 (iElder, 2022). Any nursing homes licensed after this date are not included in the discussion. Econ Medicare Center and Econ Medicare Center and Nursing Home are two companies that have more than 100 premises in the center of Peninsular Malaysia, specifically Kuala Lumpur and Selangor. For the east coast, there are only licensed nursing homes in Pahang but not in Kelantan or Terengganu. Located in the northern region are 22 licensed nursing homes in Kedah. In the Borneo region, there are five licensed nursing homes' companies in Sarawak with a total of 209 premises but none in Sabah. The states of Perlis, Penang, and Negeri Sembilan also do not have any licensed nursing homes as of 2022.

Table 4 Licensed nursing homes in Malaysia

No	Nursing homes	State	Locations
1	City Heart Care Centre	Johor	5
2	Econ Medicare Centre and Nursing Home	Johor	194
3	Jeta Care Sdn. Bhd	Johor	1
4	Kang Xin Care Centre Sdn. Bhd	Johor	15
5	Spring Valley Homecare (JB) Sdn. Bhd	Johor	8
6	TLC Nursing Home	Kedah	22
7	Econ Medicare Centre	Kuala Lumpur	189
8	KPJ Senior Living Care	Kuala Lumpur	42
9	Lecadia Primacare Centre Sdn. Bhd	Kuala Lumpur	30
10	ESP Life Nursing Care Centre Sdn Bhd	Melaka	16
11	Mediskill Nursing Centre Sdn Bhd	Pahang	14
12	Larut Care Centre	Perak	9
13	Eden On The Park Care Residence	Sarawak	24
14	Lions Nursing Home	Sarawak	60
15	Love Care Centre	Sarawak	28
16	Rejang Nursing Care Centre	Sarawak	73
17	Tabuan Healthcare & Nursing	Sarawak	24
18	Bellevue Residential Homecare (M) Sdn. Bhd	Selangor	8
19	Econ Medicare Centre and Nursing Home	Selangor	138
20	SP Nursing Care Centre	Selangor	4
21	Seavoy Nursing Home Sdn. Bhd	Selangor	1
	Total		905

Source iElder (2022)

5.2 Profit Making Model

The long-term care system should be designed with facilities and services tailored to the specific needs of the elderly (Department of Social Welfare 2024). Everyone desires a comfortable life in their later years, particularly those with medical issues who often require specialized care and support. To address these needs, the long-term care system may include various types of facilities based on the specific care requirements (MIDA 2021) in order to be profitable. The facilities are care centers, nursing homes, rehabilitation centers or services, daycare centers, and retirement homes or villages.

Facilities such as care centers for the elderly providing the personal and social needs of senior citizens are required. The care centers should offer a lifestyle that allows seniors to remain independent while accessing dedicated assistance. Services may include meal planning, housekeeping, routine medical check-ups, palliative care, therapy, medication management, and social activities.

Nursing homes providing various levels of medical care for the elderly who can no longer be cared for at home or require 24-hour nursing supervision should be offered. Residents in nursing homes would receive accommodation, meals, 24-hour nursing care, personal assistance, rehabilitation services, and social activities. For elderly individuals staying at home, nursing homes could offer personal care assistance, nursing care, home therapy, medical escorts, respite care, dementia care, and social activities. Home nursing involves professional staff providing care in the familiar environment of the individual's home. This facility provides personal and medical care services in the comfort of the elderly person's own home and allows them to recover at home with support from family members.

Offering rehabilitation services focuses on physical therapy, stroke therapy, occupational therapy, and other forms of rehabilitation. These services help seniors recover from injuries, surgeries, or illnesses. This type of center is essential for maintaining mobility and improving overall well-being. Post-operation rehabilitation programs could be offered as well as post-stroke rehabilitation programs. The primary goal of post-stroke rehabilitation is to promote maximum patient recovery. The main focus includes strengthening of muscle groups, motor re-learning, and retraining balances.

Daycare centers should provide care and companionship for senior citizens during the day while their families are at work. After work, family members can fetch the elderly to take them home. The centers should offer scheduled social activities, prepare meals, and assist with personal hygiene, much like a nursery. Throughout the day, seniors should have plenty of chances to interact with one another.

Retirement villages would provide a home and its environment that is tailor made for the elderly (Lee 2021). It should be subject to market demand, especially from the financial and location aspects. In setting the rates, the size of the relevant target market or income group and their preferences should be understood through surveys and market studies. There should be a range of choices from affordable to premium elderly care.

6 Caregivers and Qualification System

A significant initiative in the care-giving services is exhibited by the establishment of the National Caregivers' Association in 2012, with the objective of providing support and services to caregivers around the country. Equipped with a range of services, including training, education, and counseling, it aims to improve the overall well-being of both caregivers and the aging population. The introduction of the National Policy on Aging in 2011 emphasizes the importance of providing assistance and empowerment to caregivers in Malaysia. The policy acknowledges the vital role caregivers play in caring for elderly individuals and emphasizes the need to provide them with adequate support. To achieve this, the government has implemented several caregiver assistance initiatives. For instance, the Caregiver's Training Program equips caregivers with essential skills in nursing care, nutrition, and creating a safe home environment. Additionally, the government offers the Caregiver's Allowance to financially assist low-income caregivers responsible for elderly care. To further enhance caregiver support, the government collaborates with NGOs and companies. For instance, the Alzheimer's Disease Foundation Malaysia provides caregiver training, counselling services, and support programs for those caring for individuals affected by dementia.

For those planning to qualify as a caregiver for the elderly or to operate a senior care center in Malaysia, it is essential to obtain the Malaysian Skills Certificate offered by the Malaysian Skills Development Department, a public sector agency (iElder 2023). Obtaining certification standards for elderly care are crucial to ensuring high-quality care for senior citizens. While nursing and medical programs cover a range of medical skills, the Malaysian Skills Certificate specifically emphasizes expertise in elderly care. Possessing the right skills enables caregivers to offer superior care to the elderly population in Malaysia. These certification standards fall under the National Occupational Skills Standards (NOSS) and are categorized as Residential Care Activities for the Elderly and Disabled.

There are three levels of certification: Level 3 covers Elderly Care Center Operation, including skills related to residents' care, safety, hygiene, and emergency response. Level 4 (Malaysian Skills Diploma) focuses on Elderly Care Center Administration, while Level 5 (Malaysian Advanced Skills Diploma) pertains to Elderly Care Center Management. To acquire the Malaysian Skills Certification, individuals can choose from three methods: participating in training programs at Skills Development Department accredited centers, undertaking industry-oriented training through the National Dual Training System, or obtaining accreditation based on prior achievement (work or training) by providing evidence of skills competency, assessed by officers and endorsed by external verification officers appointed by Skills Development Department. Additionally, certification through Accreditation of Prior Achievement offers advantages such as quick certificate acquisition, the ability to remain employed without attending classes or training, and low cost.

The private sector also offers certifications for long-term elderly care, with varying duration depending on the course's purpose and the participant's background. Short courses are available for family caregivers and domestic helpers, providing them with knowledge on caring for seniors (Care Concierge 2024). These programs are designed to equip family caregivers, domestic helpers, and individuals with the knowledge and abilities needed to care for seniors at home. Topics cover aspects on managing Activities of Daily Living (ADLs), hygiene care, and safety, communication skills, promoting basic mobility needs, hygienic and dietary requirements, assessing general health status, and assistance in medication administration. Additionally, participants will learn about risk and safety considerations for seniors, including preventive measures for falls and pressure sores, effective management of choking incidents, and methodical hands-only CPR techniques for unconscious seniors.

As for specialized skills designed for family caregivers, the programs directly address critical subjects such as CPR and Dementia Care. Learners gain the tools to compassionately support individuals with dementia and Alzheimer's disease. The "Hands-only CPR and AED Training" technique is used to treat people suffering from sudden cardiac arrest. It involves chest compressions and rescue breaths to keep blood flowing to the heart and brain. An AED (Automated External Defibrillator) is a portable device that provides electric shocks, which can be used to restart the heart.

There is a professional care-giving certification program aimed at those pursuing a career in senior caregiving. The basics and specialized elements of caregiving are offered as a comprehensive course to become a certified caregiver. Designed for individuals interested in full-time employment as healthcare assistants, this program emphasizes kindness, compassion, and care for seniors. The basics cover topics such as an introduction to caregiving, basic safety and health precautions for caregivers, vital signs and health assessment, promoting basic mobility needs, promoting hygienic needs, dietary considerations, and risks and safety management. The specialized course includes basic medication knowledge, basic wound dressing and first aid treatment, intake and output management, respiratory care, suctioning, common elderly illnesses and diseases, and palliative care.

For caregivers with experience in nursing homes but lacking formal training, there is a course designed to enhance their skills. It aims to refresh and update clinical skills relevant to nursing home care, covering a range of topics including vital signs monitoring, promoting hygienic practices, addressing mobility needs, and understanding risk and safety. A caregiver will be equipped with the necessary skills to provide comprehensive care for seniors. In addition, a corporate workshop serves as a comprehensive guide for family caregivers, offering essential insights into care skills and knowledge. It provides participants with fundamental insights into health monitoring, risk and safety awareness, effective communication, and basic mobility awareness.

References

Advance Care Planning. (2018). Conversation about your future self and care management and finance. https://www.agedcare.com.my/acgconcept/0.2017/july/caregiverpreneurs

Asrulsani, M. S., Awang Chek, M. Z., & Ismail, I. L. (2023). Understanding a long-term care towards ageing population in Malaysia. *International Journal of Academic Research in Business and Social Sciences*, *13*(12), 4744–4754.

Bank Negara Malaysia. (2024a). Insurance key indicators. *Annual Insurance Statistics 2016*. https://www.bnm.gov.my/stats-insurance/-/asset_publisher/fEOnyB0mSi8g/content/id/1014934

Bank Negara Malaysia. (2024b). Takaful key indicators. *Annual Takaful Statistics 2016*. https://www.bnm.gov.my/-/ats2016

Batumalai, K. (2020). *What Malaysia needs for healthy ageing and care*. Codeblue. https://codeblue.galencentre.org/2020/11/17/what-malaysia-needs-for-healthy-ageing-and-care/

Care Concierge. (2024). *Certification programme*. Care Concierge Academy. https://mycareconcierge.com/academy

Chung, C. F., Pazim, K. H., & Mansur, K. (2020). Ageing population: Policies and programmes for older people in Malaysia. *Asian Journal of Research in Education and Social Sciences, 2*(2), 92–96.

Department of Social Welfare. (2024). *Senior citizen activity centres*. Ministry of Women, Family and Community Development.

Department of Statistics Malaysia. (2024a). *Household income, poverty and household expenditure*. Ministry of Economy.

Department of Statistics Malaysia. (2024b). *Demographic statistics Malaysia, First quarter 2024*. https://storage.dosm.gov.my/demography/demography_2024-q1.pdf

Hamdy, M. S., & Md Yusuf, M. (2018). Review on public long-term care services for older people in Malaysia. *Malaysian Journal of Science Health & Technology,2*(Special Issue).

iElder. (2023). *Certification standards for elderly care in Malaysia*. https://ielder.asia/blogs/news/certification-standards-for-elderly-care-in-malaysia

iElder. (2022). *List of licensed nursing home in Malaysia*. https://ielder.asia/blogs/directory/list-of-nursing-home-in-malaysia

Koris, R., Mohamed Nor, N., Haron, S. A., Hamid, T. A., Aljunid, S. M., Muhammad Nur, A., Ismail, N., Shafie, A. A., Yusuff, S., & Maimaiti, N. (2019). The cost of healthcare among Malaysian community-dwelling elderly. *Jurnal Ekonomi Malaysia*, *53*(1), 89–103.

Lai, W. H., Hon, Y. K., Pang, G. M. H., Chong, E. M. G., Nordin, N., Tiong, L. L., Tan, S. H., Abu Sapian, R., Lee, Y. W., & Rosli, N. (2022). Dementia of the ageing population in Malaysia: A scoping review of published research. *Aging and Health Research*, *2*(2), 1–9.

Lee, R. (2021). *Senior living facilities catching on in Malaysia*. The Edge Malaysia. https://theedgemalaysia.com/article/cover-story-senior-living-facilities-catching-malaysia?gclid=CjwKC

Life Insurance Association of Malaysia. (2023). *Life insurance industry performance 2023*. https://www.liam.org.my/images/liam/PR-Life-Insurance-Industry-performance-2023.Final.pdf

Malaysia National Health Accounts. (2019). *Health expenditure report 1997–2017*. Ministry of Health Malaysia.

MIDA. (2021). *Golden opportunities in senior living care - MIDA*. Malaysian Investment Development Authority. https://www.mida.gov.my/golden-opportunities-in-senior-living-care/

Pillai, S. (2023). *Elderly care insurance not commercially viable in Malaysia*. Codeblue. https://codeblue.galencentre.org/2023/08/24/elderly-care-insurance-not-commercially-viable-in-malaysia/

RinggitPlus. (2024). *Best medical card in Malaysia 2024 - Compare and buy online*. https://ringgitplus.com/en/health-insurance/medical-card/

Statista Research Department. (2023). *Share of aging population Malaysia 2014–2022*. https://www.statista.com/statistics/713529/malaysia-aging-population/

Statista Research Department. (2024). *Breakdown of life insurance companies' income in Malaysia from 2017 to 2023 by type of income*. https://www.statista.com/statistics/1078997/malaysia-breakdown-of-life-insurance-companies-income-by-type-of-income/
United Nations. (2018). *Malaysia LTC input 2018*. https://social.un.org/ageing-working-group/documents/ninth/Inputs%20Member%20States/Malaysia_LTC.pdf
World Health Organisation. (2022). *Supporting people living with dementia in Malaysia*. https://www.who.int/westernpacific/news-room/feature-stories/item/supporting-people-living-with-dementia-in-malaysia

Long-Term Care for the Aged Population the Case of Bangladesh

Muhammad Ziaulhaq Mamun and Md. Zahid Hossain

Abbreviation

ADL	Activities of Daily Living
ATCOA	Asia Training Center on Aging
BGMEA	Bangladesh Garment Manufacturers and Exporters Association
BWHC	Bangladesh Women Health Coalition
BAAIGM	Bangladesh Association for the Aged and Institute of Geriatric Medicine
CBHC	Community-based health clinic
CBHI	Community-based health insurance
EPHC	Elderly and Palliative Health Care
FDI	Foreign Direct Investment
GoB	Government of Bangladesh
HPNSP	Health Population and Nutrition Sector Development Program
HYV	High yield variety
ICESCR	The International Covenant on Economic, Social and Cultural Rights
LTC	Long-term care
MDGs	Millennium Development Goals
MHFW	Ministry of Health and Family Welfare
MTP	Medically trained providers
NCD	Noncommunicable diseases
NGO	Non-governmental organization
NSSS	National Social Security Strategy

M. Z. Mamun (✉)
Institute of Business Administration (IBA), University of Dhaka, Dhaka, Bangladesh
e-mail: mzmamun@du.ac.bd

Md. Z. Hossain
Mercantile Bank Plc, Dhaka, Bangladesh

H. Lee and G. Nicolini (eds.), *International Comparison of Long-Term Care Insurance Systems*, Contributions to Management Science,
https://doi.org/10.1007/978-981-95-7781-1_12

PDO	Predeparture orientation
PHC	Primary health care
RIC	Resource Integration Center
RCHCIB	Revitalization of Community Healthcare Initiatives in Bangladesh
RMG	Readymade Garment
SGD	Sustainable Development Goals
SSN	Social safety net
UDHR	Universal Declaration of Human Rights
VGD	Vulnerable group development
VGF	Vulnerable Group Feeding
WHO	World Health Organization

1 Long-Term Care for the Aged Population: The Case of Bangladesh

Today Bangladesh is enjoying a demographic dividend. There are 15.3 million people aged 65 or above out of 117.2 million in Bangladesh (BBS, 2023); this number was 10.2 **million out of 150.2 million** in 2011. The average life expectancy in Bangladesh stood at 72.8 years with an increase of 3.8 years from 69.0 years in 2011. The number of elderly populations is growing faster than the overall population growth rate. Over the past decade, the elderly population has increased by 50.01%, while the total population has grown by only 14.66%. That is, the increase in the number of elderly people is 3.41 times higher than the population growth.

The demographic dividend is projected to start shrinking by 2035, and Bangladesh is expected to transition from an "aging" society in 2029 to an "aged" society by 2047. The trend of a rise in the number of elderly people in the country is alarming due to the absence of any proper initiative to manage them. The elderly people in Bangladesh are facing economic, social, and health vulnerability. The fact that the economic and health benefits for the elderly have not increased in line with the increase in the number of elderly people is worrying. Without long-term care (LTC) initiatives, the elderly may become a burden to the country in the future. Keeping the above scenario in mind, this chapter has drawn an overall picture of the reality of and responses to care for the elderly in Bangladesh from the financial consumer's perspective. The topics explored include:

- *Demographic Dividend in Bangladesh: Evolution, Challenges and Prospects*
- *Service Requirements for the Aged in Bangladesh*
- *Health Care System in Bangladesh*
- *Long-Term Care (LTC) Systems in Bangladesh*
- *Health Insurance for Aged in Bangladesh*
- *Universal Pension Scheme (UPS): New Approaches by the Government*
- *Elderly Care Services and Homes in Bangladesh*
- *Concluding Remarks*

2 Demographic Dividend in Bangladesh: Evolution, Challenges and Prospects

The fiscal and economic crises enveloping many of the world's wealthiest nations have brought to light the economic challenges arising from tectonic shifts in demography in the developed world. During demographic transitions, sharp declines in fertility lead to significant changes in a population's age structure. Smaller birth cohorts reduce youth dependency ratios and mechanically increase per capita output if output per worker and the labor force participation rate remain unchanged, generating a demographic dividend. In developing societies, mortality rates decline first, followed by a fall in fertility rates, leading to changes in the age structure. As a result of declining population growth, there is a bulge in the working-age population and a shrinking dependent population, which can allow for faster economic growth when combined with effective policies and markets.

The impact of changes in a nation's age structure on its economy has been studied for decades (Bloom et al., 2003a; Coale & Hoover, 1958; Easterline, 1967; Ehlrich & Ehlrich, 1990; Mason, 2005; Simon, 1981). The underlying theory suggests that the demographic dividend positively impacts a nation's economic development and that in high-fertility societies, reducing fertility can be a powerful tool to reduce poverty (Eastwood & Lipton, 1999; Mason & Lee, 2004). Among many South and Southeast Asian countries, Bangladesh has achieved great success with family planning programs along with remarkable improvements in health status (Bloom et al., 2003b).

This section is divided into six parts to cover the different aspects of the demographic dividend in Bangladesh: (i) Issues; (ii) Demographic trends; (iii) Demographic transition; (iv) Essentials of demographic dividend; (v) Socio-economic challenges; and (vi) Policy recommendations. The analysis considers the features of demographic transition, age dependency ratio, population growth and its components (births, deaths, and international migration), age structure, and sex composition of the population. Variables such as investment, Gini coefficient, income, female labor force participation rate, crude birth rate, crude death rate, life expectancy, age dependency ratio, and population growth rate, along with other demographic factors, have been considered.

2.1 Issue

Bangladesh is a densely populated country with a population growth rate of 1.01% (BBS, 2023). Demographic change in Bangladesh is opening up new economic opportunities. The declining infant and child mortality helped to spark higher fertility, effectively resulting in a temporary baby boom. As this cohort moves into working ages, Bangladesh finds itself with a potentially higher share of workers as compared with dependents. If the working-age population can be productively employed, Bangladesh's economic growth stands to accelerate. Policy choices will be crucial in helping Bangladesh realize the economic benefits of demographic change. Failure to capitalize on these opportunities could lead to economic stagnation (Ahmed, 2019).

Most of the population in Bangladesh directly or indirectly depends on agriculture, with a very low per capita income. An industry-led agricultural transformation is essential to reduce population dependency on agriculture and substantially increase per capita incomes in the sector. People here are working in the informal sector getting lower income, little health protection, and no incentives. For sustainable progress, the country needs more flexible labor markets, especially increased literacy and greater participation of women in all socio-economic aspects. It also requires a broader societal attitude toward women working, higher female labor force participation rates, a healthier population, improved infrastructure, and technological advancement. If Bangladesh needs to progress its phase of development, one important possibility is by increasing investment in human capital and the formation of an environment of fewer people in agriculture, creation of productive jobs in the organized sector, enhancement of entrepreneurship, and fostering investments while improving strategies for increasing the productivity in agriculture. In brief, Bangladesh needs to foster decades of inclusive growth. The challenge for Bangladesh is how to reap the benefits of the demographic dividend.

2.2 *Demographic Trends in Bangladesh*

In Bangladesh, there are two opinions among analysts and demographers about the dividend's beginning period. One group believes it started in the 1990s, while another group argues it began after 2000. The Government's Eighth Five-Year Plan noted that the share of the working-age population started to increase in 1978, heralding the beginning of the demographic window of opportunity. Demographers have forecasted that Bangladesh's first demographic dividend window will close between 2033 and 2040. It is projected that Bangladesh will become an aging society by 2029 and an aged society by 2047. The country is already in a declining stage as the dependency ratio is on the rise. As the ratio of people aged 60–64 years continues to increase, the opportunity to reap the demographic dividend still exists.

Bangladesh is currently benefiting from the demographic dividend as the number of young people outnumbers the non-working-age population (Fig. 1). Presently, the foremost question for Bangladesh is whether the current momentum will continue in the coming years as well or if it will soon lose momentum. The question has arisen because the number of elderly people has increased over the years, pushing up the dependency ratio in recent years. The proportion of the working-age population declined to 65.08% in 2023 from 66.58% in 2021. A year earlier, the proportion was 65.67% (2022). Similarly, the dependency ratio for people over 65 rose to 9.4% in 2023 from 8.6% in 2022.

The speed at which Bangladesh is likely to transition from an "aging" society to the "aged" stage is faster than advanced Asian countries and rich European countries. However, the proportion of the population in the age group of zero to four is still

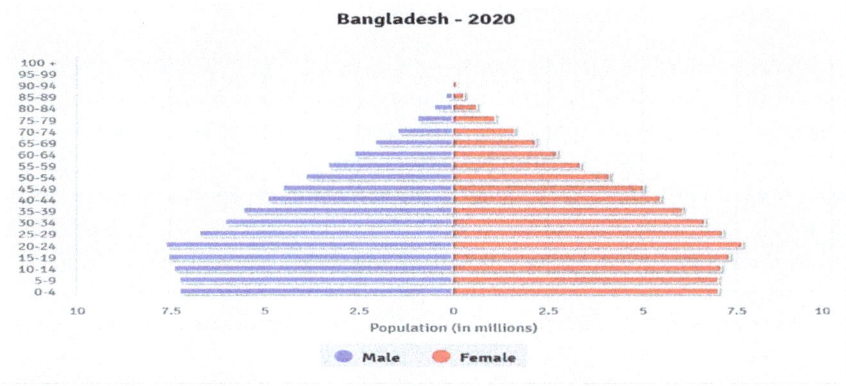

Fig. 1 Population age distribution of Bangladesh in 2020

increasing. In about 11–15 years, they will enter the workforce. Therefore, even if there is a decline in some age groups, the proportion in the 15–64 age group is not likely to fall substantially, and the potential for a demographic dividend remains, at least in the medium term. Owing to the emerging challenges stemming from Artificial Intelligence, it will be difficult to optimize the dividend. The government's investment plan for education and health is taking too long to yield results. World Bank data shows that Bangladesh is one of the 20 developing countries with the largest populations of older adults (60 or older) in the world. By 2025, Bangladesh will account for about half of the world's older adult population. By 2025, one in 10 Bangladeshis will be 60 or older, and by 2050, that number will be one in five. However, until the dependency ratio reaches 70%, it cannot be said that the demographic dividend is fading.

2.3 *The Demographic Transition in Bangladesh*

(A) **Age Dependency Ratio in Bangladesh**

In the 1970s, the growth rate of the dependent population in Bangladesh was higher than that of the working-age population. However, a significant shift occurred in the early 1980s, with the growth rate of the working-age population surpassing that of the dependent population. Over time, the dependency ratio gradually declined, indicating that Bangladesh has already entered the demographic transition phase, creating a window of economic opportunity. The age dependency ratio in Bangladesh was last measured at 47.09% in 2022, down from 53.68% in 2014 and 69.13% in 2000 (World Bank, 2023).

(B) Population Growth and Its Components

Bangladesh's annual population growth rate was 1.01% in 2023–2024, down from 1.23% in 2010–2011 (Table 1). This indicates that Bangladesh is progressing through its demographic transition. Also, the birth rates have drastically reduced to 21.6 (2022) from 31.1 (1995) per 1000 population and the death rates have decreased to 5.6 (2022) from 7.4 (1995), thereby reducing the number of dependents on the working age population. From 1995 to 2022, the Crude Birth Rate (CBR) in Bangladesh decreased smoothly from 32 per 1,000 to 18 per 1,000. The number of births in a country depends on the average number of births per woman of childbearing age and the number of women in this age range. When the number of women of childbearing age increases, the number of births can rise even if the number of births per woman decreases—a phenomenon known as "population momentum." The Total Fertility Rate (TFR) is a measure of fertility that is not influenced by the number of women of childbearing age in the population. Thus, TFR is considered a more reliable measure than CBR for comparing fertility levels between countries or time periods. The International Data Base (IDB) (2023) estimates that the TFR in Bangladesh will gradually decrease to the "replacement level"—the level needed for long-term population stabilization (approximately 2.1 children per woman)—by 2025. The Crude Death Rate (CDR) in Bangladesh is projected to remain stable at six per 1,000 from 2014 to 2025.

(C) Age-Sex Structure of the Population

Age-sex structure of the population pyramid is normally used to depict the age-sex structure of a population of a certain country. In a nation with high fertility rates, the pyramids are formed with a wide base and a large young age population, with narrow bands near the top representing an older population which are near the end of their natural lifespan. It is found that the Bangladeshi age-sex structure in 2000 is a good example of a classical pyramid shape (Fig. 2 and Table 2). The pyramid shape of the year 2020 has a thicker base than the year 2000. Due to fewer births as

Table 1 Historical population growth rate data of Bangladesh

Year	Population	Growth rate (%)	Year	Population	Growth rate (%)
1950	39,728,535	–	2015	157,830,000	1.20
1951	40,548,590	2.06	2020	167,420,951	1.15
1961	51,882,769	2.95	2021	169,356,251	1.16
1969	65,866,908	2.92	2022	171,186,372	1.08
1981	86,154,836	2.65	2023	172,954,319	1.03
2001	131,670,484	1.92	2024	174,701,211	1.01
2011	150,211,005	1.23			

Source Statistical yearbooks, BBS

forecasted, the base (age 0–4) of the pyramid for Bangladesh is not as wide as it was for 2000, but above age 20 the bars are all much wider than they are in 2000 or 2020 for those age groups. In this period the proportion of the labor force age population is increasing, providing a one-time "demographic dividend" for investing heavily in human resource development.

As measured by the proportion of the population in the labor force (15–64), this window is projected to open widely in Bangladesh over the next 10–20 years, which is a relatively short period. The labor force growth is projected to slow down and level off by 2050 and decline while labor force growth will occur after a certain period of 2025. With declining fertility and rising life expectancy, the population

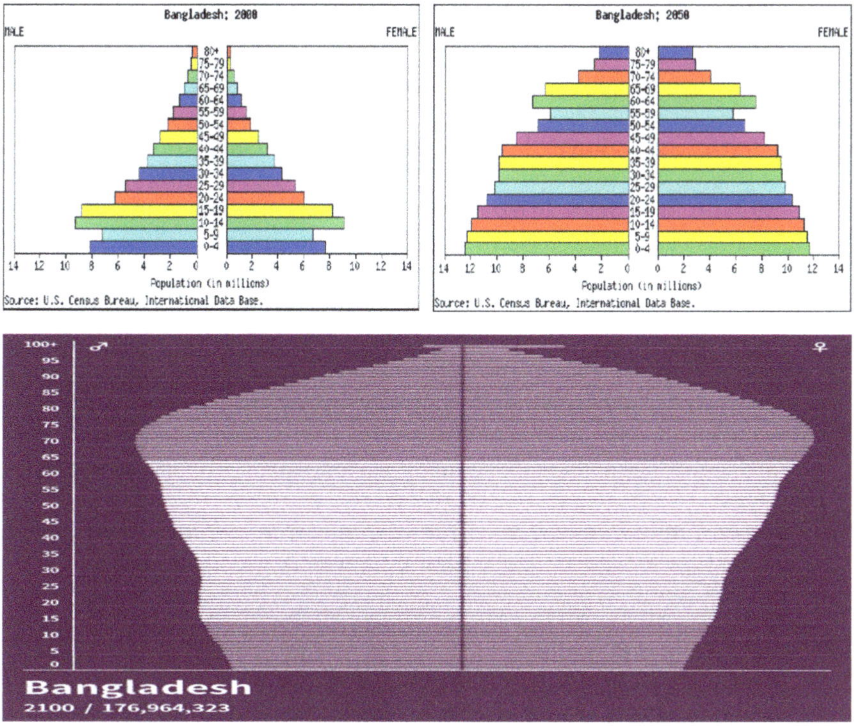

Fig. 2 Forecasted age distribution of Bangladesh over the years

Table 2 Age distribution over the years in Bangladesh (%)

Age	Year							
	1970	2000	2005	2010	2015	2020	2023	2024 (projected)
0–14 years	44.7	37.0	34.4	32.0	29.3	27.0	25.5	25.1
15–64 years	51.8	59.2	61.3	63.2	65.6	67.4	68.2	67.1
>64 years	4.5	3.9	4.3	4.8	5.1	5.6	6.3	7.8

aged 0–14 and 0–64+ will be approximately equal by 2050. After this point in time, old-age dependency will exceed youth dependency. However, now it is time to bank on Bangladesh‘s demographic dividend.

2.4 *Essentials of Demographic Dividend in Bangladesh*

To maximize economic growth, it is crucial to efficiently utilize key resources like land, labor, capital, entrepreneurship, science and technology, health, and the environment. In Bangladesh, the demographic transition has led to a surplus of labor, necessitating extensive investment to absorb this labor force. With the gap between birth and death rates narrowing, Bangladesh is experiencing slower population growth (expected to be 1.00% in 2025). To fully capitalize on the demographic dividend, the following prerequisites must be met:

(a) **Maximize Agricultural Productivity**: Increase returns from arable land through crop diversification and the use of high-yielding variety (HYV) crops.
(b) **Long-term Investment in Manufacturing**: Large-scale and sustained investment in labor-intensive manufacturing sectors to generate capital and absorb surplus labor.
(c) **Skill Development**: Provide sufficient institutional vocational training to meet the demand for efficient and skilled labor.
(d) **Enhance Female Labor Force Participation**: Increase female participation in the labor force by ensuring workplace security and other necessary amenities.
(e) **Diversify and Globalize Manufacturing**: Encourage global diversification of manufacturing units to boost earnings and sustain surplus, aiding capital formation.
(f) **Promote Capital Formation**: Capital formation is essential for combining production factors effectively, ensuring sustainable economic growth.
(g) **Support Capital Accumulation:** Provide labor with tools and implements of production to enable greater specialization.
(h) **Ensure Political Stability**: Maintain political stability to safeguard investments and prevent capital wastage.
(i) **Foster Entrepreneurship**: Promote entrepreneurship through proper policies and incentives, as entrepreneurs drive economic development and job creation.
(j) **Adopt Advanced Science and Technology**: Incorporate the latest science and technology across sectors to help local producers compete globally.
(k) **Increase Health Expenditure**: Proportionately increase per capita health expenditure alongside labor force growth.
(l) **Enhance Environmental Resilience**: Build capacity to address environmental challenges and mitigate the effects of global warming.
(m) **Improve Transportation and Infrastructure**: Develop transportation systems and agricultural infrastructure to support agro-based industries and market accessibility.

(n) **Protect Financial Sector**: Shield the internal financial sector from global fluctuations and strengthen safeguards against corruption.

Effective deployment of labor, alongside the appropriate formulation of policies, is vital. If not handled correctly, the demographic dividend could become a liability, leading to unemployment and placing unsustainable pressure on education, health, and social security systems.

2.5 Socio-Economic Challenges

Bangladesh faces several socio-economic challenges in its demographic transition, which pose significant obstacles to harnessing the demographic dividend:

(a) **Investment Policy Formulation**: Bangladesh has struggled to attract foreign direct investment (FDI) and lacks a coherent strategy to promote private investment that contributes to sustainable development, inclusive growth, and job creation. The poor quality of infrastructure, unreliable electricity supply, and inefficient transportation systems are critical barriers to development.
(b) **Poverty Reduction and Pro-Poor Policies**: Bangladesh has made notable progress in reducing poverty, with 18.7% of the population living below the national poverty line and extreme poverty at 5.6% as of 2022. Despite this, substantial efforts are still required to formulate and implement growth strategies that further reduce poverty and support the most vulnerable.
(c) **Strategic Initiatives**: The country must implement strategies that include:

- Supporting NGOs in poverty alleviation.
- Formulating export policies to incentivize agriculture and industrial growth.
- Improving labor mobility to better integrate the unemployed, underemployed, and informal sector workers into productive employment.
- Expanding social safety nets.
- Promoting urbanization to absorb surplus agricultural labor.
- Enhancing skill development and vocational training, particularly for future migrant workers.
- Developing infrastructure, including power, transportation, and IT.
- Fostering collaboration among government, academia, and industry.
- Ensuring flexibility in labor and product markets.
- Supporting rural prosperity through agro-based industries.
- Implementing equitable and pro-poor policies.
- Encouraging women's participation in economic, social, and political spheres.
- Promoting good governance and the rule of law.

2.6 Policy Recommendations

A young, healthy, and educated workforce can significantly boost economic growth, provided the right social and economic policies are in place. The demographic dividend can complement growth driven by capital investment in infrastructure, technology, manufacturing, trade policy, and market liberalization. If harnessed effectively, the demographic dividend can increase per capita income and savings rates. The following policy recommendations are proposed:

- **Investment Policies**: Formulate long-term investment policies to leverage global market opportunities.
- **NGO Support**: Assist NGOs in achieving financial sustainability.
- **Export Strategies**: Develop export strategies for agricultural products, capital goods, and raw materials to incentivize producers.
- **Global Standard Education**: Focus on improving education standards to enable Bangladesh to compete internationally.
- **Social Safety Nets**: Increase budgetary allocations to expand the scope of social safety net programs.
- **Vocational Training**: Expand vocational training and pre-departure orientation (PDO) programs in technology and foreign languages.
- **Education Rights**: Ensure the enforcement of the right to free and compulsory education for children.
- **Women's Empowerment**: Implement policies that go beyond anti-poverty programs to address childcare, transportation, and restrictions on women's work.
- **Agricultural and Industrial Strategy**: Formulate strategies for agro-industrial linkages, increasing crop productivity, access to agro-industries, agricultural credit, advanced technology, biomass power, and biofuels to create employment opportunities.
- **Administrative Reforms**: Implement administrative changes, decentralization, transparency, anti-corruption strategies, and strategic assistance to multilateral organizations.
- **Law and Order**: Prioritize law enforcement and ensure fairness in its application.

3 Service Requirements for the Aged in Bangladesh

3.1 Issue

Aging is a natural and inevitable process that everyone experiences. It refers to the biological, psychological, and social changes that occur throughout life, from childhood to adolescence, adulthood, and old age. Aging results from detrimental processes at the cellular, sub-cellular, and organ levels that are associated with the passage of time. Despite medical interventions, aging follows its own dynamic, largely beyond human control (Gorman, 1999, p. 7).

Table 3 Elderly population from 1951 to 2023 (in'000)

Year	Total population			Elderly population 60+			%
	Male	Female	Total	Male	Female	Total	
1951	21,937	19,995	41,932	1023	834	1857	4.40
1981	44,919	42,201	87,120	2751	2154	4905	5.6
1991	57,314	54,141	111,455	3298	2748	6046	5.42
2000	65,808	62,301	128,109	3544	3703	7247	5.67
2010	75,551	72,012	147,563	4901	5232	10,133	6.87
2015	80,526	76,807	157,333	5839	6212	12,051	7.66
2020	85,576	81,179	166,755	6998	7452	14,450	8.67
2024	86,031	87,769	173,800	7812	8669	16,481	9.50

Source Statistical Yearbooks, BBS

As people age, they gradually lose the ability to perform daily functions. Aging has four dimensions: physical, psychological, population-related, and social. Social aging is a multidimensional and dynamic force, encompassing the transition into and out of roles, societal expectations about behavior, resource allocation, and opportunities. It involves negotiating the implications of chronological age and the experiences of individuals as they navigate life stages (Morgan & Suzanne, 2001, p. 7).

Bangladesh is undergoing a significant demographic shift, indicating a rapidly aging population (BBS, 2023). The proportion of older people increased from 7.47% in 2011 to 9.29% in 2023, according to the latest population census (Table 3). In absolute numbers, Bangladesh now has about 15 million people aged 60 and above. By 2050, this number is expected to more than double to 36 million. Data further revealed that one in every ten citizens in Bangladesh will be 60 years old or older by 2025. By 2050, this figure is expected to rise to one in every five citizens. The rapid growth of the aging population in Bangladesh over the next few decades will require extensive efforts to carefully assess their needs and find ways to meet them.

3.1.1 Concerns and Problems of the Elderly

Elderly people in Bangladesh are commonly affected by arthritis, rheumatism, high blood pressure, and heart disease. Additionally, there is a decline in sensory functions, such as vision and hearing. Stress and deprivation, coupled with cognitive decline, also significantly impact the elderly. Social and environmental factors strongly affect their physical and mental health, with emotional disorders being prevalent among the elderly.

In traditional societies like Bangladesh, older people have historically been respected and considered valuable members of the family, receiving special care from extended family members. However, industrialization and urbanization have dramatically changed the traditional extended family structure, with Bangladesh being no exception. The average family size in Bangladesh is decreasing due to rural-to-urban migration (Table 4).

Many families have been sending their children abroad for education, employment, or permanent settlement. Consequently, many young and adult family members leave their elderly parents behind, settling either in urban centers in Bangladesh or in other countries (Rahman, 1999, p. 151). The ability of families to care for elderly members in urban settings is severely compromised by crowded housing, limited financial resources, and the increasing employment of women. This results in many elderly people living separately from their children and grandchildren. Studies have shown that an increasing number of elderly individuals are living independently (Kabir, 1994, p. 33) (Table 5). Though much data is not available in this respect, it can be assumed that self-arranged living for the elderly is increasing in Bangladesh (Erb, 2011).

As a result, the social and health status of a significant portion of the elderly in Bangladesh, whether residing in urban or rural areas, is deteriorating. Those living alone often experience severe psychological distress. Previous studies have noted that more than two-thirds of elderly men lived in nuclear families where they were likely the primary breadwinners (CPD, 2000, p. 15). In poor families, the elderly face difficulties in securing basic needs such as food, clothing, shelter, security, love, and meaningful employment or leisure activities. They live in fear and frustration due to the lack of sufficient social security programs to meet their basic needs, often depending on others for their livelihood (Table 6).

Bangladesh's poverty reduction has been supported by economic growth, sound macroeconomic policies, and a demographic dividend. The country's growth in the industrial and service sectors has also played a role in reducing poverty. However, the agricultural sector is still important for poverty alleviation, and some researchers say its significance is often overlooked. However, the pace of poverty reduction has slowed in recent years. The World Bank estimates that around 500,000 people fell

Table 4 Household size over the years (1991–2024)

Parameters	1991	2001	2011	2022	2024
(1) Number of household (million)	19.4	25.4	32.1	35.2	33.73
(2) Average household member	5.5	4.8	4.4	4.3	4.26

Source Population census 2023, BBS

Table 5 Living arrangements of aged people

Living arrangement	Year		
	1994	2000	2023
Self	55%	60%	–
With their sons	25%	20%	–
With their daughters	11%	10%	–

Source Kabir (1994), p. 33

Table 6 Old age dependency ratio over time

Year	Dependency ratio	Year	Dependency ratio
1911	8.2	1995	8.9
1931	5.8	2000	9.4
1951	8.4	2010	11.0
1981	11.7	2020	13.9
1991	11.0	2023	9.4

Source BBS (2023)

into extreme poverty between 2022–23 and 2023–2024. This is due to high inflation and weak private consumption growth, which have eroded purchasing power. Income inequality in Bangladesh has also been rising. The Gini coefficient, which measures income inequality, increased from 0.458 in 2010 to 0.499 in 2022.

Due to poverty and limited family income, most elderly people in Bangladesh cannot meet their basic needs, including food, healthcare, clothing, adequate shelter, and access to income or employment opportunities (Table 7). It is difficult for family members to provide for the basic needs of their elderly relatives. Food is the top priority for elderly people in both rural and urban areas (Help Age International, 1999, p. 137), and most are financially dependent on their children (Kabir, 1994). In wealthier families, many elderly individuals suffer from psychological issues related to social alienation, loneliness, tension, and depression.

Elder abuse is alarmingly prevalent in poor families in Bangladesh. Elderly individuals, particularly women who often have little or no property, suffer mistreatment from family members and society. Common forms of elder abuse include verbal assault, isolation, threats, reduction of personal freedom, theft of money or property, hazardous living conditions, lack of supervision, withholding of food, and inducing fear (Boudreau, 1993, p. 145). The National Aging Resource Center on Elderly Abuse (NARCEA) reports that the most frequent types of elder abuse are neglect (37.2%), followed by physical abuse (26.3%), financial or material exploitation (20%), and emotional abuse (11%) (NARCEA, 1990: 1).

Table 7 Poverty and absolute poverty according to calorie intake (%)

Type	Area	1983/84	1991/92	2000	2024
Poverty	National	62.6	47.5	44.3	18.7
	Rural	61.9	47.6	42.3	26.4
	Urban	67.7	46.7	52.5	18.9
Absolute poverty	National	36.8	28.0	20.0	6.1
	Rural	36.7	28.3	18.7	6.5
	Urban	37.4	26.3	25.0	3.8

Source Preliminary report of household income and expenditure surveys, BBS

3.2 Aged Services in Bangladesh

Traditionally, most elderly people in Bangladesh, especially in rural areas, have been cared for and nursed by their family members, religious institutions (mosques, temples), and systems like Zakat and donations. However, there has been a change due to the breakdown of the traditional extended family structure. Moreover, many families in rural areas live below the poverty line, making it difficult for them to meet the needs of their elderly members. Consequently, there is a pressing need for government and voluntary assistance for the rural aged poor.

After independence in 1971, the Bangladesh government initiated programs like pensions, gratuities, welfare funds, group insurance, and provident funds for government officials and employees. However, most of the population remains outside of these measures. Recognizing the plight of helpless rural elderly, the government introduced the Old Age Allowance program in 1998, which covers 10 elderly people in each ward, benefiting 403,110 elderly people across the country. Although the allowance is meager and the number of recipients is small, it is a positive start and a pioneering effort by the government (Rahman, 1999, p. 144).

In addition, the government provides services to the elderly, mostly women, through the Vulnerable Group Development (V.G.D) and Vulnerable Group Feeding (V.G.F) programs. Recently, the government established six old age homes (Santi Nibas) in six divisions, offering shelter, lifelong healthcare, medical care, and recreational services for these people. Bangladesh also launched the "Ashrayan" project in 1997 to house the country's homeless population, benefiting over 800,000 homeless and destitute families and touted as the world's largest housing project for the poor. So far, around 507,398 families have received such homes across the country, providing shelter to more than 3 million people.

Along with government programs, some NGOs, such as the Bangladesh Association for the Aged and Institute of Geriatric Medicine (BAAIGM), Retired Government Personnel Welfare Association, Retired Police Officers Welfare Association, Rehabilitation Center for Aged and Child, and Senakalyan Sangstha, are providing services to elderly people in Bangladesh. Resource Integration Center (RIC) and Bangladesh Women Health Coalition (BWHC), two member organizations of the Asia Training Center on Aging (ATCOA), are implementing a pilot project on the development of women's health and status. Other organizations like Rotary Club, Lions Club, Girls Guide, Zayeda Dream Care Mothers Home, Apon Ghor, Nijer Ghor, Antore Apon, etc., are also participating in aging care services.

3.3 Limitations of the Services

Though some initiatives have been taken for the welfare of elderly people, several constraints and limitations undermine these services, including:

(i) **Pension Limitations**: The pension system is limited to government employees, who represent only a small portion of the total population. Upon their death, their spouses may continue receiving the pension, but bureaucratic complexities often hinder the transfer of pension and other allowances.
(ii) **Limited Savings Programs**: There are a few government savings programs available for the elderly to invest their money. Unfortunately, these programs are gradually decreasing or becoming more limited in scope.
(iii) **Lack of Social Security Programs**: In 1998, the government introduced the Old Age Allowance and the Widowed and Destitute Women Allowance programs, benefiting 403,110 people. However, the allowance is a meager Tk. 125 (about $1.10) per month, which plays a minimal role in aiding the aged and destitute women.
(iv) **Limited Medical Services**: Although elderly people require extra medical care, there are few government initiatives that provide these services. Moreover, the elderly often receive less attention and priority in these centers, leading to increased suffering due to inadequate care.
(v) **Reliance on Family Members**: The typical caregivers for impaired elderly people are female family members, such as wives, sisters, daughters, and daughters-in-law (Montgomery & Datvyler, 1990, p. 36). These female members sometimes become impatient or reluctant, highlighting the need for institutional care as an alternative (Friedlander, 1997, p. 248).
(vi) **Limited Institutional Services**: Although the government has set up some institutions, these institutions often fail to attract enough elderly members due to a lack of awareness, accessibility, convenience, and poor service delivery.
(vii) **Shortage of Skilled Manpower**: Caregiving institutions suffer from a shortage of skilled personnel to care for the elderly. Service providers often lack professional education, knowledge, and motivation, which further diminishes the quality of care.

3.4 Service Recommendations

Aging is not only a concern for the individual and their family; it is also a societal concern. While some government and voluntary organizations are working to alleviate the suffering of the elderly, these efforts are often inadequate, insufficient, and cumbersome. Disorganization in services, social myths and prejudices, social structures and systems, negative attitudes towards the elderly, and value conflicts also exacerbate elderly problems. The following actions, if properly implemented, can improve aged services:

(i) **Expand Community Care Services**: Community care services should be expanded to provide care for the elderly. New and alternative institutions, such as aged homes, nursing homes, health complexes, care centers, and recreational centers, should be established or rearranged.

(ii) **Promote Home-Based Care**: Home-based care should be prioritized over institutional care, as elderly people often feel more comfortable at home due to accessibility and convenience. Local governments could arrange for "Paid Home Helpers" to serve elderly people in their homes.
(iii) **Adopt Social Welfare Policies**: The government should adopt social welfare policies and programs that ensure the rights of the elderly. Large-scale social security programs, such as pensions, old age allowances, and health insurance, are necessary to support the elderly.
(iv) **Implement Counseling Programs**: Micro and macro-level counseling programs should be established for both the elderly and the community. These programs will help the community overcome stigma and encourage the elderly to take advantage of available services.
(v) **Expand Awareness Campaigns**: Awareness campaigns should be expanded to ensure that family members and the community are aware of existing services and become more sympathetic towards the elderly.
(vi) **Engage the Elderly in Activities**: The government should develop programs that involve the elderly in activities that utilize their inner potential, helping to reduce their mental suffering due to loneliness and isolation.
(vii) **Strengthen Family Relationships**: Family relationships should be strengthened, with an emphasis on teaching children to respect their elders. Families can play a vital role in this regard.

4 Health Care System in Bangladesh

Bangladesh has made remarkable progress in various health indicators over the past two decades, surpassing many neighboring and developing countries. The country achieved MDG-4 ahead of schedule and is on track to meet MDG-5, despite a low health budget and numerous other challenges. Bangladesh has now transitioned to the SDG era. The 4th Health, Population, and Nutrition Sector Development Program (HPNSP) is currently in place, covering the period from January 2017 to June 2022. During the first five and a half years of the SDGs, the Community-Based Health Clinic (CBHC) program, a flagship initiative of the government, has made substantial contributions to achieving SDGs, just as it did for the MDGs, and will continue to do so until 2030. Under the 4th HPNSP, the scope of CBHC has been expanded, incorporating activities from Community Clinics (CC) and Essential Health Services (ESD) across all health facilities within the Upazila (sub-district), beyond just the CCs.

4.1 Issue

The world is undergoing a significant demographic shift, with the number of people aged 65 and above already surpassing the number of children under five years old (WB, 2024). This trend has profound implications globally and is especially relevant for Bangladesh. Bangladesh is one of the fastest-growing economies in the world, with an average GDP growth of 6–7% in recent years. Along with this economic growth, there have been significant improvements in various socio-economic indicators, including access to healthcare. Life expectancy has increased to 72 years, and there have been reductions in infant mortality, under-5 mortality, stunting, and other health-related indicators. As Bangladesh's population ages, the country must take proactive measures to revamp its healthcare sector to meet the needs of its aging population.

While the Government of Bangladesh has committed to providing many of the basic rights of older adults, their healthcare needs remain unmet. Inadequate funding and services highlight the necessity of a healthcare system tailored to the specific needs of older adults, such as long-term, integrated care. Additionally, there is a lack of supportive structures, such as a health insurance fund covering common chronic conditions faced by older adults, which would help remove barriers to accessing healthcare. The primary healthcare (PHC) system is currently more focused on treating acute illnesses rather than providing integrated, long-term, people-centered care for older adults. Barriers to accessing appropriate healthcare for older adults include high costs, limited access to medicines and transportation, insufficient numbers of trained providers, and age discrimination.

4.2 Vulnerability of the Aging Population

Bangladesh has one of the largest populations of older adults in the world, a demographic driven by increasing life expectancy. This shift is accompanied by a rise in non-communicable diseases (NCDs) and multi-morbid conditions that disproportionately affect older adults. These chronic conditions create a growing demand for healthcare services. NCDs account for 70% of all deaths in Bangladesh, and they are costly to treat, imposing financial hardships on families in low-resource settings. This surge in demand also escalates the costs of both clinical and long-term care, further burdening financially vulnerable segments of society.

Despite the significant burden of NCDs, only $0.82 is spent per capita on NCD control, far below the $1.50 recommended by the WHO. Increasing spending on NCD management can help alleviate the financial pressure on households caring for older adults. Currently, neither NCD control efforts nor PHC services adequately address the needs of older adults. For example, there are no specific protocols for older adults, data is not disaggregated by age, and the training of health professionals does not cover older adult care. Although several policies for older adults have been formally adopted, they are not consistently implemented in practice. There is also a motivation to evaluate the outcomes of service delivery for older adults, but a shortage of human resources has made it difficult to conduct formal evaluations.

Moreover, Bangladesh is highly vulnerable to climate change, which is expected to cause more frequent and severe natural disasters such as heatwaves, floods, and landslides. These events will disproportionately affect vulnerable populations, including older adults, who are more likely to suffer from health issues and have limited access to resources and support systems to cope with the impacts of climate change. These barriers can be even more severe for older adults. Innovative solutions are needed to address these challenges and improve access to healthcare for this vulnerable sub-population.

4.3 Need for the Health Care System

As the population of elderly individuals in society grows, so does the demand for increased investment in the health sector to address their health and nutritional needs. Despite this rising demand, the government's allocation to the health sector has remained below 1% of GDP for decades. This underinvestment necessitates a threefold increase in public spending to ensure adequate treatment facilities for senior citizens. Currently, hospitals lack sufficient medical facilities to care for those who have contributed to the nation throughout their lives.

There is a pressing need to establish palliative care units in all medical college hospitals, introduce modern medicines and advanced equipment, and focus on capacity development of health personnel, particularly in palliative care. Given the increasing per capita out-of-pocket healthcare expenditure, the Planning Commission has recommended the introduction of a special *health card* for elderly people to help reduce their healthcare costs.

The potential support ratio—the number of working-age individuals (15–64) required to support one elderly person (65+)—has been declining and is projected to decline even faster in the future. Historical data shows that in 1960, about 20 working-age people supported one senior dependent; by 2019, this number had fallen to 13. The population census in 2022 revealed a support ratio of 11, which is expected to drop to six by 2040 and three by 2065. Training young people to assist the elderly in accessing healthcare services could simultaneously create employment opportunities.

After the age of 60, medical expenses typically increase due to more frequent health problems. Many senior citizens lack sufficient savings to cover these costs, and government allocation for social security programs remains inadequate. To address this, it is crucial to enhance the workability of elderly individuals and reorient existing institutional arrangements for health service delivery. Increased investment—both financial and in human resources—is necessary to develop an effective Elderly and Palliative Health Care (EPHC) service system. The Ministry of Health and Family Welfare can lead multi-sector collaboration with other ministries, the private sector, NGOs, and CSOs to provide enhanced EPHC services.

4.4 Need Analysis, Coordination, and Implementation Issues of Aging Policies

Care support for the elderly population is a relatively new issue for policymakers in Bangladesh, and there is widespread ignorance about the specific care needs of older adults. Apart from a few scattered programs, mostly run by NGOs, there are no comprehensive care provisions for older adults in the country. The Government of Bangladesh (GoB) initiated the National Policy on Aging (NPA) in 2007, marking the first significant effort to ensure dignity, social security, and healthcare for the elderly. However, despite its recommendations, no specific measures have been implemented (Hamiduzzaman et al., 2018). In 2013, the government introduced the Personal Care Assistance (PCA) Act, aimed at ensuring children take proper care of their parents. This policy, however, places the responsibility solely on the family, rather than providing state-supported care for seniors.

The PCA's ineffectiveness stems from its lack of clarity in formulation and implementation, as well as social factors such as affection for children and dependence on them. By 2023, there had been little progress in the Act's implementation, primarily due to a lack of manpower, public awareness, and cultural attitudes. None of the aging care policies—be it the 2007 NPA, 2013 PCA, the 2014 Senior Citizen declaration, or the Old Age Allowance (OAA) programs—have been effectively formulated or implemented to ensure universal health and social care coverage for older adults in Bangladesh (Begum & Islam, 2019).

Abuse of older persons is a common issue in Bangladesh, driven by various factors, including economic hardship, exploitation of parents' assets, and physical and mental abuse within families. However, many victims refrain from reporting abuse due to love for their children, fear of social stigma, or lack of alternative shelter.

In 2007, the NPA designated individuals aged 60 and above as "senior citizens." This designation was reaffirmed on 29 November 2014 by the President of Bangladesh, but without any associated benefits or rights. Additionally, while 60 is the officially recognized age for entering old age, eligibility for the Old Age Allowance (OAA) program starts at 62 for women and 65 for men, highlighting a lack of coordination among government agencies.

Despite the limited impact of these policies, the current government reorganized the National Committee on Older Persons in 2017 to implement a national policy for elderly care. This committee has finalized a draft for the Probin Unnayan (Elderly Development) Foundation, an independent legal institution aimed at supporting elderly people. However, bureaucratic delays have prevented the approval of this draft.

4.5 Policy Recommendations

Bangladesh must prioritize the care of its aging population by focusing on enhancing primary healthcare services. While health indicators have improved significantly over the past five decades, more work is needed to establish universal healthcare. The challenges posed by a growing aging population can be transformed into opportunities for systemic change. With the right policies and investments, Bangladesh can develop innovative solutions to improve healthcare for its elderly population.

In terms of financing, the government should consider increasing investments in the health of older adults using an output-based budget. Cost-saving measures, such as involving non-health ministries and enforcing clear payment guidelines, should be implemented. Under the theme of innovation, digital health technologies can be leveraged to improve access to care and develop long-term care strategies that enhance senior health outcomes. For example, telemedicine can help older adults with mobility issues consult with physicians from the comfort of their homes. Additionally, training healthcare professionals to adopt age-sensitive approaches can improve the patient experience for seniors.

Regulation and oversight are crucial for enhancing quality and accountability. Reducing interruptions in the supply chain will help maintain a continuous supply of essential drugs. In health facilities, effective financial management policies can prevent waste. The establishment of an evaluation officer position could help monitor adherence to quality guidelines. These combined efforts can create a holistic healthcare system capable of supporting the aging population and maximizing the years Bangladeshis spend in good health.

5 Long-Term Care (LTC) Systems in Bangladesh

5.1 Issue

Ensuring income security for people in old age is a crucial aspect of the UN's common agenda for social security and universal social protection for all. The rights of older individuals to social security and an adequate standard of living are outlined in major international human rights instruments such as the Universal Declaration of Human Rights (UDHR), 1948, and more broadly in the International Covenant on Economic, Social and Cultural Rights (ICESCR), 1966.

The International Labor Organization (ILO) Convention No. 102 on social protection minimum standards, Convention No. 128 on invalidity, old-age, and survivors' benefits, along with its accompanying Recommendation No. 131, and Recommendation No. 202 on social protection floors collectively provide an international reference framework for pensions and other social security benefits, ensuring income security and access to healthcare in old age.

Bangladesh has a complex legislative framework for protecting the rights of elderly persons. Major regulatory instruments include the National Policy on Older Persons 2013, the Maintenance of Parents Act 2013, the National Committee on Older Persons 2017, the Action Plan to implement the National Policy on Older Persons 2013, and the draft Probin Unnayan Foundation Act 2017. The Constitution of Bangladesh, in Article 15(D), mandates the introduction of a social security program for the elderly population.

Bangladesh is experiencing a significant demographic shift with a rapidly aging population (BBS, 2023). Currently, there are about 15 million people aged 60 and above; by 2050, this number is expected to exceed 36 million. Barriers to accessing appropriate care services for older adults include high costs, lack of access to medicines and transportation, insufficient numbers of trained providers, and age discrimination. Addressing this situation, the availability of services and their needs analysis is crucial. Therefore, this section will explore the Long-Term Care (LTC) systems in Bangladesh.

5.2 Public Long-Term Care (LTC) Systems

The Bangladeshi government has implemented a range of social security programs with substantial coverage for the protection and care of the older population, such as a pension system, retirement benefits, and other initiatives under the National Social Security Strategy (NSSS). This includes the Old Age Allowance (OAA) Program, which began in 1998, allowances for freedom fighters, allowances for widows and deserted women, and the Vulnerable Groups' Feeding (VGF) program. However, a significant number of older people remain outside these programs.

To further enhance the protection of older persons, the Government of Bangladesh launched a Universal Pension Scheme (UPS) in August 2023. This scheme aims to provide a pathway to self-sustained retirement for citizens, allowing individuals with modest incomes to plan for a financially secure retirement. Effective implementation of UPS in Bangladesh will require attention to governance, accountable fund management, and digital integration. Additionally, targeting beneficiaries and addressing the diverse population and informal sector will be crucial.

5.3 Social Protection for Aged Persons: Scopes and Possibilities

Rapid urbanization, high-rise apartment living, increased workforce participation by both sexes, disintegration of joint families, and loneliness complicate caregiving options and their availability. Policy and structural deficiencies exacerbate the situation, as policymakers have yet to fully understand the extensive needs that the aging population will create in the coming decades.

As life expectancy increases in Bangladesh, older individuals require long-term care (LTC) services to address personal care needs. These services help individuals live independently and safely when they are unable to perform daily activities. LTC can be provided in various settings by different caregivers, depending on individual needs. Traditionally, most LTC in Bangladesh has been provided at home by family members, relatives, and friends, along with domestic helpers. However, LTC can also be provided in institutions such as nursing homes (commonly known as old homes in Bangladesh) or in adult daycare centers, which are yet to be established and operated effectively in the country.

LTC services also include arranging for delivery of cooked meals, attending adult daycare, and accessing transportation services. These services may be provided free or for a fee, depending on insurance benefits, availability, premium payment schemes, or government-subsidized models. Several risk factors increase the need for LTC: (i) age'; (ii) longer lifespan of women compared to men'; (iii) single individuals (both widows and widowers) needing external care; (iv) poor diet and lack of exercise; and (v) health and family history.

Many of these risk factors are already common or will become more prevalent among Bangladeshis due to longer lifespans. Bangladeshi women often marry men several years older, leading to longer widowhood. Additionally, urban residents tend to have poor dietary habits and limited opportunities for physical exercise. Rising divorce rates and the increasing number of older people living alone due to education and employment opportunities further indicate that LTC will become a significant social necessity in Bangladesh.

One alternative to institutional LTC is home-based care, which includes health, personal, and support services (e.g., assistance with bathing, dressing, medication, and supervision) to help people remain at home independently for as long as possible. In Bangladeshi society, much of this care is provided by unpaid family members, friends, and neighbors. Paid caregivers, including informal caregivers and healthcare professionals such as nurses, home health aides, therapists, and homemakers, are commonly hired through home health care agencies in other countries. Bangladesh has yet to develop and offer home-based health care agencies.

As support from family and friends may become insufficient, individuals might need to move to full residential facilities—commonly known as old homes—that provide the required services. Most old homes in Bangladesh offer only housing and housekeeping, with a few providing personal care and medical services. Specialized programs for Alzheimer's and dementia, as well as rehabilitation services like physical, occupational, and speech therapy, are not widely available in Bangladeshi old homes. Entrepreneurs in Bangladesh could explore business models to address these gaps.

The OAA program is a well-known old-age care service. However, it is a low-level flat-rate benefit (approximately $5 per month) and provides only around 30% coverage (DSS, 2021). Some view the OAA as a form of respect rather than a means of subsistence, while others consider the limited resources spent on it as insufficient for adequate support.

In addition to limitations in the amount and coverage of the OAA, issues such as political bias, nepotism, bribery, and corruption affect its management and distribution. The OAA scheme is centrally funded and regulated by local governments, with the central government distributing funds to the district level. Local governments then manage and distribute the funds, often without central government oversight.

To transform the country's health system to meet future demands, it is essential to gather evidence and understand stakeholder needs, fostering progress toward universal health coverage and better well-being for aging populations. WHO advocates for primary health care as the foundation for universal health coverage. By focusing on primary health care reform and prioritizing the health and well-being of aging populations, Bangladesh can strengthen its health system to meet the needs of all citizens, promote healthy aging, and foster social inclusion. Collaboration among policymakers, health experts, and development stakeholders is crucial to improving primary health care-centered integrated care and ensuring a better future for aging populations.

5.4 Community Clinics (CCs) in Bangladesh: A Unique Example of Health for All

Bangladesh is committed to ensuring "Health for All," a declaration adopted by member states at the Alma-Ata Conference on Primary Health Care (PHC) in 1978. This declaration marked a significant milestone in public health, identifying primary health care as essential for achieving the goal of health for all. In line with this declaration, Bangladesh aims to provide quality healthcare without financial hardship to all citizens to achieve Sustainable Development Goals (SDGs) and Universal Health Coverage (UHC). As part of its primary health care system, the government of Bangladesh established Community Clinics (CCs) in 1998, aiming for one clinic per 10,000 people in rural areas. This initiative was well-received by the rural population, who generously donated land for the construction of these clinics.

The CC project, initially introduced under the Ministry of Health and Family Welfare (MOHFW) in 1998, was later integrated into the Directorate General of Health Services through the "Community-Based Health Care: Operational Plan." The current 4th Health Population and Nutrition Sector Development Program (HPNSP) describes the CCs as the fundamental unit of the Upazila (sub-district) health system. As of June 2020, 13,812 CCs had been constructed and were operational, with 133 more under construction. The CC model represents a unique example of Public–Private Partnership (PPP), as CCs are built on community-donated land, and the government provides medicines, manpower, and service providers (including Community Health Care Providers, Health Assistants, and Family Welfare Assistants).

Unfortunately, CCs were inactive from 2001 to 2008 due to a change in government. When the previous political party returned to power, CCs were reactivated in 2009 under the "Revitalization of Community Healthcare Initiatives in Bangladesh (RCHCIB)" project. During this phase, international agencies such as WHO, JICA, Gavi, The Vaccine Alliance, UNICEF, USAID, TIKA, OMRON, and Save the Children, along with NGOs, provided financial and technical assistance for training, construction, and ensuring the availability of drugs and equipment. This support led to significant improvements in CCs and health indicators among the rural population.

Each CC is managed by a community group and two-thirds of community support groups, consisting of community members, landowners, and local government representatives. CCs serve as a "one-stop" service outlet for health, family planning, and nutrition, focusing on prevention and health promotion. In response to current epidemiological trends, CCs conduct screenings for non-communicable diseases (such as hypertension, diabetes, autism, and clubfoot) and refer emergencies and complicated cases to higher-level facilities for proper management. Some CCs now offer normal deliveries, depending on the availability of skilled health workers, local demand, and the capabilities of the Upazila health management system, with referral facilities available when necessary.

Bangladesh has made remarkable progress in improving the health status of its population, supported by CC initiatives as part of the PHC approach and improvements in social determinants of health. Rural mobility has increased for seeking essential treatment at CCs. For long-term sustainability and strengthened community participation, the government enacted the "Community Clinic Health Assistance Trust Act 2018," which transferred the government-owned CCs to a legally autonomous trust run by a Trustee Board of 13 members and an Advisory Board of 8 members, none of whom are public servants. The Prime Minister serves as the President of the Advisory Board. The Act allows the trust to raise additional funds to supplement government support. This model of best practices could be replicated in other countries.

The availability of basic healthcare services at people's doorsteps and the referral of complicated cases to higher-level facilities have been made possible by these grassroots-level health facilities. The number of CC level service seekers has increased over time gradually and it is estimated that an average of 40 patients/day receive service from each CC. CC-based service provision has led to increasing access of the poor (particularly women) to public health, population and nutrition services, and community participation. Health education and counselling through CCs have created mass awareness of many health problems and of the necessity of seeking care from the formal health professionals instead of the quacks and traditional healers. Overall, the CCs have reduced the need for extensive domiciliary services and helped women to go out of home to seek health services as a groundbreaking step in conservative Muslim society.

Despite some limitations, none of the CCs have a complete set of equipment. However, the majority of the CCs are found to function with an adequate number of primary medical kits. The overall condition and adequacy of equipment are not fully satisfactory. In terms of furniture and logistics, nearly two-thirds of CCs are rated as "good." The services and facilities at CCs are generally satisfactory concerning waiting arrangements, cleanliness, service quality, provider interaction and behavior, and health education. Also, in terms of waiting time, privacy maintenance, medicine availability, and information access, CCs are found quite satisfactory. Though the status of CCs is not up to the mark, the user's satisfaction is quite positive. It may be because, in a low-middle income country, like Bangladesh, people's expectation for the services was very low, which was fulfilled by the CCs. Community clinics are a unique example of PPP, with community engagement as a key pillar. All CCs are established on community-donated land, with government-provided services, medicines and equipment, and management jointly handled by the community and government. With the SDG for health (SDG3) and the goal of achieving UHC, CCs have become a unique instrument for both objectives, although some fine-tuning is needed. CCs have gained the community's confidence, as evidenced by increasing utilization, and now need to be repositioned to deliver comprehensive promotive, preventive, basic curative, and to some extent rehabilitative and palliative care.

Despite some limitations in the provision of healthcare service, community clinics have emerged as a flagship program of the Government of Bangladesh, aiming to make health services available at the doorstep of rural populations. However, considering the increasing workload on service providers, creating more core positions for community groups, establishing posts for service providers, strengthening domiciliary services, and further improving CCs are essential. This can be achieved through infrastructure development, employing more skilled health personnel, ensuring a steady supply of essential drugs and logistics, and enhancing supervision and monitoring. For success, revolutionizing the public–private partnership through effective community participation in operating community health facilities is crucial.

5.5 *Policies to Support an Aging Population*

To cater to the needs of the aging population of Bangladesh, some of the following key areas can be addressed by policymakers and other stakeholders:

- **Budget allocation:** The government needs to ensure budget allocations based on outputs, e.g., number of NCD (Noncommunicable diseases) screenings, health education sessions, etc. It should also establish clear guidelines and have an integrated approach by involving different ministries to share the associated costs.
- **Digital technology:** Bangladesh is now in the digital age. Digital health technologies can improve patient follow-up and accessibility to care for older adults with limited mobility. A digital database can provide disease tracking, patient follow-up through text messaging, and telemedicine functionality; for this the health workforce needs to be trained and equipped with telehealth tools.
- **Monitoring:** The government needs to increase oversight over the private sector and telemedicine for quality control and to train relevant health care professionals on financial regulation and budget management to facilitate financial management

of long-term care for older adults. They also need to ensure accountability of the health workforce by improving monitoring and supervision.
- **Evaluation:** Policymakers should consider creating a district-level NCD medical officer role to regularly monitor, evaluate, and report the long-term care program. The relevant authorities also need to better monitor and evaluate standard operating procedures, training of health professionals, database maintenance, regular report generation, clinical audits, and referral follow-up.

6 Health Insurance for the Aged in Bangladesh

6.1 Issue

Economic theory suggests that employees with health insurance coverage perform better in their roles and contribute positively to national development. More importantly, the social protection implications of health insurance are significant for both employees and the general population. The recent advancements in health facilities, coupled with high costs, have spotlighted the issues surrounding health insurance, as individuals struggle to afford these expenditures. Despite rapid economic and political progress, Bangladesh has not made significant strides in this area.

The social security scheme traditionally encompasses ensuring a minimum wage; old age/retirement benefits; unemployment protection; retrenchment compensation; therapeutic care for ailments; and emolument for employment-related harm and death; maternity security and issues specific to women; as well as social welfare programs as determined by laws, arrangements, contracts including collective bargaining agreements, and international instruments (Bartosic & Bernstein, 1973).

An effective health insurance policy and its proper management can significantly contribute to achieving optimal health outcomes. In the absence of proper health insurance, employees risk falling into poverty. A suitable health insurance model enhances employees' capabilities and well-being.

6.2 Bangladesh Perspective

Bangladesh is still in the developing phase, with the costly out-of-pocket (OOP) model of insurance being the predominant option. Some sporadic insurance facilities exist for affluent individuals, but they are neither widespread nor affordable for the general population. Feasibility studies were conducted before introducing health insurance for government employees but with no visible results. The main objective of a country's health system is to preserve health, treat illness, and prevent poverty due to health costs. In Bangladesh, the health system focuses mainly on basic health care and disease treatment, largely neglecting the issue of medical costs. There is little protection for the general population against the risk of falling into poverty due to high medical expenses.

The Constitution of Bangladesh recognizes the basic rights of people within the societal environment, including vital well-being security plans. Globalization and changing economic conditions impact traditional working environment values, business nature, working conditions, welfare offices, industrial relations, and modern social security frameworks (Swadźba, 2011). The advent of free-market economic policies and unequal economic and industrial reforms has posed serious challenges to job security and social protection for workers, particularly in health protection (Kawewe, 2000).

6.3 *Health Insurance for Government Servants*

The health insurance program for public servants provides financial benefits or facilities to cover medical costs for government employees and their families. Health insurance for government employees is considered significant in many countries. Consistent with Article 21 (2) of the Constitution of Bangladesh, the government has taken several initiatives to enhance the capacity of public servants, aiming to improve their efficiency in implementing government policies. Measures to ensure their satisfaction can lead to improved service quality for the public. Health insurance for government employees is expected to ensure their social protection, leading to increased satisfaction and productivity, which in turn facilitates efficient implementation of government social security programs.

The financial burden of out-of-pocket (OOP) payments is high and should be reduced by regulating the health sector and covering the care of government employees and chronic illnesses through prepayment-financing mechanisms. It is strongly recommended that health security schemes with a focus on government employees be introduced due to high indicators of financial hardship. The current government health insurance program for public servants involves benefits such as medical cost coverage for employees and their families. It is a type of social insurance pooling the risks of medical costs through full or partial premiums.

The government can ensure health coverage by establishing a health insurance system for government servants, requiring minimal allocation per employee. Despite the positive aspects of health insurance, it is not universally accepted as an incentive package for government employees in many countries. The importance and impact of insurance on government employee effectiveness, along with the challenges and prospects of the insurance sector in Bangladesh, reveal that although Bangladesh faces various risks, insurance coverage is limited. Insurance companies also face hurdles, including human resources and social stigma.

The government has allocated a substantial budget for public servants' remuneration and medical costs, reflecting its commitment to employee well-being and social protection. However, the government could further enhance social protection without additional costs. A health insurance model, preferably a social insurance model combining both Beveridge and Bismarck models, is recommended for government employees in Bangladesh (Bartosic & Bernstein, 1973). A pilot program should be conducted before a nationwide rollout, with the national program based on pilot testing results.

6.4 Community-Based Health Insurance in Bangladesh

Nearly half of all wage workers in Bangladesh work in unsafe environments, leading to illness and injury and reduced work productivity (Rockefeller Foundation, 2013). Several models of community-based health insurance (CBHI) and health insurance schemes have been introduced in Bangladesh to address this issue, particularly for workers in the ready-made garments (RMG) industry, which employs over four million people in 5,400 factories (Bangladesh Garment Manufacturers and Exporters Association, 2023).

Bangladesh's first National Health Policy (NHP) was approved in 2000, and revisions in 2011 introduced new issues, including a health insurance scheme for formal institutions and health cards for the ultra-poor (WHO, 2015). Existing reforms, such as community clinics and maternal care vouchers, provide limited health services (WHO, 2015). Health protection schemes for government employees are limited (Hamid, 2015; Siddiquee & Rahman, 2013).

The proposal for health insurance for formal sector workers does not cover informal and rural sector workers (WHO, 2015). The penetration of health insurance and social protection among informal workers, even with national health insurance, remains low in Bangladesh (Rockefeller Foundation, 2013). Workers in the RMG sector benefit from health micro-finance schemes offered by Cashpor and Grameen banks.

Private health insurance is nearly non-existent, existing only in some areas managed by NGOs (Molla & Chi, 2017). BRAC, an NGO, charges premiums based on individuals' economic capacity for its health insurance scheme. Challenges in implementing health insurance schemes include the lack of infrastructure for the large informal sector and issues with introducing "pre-payment" national insurance schemes. However, CBHI schemes have been shown to increase the utilization of medically trained providers (MTPs) among informal workers (Spaan et al., 2012).

Though evidence on CBHI's impact on health access and equity in Bangladesh is limited, it is reported that health insurance (i) increases access to affordable health services, (ii) improves health facilities in RMG factories, (iii) enhances workers' health-seeking behavior, and (iv) positively impacts working conditions and productivity (Uddin, n.d.).

Recent years have seen innovative low-cost health insurance schemes piloted by NGOs (e.g., SSK and HAEFA; zero-cash transaction APON and SNV Netherlands business model, and fee-based UPHCSDP). Widespread public acceptance may take time as the concept of health insurance continues to grow in Bangladesh (Islam & Biswas, 2014). Growing Corporate Social Responsibility (CSR) initiatives include partnerships between large international companies to improve health within agricultural communities (Rockefeller Foundation, 2013).

The Bangladesh Garment Manufacturers and Exporters Association (BGMEA) and Telenor Health aim to identify opportunities for innovative and affordable solutions to help RMG workers manage their health. As most RMG sector employees are female, the focus includes women's health and services benefiting their families. However, there is no data confirming that assigning health insurance responsibility to women leads to better healthcare for women and their families. Affordable health insurance schemes for the poor, elderly, disadvantaged, and disabled will benefit various Bangladeshi communities.

7 Universal Pension Scheme (UPS): New Approaches by the Government

7.1 Issue

To enhance protection for older persons, the Government of Bangladesh introduced the "Universal Pension Scheme (UPS)" on 17 August 2023. This scheme aims to provide self-sustained retirement options for citizens, allowing even those with modest incomes to prepare financially for retirement. Four distinct pension schemes have been introduced: (i) Progoti (employees of private companies); (ii) Surokkha (informal sector workers, e.g., farmers and laborers); (iii) Somota (individuals living below the poverty line); and (iv) Probash (Bangladeshi citizens living abroad).

Bangladesh is experiencing a demographic dividend with an increasing gap between working and retired people. The average life expectancy of Bangladeshis is currently 73 years, expected to rise to 80 years by 2050 and 85 years by 2075. This implies that Bangladeshis will live approximately 20 years post-retirement in the next three decades. The current dependency ratio of the elderly (65 years and above) is 9.4%, projected to rise to 24% by 2050 and 48% by 2075. Given the increasing life expectancy and dependency ratio, the UPS is a timely initiative for future elderly citizens, reflecting economic strength and a visionary approach toward a developed societal structure.

7.2 Implementation of the Universal Pension Scheme

The implementation of the UPS requires effective governance, accountable fund management, and digital integration. The National Pension Authority has been established to oversee this. The goal is to cover 10 crore citizens under the UPS, providing a well-organized social security structure. As of December 5, 2023, 16,600 people have registered, with 19 crore taka deposited.

The government emphasizes providing adequate old-age pensions at guaranteed levels, regularly adjusted to maintain purchasing power until death. Pensions may be provided through contributory schemes and/or universal "means-tested" non-contributory schemes. Contributory pensions should ensure income maintenance with at least minimum compensation rates relative to past earnings, or minimum benefit.

Non-contributory pensions, including "means-tested" old-age pensions, should guarantee that the provision offered is at least sufficient to maintain the beneficiary's family in health and decency. These benefits should collectively ensure a national social protection floor that provides a dignified life in old age as part of a comprehensive social protection system, which also offers higher levels of pensions. Social protection floors are nationally defined sets of basic social security guarantees that ensure, at a minimum, that all people in need have access to essential health care and basic income security over their lifetime, securing effective access to necessary goods and services.

Public pension schemes have proven effective in ensuring adequate income security for older people and in combating poverty and social inequality. Many countries have progressively added components to their systems to guarantee minimum pensions and, in some cases, have established supplementary mechanisms to secure higher benefits. The universal pension scheme, along with other increasingly contributory social protection schemes, will have a significant impact on the lives of Bangladeshi citizens, providing financial security from birth to old age and encouraging greater participation in pension programs. The ILO and the UN system in Bangladesh will continue to support the development of these systems for the benefit of all.

7.3 The Main Features of the Universal Pension Scheme

The Universal Pension Scheme includes the following main features:

- Beneficiaries aged 18–50 must contribute until they turn 60. Those over 50 must contribute for at least 10 years to receive a pension (based on accumulated amounts including profit) for life. Bangladeshi citizens working or residing abroad can also participate in this scheme.
- Currently, officers and employees of Government and Autonomous Institutions are excluded from the scheme, but they will be included gradually.
- The monthly pension amount will be determined based on the return on investments of the pensioners' contributions in secure and profitable sectors under the investment rules.
- Organizations can participate in the scheme, with subscription fees determined by the National Pension Authority.
- Subscription fees will be set according to real situations, law, and practice, with the pension authority ensuring maximum returns on deposits.

- Subscribers must make monthly payments to their scheme account; otherwise, the account will be frozen. Accounts can be resumed upon payment of missed fees.
- If a subscriber dies before age 75, their nominees will receive the remaining amount up to the age of 75.
- If a subscriber dies before completing at least 10 years of contributions, the deposit will be returned to their nominee along with any profit.
- The accumulated amount in a pensioner's account cannot be withdrawn in full at once. However, subscribers can obtain loans up to 50% of the total amount paid, including interest (upon request).
- Pension contributions are treated as investments eligible for tax concessions, and the monthly pension is exempt from income tax.
- The government will cover part of the subscription for those who are insolvent or below the low-income threshold.
- Subscribers can adjust the contribution rate and scheme after joining.
- The government will cover all expenses of the National Pension Authority (NPS).

7.4 Products of the Universal Pension Scheme

The Universal Pension Scheme includes four distinct products:

1. **Progoti (for employees of private companies)**: Employees or owners of privately owned institutions can participate by paying the prescribed contribution rate. If an institution participates, it will cover 50% of the contribution, with the remaining 50% paid by employees. If a private organization does not participate, employees can still join individually. Monthly subscription amounts are Tk. 2000 ($17.50), Tk. 3000 ($26.32), Tk. 5000 ($43.86), and Tk. 10,000 ($87.72).
2. **Surakkha (for self-employed citizens)**: Individuals in the informal sector or self-employed (e.g., farmers, rickshaw pullers, laborers) can join by paying the prescribed contribution rate. Monthly subscriptions are Tk. 1000, Tk. 2000 ($17.50), Tk. 3000 ($26.32), and Tk. 5000 ($43.86).
3. **Samata (for very poor self-employed citizens)**: Low-income individuals living below the poverty line (with an annual income of less than Tk. 60,000, no evidence required) can participate. The monthly subscription is Tk. 1000 ($8.77), with Tk. 500 ($4.39) paid by the subscriber and Tk. 500 ($4.39) provided as a government grant.
4. **Probash (for expatriate Bangladeshi citizens)**: Bangladeshi citizens working or staying abroad can join by paying the prescribed contribution in foreign currency. After returning to Bangladesh, they can pay the equivalent in local currency or change the scheme if needed. Monthly subscription amounts are Tk. 2000 ($17.50), Tk. 5000 ($43.86), Tk. 7500 ($65.79), and Tk. 10,000 ($87.72). Expatriates can also open a pension scheme (Surakkha) for family members in Bangladesh and pay monthly contributions.

8 Old Age Homes and Services in Bangladesh

8.1 Issue

Bangladesh has a rich cultural tradition where the elderly are an integral part of society. As society transitions from agriculture to industry, traditional family structures are changing, leading to smaller family sizes and a decline in the joint family system. With more people moving abroad for education or employment, it is becoming increasingly difficult for families to care for their elderly members.

An old age home, or retirement home, is a residential facility providing nursing and assisted living services for older adults, including meals, housekeeping, medical care, and recreational activities. With the increasing number of elderly people in Bangladesh, due to improved life quality, there is a growing need for such care facilities. However, there is a shortage of high-quality care centers in the country. To address this, both organizations and wealthy individuals need to establish standard care centers to provide the necessary healthcare and support, preserving the valuable experience of the elderly and normalizing elderly services in society.

8.2 Aging Population in Bangladesh

Policy responses to the aging population in Bangladesh have rarely been studied. It is crucial to assess the extent to which policymakers are aware of the rapidly growing older population and their care needs, and how this awareness is reflected in policy initiatives. Current statistics on older people in Bangladesh highlight emerging challenges related to medical, social, and economic issues. It is essential to adapt our health system to address the demands posed by an increasing senior population. Nutritional disorders are prevalent and significant among the elderly.

Malnutrition is associated with decreased muscle mass, higher infection rates, poor health outcomes, and impaired quality of life. It is a strong independent risk factor for short-term mortality. Studies show a high prevalence of poor nutritional status and impaired functional ability among the elderly. Additionally, the impact of factors affecting nutritional status may vary based on cultural backgrounds. The nutritional and functional status of community-dwelling elderly individuals, especially in rural areas, remains under-researched.

Approximately 77% of elderly people lack sufficient income to meet their basic needs, and 71.4% rely on siblings for financial support. Many poor families cannot provide separate living spaces for their senior members, often residing in cramped one or two-room houses with more than five family members. Currently, there are six government-run old age homes under the Ministry of Social Welfare, and several shelters and traditional old age homes operated by private institutions. These circumstances highlight the growing demand for elderly care homes and services in Bangladesh.

8.3 Professional Elderly Care Services in Bangladesh

In Bangladesh, elderly care is often perceived as a last resort for older individuals who cannot manage independently or are unable to perform daily tasks. Leaving home for institutional care is a distressing prospect for many seniors, who prefer to stay at home as long as possible. It is also considered unethical to relocate them against their will. However, increasing numbers of younger people have rigid routines that prevent them from caring for elderly family members.

Elderly care encompasses a wide range of services designed to meet the special needs of senior citizens requiring assistance with daily activities. This includes adult daycare, nursing care, home care, hospice care, and long-term care. Globally, the term "elderly care" covers various aspects, and it is not solely driven by aging but also by specific diseases and physical conditions. The need for elderly care in Bangladesh is becoming more urgent, but such services remain limited.

Professional elderly care can be provided at home, which allows seniors to remain in their own environment while receiving the necessary support. Caregivers can assist with healthy diets, fall prevention, physical activity, regular doctor visits, dementia care, personal care, and Parkinson's care. Elderly care services can address various physical and emotional challenges:

- **Physical Problems**: Chronic health issues can limit the activities seniors can perform. Caregivers can help with:
  - Gait or walking problems
  - Sensory issues such as hearing, vision, or smell impairments
  - Serious health conditions like diabetes and heart disease
  - Permanent or temporary physical limitations
  - Cognitive issues that impact safety, such as memory loss, attention problems, confusion, and forgetting to take medications
- **Emotional Problems**: Loss of a spouse or children can lead to emotional distress. Moving to an old age home might not be effective in such cases. In-home care can address emotional problems such as:
  - Depression
  - Social withdrawal
  - Loneliness
  - Personality changes
  - Loss of interest in activities

8.4 Need for Old-Age Homes in Bangladesh

Bangladesh lacks a comprehensive social welfare system, leading to competition for limited resources, particularly for the elderly. Although Bangladesh has traditionally been a young nation demographically, it is now experiencing rapid growth in its older population. This demographic shift is likely to result in significant health and social challenges and substantial government expenditures (Barikder et al., 2016; Hamiduzzaman et al., 2018; Rahman, 2017). Like many developing countries, Bangladesh has traditionally relied on unpaid family care for older adults, supported by social, cultural, and religious norms (Kabir et al., 2002).

Despite this, the elderly have not been a primary focus for government or third-sector organizations. This lack of attention has been mirrored by a lack of research, with few studies addressing aging and care for older adults in Bangladesh (Barikder et al., 2016; Tareque et al., 2015). Healthcare for older adults is often unavailable and expensive, and formal long-term care options are almost non-existent (HEU, 2012). Despite a large elderly population (over 15.3 million), publicly funded formal home care is unavailable, and institutional care for older adults is rare and relatively new in Bangladesh (Barikdar & Lasker, 2016). Consequently, long-term care in Bangladesh is largely dependent on informal family care.

8.5 *Home Care Versus Care Homes: Unexplored Vulnerability for Older Adults*

Old age inevitably involves biological health deterioration and various life challenges. These needs cannot be adequately addressed by modest economic benefits such as the Old Age Allowance (OAA). Significant demographic and socio-economic changes, including rural-to-urban migration and international migration, have left many older adults alone at home. Consequently, support for basic Activities of Daily Living (ADLs) and instrumental activities of daily living has become very limited. Many older adults also face gerontological health conditions that require additional care. The government has established only six old-age homes in six regions, providing minimal shelter, healthcare, and medical care, which is insufficient relative to the total need. Furthermore, the quality of these institutions is often poor, leading many older adults to avoid them, leaving several facilities vacant.

While some national and international NGOs have been developing residential care for the elderly, their combined efforts remain inadequate in both quantity and quality. Private care homes operate commercially, charging fees that exclude economically disadvantaged older adults. Financially secure older adults often prefer private care homes over government facilities if family support is unavailable. Culturally, older adults in Bangladesh generally prefer to live with their children or grandchildren. However, many children migrate to cities or abroad for education or work, and an increasing number of women are joining the labor market, reducing the availability of unpaid family caregivers. Consequently, many older adults remain at home with inadequate care from health or social services, often exacerbated by family poverty.

The government's Parental Care Allowance (PCA) program has not been very effective. In some cases, busy young parents may bring their parents to live with them, so they can spend time with their grandchildren. Some NGOs have initiated programs where older adults are accommodated in care homes alongside orphans and street children, providing a family-like environment for both groups. While these initiatives can have positive social outcomes, many are still in the planning stages. Overall, societal perceptions of old-age homes are often negative due to cultural values and family ties, making it unlikely for older parents to move away from their children. Policymakers are divided on establishing residential care for older adults, with many believing that children should care for their parents due to societal norms and the government's limited resources (Aminuzzaman, 2013). Despite mixed opinions, there remains a need for old-age homes because not all older adults have children, or some may prefer the privacy and support offered by care homes.

Cultural and religious issues also impact the provision of health and social care services. Providing diverse care for older adults is challenging, especially for women, who may face additional difficulties if they have disabilities. For instance, many Muslim women are reluctant to receive physical treatment from male caregivers, and the lack of digital equipment often means that health workers provide many services manually, which can be problematic.

8.6 Retirement Homes for an Industrializing Bangladesh

As Bangladesh approaches the intermediate stage of aging, the number of nuclear families is rising. Many older people, with savings and valuable experience, could become assets to society. However, there is a significant gap in providing the necessary support facilities to help them lead peaceful and productive lives. Not all seniors have the same care needs, so a balanced and holistic care system should be designed to promote healthy lifestyles, including nutritious diets, regular exercise, and strong social connections.

Senior citizens are valued for their contributions and experience. To provide the necessary support, various organizations or businesses could establish care centers with different tiers:

- **Premier Living**: For high-income elderly individuals
- **Seniors Living**: For middle-income elderly individuals
- **Retired Living**: For low-income elderly individuals

This model could be cost-effective and self-sustainable, with the Retired Living group paying a nominal fee, the Seniors Living group covering actual costs, and the Premier Living group paying a premium for enhanced services. Surplus funds from the Premier Living group could subsidize the Retired Living group.

Due to the social stigma surrounding old-age homes, initial challenges may include convincing people to use these facilities. Active campaigning, both online and offline, highlighting the importance of elderly care and the benefits of care facilities, could help overcome this challenge. The socio-economic implications of an aging population are emerging issues in Bangladesh, making it essential to develop new policies and increase awareness. Integrated, assisted-living facilities need to address the needs of the growing elderly population.

9 Concluding Remarks

Bangladesh's demographic dividend is currently contributing to economic growth, complementing investments in infrastructure, technology, manufacturing, and trade policies. The abundant supply of young, healthy, and educated workers has the potential to boost economic growth and socio-economic development. If effectively harnessed, this demographic dividend could lead to increased per capita income and higher savings rates as more people become economically active. Achieving this requires policies that provide mechanisms and incentives for savings during working years. However, the rapid increase in the elderly population due to improved quality of life necessitates comprehensive planning and attention.

Aging is a natural and inevitable process that affects everyone, making it a significant social concern beyond individual and familial issues. Although some government and voluntary organizations are working to address the challenges faced by the elderly, these efforts are often fragmented, inadequate, and cumbersome. Social myths, prejudice, structural issues, and negative attitudes toward the elderly further exacerbate their problems.

Bangladesh has made significant progress in health indicators, achieving MDG-4 ahead of schedule and making substantial progress towards MDG-5 despite budgetary constraints. The country's 4th Health Population and Nutrition Sector Development Program (HPNSP) includes community-based health clinics that have contributed to achieving Sustainable Development Goals (SDGs) and will continue to do so until 2030. The 4th HPNSP expands community-based health care (CBHC) activities to include all health facilities within Upazilas (sub-districts) beyond community clinics.

To address the needs of its aging population, Bangladesh must focus on enhancing primary health care. While health indicators have improved significantly over the past fifty years, there is still progress needed to achieve universal health care. Countries like Bangladesh can turn the challenge of a growing aging population into opportunities for systemic transformation. With appropriate policies and investments, innovative solutions can be developed to improve health care for the elderly.

The nutrition and health status of the elderly depend on access to adequate food, safe water, proper sanitation, and hygienic standards. Establishing WHO-recommended Age-Friendly Primary Health Care centers and dedicated wards or units in hospitals is essential. Additionally, to reduce the vulnerability of older women, asset distribution according to the law is necessary. New generations must be informed and responsive to their responsibilities toward the elderly, as caring for older adults is both an ethical duty and a societal responsibility.

Economic theory suggests that employees with health insurance perform better and contribute more to national development. The rising costs of health care highlight the importance of health insurance, as many individuals cannot afford these expenses. Health insurance plays a crucial role in social protection, but Bangladesh has yet to achieve significant progress in this area despite rapid economic and political advancements.

An effective health insurance policy can greatly enhance overall health outcomes. Without proper health insurance, employees risk falling into poverty due to high medical costs. Nearly half of all wage workers in Bangladesh work in unsafe environments, leading to illness and decreased productivity. Several community-based health insurance models and schemes have been introduced to address this issue. A suitable health insurance model can improve employee well-being and protection for older people. The "Universal Pension Scheme" initiated by Bangladesh represents a significant step towards communal welfare, offering a path to self-sustained retirement for citizens, even those with modest incomes.

The most concerning prospect for many elders is being forced to leave their homes when their children are unable to care for them. As more young people become unable to provide care due to demanding routines, old-age homes present a potential solution. Social stigma surrounding old-age homes may pose a challenge, but this can be mitigated through active campaigning that highlights the importance of elderly care and the benefits of care facilities.

Professional elderly care can provide support without requiring seniors to leave their homes. Caregivers can assist with various needs, including diet management, fall prevention, physical activity encouragement, regular doctor visits, dementia care, personal care, and support for conditions like Parkinson's disease. Developing new policies and increasing awareness in this area is crucial.

As Bangladesh enjoys its demographic dividend, it will begin to transition from an "aging" society in 2029 to an "aged" society by 2047. This shift will lead to changes in the demographic structure and pose new challenges, as increasing numbers of elderly individuals will require specialized care and services. Without a robust social welfare system, competition for resources, particularly in health and medical services, will intensify.

Ensuring income security for the elderly is a key aspect of the UN's social security and universal protection agenda. Barriers to adequate care include high costs, limited access to medicines and transportation, insufficient trained providers, and age discrimination. Addressing these issues requires a comprehensive analysis of service availability and needs. Policymakers and stakeholders should focus on budget allocation, digital technology, monitoring, and evaluation to support the aging population.

The government should invest more in elderly health care through an output-based budget. Leveraging digital health technology can improve care accessibility and create a long-term care framework. Effective regulation and oversight can enhance quality and accountability, and reducing supply chain disruptions is essential for a consistent drug supply. Creating a dedicated evaluator position to monitor adherence to quality guidelines can further strengthen the health care system. Together, these strategies can build a foundation for a holistic health care system that supports the aging population and enhances their quality of life.

References

Ahmed, I. (2019). The impact of ageing on population structure and development process of different levels of Bangladesh. *European Journal of Medical and Health Sciences*, 50–58, https://doi.org/10.34104/ejmhs.01950058: Universe Publishing Group – UniversePG.

ARC. (2023). ARC Centre of Excellence.

Aspin, J. (2014). *Universal health coverage for inclusive and sustainable development: Country summary report for Bangladesh*. Health, Nutrition and Population Global Practice, World Bank Group. https://doi.org/10.11588/xarep.00003510.

ATCOA (2000, July). Asia Training Center on Aging, ATCOA News, Issue 13.

Barikder, A., Tahera, A., & Lasker, S. (2016). The situation of the elderly in Bangladesh. *Bangladesh Journal of Bioethics*, *7*(1), 27–36. https://doi.org/10.3329/bioethics.v7i1.29303.

Barkat, A., Gupta, S. K. S., Hussain, A. A., Rahman, M., & Ahamed, F. M. (2013). Improving the targeting effectiveness of social safety nets in Bangladesh. Paper presented at Extreme Poverty Research Group (EPRG) 11, Social Protection of the Poorest, Dhaka.

Bartosic, F., & Bernstein, J. (1973). Group legal services as a fringe benefit: Lawyers for forgotten clients through collective bargaining. *Virginia Law Review*, 410–461.

BBS. (2023). *Bangladesh population and housing census 2022*. Bangladesh Bureau of Statistics, Ministry of Planning, Government of Bangladesh.

Begum, A., & Islam, R. (2019). *An inclusive approach to care of the elderly in Bangladesh*. BIDS-REF Study Series No. 19–04, Bangladesh Institute of Development Studies. Dhaka.

Bloom, D. E., Canning, D., & Malaney, P. N. (2003a). Population dynamics and economic growth in Asia. *Population and Development Review*, *26*, 257–290.

Bloom, D. E., Canning, D., & Sevilla, J. (2003b). *The demographic dividend: A new perspective on the economic consequences of population change*. RAND Corporation.

Boudreau, A. (1993). *Elder abuse, family violence: Prevention and treatment*. Edited by Robert. L. Hampton & others. Sage Publication.

Coale, A. J., & Hoover, E. M. (1958). Population growth and economic development in low-income countries. *Princeton University Press*, 6–25.

Cockcroft, A., Milne, D., Oelofsen, M., Karim, E., & Andersson, N. (2011). Health services reform in Bangladesh: Hearing the views of health workers and their professional bodies. *BMC health services research*, *11*(2), 1–8.

Coleman, J., William, C., & Donald. R. (1990). *Social problems*. Harper Collins Publishers.

CPD. (2002). *Center for policy dialogue, report-23, Aging in Bangladesh: Issues and challenges*.

Easterline, A. (1967). Effects of population growth on the economic development of developing countries. *The Annals of the American Academy of Political and Social Science*, *36*(9), 98–108.

Eastwood, R., & Lipton, M. (1999). The impact of changes in human fertility on poverty. *Journal of Development Studies, Taylor & Francis Journals*, *36*(1), 1–30.

Ehlrich, P. R., & Ehlrich, A. H. (1990). The population bomb revisited. *The Electronic Journal of Sustainable Development*, *1*(3), 1–13.

Erb, S. (2011). A study of older people's livelihoods in Bangladesh. HelpAge International, Cordaid, HelpAge Bangladesh.

Friedlander, W. A. (1997). *Introduction to Social Welfare*. 5th ed. Prentice Hall of India.

Gorman, M. (1999). *Development and the rights of older people, The aging and development report: poverty, independence and the World's older people*. Earthscan Publications Limited.

HAI. (2000). Help Age International, A situation of older people in Bangladesh. *Bangladesh Journal of Geriatrics*, *37*(1&2), 137.

Hamid, S. A. (2014). *Designing a health insurance scheme for government employees in Bangladesh: A concept paper*.

Hamiduzzaman, M., Torres, S., Fletcher, A., Islam, M. R., Siddiquee, N. A., & Greenhill. J. (2022). Aging, care and dependency in multimorbidity: How do relationships affect older Bangladeshi women's use of homecare and health services? *Journal of Women & Aging*, *34*(6), 731–744. https://doi.org/10.1080/08952841.2021.1951115.

Hassan, M. Z., Fahim, S. M., Zafr, A. H. A., Islam, M. S., & Alam, S. (2016). Healthcare financing in Bangladesh: Challenges and recommendations. *Bangladesh Journal of Medical Science, 15*(4), 505–510. https://doi.org/10.3329/bjms.v15i4.21698.

Hossain, M. I., Alam, M. J., Islam, N., & Mamun, M. Z. (2006). Service requirement for the aged people in Bangladesh. *Journal of Business Studies, Center for Business Research, Southeast University*, II(1), 152–163.

Hossen, M. S., & Mohd Pauzi, H. B. (2023). Embracing housing alternatives for the enhancement of wellbeing in the aging population: A qualitative study. *J Aging Neuro Psychol*, *4*. 120. https://doi.org/10.29011/2688-6499.100020.

IDB. (2023). International database: World population estimates and projections. International Database (IDB), US Census Bureau.

Islam, K. (2023). *Time to focus on healthy aging: Challenges, opportunities, and recommendations for Bangladesh: Silver opportunity case studies.* World Bank Group.

Kabir, H. (1994). Local level policy development to deal with the consequences of population aging in Bangladesh. United Nations.

Khan, J. A., Ahmed, S., & Evans, T. G. (2017). Catastrophic healthcare expenditure and poverty related to out-of-pocket payments for healthcare in Bangladesh—An estimation of financial risk protection of universal health coverage. *Health policy and planning*, *32*(8), 1102–1110.

Mason, A. (2005). Demographic Dividends: The past, the present, and the future. Paper presented in the Joint International Conference of the 21st Century COE (Center of Excellence) Program of Kobe University and the Japan Economic Policy Association (JEPA), "Towards a New Economic Paradigm: Declining Population Growth, Labor Market Transition and Economic Development under Globalization." Awaji Yumebutai International Conference Center near Kobe, Japan, December 17–18, 2005.

Montgomery, R. J. V., & Datvyler, M. M. (1990). Women and men in the care giving role. *Generations*, *14* (Summer), 36.

Morgan, L., & Suzanne, K. (2001). *Aging: The social context*. Pine Forge Press.

Rabbani, G., & Hossain, S. (1981). Population projection of Bangladesh (1975–2025). Bangladesh Bureau of Statistics.

Rafin, S. M. S. (2023). A critical analysis of the social security of the aged citizens of Bangladesh. *Law and Society Students' Journal*, *1*(1). https://doi.org/10.5281/zenodo.7654470.

Rahman, H. M. (1998). International year of the older persons and the cases of Bangladesh. *Bangladesh Journal of Geriatrics*, *36*(1&2), 144.

Rahman, K. M. M. (2007). Living arrangements and health status of the rural elderly of Naogaon District, Bangladesh. *Indian Journal of Gerontology*, *21*, 378–393.

Riaz, B. K., Ali, L., Ahmad, S. A., Islam, M. Z., Ahmed, K. R., & Hossain, S. (2020). Community clinics in Bangladesh: A unique example of public-private partnership. *Heliyon*, *6*(5), e03950.

Rockefeller Foundation. (2013, May). Health vulnerabilities of informal workers. https://assets.rockefellerfoundation.org/app/uploads/20130528214745/Health-Vulnerabilities-ofInformal-Workers.pdf.

Roy, M., & Kayesh, M. S. (2016). Reaping demographic dividend in Bangladesh: Challenges and prospects. *Global Journal of Human-Social Science*, *16*(2), 11–20.

Sheikh, N., Sarker, A. R., & Sultana, M. (2022). Disease-specific distress healthcare financing and catastrophic out-of-pocket expenditure for hospitalization in Bangladesh. *International Journal of Equity Health, 21*, 114. https://doi.org/10.1186/s12939-022-01712-6.

Simon, J. (1981). *The ultimate resource*. Princeton University Press.

World Bank. (2024). *Global economic prospects 2024.*

Long-Term Care Insurance in Vietnam

Huong Thi Thu Phung, Van Dinh, and Thai Hong Le

1 Introduction

In Vietnam, long-term care refers to the continuous provision of health-related and social support services for individuals who are unable to perform daily activities independently because of chronic illness, disability, or old age. Such care encompasses a broad range of services, including personal care, medical supervision, rehabilitation, and assistance with activities of daily living (ADLs). As one of the fastest-transforming economies in East Asia, Vietnam has achieved substantial socioeconomic progress and sustained GDP growth in recent decades (World Bank, 2024a, 2024b); however, these gains have unfolded alongside rapid population ageing and a rising prevalence of chronic conditions, placing increasing pressure on health and social protection systems. In this context, demand for long-term care services is rising rapidly, highlighting the need for a comprehensive long-term care system that can provide accessible, affordable, and high-quality services for older persons. Yet, despite continued economic growth, Vietnam has not established a fully integrated long-term care system or a dedicated long-term care insurance framework, leaving care provision fragmented across families, health services, and social assistance arrangements. To respond effectively to changing demographic and epidemiological patterns, Vietnam needs to strengthen geriatric and rehabilitative capacity,

H. T. T. Phung (✉)
Banking Academy of Vietnam, Hanoi, Vietnam
e-mail: huongphung@hvnh.edu.vn

V. Dinh
University of Wisconsin, Superior, WI, USA
e-mail: vdinh@uwsuper.edu

V. Dinh · T. H. Le
University of Economics and Business, Vietnam National University, Hanoi, Vietnam
e-mail: thailh@vnu.edu.vn

H. Lee and G. Nicolini (eds.), *International Comparison of Long-Term Care Insurance Systems*, Contributions to Management Science,
https://doi.org/10.1007/978-981-95-7781-1_13

expand professional home-based and institutional care services, and improve coordination between health care and social care systems. The Vietnamese government has increasingly recognized the urgency of population ageing and older-person care, but major challenges remain in financing, service capacity, workforce development, and equitable access (Ministry of Labour, Invalids and Social Affairs, 2020).

2 Drivers of Long-Term Care Need in Vietnam

2.1 *Demographics and Aging*

Vietnam has seen consistent population growth historically, characterized by fluctuating growth rates, birth rates, and mortality rates over different periods. Population statistics also illustrate the historical context, living standards, and governmental focus on population and development matters. The General Statistics Office, Ministry of Planning and Investment reported in early January 2023 that Vietnam's overall population was 99.46 million, with men comprising 49.9% and women 50.1% (General Statistics Office of Vietnam, 2023). The 2022 population change study conducted by the General Statistics Office indicates that the average life expectancy in the country was 73.6 years, with men averaging 71.1 years and women averaging 76.4 years. In 2024, Viet Nam's total population was estimated at 100,987,686 (World Bank, 2024c), underscoring the scale and urgency of ageing-related care needs.

The projected population pyramid for Vietnam from 2019 to 2069 in Fig. 1 (General Statistics Office of Vietnam, 2020) clearly shows a shift towards an older population structure. By 2069, the base of the pyramid is projected to narrow significantly, and the top will expand, indicating increased life expectancy and a substantial proportion of the population aged 80 and older. This rapid aging is exacerbated by Vietnam's low fertility rate and unclear fertility policies, leading to an increasing dependency ratio and escalating demand for LTC services.

Figure 2 illustrates the distribution of the elderly population by urban and rural residence in 2015, showing that over 66% of the elderly resided in rural areas (MoH,

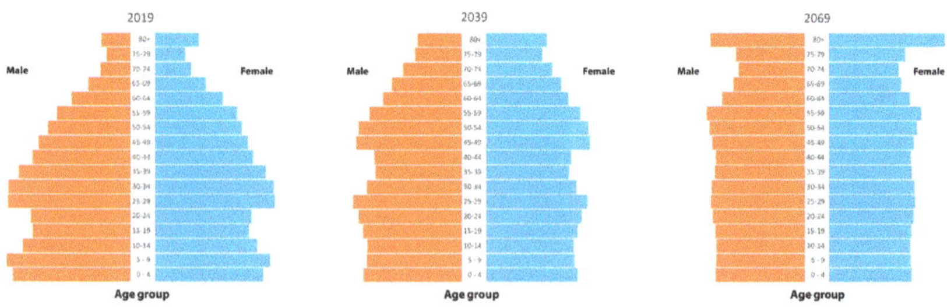

Fig. 1 Projected population pyramid of Vietnam, 2019–2069. *Source* General Statistics Office of Vietnam (2020)

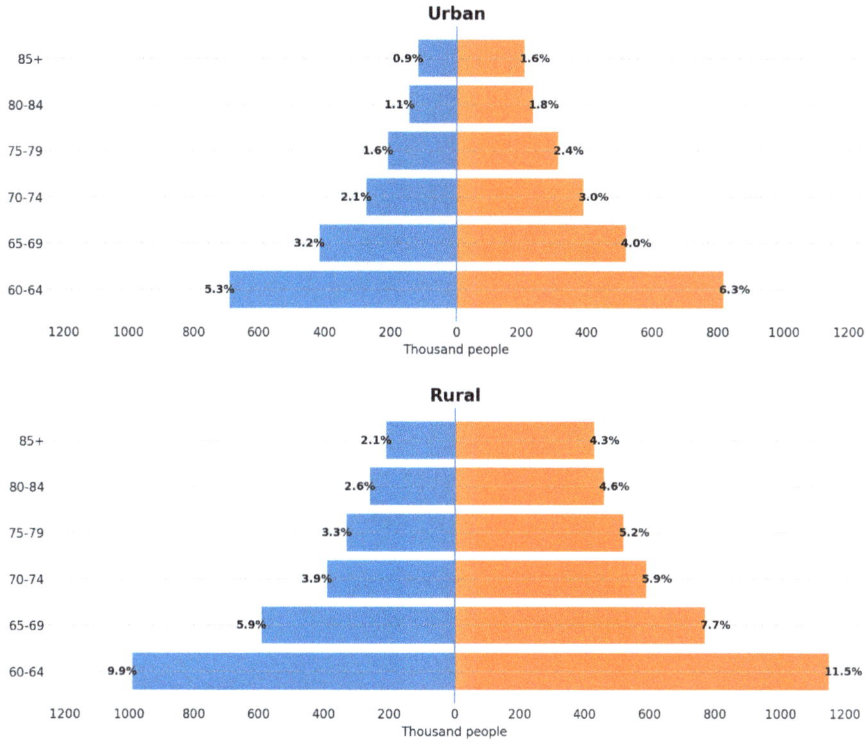

Fig. 2 Population pyramid for older persons by urban and rural residence. *Source* Ministry of Health and Health Partnership Group (2018)

2018). This rural concentration, coupled with the out-migration of the working-age population, reduces the pool of informal caregivers and strains formal care access due to poor rural infrastructure and urban concentration of skilled healthcare professionals.

The percentage of women in the overall population showed a decreasing trend from 2016 to 2020 (Table 1). The female population in urban regions declined by 0.7%, whilst in rural regions, it reduced by 0.3%. By 2049, the male-to-female ratio is projected to rise markedly across all age demographics (Pham & Do, 2009).

Besides, over 60% of elderly adults have at least one child, peaking at 73% among the oldest seniors (Giang et al., 2022). Walker and Wyse (2022) highlight the critical role of informal caregivers, typically family members, driven by strong cultural expectations. However, these social norms are changing, and by 2050, when an estimated 25% of the population will be over 60, relying solely on adult children as primary caregivers will no longer be feasible. This necessitates government and private sector intervention to fill the care vacuum.

Table 1 Female population of Vietnam in the period 2016–2020

No	Content	Data	
1	*Percentage of female population in total population (%)*	*Year 2016*	*Year 2020*
	– Nationwide	50.6	50.20
	+Urban female population	51.3	50.63
	+Rural female population	50.3	49.95
2	*Percentage of female population in total population by age group (%)*	*Year 2016*	*Year 2019*
	– Females of working age (15–55 years)		49.43
	– Females aged 18 and older	51.7	51.14
	– Female youth (16–30 years)	49.2	48.86
	– Females in middle age (15–49 years)	49.5	49.19
	– Females aged 60 and older	61.0	58.13
3	*Population growth rate (%)*	Total	*Female*
	– Average population growth rate from 2016–2020	1.13	1.06

Source VWU (2022)

2.2 *Income and Long-Term Care*

As individuals age, their health often declines, income sources diminish, and the ability to work ceases. Rapid population aging in Vietnam is projected to increase medical costs, insurance expenditures, and social security demands, posing significant challenges to pension systems. The increasing dependency ratio strains Vietnam's social security and pension systems, leading to rising pension and healthcare expenditures and decreasing public pension fund budgets.

Despite Vietnam's economic expansion, many older individuals still face financial struggles. HelpAge International reports that 60% of Vietnamese seniors are economically disadvantaged, with many living in poverty. An ILO survey from 2019 indicated that most elderly Vietnamese reside in low-income households. In 2016, up to two-thirds of the elderly lived in families with an average per capita income of less than 100,000 VND (less than $2) per day. Most elderly people are unable to work or have a stable income; for instance, 48% of women and 35% of men aged 65–69 are no longer in the labor force, a trend that intensifies with age. Figure 3 (ILO, 2019) visually represents the significant proportion of elderly individuals living below the average income per capita.

According to the General Statistics Office (2023), Vietnam's estimated national average per capita income for 2022 was 4.6 million VND per month, an 11.1% increase from the previous year. Income levels consistently rose in both urban (5.9 million VND/month) and rural areas (3.0 million VND/month), as depicted in Fig. 4. Despite this, a significant income gap persists, and the elderly population faces particular economic hardship, earning only 538,000 VND per month from social protection and pensions. Furthermore, only 62.79% of seniors had health insurance.

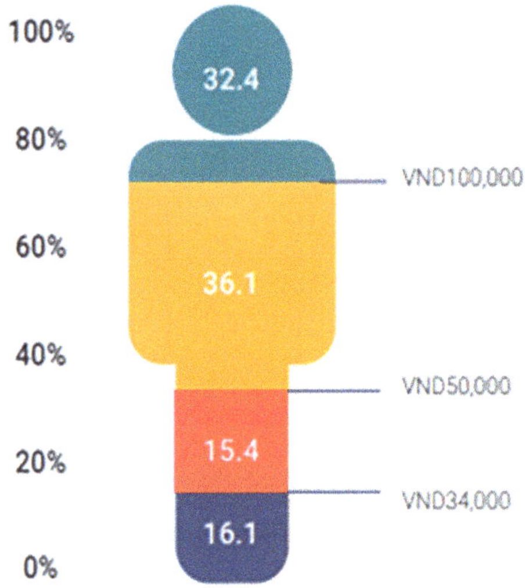

Fig. 3 Proportion of elderly people living below the average income per capita. *Source* ILO (2019)

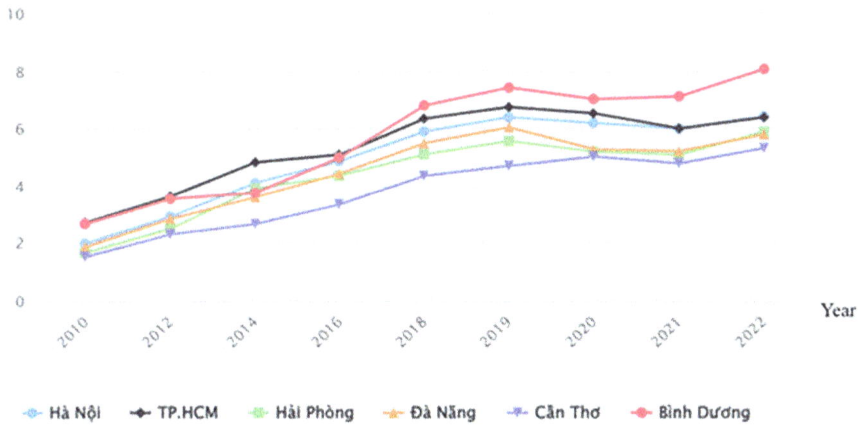

Fig. 4 Changes in per capita income of selected cities during the period 2010–2022. *Source* General Statistics Office of Vietnam (2023)

Besides, the average per capita expenditure in Vietnam decreased from pre-pandemic levels, reaching approximately 2.8 million VND per month in 2022 (General Statistics Office, 2023). Households, particularly in metropolitan areas, reduced spending due to the economic impact of COVID-19. While the average per capita expenditure in metropolitan regions was 3.3 million VND per month, rural areas exhibited a lower figure of 2.5 million VND.

Living expenses constituted a significant portion of household expenditures in 2022, averaging 2.7 million VND per person per month. Food accounted for 1.3 million VND of this, while non-food expenses totaled 1.4 million VND (Ngoc, 2024). The disparity in monthly per capita living expenses between the wealthiest and poorest groups narrowed from 5.7 times in 2020 to 3.2 times in 2022, primarily due to reduced living costs among the affluent.

The Health Insurance Law has provided significant healthcare benefits for the elderly, including complimentary examinations, partial payments, and full coverage for those receiving monthly death or social protection benefits. As a result, the proportion of elderly individuals enrolled in medical insurance has steadily increased. According to the Ministry of Labor, War Invalids, and Social Affairs, the total number of individuals enrolled in social insurance grew by approximately 1.1 million between 2019 and 2020, with a majority being elderly. Vietnam Social Security witnessed a corresponding rise in medical insurance issuance, from 8.8 million in 2016 to 12.1 million in 2020 (VSS, 2023).

Despite these advances, 5% of older people—over 500,000 individuals—remain uninsured. This group primarily consists of people aged 60–79 who do not come from poor, near-poor, or socially privileged households. Despite financial support, many older people continue to struggle with enrolling in medical insurance.

As the elderly population grows, healthcare and social welfare systems struggle to keep up, creating a rising demand for long-term care services, particularly for those with chronic diseases. The country's infrastructure, especially in rural areas, is insufficient to meet these needs (UNFPA, 2021). Many older adults in Viet Nam continue to rely on co-residence with or financial support from their children because pension coverage remains limited, while formal social assistance provides only modest protection against old-age poverty (Pfau & Giang, 2010; Giang & Pfau, 2009). The absence of comprehensive LTC insurance further burdens families, particularly low-income ones, as they must bear the full cost of care. These financial pressures strain society, highlighting the urgent need for policy reforms, better LTC infrastructure, and financial support to ensure seniors have access to necessary care and resources for healthy aging.

3 Public Long-Term Care Arrangements in Vietnam

3.1 System Structure

3.1.1 Operational Structure

Since the enactment of the 1945 Constitution, Vietnamese law has stipulated that families bear the primary responsibility for the care of their elderly relatives. The 2009 Law on the Elderly further codified these duties, mandating that descendants and grandchildren provide housing and financial support and cover healthcare costs. When families are unable to meet these obligations, individuals and organizations may provide home or facility-based care. Social protection centers offer specialized assistance for particularly vulnerable elderly adults, including those who live alone or in poverty.

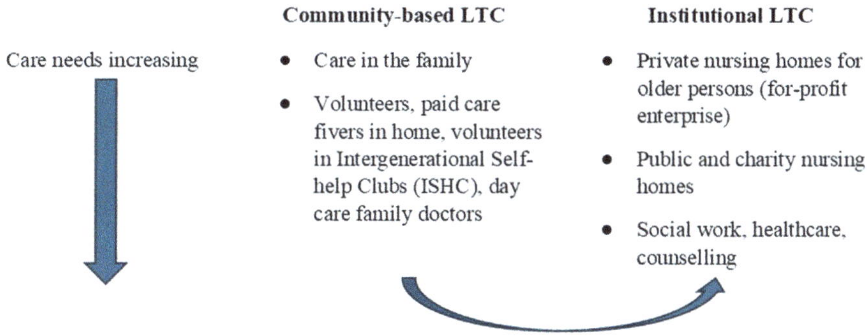

Fig. 5 Vietnam long-term care model. *Source* Synthesized by the authors

Government programs have consistently aimed to improve the welfare of the aging population. The National Action Program for the Elderly (2012–2020) was approved by Prime Minister of Vietnam (2012) targeted ethnic minority groups, while the Ministry of Health's healthcare plan for 2017–2025 aimed to help all elderly adults achieve self-care capabilities. The Prime Minister's 2020 decision extended the focus on elderly healthcare until 2030, in line with Vietnam's comprehensive population aging policy.

Alongside Vietnam's long-term care model (Fig. 5), public long-term care insurance in Vietnam is primarily situated within the broader social insurance framework. It is regulated by the Ministry of Labour, Invalids, and Social Affairs and implemented by Vietnam Social Security. The system operates through a network of local social insurance offices, which oversee the delivery and administration of long-term care services across different regions (as shown on Table 2).

3.1.2 Financial Resources

At present, Vietnam does not have a dedicated public LTC insurance scheme; LTC-related support is mainly provided through the public healthcare system and government assistance programs for older people. If a public LTC insurance program were to be developed, potential funding sources could include payroll-based contributions (providing reliable and stable revenue but potentially seen as a burden on employers and employees), allocations from general taxation (able to generate substantial revenue but less directly linked to LTC needs), individual premiums or specific contributions (more closely tailored to LTC risks and costs but potentially burdensome for individuals), and government subsidies (supporting affordability for all but requiring significant public expenditure) (Table 3).

Table 2 Public LTC insurance operational structure

Level	Organization	Responsibilities
Central	Ministry of Health	Oversees planning, development, and implementation. Sets policies, standards, and regulations. Monitors system performance
Central	National Social Insurance Agency (NSIA)	Administers the insurance program. Develops and maintains national database
Central	Health Insurance Fund	Collects and manages financial resources. Allocates funds to providers
Provincial	Provincial Health Department	Coordinates implementation at provincial level. Oversees provider network. Ensures compliance with standards
Provincial	Provincial Social Insurance Agency	Handles enrollment, premium collection, and benefit payments for individuals in the province. Maintains provincial database
Local	District/City Health Department	Provides administrative support at local level. Assists in enrollment and coordination of services
Local	Community Health Centers	Serve as points of contact for individuals. Assist in assessment and referral
Providers	Nursing Homes	Provide 24-h nursing care and assistance with daily living activities
Providers	Home Health Agencies	Offer a range of services, including skilled nursing care, physical therapy, occupational therapy, and home health aides
Providers	Community-Based Organizations	Provide social support, respite care, and other community-based services

Source Synthesized by the authors

3.1.3 Payment of Benefit Costs

Based on Table 4, the payment of benefit costs for LTC in Vietnam's public system can be described as a sequence of key administrative and financial steps. Payments typically begin with eligibility determination (commonly linked to age, disability status, and assessed care needs), followed by benefit calculation according to the level of required care, and disbursement either directly to service providers or to insured individuals/beneficiaries. Effective implementation would rely on coordination between local social insurance offices and Vietnam Social Security (VSS) to ensure consistent administration. The main factors shaping benefit expenditures and payment efficiency include the benefit structure (types and levels of benefits and eligibility criteria), payment mechanisms (direct payment, reimbursement, prepaid cards), payment rates (fee schedules, negotiation, quality incentives), claims processing (administrative efficiency and appeals), cost-sharing (co-payments and deductibles), and provider networks (network development and provider contracting).

Table 3 Funding sources for public LTC insurance in Vietnam

Mechanism	Description	Advantage	Disadvantage
Payroll taxes	Employers and employees contribute a portion of their wages to a dedicated fund for LTC insurance	Reliable and stable revenue	Perceived as a burden on employers and employees
General taxation	The government collects taxes from various sources, such as income tax, corporate tax, and property tax, and allocates a portion of the revenue to the LTC insurance program	Can generate substantial revenue	Less directly linked to LTC needs
Specific premiums	Individuals purchase LTC insurance policies and pay premiums directly to the insurance provider. The government may offer subsidies or tax incentives to make premiums more affordable	Tailored to LTC risks and costs	May be perceived as a burden on individuals
Government subsidies	The government provides financial assistance to individuals who cannot afford to purchase LTC insurance or to LTC providers to reduce the cost of services	Ensures affordability for all	Requires significant government expenditure

Source Synthesized by the authors

Table 4 Payment of benefit costs in public long-term care insurance in Vietnam

Factor	Considerations
Benefit structure	Types of benefits, benefit levels, eligibility criteria
Payment mechanisms	Direct payment, reimbursement, prepaid cards
Payment rates	Fee schedules, negotiation, quality incentives
Claims processing	Efficiency, appeals process
Cost-sharing	Co-payments, deductibles
Provider networks	Network development, provider contracting

Source Synthesized by the authors

3.1.4 Procedures for Using Services

In Table 5, access to public LTC services in Vietnam generally follows a structured process. First, eligible individuals (or their representatives) submit an application through local social insurance offices, together with required documentation such as proof of disability or care needs. Next, a formal assessment—often involving medical evaluations and consultations—is conducted to determine eligibility and the appropriate level of care. Once approved, beneficiaries may receive LTC services in different settings, including in-home care, institutional care, or community-based services, with providers selected according to the required care type and contracted

Table 5 Procedures for using services

Step	Description	Detail
Application	Eligible individuals or their representatives must apply for LTC benefits through local social insurance offices	The application process involves submitting required documentation, such as proof of disability or care needs
Assessment	An assessment is conducted to determine the individual's level of care needs and eligibility for benefits	This may involve medical evaluations and consultations
Service provision	After approving, individuals can access LTC services, which may include in-home care, institutional care, or community-based services	Service providers are selected based on the type of care required and may be contracted by VSS or local authorities
Monitoring and evaluation	The provision of LTC services and benefit payments is regularly monitored and evaluated to ensure service quality, proper use of funds, and compliance with established regulations	The quality of services and the effectiveness of benefit payments are monitored by the VSS and local social insurance offices to ensure compliance with regulations and standards

Source Synthesized by the authors

by VSS or local authorities. Finally, service delivery and benefit payments are continuously monitored and evaluated to ensure service quality, proper use of funds, and compliance with relevant regulations and standards.

3.2 *Certification of Need for Long-Term Care*

3.2.1 Certification Mechanism

Vietnam currently lacks a standardized and formalized mechanism for certifying LTC needs. As a result, procedures for assessing an individual's need for LTC and issuing official certification remain unclear and are not widely implemented. In practice, the public healthcare system is often treated as the main reference point for public LTC in Vietnam. The certification process typically includes: (1) application submission to a local social insurance office or a designated healthcare facility with supporting documents (personal information, medical records, and evidence of care needs); (2) medical evaluation to assess health status and disability level, often involving clinicians and specialists and considering the individual's ability to perform activities of daily living (ADLs); (3) care needs assessment to determine the required level of care, including functional evaluation and consideration of living conditions and available support; (4) issuance of certification for those meeting eligibility criteria, specifying care level and eligible services; and (5) periodic reassessment to ensure the certification remains appropriate as needs change (Table 6).

Table 6 Certification mechanism of LTC in Vietnam

Step	Description
Application submission	Individuals or their representatives apply to the local social insurance office or a designated healthcare facility. The application includes personal information, medical records, and evidence of care needs
Medical evaluation	A medical evaluation is conducted to assess the individual's health status and level of disability. This typically involves consultations with healthcare professionals, including doctors and specialists, who evaluate the individual's ability to perform Activities of Daily Living (ADLs)
Assessment of care needs	Based on the medical evaluation, a care needs assessment is performed to determine the level of care required. This assessment may include physical and functional evaluations, as well as considerations of the individual's living conditions and support network
Certification issuance	If the individual meets the eligibility criteria, a certification of need for LTC is issued. This certification outlines the level of care required and the type of services eligible for support. It is used to access LTC benefits and services
Periodic reassessment	Certifications are periodically reviewed and reassessed to ensure that the care provided remains appropriate to the individual's changing needs

Source Synthesized by the authors

3.2.2 Insurance Benefits and Categories of Care Required

Vietnam has not yet established a stand-alone, detailed public LTC insurance scheme comparable to those found in several other countries. In the current regulatory and policy landscape, there is no clearly defined package of LTC benefits financed specifically through social insurance contributions or a dedicated state budget line. Instead, support for people with long-term care needs is delivered through a combination of general social protection and sectoral programs. These include cash allowances and social assistance for older people and persons with disabilities, the provision of care in social protection facilities (e.g., nursing homes), home-based support programs in some localities, and related measures in health, education, and employment policy. In practice, the scope, generosity, and accessibility of these supports vary, and they do not constitute a unified LTC insurance benefit structure with standardized eligibility levels and clearly priced service entitlements.

3.2.3 Dementia

Vietnam does not currently have a specific law dedicated to protecting the rights and needs of people living with dementia. Nonetheless, certain rights and protections may be addressed indirectly through broader legal provisions, including civil law frameworks, mental health-related regulations, and social insurance regulations. In particular, where cognitive impairment severely affects decision-making capacity, legal procedures may allow a court to determine limitations in civil capacity, which can then shape guardianship arrangements and access to support. While these mechanisms offer partial protection, the absence of a dementia-specific legal framework can leave gaps in areas such as early diagnosis pathways, caregiver support, service standards, and safeguards for autonomy.

3.3 Long-Term Care Services

3.3.1 Overview

LTC services in Vietnam aim to support individuals who require sustained assistance due to population aging, chronic illness, or disability. Service provision is characterized by a mixed landscape in which public programs, private providers, families, and communities each play important roles. LTC services may take multiple forms depending on needs and preferences, including in-home care, facility-based care, and community-based support. However, availability and quality often differ across regions. Urban areas generally have greater service density and provider choice, while rural and remote areas may face constraints such as limited workforce capacity, fewer specialized services, and weaker referral and coordination mechanisms.

3.3.2 In-Home Services

In-home services include both professional health-related care and non-medical assistance delivered in the person's home. Professional inputs may involve nursing care, basic rehabilitation (such as physical therapy), medication management, and monitoring of chronic conditions. For individuals with serious illness, home-based palliative support can also be important. Alongside these services, many people require help with activities of daily living, such as bathing, dressing, eating, mobility, and household tasks. In Vietnam, families often provide the bulk of this support, supplemented in some settings by community health workers or paid caregivers where available and affordable.

3.3.3 Facility Services

Facility-based services provide structured living environments for individuals who need substantial, continuous support. This includes nursing homes or social protection facilities that offer 24-h care, as well as assisted living-style arrangements that combine accommodation with meals, housekeeping, and social activities. For people with dementia or Alzheimer's disease, specialized memory care, where it exists, may provide enhanced supervision, behavioral support, and caregiver guidance. Facility services can reduce caregiver strain and improve safety for high-need individuals, but access is often shaped by cost, eligibility criteria, local supply, and social preferences that continue to favor family-based care.

3.3.4 Community-Based Services

Community-based services can bridge the gap between home care and residential care by offering flexible support within the local community. Day care centers provide daytime supervision, activities, and basic assistance for individuals who need support but do not require 24-h care. Respite care offers temporary relief for primary caregivers, helping to prevent burnout and sustain home-based care. Community meal programs may provide nutritional support and social contact, especially for older people living alone. In addition, social support groups can reduce isolation by offering companionship, emotional support, and practical information for both care recipients and caregivers.

3.4 Prevention of Nursing Care

Preventing or delaying the need for intensive nursing care is an essential pillar of long-term care planning. Government communications often emphasize healthy aging strategies, including balanced nutrition, regular physical activity, and avoidance of harmful substances. In addition, early support for people living with chronic conditions or disabilities can help slow functional decline and reduce avoidable complications (Ministry of Health, 2023). Community-based initiatives are increasingly recognized as promising approaches to promote social participation, cognitive stimulation, and physical activity among older adults. Over time, these prevention-oriented measures can reduce demand for high-cost institutional care and improve quality of life.

3.5 Users' Cost Burden

3.5.1 Limits by Level of Care Required

Despite ongoing initiatives to support older people and those with illness, such as health insurance coverage for some older age groups and targeted social support, many individuals continue to face barriers in accessing appropriate services. These barriers are often geographic (e.g., distance to facilities in remote areas), informational (limited awareness of available policies and eligibility), and capacity-related (shortage of services and trained personnel). Public provision tends to prioritize primary healthcare and acute disease management, while long-term care, home care, rehabilitation, mental health care, and sustained social support remain comparatively underdeveloped. As needs become more complex, particularly for frail older adults and people with cognitive impairment, gaps become more visible, especially where service intensity must increase with higher care levels.

3.5.2 User's Burden

For users of publicly supported LTC-related services, the most common constraint is financial. Even when services are partially subsidized, individuals and families may still face spending for items not covered, for services beyond coverage limits, or for private care used to compensate for limited public supply. Costs can include paid caregiving, transport, medicines and supplies, home modifications, and supplementary rehabilitation. As a result, financial burden frequently falls on households, particularly where income is low, needs are long-term, or caregiving demands limit family members' ability to work.

3.6 Relationship with Public Assistance

The relationship between a future public LTC insurance model and existing public assistance programs in Vietnam would depend on policy design, financing rules, and eligibility coordination. At present, public health insurance and social assistance programs for older people and persons with disabilities can provide partial financial support for medical needs and basic living expenses. If LTC coverage were expanded, LTC services could complement these schemes by addressing the costs of daily care and support services rather than primarily medical treatment. Over time, the interaction between LTC coverage and social assistance would likely evolve as policies mature. Policymakers would need to determine how benefits are layered (e.g., whether social assistance acts as a safety net for those unable to contribute, while LTC insurance provides broader service entitlements) and how to avoid duplication while ensuring that vulnerable groups are protected.

3.7 Achievements and Issues

3.7.1 Care Prevention

Although Vietnam does not yet operate a fully defined public LTC insurance scheme, prevention-oriented approaches within health and social policy can still contribute to reducing future care needs. Promoting healthier lifestyles and strengthening early detection of functional decline may prevent complications of chronic disease and delay disability. Early intervention is especially important for individuals with emerging frailty or cognitive changes, where timely support can help maintain independence and reduce the intensity of later care needs.

3.7.2 Dementia

Dementia is becoming an increasingly important issue as Vietnam's population ages. A comprehensive LTC approach could play a vital role by supporting services tailored to dementia-related needs, including caregiver training, respite care, community support, and where feasible—specialized supervision and safety measures. Public awareness is also essential, particularly regarding early symptoms and the value of timely assessment, both to improve outcomes and to reduce stigma.

3.7.3 Challenges

A major challenge is the absence of a detailed, unified LTC insurance program with clearly defined eligibility criteria, benefit levels, and financing arrangements. Current support is fragmented across different policies and programs for older people, persons with disabilities, and healthcare services. This fragmentation can make access pathways unclear, create uneven coverage across regions, and limit the ability to plan sustainably for the growing demand associated with population aging.

3.8 Problems and Issues

Vietnam's long-term care system faces structural constraints, including limited recognition of LTC as a distinct policy field, insufficiently clear guidance on care responsibilities, and uneven resource allocation that can weaken implementation. Demographic change—especially the rapid increase in the older population—creates pressure on public budgets that are already constrained, making sustainable financing a central concern. Geographic disparities further shape access: people in rural or remote areas may face fewer services and longer travel times, while service networks and workforce capacity remain concentrated in urban settings.

Evidence also points to a gap between need and receipt of care. In 2011, despite substantial need for LTC among older people, only 36% reportedly received the necessary support for activities of daily living, while 27% of those in need received no care, with particularly severe gaps in some regions. In addition, as of early 2024, Vietnam recorded approximately 3.3 million social welfare beneficiaries (Government of Vietnam, 2024b), alongside around 400,000 people requiring specialized care due to severe mental illness, disability, or a combination of both. Financial adequacy remains a key concern: a social allowance of 360,000 VND per month was far below basic living standards—around 24% of the rural poverty threshold for 2021–2025 (1.5 million VND per month)—and about 20% of the base pay as of July

1, 2023. To address this, the Ministry of Labour, Invalids and Social Affairs proposed increasing support to 500,000 VND per month (Vietnam News Portal, 2024). From 1 July 2024, Decree No. 76/2024/ND-CP raised the standard monthly social assistance level to VND 500,000 and amended key provisions of Decree No. 20/2021/ND-CP (Government of Viet Nam, 2024a).

Addressing these challenges will require coordinated action across government agencies, healthcare and social service providers, and communities. Priority areas include clarifying policy leadership and service responsibilities, strengthening assessment and referral pathways, expanding and professionalizing the care workforce, improving service availability in underserved areas, and ensuring sustainable financing that can meet the rising demand for long-term care in an aging Vietnam.

4 Private Long-Term Care Insurance

4.1 History

Private LTC insurance in Vietnam is a relatively new line of business. It began to emerge in the 2010s as households increasingly sought financial protection against prolonged care needs. Several structural shifts have contributed to this demand. Vietnam's population has been aging, while family arrangements have gradually moved toward smaller, more nuclear households, reducing the availability of informal care at home. In this context, private insurers started to introduce LTC related products—often positioned as a complement to health and life insurance, aimed at easing the financial and caregiving burden that long-term dependency can impose on families.

4.2 Current Status

Despite growing interest, private LTC insurance remains at an early stage of development in Vietnam. Demand is most visible among middle- and higher-income groups, but overall penetration is still limited compared with mainstream life and health insurance. Adoption has been constrained by low public awareness, relatively high premiums, and the complexity of policy terms and benefit conditions. Industry discussions commonly note that contracts specifically oriented to LTC represent only a small share of life insurance portfolios.

In practice, the Vietnamese market tends to offer LTC coverage through hybrid or rider-based designs rather than stand-alone LTC insurance. Major insurers—including Bao Viet, Prudential, and Manulife—have offered packages that can support care at home, in medical facilities, or in nursing homes. These packages may include cash benefits or reimbursement for daily assistance, facility-based care, and selected medical expenses during periods of long-term dependency. For instance, some Prudential offerings have bundled LTC-related benefits with life insurance, enabling broader financial protection across longevity, health shocks, and extended care needs.

4.3 Benefit Design and Payment Methods

Benefit structures in Vietnam's private LTC-oriented products generally aim to cover the costs associated with prolonged assistance in activities of daily living and ongoing care needs. Policies may provide (i) cash allowances to support home-based care, (ii) payments linked to nursing or caregiving services, and/or (iii) reimbursement for eligible expenses in long-term care facilities, depending on plan design. Benefits are typically differentiated by level of dependency, care setting (home versus facility), and selected coverage amounts. Larger insurers often emphasize flexible benefit packages, allowing policyholders to align protection with anticipated care preferences and affordability constraints. While such customization can improve suitability, it also increases the need for transparent communication about eligibility triggers, exclusions, and claim documentation.

4.4 Relationship with Public Schemes and Care Facilities

Vietnam does not currently operate a comprehensive public LTC insurance system. Social health insurance primarily covers medically necessary services for illness and injury treatment, but it generally does not cover long-term personal care services for older persons with functional limitations or people with chronic dependency. This gap leaves many households exposed to substantial out-of-pocket expenses when long-term assistance is required. Private LTC insurance therefore has a potential role as a supplementary mechanism, offering additional options for financial protection where public coverage is limited.

Nevertheless, coordination between public programs and private LTC insurance remains underdeveloped. Stronger linkages—such as clearer definitions of LTC services, standardized care needs assessment, and shared service quality standards—could reduce fragmentation and improve the feasibility of private coverage.

Private LTC insurance is also closely tied to the availability and capacity of care providers, since benefits ultimately depend on service delivery. When care needs arise, policyholders may choose home-based services or professional nursing facilities, with costs covered fully or partially depending on policy terms. As the network of nursing care services in Vietnam continues to expand, rising demand from insured clients could further stimulate market growth and professionalization of care provision.

4.5 Problems and Regulatory Issues

Although private LTC insurance offers a promising approach to mitigating long-term care risks, multiple barriers remain. First, affordability is a central constraint: premiums for meaningful LTC protection can be high relative to the income of low- and middle-income households. Second, limited public understanding of LTC risk and insurance value reduces demand, particularly when families expect to rely on informal caregiving. Third, consumer protection concerns persist where product terms are complex and benefit triggers are not well understood.

From a regulatory perspective, more comprehensive guidance is needed to support market development and protect policyholders. Priority areas include (i) clearer standards for benefit eligibility and care-need assessment, (ii) strengthened disclosure requirements to ensure that consumers understand exclusions and claims procedures, and (iii) supervision mechanisms tailored to LTC-related products, given their long duration, uncertain utilization patterns, and reliance on care provider networks. Addressing these challenges is essential if private LTC insurance is to expand responsibly and contribute to broader long-term care financing in Vietnam.

5 Long-Term Care Facilities and Nursing Care Providers

Vietnam's long-term care infrastructure remains limited. Available evidence suggests that only a small proportion of older persons reside in long-term care facilities, estimates indicate that approximately 0.6% of older people live in LTC institutions (World Health Organization, 2020). This low rate reflects both constrained service supply and the continuing dominance of family-based care. As population aging accelerates and household caregiving capacity declines, demand for formal care services, home care agencies, community-based support, and residential nursing facilities is likely to increase. The pace and quality of this expansion will be a decisive factor shaping the practical value of private LTC insurance, since insurance benefits must translate into accessible and reliable care services.

5.1 Public Facilities

5.1.1 History

Vietnam's public LTC facilities have a long institutional trajectory, closely intertwined with broader reforms in the national health and social protection systems. As summarized in Table 7, the development of publicly supported care services can be understood through three major periods.

Table 7 History of public LTC facilities

Before Doi Moi (1975–1986)	After Doi Moi (1986–2000)	From 2000 till now
Vietnam's public healthcare system is established under the complete management of the state, with the goal of providing free healthcare to the people	Starting from the policy Doi Moi, the state is implementing reforms in the healthcare system, expanding its scale and improving infrastructure. Major hospitals such as Bach Mai, Viet Duc, and Cho Ray have been upgraded and equipped with more modern facilities. At the same time, the government began to encourage public–private partnership models in healthcare	The government continues to invest heavily in public healthcare infrastructure, with support from international aid programs and private partners. The national health insurance system was established and developed, helping to increase access to healthcare services for the people. Public hospitals at the provincial and district levels are gradually being better equipped with facilities and medical equipment

Source Synthesized by the authors

Before Đổi Mới (1975–1986), Vietnam's public service model was shaped by a centrally managed system in which the state assumed primary responsibility for organizing healthcare and related welfare services. During this period, the overarching objective was to expand access and provide basic care through a state-led approach, reflecting the country's post-war reconstruction priorities.

After the launch of Đổi Mới (1986–2000), reforms in the healthcare sector accelerated. The state began to expand the scale and scope of service delivery, while simultaneously upgrading infrastructure in key hospitals and encouraging new models of service provision. An important feature of this period was the gradual introduction of public–private partnerships, which created conditions for diversified financing and expanded service options, even though formal LTC services remained limited and unevenly distributed.

From 2000 to the present, public investment in healthcare infrastructure has continued, supported in part by international cooperation and donor-funded programs. Over time, the development of social health insurance contributed to improved access to medical services, and provincial-level hospitals increasingly benefited from better facilities and equipment. However, the expansion of medical coverage has not automatically translated into comprehensive coverage for long-term care, particularly for non-medical supportive services required by older persons with functional limitations.

Within this broader evolution, Vietnam's public LTC institutions began to take shape earlier in the early twentieth century, when the state initiated the establishment of residential care settings, commonly nursing homes or welfare facilities, primarily intended for older persons and people with disabilities. Over time, these facilities expanded their service scope beyond basic accommodation to include a combination of medical support, rehabilitation, and social care activities, depending on institutional capacity and local resources.

In terms of current capacity, as of 2023 Vietnam operates approximately 230 state-run long-term care institutions, commonly organized as social protection centers providing residential and supportive services for vulnerable groups, including at-risk older persons (Ministry of Labour, Invalids and Social Affairs, 2023). Despite these efforts, the overall long-term care infrastructure remains limited relative to demographic needs; for example, available estimates indicate that only a very small share of older persons reside in LTC facilities, around 0.6% (World Health Organization, 2020). This gap underscores a continuing reliance on family-based care and highlights the importance of strengthening both formal service provision and sustainable financing mechanisms for long-term care in Vietnam.

5.1.2 Types and Operators

In Vietnam, LTC services are delivered primarily through two channels: institutional care and community-based care, with provision involving both public authorities and social organizations.

Institutional care generally refers to residential settings such as social protection centers and nursing homes. These facilities are predominantly operated and managed by government agencies and are intended for older adults who cannot live independently—often because family caregiving capacity is limited or household resources are insufficient. Institutional care providers typically deliver accommodation and daily living assistance alongside basic health monitoring and social support. As of 2023, Vietnam operated approximately 230 state-run long-term care institutions, commonly referred to as social protection centers, providing residential services for vulnerable groups, including older persons (Ministry of Labour, Invalids and Social Affairs, 2023).

Alongside institutional provision, community-based care has become increasingly prominent as Vietnam seeks to maintain older persons within their communities, reduce pressure on residential facilities, and mobilize local networks for support. A widely recognized model is the Intergenerational Self-Help Club (ISHC) approach. Initiated in 2005 and scaled nationally by 2020, ISHCs aim to improve the well-being of older persons—particularly those in disadvantaged circumstances—through an integrated package of support that commonly includes health promotion, livelihood assistance, social participation, and volunteer-supported home care. The model has expanded rapidly: by 2021, there were approximately 3,500 ISHCs nationwide, and by the end of 2024 the number reportedly reached 8,435 clubs with more than 484,000 members (HelpAge International in Vietnam, 2025). In practice, ISHC development has involved coordination with organizations such as the Vietnam Association of the Elderly and the Red Cross, including pilots of compensated home-based care models within broader LTC initiatives. Policy support has also strengthened in recent years; in 2024, the Ministry of Labour, Invalids and Social Affairs issued Decision No. 1335/QD-LDTBXH outlining a 2024–2025 plan to further scale up the ISHC model

(Ministry of Labour, Invalids and Social Affairs, 2024). In parallel, the World Bank–Japan Social Development Fund partnership reported supporting more than 24,725 older people through 186 ISHCs since 2021 (World Bank, 2024d).

5.1.3 Operational Status

Operational capacity for older-person care in Vietnam remains constrained relative to the pace of population aging, particularly in geriatric medicine and specialized service delivery. As of 2019, national-level reporting indicated that the country had insufficient geriatric hospitals and geriatric departments to meet growing demand. The National Geriatric Hospital has been described as the only hospital in Vietnam dedicated specifically to older persons, while geriatric departments were present in only 49 of 63 provinces within general hospitals (Uyen Nguyen, 2023). This suggests a significant gap in specialized clinical capacity for diagnosis, treatment planning, and management of chronic conditions that commonly drive long-term care needs.

At the same time, Vietnam has maintained a broad primary care network, with more than 11,400 communal health stations across communes, wards, and districts. These facilities function as the nearest point of contact for many residents and play a frontline role in health protection and basic service delivery (Thủy Bình, 2024). However, strong geographical coverage does not necessarily translate into geriatric specialization or integrated long-term care coordination, particularly for individuals requiring assistance with daily living activities over extended periods.

On the social care side, residential care supply remains limited and unevenly distributed. As noted above, Vietnam operated around 230 state-run social protection centers in 2023 (Ministry of Labour, Invalids and Social Affairs, 2023). Yet, only a small subset of these institutions reportedly focuses primarily on older persons, indicating that many centers serve multiple vulnerable groups and may not be equipped with geriatric-trained staff or age-friendly infrastructure. In response to rising demand, government planning has included the ambition to establish a nursing home in each province by 2025, reflecting recognition that facilities are currently scattered and that aging is accelerating. Overall, Vietnam continues to rely on a mixed trajectory of public provision, community-based models, and selective private initiatives to expand LTC infrastructure and improve service readiness.

5.1.4 Funding and Cost Recovery

Financing for Vietnam's public long-term care facilities is largely framed around social welfare objectives rather than commercial performance. Because these institutions are intended to support older persons and other groups facing vulnerability, particularly those with limited family support or chronic care needs, operations are generally not designed to generate profit. Instead, public facilities typically depend on government funding allocations and related social assistance mechanisms to sustain basic services, with cost recovery constrained by the policy aim of maintaining affordability and access for low-income beneficiaries. This financing logic reinforces the protective role of the state but also creates structural pressures: when demand rises faster than public budgets and staffing capacity, facilities may experience limitations in service scope, infrastructure quality, and the ability to professionalize long-term care delivery.

5.2 *Private Facilities*

5.2.1 History

Vietnam's private long-term care (LTC) market has expanded in recent years, driven by rising incomes in major cities, changing family structures, and increasing expectations regarding service quality. Compared with public provision, private services are more strongly shaped by market-based pricing and consumer choice, and they remain concentrated in urban and economically dynamic provinces. Private LTC provision in Vietnam can be grouped into three main types: institutional care, community-based care, and home-based care, delivered by a mix of commercial operators and partnership-based initiatives (Table 8).

Table 8 History of private LTC facilities

Before 2000	2000–2010	2010–2020	2020–now
Care for older persons in Viet Nam was predominantly family-based. Institutional care remained limited and was provided mainly through public social protection facilities and a small number of charitable or religious homes, rather than a developed commercial LTC market.	Early non-state residential elder-care models began to emerge on a small scale, especially in major urban areas. This period was characterized more by initial experimentation than by broad market expansion, alongside the rise of community-based care initiatives.	The non-public residential care segment expanded, particularly in Hanoi and Ho Chi Minh City, and increasingly targeted households able to pay for specialized services. However, supply remained limited: by 2019 there were 102 centers with elderly-care subdivisions nationwide, but only 32 specialized elderly-care facilities; by 2021 the number was about 40, most of them privately operated.	Private and mixed-model LTC services have continued to expand, while policy attention has increasingly shifted toward integrated care, home- and community-based care, and stronger private-sector participation. Nevertheless, the system remains fragmented, urban-centered, and constrained by affordability and an incomplete incentive framework.

Source: Based on Van, Tuan and Oanh (2021)*, UNFPA* (2021)*, and recent policy updates*

Institutional care in the private sector has become increasingly visible through the emergence of private nursing homes and retirement-oriented communities (Vietnam News Agency, 2024), although the segment is still relatively new compared with public social protection centers. Private facilities generally position themselves as higher-end alternatives, offering improved infrastructure, closer medical supervision, and more personalized care plans. Services often combine assistance with activities of daily living, rehabilitation support, and structured social activities, with an emphasis on comfort, privacy, and responsiveness. These features come at a substantially higher cost than public provision and therefore primarily serve middle- and high-income clients. Estimates suggest that by 2023 approximately 80 private nursing homes were operating in Vietnam (Uyen Nguyen, 2023), indicating a growing, yet still limited, market footprint relative to the size of the aging population.

Community-based care provided by private actors remains less developed than institutional provision, but a number of commercial and semi-commercial initiatives have begun to supplement local services for older persons. In practice, private entities sometimes collaborate with community organizations to deliver programs that include health screening, social engagement activities, and volunteer-supported assistance. Such initiatives are typically concentrated in more developed urban areas where demand for organized community support is stronger and where households are more able to pay for services. In addition, some private community centers have introduced day-care services and senior clubs designed to promote active aging. These clubs commonly provide periodic health assessments, physical activity or fitness sessions, and opportunities for social participation, offering a lighter-touch support model for relatively independent older adults.

Home-based care has expanded rapidly and is increasingly viewed as a preferred alternative to residential care, particularly for families who wish to keep older relatives at home while supplementing family caregiving with professional support. Private providers offer a spectrum of services ranging from personal care and household assistance, such as bathing, dressing, feeding, and mobility support, to more health-oriented functions including medication support, basic nursing tasks, rehabilitation exercises, and monitoring of chronic conditions. Care workers are often trained to provide companionship and routine supervision, which can be particularly valuable for older persons living alone or those with limited daily family support. Importantly, many private home-care models in Vietnam are designed not to replace the family's role but to extend and reinforce it, helping to reduce the time burden and emotional strain that households frequently experience in caring for aging relatives.

5.2.2 Operational Status

The operational scale of private LTC in Vietnam remains modest, but it has expanded quickly and is increasingly concentrated in urban and economically dynamic localities. By 2021, Vietnam reportedly had around 80 private elderly care facilities, while only 32 out of 63 provinces and centrally governed cities had nursing homes, with most of these facilities operated by private providers (Jill Lai, 2023). This uneven distribution underscores both the early-stage nature of the market and the tendency for private providers to locate where purchasing power, demand, and supporting medical infrastructure are stronger.

Despite limited geographic coverage, the segment is widely viewed as a high-growth area for domestic private providers as well as international operators seeking entry into Vietnam's aging-related service economy. Service prices reflect this market positioning. Reported costs for residence-based care in private nursing centers commonly range from 6 to 13 million VND per month, depending on service intensity, accommodation standards, and medical supervision levels (Ngan, 2024). In parallel, the growth of private home-care services has been accompanied by relatively high labor costs for trained caregivers and nursing personnel, particularly for packages that include clinical monitoring, rehabilitation support, or round-the-clock assistance. Taken together, these patterns suggest that private LTC services are expanding primarily as a premium market, while affordability remains a key barrier to broader coverage.

5.2.3 Funding and Cost Recovery

Private long-term care services in Vietnam are largely financed through direct household payments, with providers relying on market-based pricing to recover costs and generate returns. In this sense, the sector has increasingly been characterized as commercially attractive, especially in major cities where demand for higher-quality, professional care is rising. Unlike public social protection centers, which typically operate under welfare objectives, private facilities and home-care agencies are structured to achieve cost recovery through user fees and, in many cases, to deliver profits to investors. This profit orientation can encourage investment in infrastructure and service innovation, but it also reinforces segmentation in access, with formal private long-term care remaining most feasible for households with stable middle-to-high incomes or those able to pool resources among family members.

5.3 Nursing Care Providers

5.3.1 Current Status

Public nursing care institutions primarily serve elderly individuals without family or financial support, with only 13 of 230 state-operated social protection centers specifically providing aged care (Ministry of Labour, Invalids and Social Affairs, 2023). The government plans to build public nursing homes in each province by 2025, but these are often underfunded, limiting service quality. Rural areas lack skilled nurses and carers, and many urban facilities are overwhelmed.

The LTC sector has grown rapidly in Vietnam's private sector, especially in Ho Chi Minh City and Hanoi. Wealthier residents receive superior care in private nursing homes, which often resemble upscale retirement homes and typically charge 10–15 million VND per month, making them accessible only to affluent families (Uyen Nguyen, 2023). Private providers generally offer better infrastructure, more skilled carers, and specialized rehabilitation and health monitoring services.

Private companies and community organizations are increasingly providing home care for the elderly, a growing trend that allows older people to receive care at home, often with family assistance. However, home-based care can be expensive and faces a shortage of qualified workers, especially in rural areas, and lacks sufficient infrastructure. The Vietnamese government and non-governmental organizations like the Vietnam Association of the Elderly (VAE) and Intergenerational Self-Help Clubs (ISHCs) prioritize community-based care.

5.3.2 Profit-Making Model

Fee-for-service, premium offerings, and strategic alliances drive Vietnamese nursing care providers' revenue. Private nursing homes rely on monthly fees, which range from 6 to 13 million VND depending on services and care quality (Ngan, 2024). Premium facilities often charge more for specialized care like 24-h nursing or dementia care. Many nursing homes offer basic to premium packages with varying levels of medical care, rehabilitation, and personalized services.

Besides standard fees, nursing homes earn a lot from premium services like healthcare, rehabilitation, and wellness programs, which are invoiced separately. Certain facilities have partnered with private hospitals and clinics to offer on-site medical care, attracting wealthy clients seeking better health services. These partnerships may involve outsourcing specialized services, with nursing homes receiving referral fees or commissions from medical facilities.

The Vietnamese government also encourages long-term care investment with tax incentives and PPPs. Tax incentives, land-use concessions, and other favorable regulations lower private operators' operational costs, while public–private partnerships allow private entities to use public funding for infrastructure development, increasing profitability.

6 Caregivers and Qualification System

Caregivers play a crucial role in providing long-term care services, with specific tasks and responsibilities varying by organization and care level.

As shown in Table 9, Vietnam's LTC workforce is diverse (Walker & Wyse, 2022). Informal caregivers often provide care without formal training, while trained volunteers receive structured training. Formal training programs offer theoretical and practical knowledge in geriatric care, psychological support, and first aid. Despite their crucial role, Vietnam faces a shortage of healthcare professionals, especially geriatric specialists, and training programs are inadequate. Geographical disparity in workforce distribution, concentrated in urban areas, hinders quality care in rural regions, posing a significant challenge as the government aims to strengthen primary healthcare.

Table 9 Vietnam's LTC workforce

Type of workforces	Long-term care task	Workplace	Qualification and training
Family members, relatives, neighbors	Informal care, help with ADLs and IADLs	Family, community	Untrained, no specific training programs
Volunteers	Companionship, help with ADLs and IADLs, housework	Self-help clubs and other community-based models for older people	ISHC volunteers receive 20 h of training; other volunteer models may have some degree of training
House helpers	Informal care, help with ADLs and IADLs, housework	In the home, family	Untrained, no specific training programs
Health professionals at public and private health facilities	Health care	Public and private health facilities	Trained by medical schools, colleges, licensed
Other nurses	Nursing care, palliative care, health promotion	Social welfare centers Private centers for older people care Private practice as individual providers	Full-time degree-level course; can be licensed or not licensed
Social workers	Assessment, care planning, case management, help with ADLs and IADLs	Social welfare centers Social works centers Private centers for older people care Social welfare centers	Full-time degree-level course
Physiotherapists, speech therapists, occupational therapists, rehabilitators	Rehabilitation, fall prevention		Full-time degree-level course
Pharmacists	Medication review, drug management		Full-time degree-level course
Manager	Planning, training, supervision, monitoring, reporting		No standardized qualifications; based on experience

Source Walker and Wyse (2022)

7 Cross-Cutting Issues, Market Outlook, and Conclusions

7.1 Analysis of Public and Private Long-Term Care Insurance

The Vietnamese government has prioritized the elderly through various policies, notably the Law on the Elderly (National Assembly of Viet Nam, 2009), which defines the rights and obligations of seniors and the roles of families, government, and society in their support. This law mandates government provision of allowances and health insurance for individuals over 80 and vulnerable elderly, and stipulates family and societal care, with the Ministry of Health providing healthcare. It also promotes the establishment of elderly nursing homes. Further policies include the National Agenda for the Elderly for 2012–2020 and Ministry of Health circulars regulating primary healthcare and chronic disease management. The government has also promoted primary and grassroots healthcare by strengthening organizational structures, human resources, pharmaceuticals, healthcare financing, and service delivery (Van Minh et al., 2017).

The Ministry of Labour, Invalids, and Social Affairs proposed increasing the monthly social assistance rate to 500,000 VND for social protection beneficiaries starting July 1, 2024, an increase of 140,000 VND per month. Provincial and municipal People's Committees may propose higher local social assistance rates. Decree 20/2021.ND-CP lists eight groups of social protection beneficiaries, including abandoned children, orphans, children with HIV/AIDS from poor households, and various categories of elderly individuals (Government of Viet Nam, 2021).

Comparison on Structure of Public and Private Long-Term Care Insurance

Public and private LTC insurance in Vietnam differ significantly in structure, accessibility, and service quality. Government-funded programs provide basic long-term care for low-income and vulnerable populations but face substantial challenges (World Bank, 2021). These include chronic underfunding, leading to overcrowded facilities, severe staff shortages, and limited coverage for chronic conditions or disabilities (UNFPA, 2022; World Bank, 2021). The public system, while more affordable, struggles with maintaining consistent quality and expanding capacity to meet the rapidly growing demand. Its fragmented nature, relying on connections between existing policies rather than a dedicated LTC insurance program, creates inconsistencies in service provision and administrative complexities.

In contrast, private LTC insurance offers a higher standard of services, including assisted living, comprehensive rehabilitation programs, and personalized home-based care (Anh, 2020). These private facilities boast superior infrastructure and more skilled and specialized staff, and often resemble upscale retirement homes, providing a more comfortable and tailored experience. However, this higher quality comes at a significant cost, with monthly fees ranging from 10 to 15 million VND (Nguyen, 2022; Vietnam Investment Review, 2023), making private LTC largely inaccessible to the majority of the population, particularly low and middle-income families. This creates a two-tiered system where access to quality care is determined by financial capacity. Public–private partnerships are seen as a potential solution to bridge this gap, aiming to ensure both affordability and quality as Vietnam's elderly population continues to grow.

7.2 Comparison on Role of Public and Private Long-Term Care Insurance

A large portion of long-term care in Vietnam is still provided by family members, often without formal training or assistance, reflecting deeply ingrained cultural expectations (UNFPA, 2022; Teo et al., 2018). While the Ministry of Health, the Ministry of Labour, Invalids, and Social Affairs, along with numerous mass organizations and private entities, contribute to long-term care provision, there is currently no unified national model for community-based long-term care. Vietnam is actively exploring and developing long-term care models that aim to improve family caregiving through enhanced home-based services and viable residential care alternatives. A leading example is the Intergenerational Self-Help Club (ISHC), the largest home and community-based care program, which currently serves over 17,000 people and has ambitious plans for expansion. The National Program of Action on Aging, ratified in December 2021, aims to establish one ISHC in 80% of communes by 2030, significantly expanding from the current 3,400 clubs. In terms of institutional care, Vietnam has 134 social welfare centers serving 2,458 elderly individuals and 13 nursing homes (eight public and five private) available for those who can afford them.

Financing long-term care services for the elderly in Vietnam primarily relies on personal savings and household budgets (World Bank, 2021). Seniors often fund their own care services or depend on financial support from family members. For those without sufficient financial resources or the ability to care for themselves, assistance is available through government programs or charitable organizations, primarily targeting impoverished elderly individuals lacking familial support. Vietnam does not currently have a dedicated long-term care insurance system, and existing sick leave benefits from the Vietnam Social Security Agency (VSS) exclude workers requiring time off to care for elderly relatives. This often leads to significant financial strain on families, especially when caregivers must forego employment and lack social assistance. Although social benefits exist for both elderly individuals and their caregivers, the financial support is minimal and generally insufficient to cover basic care needs, despite varying by age or level of infirmity.

Public social welfare centers play a critical role in supporting older adults in difficult circumstances, particularly those without family care. These centers, funded by the state budget, provide essential services such as health check-ups, basic healthcare, lodging, food, and other necessities for the elderly. Alongside public facilities, private care centers are expanding rapidly, but their costs are significantly higher, with fees ranging from 6 to 13 million VND per month for basic services (Nguyen, 2022), making them inaccessible to many average or low-income families. These private centers are funded through a combination of government allocations, charitable donations, and payments from the families of the elderly. The state budget also finances social work services for the elderly within the social welfare system, encompassing counselling, healthcare, and instruction in daily life skills. However, aged adults who do not meet the criteria for social assistance do not receive reimbursement for these services, and the absence of explicit standards governing the pricing of social work services results in discrepancies in service delivery and expenses. Furthermore, Vietnam currently lacks explicit legal provisions for financing volunteer caregiving activities, leading to substantial financial challenges for voluntary carers who forfeit prospective earnings when dedicating time to elderly care. This situation underscores the urgent need for a clear mechanism for LTC insurance in Vietnam to protect the rights of participants, especially in the context of the increasing aging trend. To support successful aging, Vietnam can combine the strength of family and community solidarity with global best practices in long-term care, which will involve enhancing the coordination of efforts among key stakeholders. In a country with strong family traditions, support from family members, along with healthcare assistance from both public and private sectors, will contribute to creating value and protecting the rights, dignity, and well-being of elderly Vietnamese citizens.

Advantages and Disadvantages of Public Long-Term Care Insurance

The primary advantage of public long-term care provisions in Vietnam lies in their intention to provide basic support and healthcare access for vulnerable populations, particularly those without familial or financial means. The existing public health insurance system offers some benefits, including complimentary examinations and partial or full coverage for certain elderly groups, aiming to ensure a fundamental safety net.

However, the disadvantages are significant. Public programs are critically underfunded, leading to limitations in service quality and infrastructure. There is a severe shortage of specialized geriatric facilities and departments, with only one dedicated geriatric hospital nationwide and limited geriatric departments in provincial hospitals. Public nursing homes are often overwhelmed and lack skilled staff, especially in rural areas. Furthermore, the current public system primarily focuses on acute disease management and primary healthcare, leaving substantial gaps in long-term care, home care, rehabilitation, mental health care, and social support for the elderly. The existing social payment for beneficiaries is markedly inadequate, representing only a fraction of the rural poverty threshold, creating a significant gap between the need for care and actual provision, with many elderly, particularly in rural areas, receiving no necessary support.

Advantages and Disadvantages of Private Long-Term Care Insurance

The primary advantage of private long-term care insurance and facilities is the provision of higher quality services, superior infrastructure, and personalized care, often resembling upscale retirement homes. Private providers offer comprehensive packages, including financial support for daily care, nursing home treatment, and medical expenses, with options for both inpatient and home care services. This sector is growing rapidly, driven by market demand and government encouragement through tax incentives and public–private partnerships, signaling a promising market for investors. Private insurance also fills a critical gap left by the absence of a comprehensive public LTC insurance system, offering financial protection and choices not available through public means.

However, the disadvantages are substantial, primarily revolving around accessibility and regulation. The high cost of private insurance packages and nursing home fees (ranging from 6 to 15 million VND per month) makes them largely inaccessible to low and middle-income individuals, confining their benefits primarily to the affluent. Public awareness of private LTC insurance benefits remains limited, contributing to low subscription rates. Critically, the government's monitoring policies and regulations for private LTC insurance are incomplete, creating a regulatory vacuum that puts consumers at risk when choosing products that are unclear or lack full guarantees regarding benefits. This lack of oversight hinders market maturity and consumer trust.

Limitations and Future Issues of Public and Private Long-Term Care Insurance

The primary limitation for both public and private LTC in Vietnam is the fundamental absence of a comprehensive, dedicated national long-term care insurance system. This leads to a fragmented landscape where care is either informally provided by families (which is becoming unsustainable), minimally supported by underfunded public programs, or privately financed at prohibitive costs.

Public LTC in Vietnam remains constrained by the lack of a dedicated national LTC insurance scheme, which leaves the system dependent on fragmented social assistance measures and limited health-sector capacity. A central limitation is insufficient and unstable public financing, as state budgets allocated to social protection and elderly care are modest relative to the speed of population aging. This financial constraint translates into low levels of social support and a weak ability to expand services, improve quality, or subsidize care costs for households facing long-term dependency. As demand rises, underfunding also reduces the government's capacity to create predictable entitlements and to sustain recurrent expenditures for staffing, training, and facility operations.

A second major limitation is the infrastructure deficit and unequal geographic access. Vietnam faces a shortage of geriatric hospitals, rehabilitation units, and specialized LTC facilities, with rural and remote areas particularly underserved. Even where services exist, they are often concentrated in major cities, creating a large access gap for older persons living outside urban centers. This spatial imbalance reinforces inequity: families in rural areas are pushed toward informal care, delayed treatment, or out-of-pocket spending to seek services elsewhere.

Third, the public LTC landscape is limited by weak standardization and coordination across policies and providers. In the absence of a formal and unified certification mechanism for determining care needs, service eligibility and benefit levels can be inconsistent, and administrative procedures may depend on disconnected programs rather than an integrated care pathway. This fragmentation complicates management and monitoring, and it makes it difficult to ensure continuity of care between community support, medical services, and institutional care. The result is uneven service quality and inefficiencies in resource allocation, especially as different agencies may share responsibility without clear coordination.

Finally, the public system is constrained by a workforce shortage and skills gap, especially in public facilities and rural settings. Vietnam lacks sufficient numbers of trained geriatric nurses, professional caregivers, and social care workers, which limits both the availability and the quality of services. Workforce constraints also undermine the ability to scale up home-based and community-based care, models that are typically more cost-effective and better aligned with aging-in-place preferences. Without sustained investment in training, career pathways, and retention incentives, public LTC capacity will remain inadequate relative to rapidly increasing needs.

Private LTC insurance and private LTC services in Vietnam are constrained primarily by exclusivity and affordability barriers. The high cost of private insurance premiums and fee-based care services places them beyond the reach of most households, particularly outside higher-income urban populations. This creates a two-tiered care structure in which higher-quality services are accessible mainly to affluent groups, while the majority remain reliant on family care or limited public support. Because private coverage does not meaningfully pool risk across the broader population, it cannot serve as a mass solution to aging-related care needs, and it risks widening inequality in later-life wellbeing.

A second limitation is low public awareness and limited demand maturity. Many households have incomplete understanding of what private LTC insurance covers, how it differs from health insurance, and why it matters for long-term dependency risks. This weak awareness contributes to low participation rates and a narrow customer base, which in turn restricts market growth and discourages insurers and providers from investing in product innovation, wider distribution, and long-term service networks. In practice, low uptake reinforces the affordability problem: without scale, private products remain expensive and targeted toward a small segment.

Third, the private LTC sector faces regulatory and consumer-protection gaps. Incomplete oversight and unclear standards, covering areas such as benefit definitions, claims processes, service quality benchmarks, and disclosure requirements can leave consumers vulnerable and reduce trust in private LTC products. Weak regulation also limits the development of a stable, credible market, because insurers and providers operate without a robust framework that aligns incentives, ensures transparency, and enforces quality. Over time, this reduces both the legitimacy and the expansion potential of private LTC insurance as a complement to public provision.

Taken together, private LTC in Vietnam remains constrained as a niche market: it can offer options for those who can pay, but its current structure does not provide broad risk-sharing or equitable access. Without stronger regulation, awareness-building, and policy mechanisms that encourage affordability and scale, private LTC insurance and services are unlikely to close the national care gap on their own.

Future issues for Vietnam's LTC landscape will revolve around addressing these limitations. The rapid aging population will intensify demand, exacerbating existing resource and infrastructure deficits. Without significant policy reforms and investment, the financial burden on families will continue to grow, potentially leading to widespread elder poverty and unmet care needs. The challenge lies in developing a sustainable financing mechanism that can bridge the affordability gap and ensure equitable access to quality LTC for all citizens. This will likely require a strategic blend of public investment, robust regulatory frameworks for the private sector, and innovative public–private partnerships to scale up services and workforce development across the country.

7.3 Analysis of Long-Term Care Businesses and Nursing Homes

Current Status and Awareness of Long-Term Care Business and Nursing Homes

The LTC industry in Vietnam is currently in a developmental phase, yet it is experiencing rapid growth driven by the country's aging population and ongoing socio-economic transformations. Historically, elderly care was predominantly provided within families. However, the capacity for family-centered care has diminished due to increasing urbanization, smaller family sizes, and economic constraints. As a result, there is a growing awareness of the importance of professional nursing and long-term care facilities, particularly in urban centers such as Hanoi and Ho Chi Minh City (Minh & Huong, 2021).

Currently, Vietnam has approximately 80 private nursing homes and several government-run social protection centers that provide care for the elderly (Uyen Nguyen, 2023). Despite this, public awareness of professional caregiving services remains relatively low, especially in rural areas, where families still primarily rely on informal care. Cultural expectations and economic factors continue to hinder the widespread acceptance of professional nursing homes, which has slowed the overall response to the escalating demand for long-term care services.

Long-Term Care Business Market Size and Economic Effect Analysis

Vietnam's long-term care industry is projected to experience significant growth in the coming years. The 2022 population change study conducted by the General Statistics Office indicates that the average life expectancy in the country is 73.6 years, with men averaging 71.1 years and women averaging 76.4 years (General Statistics Office of Vietnam, 2023). This demographic shift is a primary driver for the demand for professional long-term care services, encompassing nursing homes, assisted living facilities, and home-based care. Projections suggest that the elderly care market will grow significantly by 2025, creating substantial opportunities for both domestic and international investors.

Investors are increasingly focusing on the private long-term care sector in Vietnam. Private nursing homes typically charge monthly fees averaging about 15 million VND (663 USD) for a single room and 19 million VND for a double room per month (Vietnam News Agency, 2021), while premium retirement communities command even higher fees. This makes the industry lucrative, particularly in urban areas where wealthier families are more likely to invest in high-quality medical care. The expansion of medical tourism in Vietnam, combined with the rising demand for long-term care services, is contributing to the growing economic impact of this business sector. Due to Vietnam's lower cost of living compared to Western nations, the country has become an attractive retirement destination for expatriates and retirees from abroad. This trend is expected to further facilitate the growth of the long-term care business market.

Policy Direction on Long-Term Care Businesses and Nursing Homes

Recognizing the growing demand for long-term care services, the Vietnamese government has begun implementing policies to promote the development of this industry. A key initiative is the establishment of a nursing home in every province by 2025, which will include both public and private facilities. Additionally, the government has encouraged public–private partnerships (PPPs) to foster investment in the infrastructure of elderly care institutions.

Moreover, policies are being developed to regulate and improve the quality of long-term care services, including the creation of standards for private nursing facilities. According to the Asian Development Bank (2022), the comprehensive policy framework designed to stimulate sector growth includes tax incentives, land-use concessions, and subsidies for eldercare programs. Despite these efforts, challenges remain, such as inadequate resources for public facilities and the ongoing requirement to improve access to high-quality medical care in more rural locations. While the government is actively seeking ways to improve the quality of long-term care services, it is also working to ensure their affordability, striving to reconcile these two competing priorities.

Future Prospects of Long-Term Care Business

Due to rapid demographic changes, Vietnam's long-term care sector holds significant potential. By 2030, over 10 million elderly Vietnamese will require daily care, a substantial increase from 4 million in 2019. The increasing demand for private nursing homes, assisted living facilities, and home-based care services is a positive indicator for the sector. Vietnam is also expected to attract more foreign investment in long-term care, particularly in high-quality elderly care and retirement communities.

Community-based care models, such as Intergenerational Self-Help Clubs (ISHCs), which blend community support with professional healthcare, show great promise. Technological innovations like telemedicine and remote healthcare have the potential to significantly benefit rural and underserved populations within the LTC market, offering solutions to geographical barriers and improving access to care.

7.4 Conclusions

Vietnam is undergoing a profound demographic transition marked by rapid population aging and a consequent surge in demand for long-term care (LTC). This trend is fundamentally reshaping the country's care landscape and exposing structural weaknesses in the traditional model of family-based informal care. While family support has historically served as the core pillar of elder care, it is becoming increasingly difficult to sustain in the context of urbanization, declining fertility, smaller household sizes, and internal and international migration. At the same time, existing public health and social welfare arrangements, though providing partial support, remain fragmented and under-resourced, and Vietnam still lacks a comprehensive, dedicated LTC insurance framework. As a result, significant unmet care needs persist, particularly among vulnerable older adults in rural and underserved areas, while the financial and emotional burden borne by families continues to intensify.

In response to these unmet needs, Vietnam has witnessed the emergence of a private LTC sector encompassing private facilities and nascent insurance products. Private provision has introduced service models that are often more individualized, higher in perceived quality, and better aligned with consumer preferences in urban markets. However, private options remain inaccessible for most households due to high costs, uneven service availability, and limited public awareness of LTC insurance and related products. Moreover, gaps in regulatory oversight, such as inconsistent standards on service quality, consumer protection, benefit definition, and market conduct, constrain the credibility and sustainable development of private LTC, while also increasing risks for users in a market that is still at an early stage of institutional formation.

Taken together, the evidence in this chapter underscores the urgency for Vietnam to move from a piecemeal, reactive LTC approach toward a more integrated and financially sustainable system. A central priority is the establishment of a dedicated public LTC insurance scheme with stable funding and clear entitlements, designed to reduce catastrophic out-of-pocket expenses and to ensure broader, more equitable access to care. Such a system would represent a shift away from reliance on general social assistance and acute health insurance mechanisms, which are not structured to address long-duration dependency risks. In parallel, Vietnam must invest substantially in both infrastructure and human resources: expanding geriatric and rehabilitative capacity, increasing the supply of specialized LTC facilities and community-based services, and developing a skilled caregiving workforce through standardized training, certification pathways, and incentives to improve retention and address uneven distribution, especially in rural areas.

Strengthening regulatory frameworks is equally essential. Clearer rules and enforcement mechanisms are needed to ensure transparency, quality assurance, and consumer protection in private LTC services and insurance products. Robust regulation would not only reduce risks faced by households but also foster trust and create conditions for healthier market development. Within this broader reform agenda, public–private partnerships can play a strategic role by mobilizing private capital and operational expertise to accelerate service expansion, while public policy tools such as targeted subsidies, tiered service packages, and contracting mechanisms can help preserve equity and prevent further widening of access gaps.

Finally, Vietnam's long-term sustainability will depend not only on expanding care capacity but also on reducing avoidable demand through prevention and early intervention. Continued emphasis on healthy aging, chronic disease management, disability prevention, and community-based screening can delay the onset of functional dependency and lower the intensity of care required. This prevention-oriented approach is critical for containing costs over time and supporting an LTC system that remains resilient as demographic pressures accelerate. Recent 2024 policy updates, most notably the increase in the social assistance standard under Decree No. 76/2024/ND-CP and continued scaling of community-based ISHCs, signal incremental progress, but they do not yet constitute a comprehensive national long-term care insurance system (Government of Viet Nam, 2024a; HelpAge International in Vietnam, 2025; World Bank, 2024d).

Ultimately, Vietnam's ability to navigate its aging transition will be determined by its capacity to build a robust, equitable, and fiscally sustainable LTC system—one that balances the enduring strengths of family and community solidarity with institutional mechanisms that guarantee access, protect households from financial hardship, and uphold the dignity and well-being of older people. This requires coordinated and sustained commitment from government, providers, insurers, and communities, as well as policy learning from international experience adapted to Vietnam's social and economic context.

References

Anh, T. V. (2020). Long-term care for older people in Vietnam: The current situation and a proposed future model. Journal of Aging & Social Policy, 32(3), 257–271. https://doi.org/10.1080/08959420.2020.1738541.

Asian Development Bank. (2022). Long-term care for older people in Viet Nam: The current scenario, and next steps toward a healthy, aging population. https://www.adb.org/publications/long-term-care-older-people-viet-nam.

General Statistics Office of Vietnam. (2020). Population projections for Vietnam, 2019-2069. https://portal.thongke.gov.vn/khodulieudanso2019/TaiLieu/AnPham/S%C3%A1ch%20d%C3%A2n%20s%E1%BB%91%20v%C3%A0%20d%E1%BB%B1%20b%C3%A1o%20d%C3%A2n%20s%E1%BB%91%20final.pdf.

Giang, T. L., & Pfau, W. D. (2009). Ageing, poverty and the role of a social pension in Vietnam. Development and Change, 40(2), 333–360.

Giang, T. L., Bui, D. T., & Trinh, T. Q. (2022). Long-term care development in Vietnam. In Shaping long-term care in emerging Asia: Policy and country experiences (pp. 73–103). Taylor & Francis. https://doi.org/10.4324/9781003131373-5.

Government of Viet Nam. (2021). Decree No. 20/2021/ND-CP providing social assistance policies for social protection beneficiaries. https://datafiles.chinhphu.vn/cpp/files/vbpq/2021/03/20.signed.pdf.

Government of Viet Nam. (2024a). Decree No. 76/2024/ND-CP amending and supplementing certain articles of Decree No. 20/2021/ND-CP on social assistance policies for social protection beneficiaries. https://datafiles.chinhphu.vn/cpp/files/vbpq/2024/7/76-cp.signed.pdf.

Government of Viet Nam. (2024b). Increase pensions and social insurance benefits. Chinhphu.vn. https://xaydungchinhsach.chinhphu.vn/de-xuat-muc-tang-luong-huu-tro-cap-bao-hiem-xa-hoi-cao-nhat-tu-truoc-toi-nay-119240623231710275.htm.

HelpAge International in Vietnam. (2025). Intergenerational self-help clubs: A sustainable solution to population ageing. https://helpagevietnam.org/en/blog/2025/intergenerational-self-help-clubs-a-sustainable-solution-to-population-ageing/.

International Labour Organization. (2019). Potential impacts of social pensions in Viet Nam.

Lai, J. (2023). Aging goldmine: Unveiling Vietnam's elderly care revolution. SourcingCares. https://www.sourcingcares.com/post/aging-goldmine-unveiling-vietnam-s-elderly-care-revolution.

Minh, N. H., & Huong, P. T. M. (2021). The care of older adults in the Vietnamese family and related issues. In Aging and the family: Understanding changes in structural and relationship dynamics (pp. 39–61). Emerald Publishing.

Ministry of Health. (2023). Practice health promotion and disease prevention to change lives. https://moh.gov.vn/tin-noi-bat/-/asset_publisher/3Yst7YhbkA5j/content/bo-truong-ao-hong-lan-thuc-hanh-nang-cao-suc-khoe-phong-chong-benh-tat-e-thay-oi-cuoc-song.

Ministry of Health, & Health Partnership Group. (2018). Joint annual health review 2016: Towards healthy aging in Viet Nam. Medical Publishing House.

Ministry of Labour, Invalids and Social Affairs. (2020). Summary report on the situation of older persons and older-person affairs in Viet Nam.

Ministry of Labour, Invalids and Social Affairs. (2023). Summary of the implementation of Decree No. 20/2021/ND-CP dated March 15, 2021, regulating social assistance policies for social protection beneficiaries.

Ministry of Labour, Invalids and Social Affairs. (2024). Plan to implement the project for scaling up the Intergenerational Self-Help Club model for the period 2024–2025 (Decision No. 1335/QD-LDTBXH). LawNet. https://lawnet.vn/en/vb/Decision-1335-QD-LDTBXH-2024-scaling-up-the-intergenerational-self-help-club-model-2024-2025-9A714.html.

National Assembly of Viet Nam. (2009). Law on older persons (Law No. 39/2009/QH12). https://vanban.chinhphu.vn/?docid=92321&pageid=27160.

Ngan, D. (2024). Development trends of nursing homes in Vietnam. Investment Paper. https://baodautu.vn/xu-huong-phat-trien-vien-duong-lao-o-viet-nam-d216049.html.

Ngoc, B. (2024). How has the income of people in Hanoi and Ho Chi Minh City increased over the past 10 years? Tuoi Tre. https://tuoitre.vn/thu-nhap-cua-nguoi-dan-ha-noi-tp-hcm-tang-ra-sao-trong-hon-10-nam-qua-20240419112824854.htm.

Nguyen, U. (2023). Investing in Vietnam's senior care market: Assisted living and retirement. Vietnam Briefing. https://www.vietnam-briefing.com/news/investing-in-vietnam-senior-care-market-assisted-living-and-retirement.html.

Nguyen, V. (2022). Nursing homes in Vietnam: Costs and things to know. The Smart Local Vietnam.

Pfau, W. D., & Giang, T. L. (2010). Remittances, living arrangements and the welfare of the elderly in Vietnam. Asian and Pacific Migration Journal, 19(4), 447–472.

Pham, T. and Do, T. K. H. (2009). Overview of the policy to adapt to the changing age structure in Viet Nam. National Geriatric Hospital.

Prime Minister of Viet Nam. (2012). Decision approving the national action program on older persons in Viet Nam for the period 2012–2020 (Decision No. 1781/QD-TTg). https://thuvienphapluat.vn/van-ban/Van-hoa-Xa-hoi/Quyet-dinh-1781-QD-TTg-nam-2012-phe-duyet-Chuong-trinh-hanh-dong-quoc-gia-151877.aspx.

Teo, P., Mehta, K., & Chan, A. (2018). The construction of old age and the experience of ageing in Southeast Asia: The case of Vietnam, Thailand, and Singapore. In The Routledge handbook of Southeast Asian development (pp. 377–388). Routledge.

Thủy Bình. (2024). Primary healthcare - The frontline in protecting and caring for public health. Communist Party of Vietnam. https://dangcongsan.vn/cham-soc-va-nang-cao-suc-khoe-nhan-dan-trong-tinh-hinh-moi/y-te-co-so-tuyen-dau-trong-bao-ve-cham-soc-suc-khoe-cong-dong-660586.html.

UNFPA. (2021). Market outlook for elderly care services in Vietnam. https://vietnam.unfpa.org/en/publications/market-outlook-elderly-care-services-vietnam.

UNFPA. (2022). Support for older persons in Viet Nam: Key findings from a 2021 review and recommendations.

Van Minh, H., Giang, K. B., Ng, N., Juvekar, S., Razzaque, A., & Ashraf, A. (2017). Primary health care system in rural Vietnam: Perception of health care workers and their patients. BMC Health Services Research, 17(1), 585. https://doi.org/10.1186/s12913-017-2521-1.

Van, P. H., Tuan, K. A. & Oanh T. T. M. (2021). Older Persons and Long-term Care in Viet Nam, in Komazawa, O. and Y. Saito (eds.), Coping with Rapid Population Ageing in Asia. Jakarta: ERIA, pp. 45–56. https://www.eria.org/uploads/media/Books/2021-Coping-with-Rapid-Population-Ageing-Asia/11_Part1-Ch-7-Long-term-Care-Viet-Nam.pdf.

Vietnam Investment Review. (2023). Nurturing prospects in elderly care market. https://vir.com.vn/nurturing-prospects-in-elderly-care-market-101155.html.

Vietnam News Agency. (2021). Nursing home market nascent in Vietnam: Savills. VietnamPlus. https://en.vietnamplus.vn/nursing-home-market-nascent-in-vietnam-savills-post215487.vnp.

Vietnam News Agency. (2024). Rapidly aging population offers opportunities for nursing home developers. VietnamPlus. https://special.vietnamplus.vn/2024/08/30/rapidly-aging-population-offers-opportunities-for-nursing-home-developers/.

Vietnam News Portal. (2024). Increase social allowance standards for the elderly. https://www.vietnam.vn/en/nang-muc-chuan-tro-cap-xa-hoi-cho-nguoi-cao-tuoi/.

Vietnam Social Security. (2023). Health insurance – A health "fulcrum" for the elderly. https://soctrang.baohiemxahoi.gov.vn/tintuc/Pages/bao-hiem-xa-hoi.aspx?CateID=0&ItemID=4472.

Vietnam Women's Union. (2022). Report on data for the 2017–2022 term of the Women's Union of provinces/cities. https://vwu.vn/web/guest/tin-chi-tiet/-/chi-tiet/phu-luc-so-lieu-51509-6801.html.

Walker, W. M., & Wyse, M. (2022). Long-term care for older people in Viet Nam: The current scenario, and next steps toward a healthy, aging population. Asian Development Bank. https://www.adb.org/publications/long-term-care-older-people-viet-nam.

World Bank. (2021). Vietnam: Adapting to an aging society. World Bank.

World Bank. (2024a). GDP of Viet Nam from 1985–2023. https://data.worldbank.org/indicator/NY.GDP.MKTP.CD?locations=VN.

World Bank. (2024b). World Bank in Viet Nam. https://www.worldbank.org/en/country/vietnam/overview.

World Bank. (2024c). Population, total – Viet Nam. https://data.worldbank.org/indicator/SP.POP.TOTL?locations=VN.

World Bank. (2024d). How intergenerational self-help clubs transform elderly care in Viet Nam. https://www.worldbank.org/en/news/feature/2024/05/28/how-intergenerational-self-help-clubs-transform-elderly-care-in-viet-nam.

World Health Organization Regional Office for the Western Pacific. (2020). Guidance on COVID-19 for the care of older people and people living in long-term care facilities, other non-acute care facilities and home care. https://iris.who.int/bitstream/handle/10665/331913/COVID-19-emergency-guidance-ageing-eng.pdf.

Responding to Long-Term Care for an Aging Society: Insights from Medical and Care Platform Initiatives in Asia and Europe

Kayo Uemura

1 Utilization of Medical and Care Platforms to Respond to an Aging Society

In Japan, the elderly share of the population will peak around 2040. Recently, with the increase in the elderly population, there has been an increase in national medical and nursing care costs and a shortage of, and increased burden on, medical and nursing care workers. Therefore, there is a need to promote the use of digital health, using, for example, IoT, AI, and robotics, and to create next-generation healthcare services focusing on three points: consolidation of healthcare resources, regional expansion and efficiency of healthcare services, and active involvement of users. The Government of Japan set up the "Medical DX Promotion Headquarters" in 2022, aiming to establish a "National Medical Information Platform" that can comprehensively collect and share health, medical, and nursing care information. They decided on a plan in 2023 to promote the sharing of electronic medical record information between medical institutions by 2030 (Fig. 1). Efforts for these initiatives are just beginning in Japan, but they are progressing in Asia (for example, in Singapore and China), where the elderly population is rapidly increasing, and in Europe (for example, in the Netherlands and Finland), where the integration of medical and nursing care information is advanced. In this report, we will introduce these leading overseas examples.

K. Uemura (✉)
Economic & Industrial Research Department, Development Bank of Japan, Tokyo, Japan
e-mail: kyonits@dbj.jp

H. Lee and G. Nicolini (eds.), *International Comparison of Long-Term Care Insurance Systems*, Contributions to Management Science,
https://doi.org/10.1007/978-981-95-7781-1_14

Establishment of a national medical information platform		
Introduction of electronic medical records	Before FY 2030	Introduction of electronic medical records to share medical information at all medical institutions
Information sharing in electronic medical records	During FY 2024	By registering for the Electronic Medical Record Information Sharing Service (tentative name), a system is established to share and exchange electronic medical record information between medical institutions and pharmacies, and operations are initiated from medical institutions that have realized standardization.
	Before FY 2026	Introduced in almost all medical institutions and pharmacies
Standardized electronic medical record information (3 documents, 6 datasets)	During FY 2023	Standardize code information for allergenic substances 3 documents: 1. Medical information form, 2. Summary at discharge, including key images, etc. 3. Medical checkup result report 6 datasets: 1. Injury/disease name, 2. Allergy info, 3. Infection Information 4. Drug contraindication info, 5. Examination info (tests useful in emergencies, tests related to lifestyle-related diseases), 6. Prescription info
Developed standards-based electronic medical records	During FY 2024	Development begun, mainly for small medical institutions
Local governments, medical institutions, and nursing care services Cooperation among institutions	Before FY 2025	Standardization of municipal systems, and standardization and cloud-based transition of documents to be shared
	After FY 2026	Nationwide operation will have begun for public medical expenses, local medical expense subsidies, vaccinations, maternal and child health information, nursing care, municipal health examinations, and infectious disease notifications.

Fig. 1 Japan's main steps for digital health initiatives in medical and nursing care. *Note* Prepared by Development Bank of Japan based on Cabinet Secretariat (Japan), Medical DX Promotion Headquarters Document

2 Singapore Initiatives: Transformation to a Service-Based Healthcare System

In Singapore, the COVID-19 pandemic exposed a lack of healthcare infrastructure. The government of Singapore is rushing to build healthcare facilities and is taking advantage of the increased digital usage during the COVID-19 pandemic as an opportunity to build a health, medical, and long-term care information platform that will serve as the foundation for digital health.

2.1 Singapore's Healthcare Delivery System

Singapore's healthcare delivery system consists of three public healthcare groups operated as not-for-profit joint-stock companies under the Ministry of Health, Singapore, and a number of other private institutions (Fig. 2). The three public healthcare groups are Singapore Health Services (Sing Health), the largest group in Singapore; National University Health System (NUHS), which focuses on university hospitals; and National Healthcare Group (NHG), which is considered to be the leader in public healthcare. The Government has promoted a healthcare delivery system that achieves maximum effectiveness with minimum resources. As of 2021, there were only 29 acute and community hospitals for a population of approximately 5.5

million people, and the shortage of healthcare infrastructure was exposed during the COVID-19 pandemic.

Therefore, the government is planning to open 10 new hospital institutions by 2030. Among them, the largest in the country, Woodlands Health Campus (NHG Group), began a gradual opening of its facilities at the end of 2023. Set on a 7.7 ha site with 1.8 k beds and a total floor area of 270 ksqm, the hospital includes four different

	Public Aircraft			Minma Aircraft
Group name	Singapore Health Services (Sing Health)	National University Health System (NUHS)	National Healthcare Group (NHG)	IHH Healthcare and others
Characteristics	· Largest public healthcare cluster in Singapore · Aiming to provide quality affordable and accessible healthcare	· Linking university and community hospitals · Aiming to provide innovative and sustainable healthcare	· Singapore's leader in public healthcare · Extending healthy life expectancy	· Singapore's largest private healthcare provider group · Aiming to become the world's most trusted healthcare service network
Central organization	Singapore General Hospital (SGH)	National University Hospital (NUH)	Tan Tock Seng Hospital (TTSH)	Gleneagles, Mount Elizabeth, Parkway
Major medical institutions	· Changi General Hospital · KK Women and Children's Hospital	· Ng Tenfong General Hospital · National University Heart Center Hospital	· Tantoksen Hospital · Johns Hopkins Singapore	· Gleneagles Hospital · Mount Elizabeth Hospital · Parkway East Hospital
Number of institutions, including those under construction	· Tertiary care / acute care hospitals: 5 · National specialty centers: 5 · General community hospitals: 3 · Clinics: 10	· Tertiary care / acute care / community hospitals: 3 · National specialty centers: 3 · Clinics / medical centers: 3 · Health institutions: 3	· Tertiary care / acute care / community hospitals: 5 · Center/Research Institute (4) · Clinic · Pharmacy · Academy, etc.	· Tertiary care / acute care hospitals: 4 · Primary care clinics: over 30 · Labs: 6 · Others
New hospitals and new investment	■Younos General Hospital · 2023: establishment of centralized Telemedicine Hub ■Singapore General Hospital · Elective Care Center (ECC) · Scheduled to open around 2026. Approximately 500 beds (25~50 operation rooms) · Constant RFID monitoring of patients' location, blood pressure, temperature, and oxygen levels · Home monitoring organization established for home care after discharge ■General hospital in Bedok (scheduled to open in 2030)	■National Skin Centerl · 2022 ■Jurong General Clinic · Scheduled to open in 2027 · Integrated polyclinic and 700 bed nursing home · Wide hallways with easy wheelchair access · Includes a second facility with nursing home and polyclinic	■Integrated Care Hub · Opened in 2022. 500 beds · Smart rehabilitation is provided. Utilizes technologies such as robotics and virtual reality programs ■Woodlands Health Campus · Opened in 2023. 1,800 beds · Provides seamless health care access for acute care, community care, and geriatric care. Uses AI · Medical team plans to monitor home patients	■IHH Healthcare · Invests in Doctor Anywhere, a telemedicine venture · Invests in Intellect, a digital mental health venture. Launched at Gleneagles Hospital · In partnership with Accredify, which introduced blockchain technology to directly issue results of the novel coronavirus tests from a mobile app
Digital platform–related	· 2019: The old system was transferred to an electronic database. Data sharing between facilities ① Bedside MyCare app: access to medical information and recovery schedule, and communication with staff ② Digital medical certificates: paperless for greater patient convenience (helps prevent loss and forgery, streamlines clinical management workflow) ③ In pilot: adding booking and payment management capabilities to the app.; recording voice orders from doctors and nurses	· NUHS takes about five years to launch medical information system, NHG joins in 2022 · Linking community healthcare with acute and convalescent hospitals · Promoting the introduction of the NEHR, which will centrally manage patient data. (Note: NUH is planning to take the lead in connecting data from the NEHR to the ENDEAVOUR AI platform.)		· Quickly responded to the COVID-19 pandemic outbreak by enabling the use of virtual consultations and making access to reservation services, medical records, and health information available via mobile applications · In October 2022, launched the MyHealth360 mobile app. It includes features for booking, phone consultation, payment, health check-up and screening reports, and a symptom checker

Fig. 2 Singapore's healthcare delivery system. *Notes* 1. Prepared by Development Bank of Japan based on various materials and interviews. 2. RFID: Radio Frequency Identification (automatic recognition technology that uses radio waves to read and write IC tag information without contact)

types of institutions: acute hospitals, community hospitals, specialized outpatient clinics, and medium- to long-term care facilities. Through integrated health, medical, and nursing care information, this first smart hospital in Singapore continuously accumulates acute, subacute, outpatient, and nursing care information, as well as other user information, across different healthcare facilities within the campus. Also planned is a remote management base where a medical team can monitor medication time, heart rate, and sleep status of patients wearing electronic wristbands at home.

In the private sector, IHH, the largest private group in Singapore, has invested in startup telemedicine service provider Doctor Anywhere. Also, in October 2022, they started mobile app service MyHealth360, which has reservation, phone consultation, and AI-equipped symptom checker functions. These services are part of IHH's plan to invest USD 100 million over three years up to 2025 in digital transformation initiatives.

2.2 Health, Medical and Long-Term Care Information Platform Initiatives: State-Run Hybrid Platform

The Government has a "One patient, one health record" vision. A hybrid method platform is being developed to manage personal health records with two systems: Next Generation Electronic Medical Records (NGEMR) and National Electronic Health Records (NEHR).

2.2.1 NGEMR (Detailed Version)

The Ministry of Health is introducing NGEMR, an advanced centralized medical record system (Fig. 3). NGEMR records both medical and administrative data on the course of hospital admissions, discharges, and outpatient appointments, allowing medical teams to quickly access the latest medical information without having to request records from another agency, saving time and money. It also reduces the need for duplicate testing and the burden on patients, because their care can be adjusted appropriately. NGEMR began operating an integrated NHG and NUHS system in 2023, starting with the NHG in 2020 during the COVID-19 pandemic. The aim is to consolidate the medical records of more than 640,000 people in more than 20 hospitals. More than 8000 health professionals were trained to run the system.

2.2.2 NEHR (Overview)

In 2011, Singapore began building a centralized, regional, electronic health record (EHR) system called National Electronic Health Records. NEHR only stores an overview of patient information, and detailed data is stored in the electronic medical

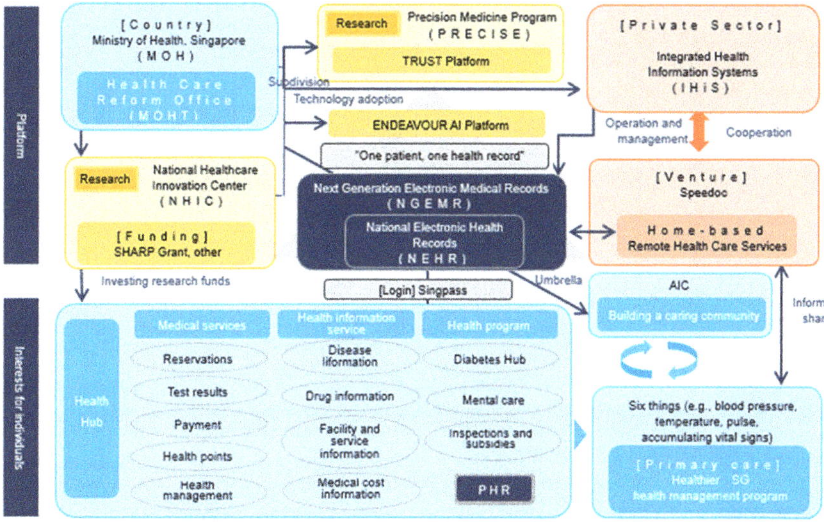

Fig. 3 Singapore's health, medical, and long-term care information platform. *Notes* 1. Prepared by Development Bank of Japan based on various materials and interviews. 2. MOHT: MOH Office for Healthcare Transformation; specialized organization dedicated to ICT utilization; established in 2018. 3. PRECISE: Precision Health Research Singapore. 4. TRUST platform: Accumulation of all data. Privacy code for Personal Data Privacy Act (PDPA) and clinical trials. 5. IHiS: Integrated Health Information Systems Pte Ltd. 6. NHIC allows physicians to participate in the innovation process and commercialize their ideas. NHIC is also responsible for the development of privacy technologies (National Health Innovation Center). 7. SHARP: Singapore Health Assistive & Robotics Programme. 8. Speedoc: Vertex investment venture. In April 2023, all medical institutions in Japan began offering Speedoc services. 9. AIC: Taking charge of building a care community (Agency for Integrated Care)

records of each medical institution so it can be retrieved as needed. This method is aimed at reducing the cost of the central platform. Based on the Medical Services Act, the Government has made it mandatory for medical practitioners authorized by institutions registered with the NEHR to provide patient data to the NEHR from 2020. Approximately 80 percent of public and private hospitals, clinics, nursing care facilities, dentistry, pharmacies and other such institutions (2455 in total as of December 2023) are participating in the NEHR, and the number of registrations continued to increase in 2023, after the coronavirus (Fig. 4).

Furthermore, to prevent healthcare professionals from accessing information inappropriately, the Government conducts regular audits and has established a strict security management system (Fig. 5).

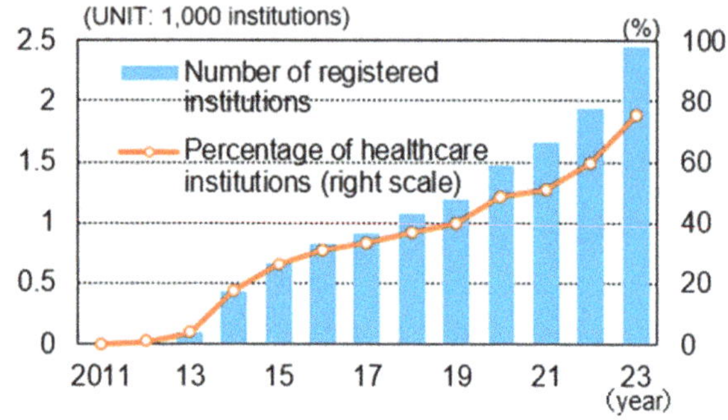

Fig. 4 Number of institutions registered with NEHR. *Note* Prepared by Development Bank of Japan based on the Ministry of Health, Singapore

Medical records ID	•Management of medical records via National Registration Identification Card number •Citizens present the NRIC number when visiting a medical institution, and doctors check the patient's medical records.
NGEMR	•Only authorized providers directly involved in the patient's care, such as physicians, have access to the data. •All access is logged and tracked to strictly protect confidentiality and privacy. •Patient privacy protection: Unauthorized access or alteration of data is punishable under the Computer Misuse Act.
NEHR	[Access authorization] •With the introduction of the Medical Services Act in 2018, the provision of patient data to the NEHR has become mandatory for all healthcare providers who have received approval from an organization registered with the NEHR since 2020. The goal is to advance the storage of medical records of all citizens in the NEHR. •Patients' NEHR records are confidential and can only be accessed for patient care purposes (not for other purposes such as insurance or employment). Certified healthcare professionals can access the NEHR to track medical history. •Access to one's own records in the NEHR via HealthHub started in November 2021. •[Periodic Audit] The Ministry of Health has put in place safeguards to prevent inappropriate access to NEHR data. Patient access logs are checked regularly and audited regularly to prevent unauthorized access (with unauthorized access subject to significant fines by the MOH). •[Opt-out method] Patients who do not wish to participate in the NEHR can opt out of the service. If a patient opts out of the NEHR, their data will continue to be sent to the NEHR (unless they request that it not be sent) but viewing will be blocked. If a patient wants to opt back into the NEHR, they can quickly restore their data without data gaps.

Fig. 5 Singapore's healthcare data security management system. *Notes* 1. Prepared by Development Bank of Japan based on various materials and theMinistry ofHealth, Singapore. 2. HealthHub:A health portal that provides one-stop access to government-provided health services and health records. Details are provided in section (3) on the next page. 3. Opt-out method: A method whereby a patient opts to stop automatic sharing of their medical and other information

2.2.3 Transition from Facility-Based to Service-Based Provision of Care: Licensing Based on the Medical Services Act

With increased access to healthcare data, the provision of medical services is no longer limited to premises where physical buildings exist, making possible the adoption of new care services such as telemedicine and home medical care. In order to flexibly respond to changes in medical services, from 2022 to 2023 the Government

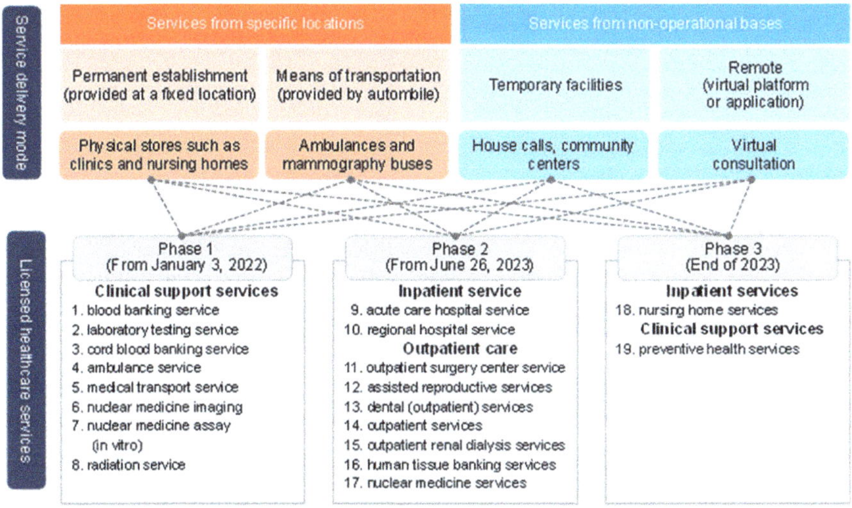

Fig. 6 Licensed health care services in Singapore. *Note* Prepared by Development Bank of Japan based on the Ministry of Health, Singapore

began transitioning from facility-based to service-based granting of medical licenses, based on the Medical Services Act (Fig. 6).

2.3 Utilization of Users' Healthcare Information: Transformation of Primary Care

(Routine Medical Care)

Since 2003, citizens have been able to log into their personal medical records using their national ID for digital services, "Singpass." From 2020, citizens' medical records have been accumulated in the NEHR. Individuals may opt out of the NEHR, whereby their data will continue to be accumulated by the NEHR (unless an individual requests otherwise) but medical service providers will not be able to view it.

In addition, the Government in mid-2022 launched the Healthier SG program, which uses digital health to manage citizens' health. For long-term health management, the company offers HealthHub, a health portal that provides one-stop access to all medical services and health records. The government manages HealthHub, a health portal that provides one-stop access to all medical services and health records. This is also available in an app that allows users to easily add vital records, such as their blood pressure and temperature, and take the initiative to work on their personal health records.

When the program started	Plans for future initiatives (from early 2024)
• One free initial health plan consultation at selected clinics • Earn health points (3,000 health points worth SGD 20) through the Healthy 365 app (registration of health-related life data, offering of exercise classes, etc.) after the initial health plan consultation • Fully subsidized state-recommended testing and vaccinations (Singapore citizens only)	• Healthier SG Chronic Tier enrollees can receive subsidies of up to 87.5% for selected chronic medications and up to SGD 360 annually for consultation, exams and other components of their care, depending on income level. • Under the Chronic Disease Management Program (CDMP), Singapore residents can use Medisave to pay for treatment without paying out-of-pocket cash.

Fig. 7 Benefits of the Healthier SG program in Singapore. *Notes* 1. Prepared by Development Bank of Japan Based on "HealthHub,"the Ministry of Health, Singapore. 2. Medisave: The medical account of the Central Provident Fund (CPF) that all Singaporeans and permanent residents are required to join. It can be used for hospitalization costs and specific outpatient treatments

In addition, as part of the Healthier SG initiative, the Government has made it mandatory for general practitioners to develop health plans for residents to manage their preventive health, including lifestyle adjustments, checkups, and vaccinations. A program allowing individuals to choose from among registered general practitioners is also being implemented. Starting in July 2023, people aged 60 and over were registered, and from 2024, those aged 40–59 are being registered. Individuals who participate in the health consultation after registration will receive a full subsidy for testing and vaccination recommended by the Government, as well as 3000 health points (worth SGD 20) that can be used at supermarkets (Fig. 7).

In Singapore, the transition to a system that promotes digital utilization first addresses elderly people with high needs for chronic disease responses and caregiving, aiming to control medical and caregiving costs. The health record information of elderly people adapted to digitalization can be shared with family and caregivers, thus enhancing the caregiving environment. The development of care communities that promote these Healthier SG–related programs is carried out by the Agency for Integrated Care under the Ministry of Health.

3 China's Healthcare Delivery System

3.1 National Policy "Internet + Medicine and Health"

In China, public hospitals are mainly covered by public medical insurance, and there are mainly third-level hospitals, second-level hospitals, first-level hospitals, and Xiao district hospitals (community hospitals). Because third-level hospitals, which provide advanced medical care, are full of patients, the Central People's Government of the People's Republic of China has jurisdiction over the use of familiar regional institutions such as Shachiku Hospital. In addition, to make up for the shortage of healthcare resources, the Government formulated the "Healthy China 2030" strategy in 2016, the master plan of the medium- to long-term national promotion of internet-based healthcare services and individualized health management services (Fig. 8).

2015	■ (National People's Congress) "Internet Plus" strategy proposed · China's first virtual hospital, Wuzhen Internet Hospital, opened in Zhejiang · Launch of an official website and mobile app to provide online medcal services focusing on follow-up visits
2016	■ Healthy China 2030 · The first medium-to long-term national plan in the field of health (the master plan for promoting the improvement of national health) · One of the main plans to develop the health (healthcare) industry · New business development for health insurance services: development of internet-based health services, personalized promotion of development of health management services, wearable devices, smart health electronics, healthcare and medical services for mobile applications
2018	■ Opinion of the Office of the State Council on Promoting "Internet + Medicine and Health" · Promotion of the "Healthy China" strategy, improvement of the level of modern medical care and health management, optimization of resource allocation, innovation of service models, improvement of service efficiency, and targeting of reduced service costs · Specification of conditions for deregulation to encourage the opening of internet hospitals
2020	■ National Health Insurance Bureau · Announcement of documents aimed at improving health insurance payment policies for internet and medical services · Implementation by major hospitals, especially public hospitals, of efforts to make internet diagnosis and treatment reasonable and legal
2022	■ State Council: Digital Economic Development Plan for the 14th Five-Year Plan (2021–2025) · Acceleration of the development of virtual hospitals and promotion of internet medical services such as health counseling, online medical care, and remote medical care ■ Central Committee of the Communist Party of China, State Council: Outline of Strategic Plan for Increasing Domestic Demand (2022–2035) · Proposal for active development of Internet + Medicine and Health services · Making internet medical services eligible for medical insurance payments based on internet fee regulations and paid items (explicitly stating that internet medical services are included)
2023	■ Central Committee of the Chinese Communist Party, State Council: Opinion on Further Improvement of the Medical and Health Service System · Emphasis on the role of information technology in developing "Internet + Medicine and Health" · Targeting 2035 as the date for completion of the "health services system"

Fig. 8 China's digital health policies. *Note* Prepared by Development Bank of Japan based on various materials and interviews

In 2018, Internet + Medicine and Health was formulated to embody this strategy. As a result, internet hospitals became covered by medical insurance, and major public hospitals began to open online hospitals. Subsequently, China's 14th Five-Year Plan (2021–2025) included measures to accelerate the establishment of not only physical medical institutions but also online hospitals to address problems such as the concentration of patients in advanced medical institutions, the lack of healthcare resources, and regional disparities. As an initiative for the future, the Government announced that it would build more internet platforms in 2023, gradually innovate medical and health service models, and aim to form a next-generation healthcare service system by 2035.

3.2 *Virtual Hospitals: Three Major Forms*

Because virtual hospitals are such a shallow field, there are various issues, such as related laws and the safety of patient information. However, due to the COVID-19 pandemic, IT literacy among the elderly has improved and usage rates have increased.

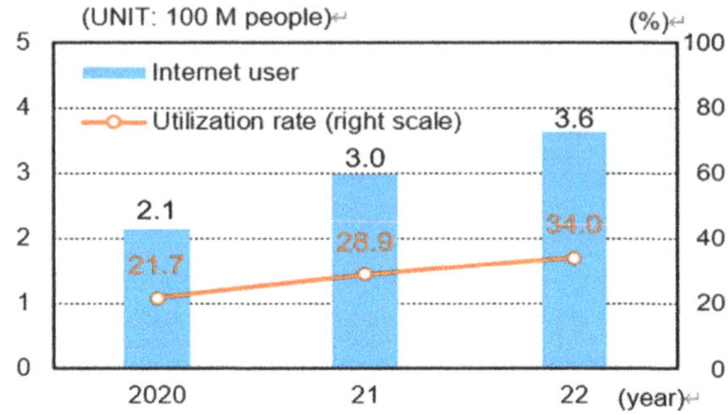

Fig. 9 (China) Trends in the number of users and usage rate. *Note* Prepared by Development Bank of Japan based on the China Internet Development Statistics Report

The number of virtual hospitals has increased from some 100 institutions in 2018 to more than 1600 in 2021. As of December 2022, the users of China's internet-based health services numbered 363 million (up 21.7% YoY), accounting for about 30% of Chinese internet users (Fig. 9). There are three types of virtual hospitals: (1) those established by an existing hospital as a secondary hospital; (2) those established in partnership with a third-party organization; and (3) those established independently by a company.

3.2.1 Virtual Hospitals Established by Medical Institutions as Secondary Hospitals

Many public hospitals establish virtual hospitals as secondary hospitals that use the brick-and-mortar hospitals as the means to provide healthcare resources. For example, the virtual hospital of Peking Union Medical College Hospital, a grade 1 hospital approved in Beijing, started diagnosis and treatment in 19 departments, including cardiovascular medicine, endocrinology, and dermatology, in March 2021 during the COVID-19 pandemic. Internet access to hospitals' virtual establishments varies by medical institution, including official accounts, apps, and WeChat mini-programs.

3.2.2 Virtual Hospitals Affiliated With Third-Party Organizations

Some virtual hospitals are operated by real medical institutions using a platform provided by a third party, such as a drugstore company.

Cowell Health, China's largest drugstore chain (Fig. 10), with 13,000 stores across 330 cities in 20 provinces, and a membership reaching over 84 million since its establishment in 2017, has six virtual hospitals. The COVID-19 pandemic promoted the digitalization of services for users, resulting in drugstore business accounting for 70% of sales and digital-related business accounting for 30% as of 2022, with digital-related business growing significantly.

Fig. 10 (China) Cowell Health. *Note* Photo by Development Bank of Japan

Virtual hospitals partnered variously with six physical medical institutions in Tianjin, Chengdu, and Hainan serve 14 million people. The services provided, which users can receive at home, include community-based smart diagnostic and medical services, family doctor services, health management services for chronic diseases, and prescription distribution services for medical institutions. Although Cowell Health does not have a partnership with public hospitals, it provides vital data such as blood pressure and blood sugar records that users have recorded using Cowell Health services when they visit public hospitals.

3.2.3 Virtual Hospitals Opened Solely by Companies

Other virtual hospitals have been opened independently by private IT companies, including JD Health, a subsidiary of China's e-commerce giant Jingdong Group (JD. com); Ali Health, a subsidiary of Alibaba; and Ping An Good Doctor, a subsidiary of China's Ping An Insurance. An app provides users access to a consultation service that matches patients with doctors 24 hours a day. In some cases—for example, sudden onset of fever—doctors' diagnoses are used as reference information to determine whether a user needs to visit a hospital. During the COVID-19 pandemic, IT literacy among the elderly increased and usage increased.

Ping An Good Doctor, the top user of virtual hospitals in China, offers a comprehensive health platform for people who are healthy, in recovery, chronically ill, or otherwise in need of care. The platform's 440 million users (registered through a system based on families' general practitioners) have 24-hour access to 750 types of service. The platform'score digital health service, "online health counselling" (Fig. 11), has been utilized more than 1.3 billion times.

The medical team consists of about 50,000 people, including full-time doctors and part-time outside doctors, dietitians, psychological counselors and trainers. The online consultation service is staffed by real doctors, but it also has an AI system to help patients inquire about their health, to make their visits more efficient. Through these activities, family doctors are able to add independent bits of data for integration into an overall personal health record.

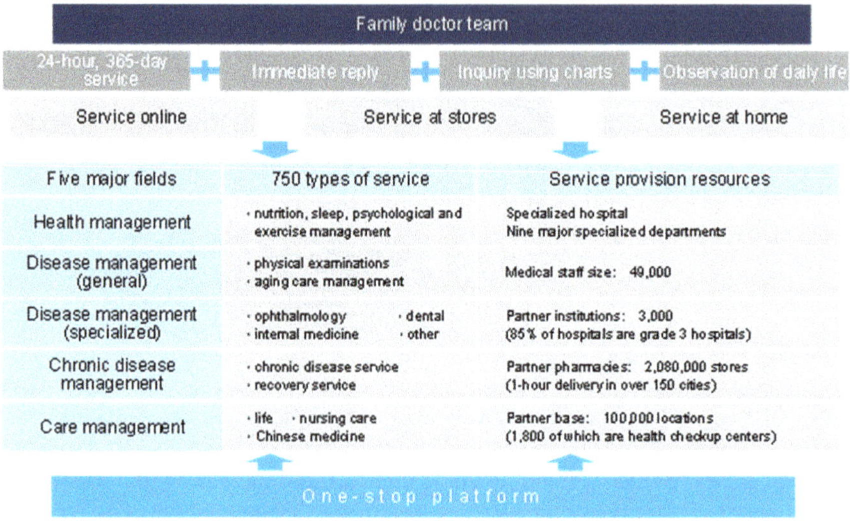

Fig. 11 (China) Online health counseling service for Ping An Good Doctor. *Notes* 1. Prepared by Development Bank of Japan based on Ping An Good Doctor. 2. As of June 30, 2022

China is working to provide integrated medical services online and offline by integrating online hospitals into medical services (Fig. 12).

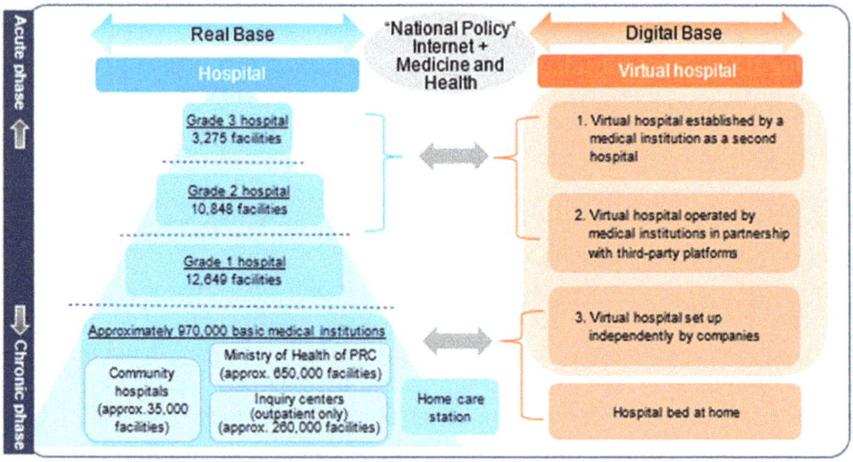

Fig. 12 Integrated online and offline medical services in China. *Note* Prepared by Development Bank of Japan based on The Central People's Government of the People's Republic of China,"Statistical Bulletin on the Development ofMedical Care in our country in 2021," and other sources

4 The Netherlands: A Decentralized Platform Operated by the Private Sector

In 2013, the Netherlands shifted itself a comprehensive to a participatory healthcare system (in which all of the Dutch people make self-help efforts) and strengthened the utilization of digital technology and preventative efforts.

The Netherlands' platform is an opt-in system, allowing users to choose whether or not to enroll in the system. It is a decentralized platform where family doctors manage electronic medical record (EMR) information. VZVZ (acronym for "Association of Healthcare Providers for Healthcare Communication" in Dutch), a private institution funded by insurance companies, operates the LSP (acronym for the name of the platform in Dutch), which manages and links information. The National ICT Institute in Healthcare (Nictiz), funded by the government, is in charge of standardizing data (Fig. 13). Under this framework, community-based sharing of electronic health record (EHR) information among healthcare providers (medical institutions, pharmacies, nursing homes, etc.) has advanced, and over 80 percent of relevant institutions are currently participating in the framework.

In addition, the government is working on spreading apps developed by private companies to promote the use of personal health records (PHRs). Users can choose from among multiple apps based on their purpose of use (e.g., measurement of heart rate or blood level, or focused on diet or sleeping habits). Further, the government requires companies that develop apps, as well as medical institutions that share information, to obtain government certification called "Medmij." Through this certification system, the security and quality of PHR are ensured.

The Netherlands plans to utilize this platform to create new services for people with chronic illness and for in-home nursing care, and to implement initiatives related to virtual care (Fig. 14).

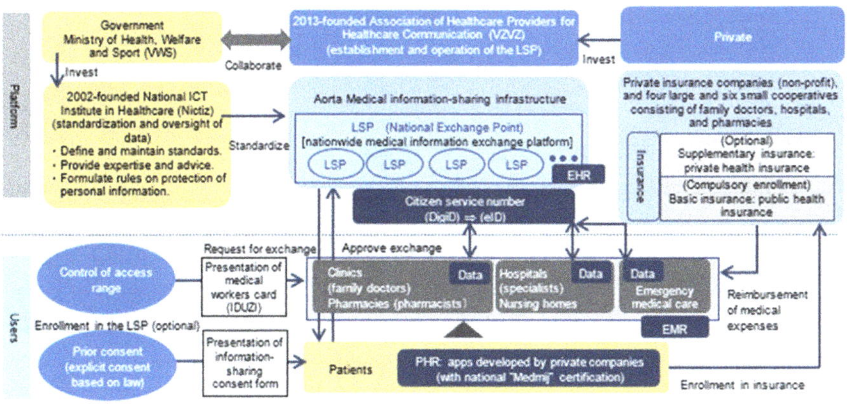

Fig. 13 Framework of the Netherlands' health, medical, and nursing care information platform. *Note* Prepared by Development Bank of Japan based on interviews with and materials obtained from Nictiz and VZVZ

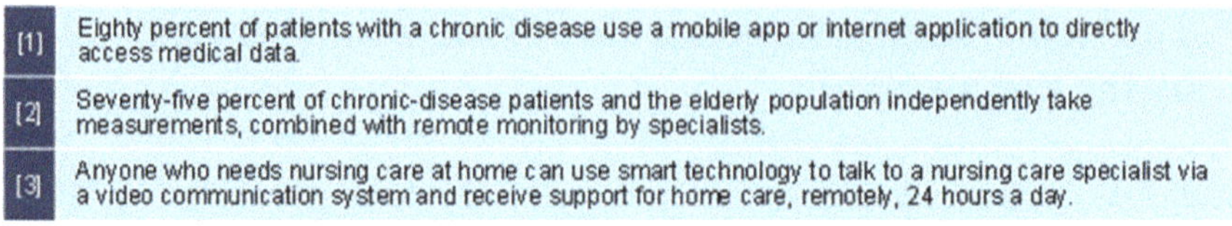

Fig. 14 The Netherlands' initiatives plan. *Note* Prepared by Development Bank of Japan based on interviews with and materials obtained from Nictiz and VZVZ

5 Finland: A Centralized Platform Operated by the Government

In Finland, the Social Insurance Institution of Finland (Kela) started operating a centralized platform called "Kanta Platform" in 2007, based on the Act on the Electronic Processing of Client Data in Social and Healthcare Services. The Kanta Platform centralizes electronic health record (EHR) information held by each medical area (Fig. 15).

Currently, the electronic medical record (EMR) adoption ratio among hospitals and clinics is close to 100%, and Kanta stores data such as medical records, nursing care information, electronic prescriptions, and test results. In 2010, Finland also opened a "My Kanta Page" where users can check their medical information and other information from their PC, and in 2017, the country started operating a personal health record system to which health data can be added. To promote the use of secondary data

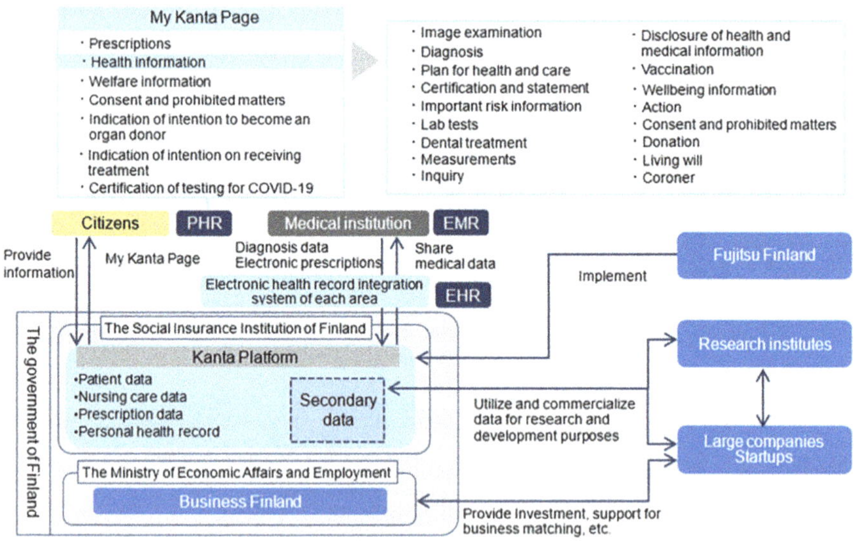

Fig. 15 Framework of Finland's health, medical, and nursing care information platform. *Note*Prepared by Development Bank of Japan based on interviews with and materials obtained from Business Finland

Founded	2018	Services provided to:	All citizens, including healthy people
Operated by	Government	Primary virtual care	• Virtual Hubs: Consultation services (for healthy people). 32 virtual hubs for rehabilitation, cancer, etc. The hubs have an AI chat bot function that users can use anonymously. • Digital care management programs: Approximately 300 programs (for patients). Programs can be used with a "My Path" account for digital services. They provide health consultation services using a monitoring device, and self-care services utilizing images and videos at each treatment stage. • Digital Health Village PRO: Electronic coaching (for specialists), online support for daily work.
Objective of establishment	Transformation of health, medical, and nursing care services through digital technology		
Target area	Health, medical, and nursing care		
Provision system	Virtually gathered experts		
	2,000 people		

Fig. 16 Digital health village (Finland). *Note* Prepared by Development Bank of Japan based on various materials

created by anonymizing the data stored on Kanta, Business Finland, a government agency operated under the Ministry of Economic Affairs and Employment, supports the creation of new businesses in the healthcare industry by investing in businesses of any size and by conducting business matching.

From around 2020, it became possible to link electronic prescriptions and CT scan images created in countries such as Estonia and Germany to Kanta, enabling cross-border information sharing. In addition, the centralized platform is utilized to provide in-home nursing care services remotely 24 hours a day, 365 days a year.

"Digital Health Village," which started as a national policy in 2014, is a particularly notable example of a virtual hospital (Fig. 16). Digital Health Village is a digital service platform jointly developed by medical experts, IT specialists, and patient organizations, and all citizens can use the platform regardless of their place of residence. Currently, approximately 2000 healthcare specialists are providing support.

Digital Health Village has three key functions. The first function is called "Virtual Hubs," which provides specialist consultation service to healthy (pre-symptomatic) citizens, helping them prevent disease and practice self-care. As of 2022, there are 32 virtual hubs on the web for topics such as rehabilitation, surgery, cancer, and heart disease.

6 Expectations for the Long-Term Care Utilization of Medical and Nursing Care Platforms in Japan Towards 2040

The transition to digital health is a global trend. In Japan as well, efforts are needed that go beyond just a digital shift to replace traditional healthcare services with online ones. In doing so, it is crucial to establish a digital foundation related to health, medical care, and nursing care, set up digital bases that aggregate healthcare resources, and aim for the wide-area and efficiency of services, which will lead to a reduction in the burden on healthcare workers. Additionally, like Singapore and

China, starting with the accumulation of healthcare information from the elderly and creating a system where individuals can be actively involved in prevention based on their healthcare data which can lead to a reduction in the country's medical and nursing care costs.

Once again, as the digital shift focusing on the elderly is expected to continue in Asia and Europe, there is a possibility that Japan's digital response may lag behind. In Japan as well, with the peak of the elderly population around 2040 as one target period, it is necessary to advance the creation of next-generation healthcare services that utilize digital health, not solely dependent on physical locations such as medical and nursing care facilities, in response to long-term care for an aging society (Fig. 17).

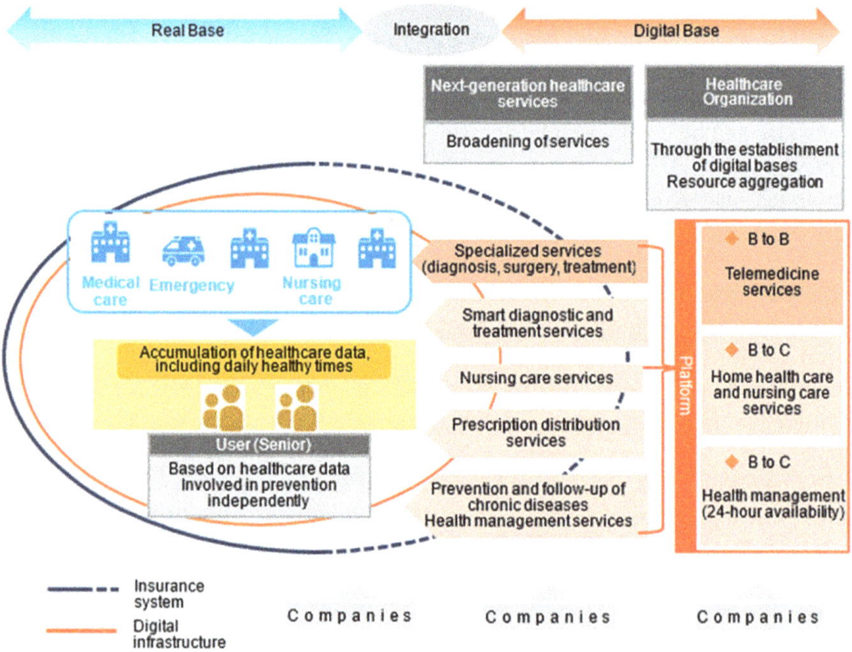

Fig. 17 Building next-generation, long-term care services in Japan for 2040. *Note* Prepared by Development Bank of Japan

www.ingramcontent.com/pod-product-compliance
Ingram Content Group UK Ltd.
Pitfield, Milton Keynes, MK11 3LW, UK
UKHW020631260926
475829UK00003BA/32
9789819577804